Study Guide & Reader for American Government and Politics in the New Millennium

Tenth Edition

D1122667

Study Guide & Reader for American Government and Politics in the New Millennium

Tenth Edition

Karen Sunshine
SUNY Rockland Community College
Suffern, New York

Virginia Stowitts-Traina
Palo Alto College
San Antonio, Texas

Christine Schultz
Santa Monica College
Santa Monica, California

Abigail Press   **Wheaton, IL 60189**

Design and Production: Abigail Press
Typesetting: Abigail Press
Typeface: Garamond
Cover Art: Sam Tolia

Study Guide & Reader for American Government and Politics in the New Millennium

Tenth Edition, 2017
Printed in the United States of America
Translation rights reserved by the authors
ISBN 1-890919-01-2
       978-1-890919-01-6

TABLE OF CONTENTS

FOR STUDY GUIDE

TABLE OF CONTENTS

FOR READER

PART I: FOUNDATIONS OF GOVERNMENT

PART II: THE POLITICAL PROCESS

PART III: SOCIAL AND ENVIRONMENTAL ISSUES

PART IV: SOCIAL AND CULTURAL PERSPECTIVES

HOW DO POLITICAL SCIENTISTS KNOW WHAT THEY KNOW? A BRIEF LOOK AT APPROACHES AND METHODS

INTRODUCTION SUMMARY:

The Introduction provides an overview of three of the most common techniques (surveys, statistics, and content analysis) used by political scientists and a rudimentary examination of two behavioral approaches (game theory and systems analysis). The differences between methods, techniques, and approaches and between micro and macro approaches are also explained.

IDENTIFICATION:

Briefly describe each term.

Epistemology

Empirical

Behavioral revolution

Method

1

Technique

Statistics

System

Systems analysis

Salience

Traditional approach

Matrix

Cells

Demands

Support

TRUE/FALSE:

Indicate whether each statement is true (T) or false (F). The correct answers are given at the end of the chapter.

_____1. One of the ultimate goals of any statistical analysis is to provide feedback to policy makers.

_____2. Statistics are used to simplify communication.

_____3. A win or lose political game, in which cooperation between the players is not an option, is called a zero-sum game.

_____4. Statistical procedures and polling techniques make it virtually impossible to come up with inaccurate information.

_____5. The approach a researcher takes limits what she/he finds.

_____6. Knowledge based on myths, hunches, intuition, or common sense is useless and must be rejected.

_____7. An "approach" refers to how information is obtained.

_____8. Polling methodology and results vary from organization to organization.

_____9. Game theory is a traditional approach.

_____10. A political system is made up of two related components: a set of interdependent parts and environments.

_____11. The process of studying for a test or a final exam is an example of a non-political technique.

_____12. The mean average is the measurement of the standard deviation.

_____13. If a voter researches an issue position taken by a candidate prior to casting his/her vote, the voter is said to have a heighten level of salience because the issue is so important to his/her voting decision.

_____14. Aristotle and John Locke are recognized as being systematic or scientific thinkers.

_____15. In a political system, support reflects the degree of satisfaction or dissatisfaction one feels about how the government has responded to an identifiable demand.

FILL-IN-THE-BLANKS:

Write the appropriate word(s) to complete the sentence. The correct answers are given at the end of the chapter.

1. As a result of the behavioral revolution in the 1950s, the study of politics became more _____ and _____ .

2. _____ is another term for information.

3. The structure of a political leader's speech is one of the major concerns in which technique? _____

4. An _____ is defined as "an orientation" or way of looking at something.

5. Statisticians use data as a means of testing the strength of the _____ between and among variables.

6. A basic assumption of game theory is that the players of the game are playing to win and hence are _____ .

7. The U.S. government has two major environments; one is its _____ environment and the other is its _____ environment.

8. The four forms of governmental decisions or outputs are: _____, _____, _____, and _____.

9. Political theorist _____, (provide the author's name) introduced the systems approach to political science.

10. A _____ is any item subjected to examination or testing.

11. _____ are educated guesses about what a researcher expects to find.

12. A _____ includes people, political institutions, political processes and interactions.

13. In a political system, laws, executive orders, judicial decisions and regulations are collectively known as _____.

14. The never-ending cycle of government converting inputs into outputs is simply referred to as the _____.

MULTIPLE CHOICE:

Circle the correct response. The correct answers are given at the end of the chapter.

1. Systems analysis is

   a) a technique.
   b) a micro approach.
   c) a macro approach.
   d) a game.

2. The most widely used technique for obtaining current data about the government is

   a) surveys.
   b) systems analysis.
   c) content analysis.
   d) game theory.

3. Statistical procedures are **NOT** used to

   a) make projections.
   b) measure data.
   c) indicate clinical depression.
   d) test the strength of the relationship between variables.

4. Behavioral approaches to politics

   a) focus on what "is."
   b) are normative.
   c) include the historical approach.
   d) include the constitutional/legal approach.

5. Game theory is an approach that originated in which academic discipline?

   a) political science
   b) history
   c) philosophy
   d) economics

6. In systems analytic terms, "demands" and "support" are both types of

   a) impact.
   b) input.
   c) output.
   d) decisions.

7. According to the boxed insert "Summary of Polling Methodology," it is not possible to

   a) include "undecided" voters, or voters "leaning" toward one of the candidates, in the sample of the population polled.
   b) take demographics, such as the age and sex of the individuals polled, into account in the sample selected.
   c) obtain a sample that reflects the characteristics of the entire adult population in the U.S.
   d) design a perfect poll.

8. In order to enhance reliability in coding material used in content analysis

   a) emotional material is not used.
   b) oral reports are not evaluated.
   c) more than one coder is used.
   d) only one coder is used.

9. Which of the following political philosophers/authors relied more on subjective impressions than objective experiences?

   a) Plato
   b) Aristotle
   c) Locke
   d) Easton

10. Game theory

   a) helps the decision-maker to make the right choice.
   b) has been used by decision-makers dating back to ancient Greece.
   c) allows the decision-maker to make the best possible decision with the given information.
   d) cannot be used to make military decisions.

11. The _____ is obtained by adding up the values of all of the indicators and dividing the total by the number of indicators.

   a) Mean
   b) Bell curve factor
   c) Standard deviation
   d) Central tendency

12. The book *The War of the Worlds*, was written by

   a) George Wells.
   b) H.G. Wells.
   c) John Steinbeck.
   d) Orson Wells.

13. Mystical thinkers who relied more on subjective impression and objective experiences include:

   a) Thomas Hume and Karl Marx.
   b) Charles Montesquieu and John Stuart Mill.
   c) Plato and Jean Jacques Rousseau.
   d) Aristotle and John Locke.

14. A _____ is a selection according to the same system, depriving the interviewer of the choice of the respondent.

   a) Random digit dialing
   b) Systematic selection
   c) Random selection
   d) Likelihood selection process

15. In 1948, the *Literary Digest* published a poll incorrectly predicting a White House victory for

   a) Harry Truman over Thomas Dewey.
   b) Thomas Dewey over Harry Truman.
   c) Harry Truman over Dwight Eisenhower.
   d) Dwight Eisenhower over Harry Truman.

ESSAY QUESTIONS:

1. Fully explain, using specific examples from the chapter, the importance of knowing how information, particularly political information, is acquired.

2. What are the component parts of a political system?

3. Describe the specific uses and limitations of statistical and polling methodology.

ANSWERS TO INTRODUCTION

TRUE/FALSE:

1. True	6. False	11. True
2. True	7. False	12. False
3. True	8. True	13. True
4. False	9. False	14. True
5. True	10. True	15. True

FILL-IN-THE-BLANKS:

1. scientific, empirical
2. data
3. content analysis
4. an approach
5. relationship
6. rational
7. domestic and international
8. laws; executive orders; judicial decisions; bureaucratic rules and regulations
9. David Easton
10. variable
11. hypotheses
12. political system
13. outputs
14. conversion process

MULTIPLE CHOICE:

1. c - a macro approach
2. a - surveys
3. c - indicate clinical depression
4. a - focus on what "is"
5. d - economics
6. b - input
7. d - design a perfect poll
8. c - more than one coder is used
9. a - Plato
10. c - allows the decision-maker to make the best possible decision with given the information
11. a- mean
12. b- H.G. Wells
13. c- Plato and Jean Jacques Rousseau
14. b- systematic selection   15. b- Thomas Dewey over Harry Truman

THE LANGUAGE OF POLITICAL SCIENCE

CHAPTER SUMMARY:

Chapter One focuses on the language used by political scientists and the need for students of American Government to learn it. After distinguishing the differences among the components of language, including concepts, theories and definitions, the remainder of the chapter is devoted to defining and explaining some of the most often used terms in the discipline of political science.

IDENTIFICATION:

Briefly describe each term.

<u>Concepts</u>

<u>Nominal definitions</u>

<u>Politics</u>

<u>Political science</u>

<u>Government</u>

Democracy

Political spectrum

Power

Hyperpluralism

Authority

Direct Democracy

Representative Democracy

Direct Initiative

Status Quo

Intensity

TRUE/FALSE:

Indicate whether each statement is true (T) or false (F). The correct answers are given at the end of the chapter.

_____ 1. Theories are the words or names used to symbolize or represent ideas.

_____ 2. A nation's power base or assets include its wealth, a large military establishment, abundant natural resources, international status, etc.

_____ 3. Hyperpluralism is associated with conflicting sets of policies, stalemate, and gridlock.

_____ 4. Governmental decision-making is the essence of the concept of politics.

_____ 5. The "majoritarian theory" of democracy is one of three theories of who holds "formal" or governmental power in a democracy.

_____ 6. The roots of American political thought are found within the Western tradition and culture.

_____ 7. Communists are on the right of the political spectrum and fascists are on the left.

_____ 8. Time, place and culture comprise the context within which political concepts, theories, and definitions emerge.

_____ 9. The three essential elements to maintaining a democratic regime are holding regular elections, creating nationalism, and protecting citizens' rights.

_____ 10. The United States is a pluralist country.

_____ 11. In *The Process of Government*, Thomas Dye set forth the basic argument in support of actual governing power residing with groups.

_____ 12. The elite theory rests on the premise that the decision making process in the United States is controlled by a handful of powerful individuals who are connected to the nation's corporate enterprises.

_____ 13. In *Politics: Who Gets What, When and How*, Harold Lasswell develops the concept of pluralism.

_____ 14. The political right includes those who bend towards conservatism and protectionism.

_____ 15. The Congress, the court, the presidency and the bureaucracy are several of the political institutions in the United States that allocate value.

_____ 16. The degree to which an individual is placed to the right or the left of the status quo line is determined by the intensity (how fast or slow the change is wanted) and the preferred speed (how strong the change is wanted).

_____ 17. By definition, an elite consists of relatively few individuals as compared with the large memberships found in the powerful interest groups.

FILL-IN-THE-BLANKS:

Write the appropriate word(s) to complete the sentence. The correct answers are given at the end of the chapter.

1. There are many types of definitions but, for the most part, political scientists use _____ definitions.

2. David Easton defined the term politics as "the _____ allocation of values."

3. Another name for a "direct" democracy is _____ democracy.

4. The degree to which an individual is placed to the right or left of the status quo line on the political spectrum is determined by both the intensity and the preferred_____ of the desired policy change.

5. Authority is a form of _____ .

6. The United States has a _____ regime.

7. The term "government" is formally defined as the _____ and the institutions that decide who gets what.

8. Applying Lasswell's definition of politics, the recipients of governmental policies are members of the _____.

9. A _____ is defined as "a way of governing."

10. Greek philosopher _____ wrote "*The Politics,*" an analysis of governing systems.

11. In _____, Plato discussed the attributes of an ideal or utopian government.

12. _____ democracy is another term for direct democracy.

13. Representative or _____ democracy occurs when the citizenship elects a small body to represent the needs of the entire nation.

14. A _____ is an attempt made to explain rather than just name political phenomena.

15. Members of the _____ include liberals, socialists, communists, and radicals.

16. According to Bertrand Russell, producing the _____ of power involves the promise of rewards or the treat of penalties.

MULTIPLE CHOICE:

Circle the correct response. The correct answers are given at the end of the chapter.

1. Political science is a

   a) hard science.
   b) physical science.
   c) biological science.
   d) social science.

2. Herodotus coined the term

   a) government.
   b) politics.
   c) democracy.
   d) constitution.

3. Registered voters may vote their approval or disapproval of proposed constitutional changes through a process called the

   a) direct initiative.
   b) recall.
   c) popular referendum.
   d) none of the above.

4. The process by which registered voters may amend their state constitution is called the

    a) direct initiative.
    b) recall.
    c) popular referendum.
    d) none of the above.

5. Registered voters may remove a government official during his/ her term of office by a process called

    a) direct initiative.
    b) recall.
    c) popular referendum.
    d) none of the above.

6. The five principal fields of political science are American government, public administration, political philosophy or theory, international relations and

    a) state government.
    b) political parties.
    c) comparative government.
    d) governing institutions.
    e) multinational corporate studies.

7. According to Lutz, in the boxed insert "The Government's Doublespeak of War" the first casualty in a war is

    a) troops.
    b) money.
    c) language.
    d) government.

8. The theory of democracy that holds that power resides with the people or voters is called

    a) majoritarian theory.
    b) group theory.
    c) pluralist theory.
    d) hyperpluralism.

9. The political left includes:

   a) liberals.
   b) Socialists and Communists.
   c) radicals.
   d) all of the above.

10. The political right includes conservatives and

   a) anarchists.
   b) Fascists.
   c) Libertarians.
   d) radical environmentalists.

11. The elite theory of politics was developed by

   a) Thomas Dye.
   b) David Hume.
   c) Theodore Lowi.
   d) Arthur F. Bentley.

12. In *The Process of Government*, Arthur F. Bentley developed the _____ theory of government.

   a) hyperpluralistic
   b) elite
   c) group
   d) individualist

13. The catchy phrase that politics is "who gets, what, when and how" was coined by

   a) Harold Lasswell.
   b) David Easton.
   c) James B. Whisher.
   d) Thomas Dye.

ESSAY QUESTIONS:

1. Fully explain, using specific examples from the chapter, the importance of knowing political definitions and understanding the language used by political scientists.

2. Define the term "power" and list and explain its four distinguishing qualities or characteristics.

ANSWERS TO CHAPTER ONE: THE LANGUAGE OF POLITICAL SCIENCE

TRUE/FALSE:

1.	False	5.	False	9.	False	13.	False
2.	True	6.	True	10.	True	14.	True
3.	True	7.	False	11.	False	15.	True
4.	True	8.	True	12.	True	16.	False
						17.	True

FILL-IN-THE-BLANKS:

1. nominal
2. authoritative
3. participatory
4. speed
5. power
6. democratic
7. people
8. elite
9. regime
10. Aristotle
11. *The Republic*
12. participatory
13. indirect
14. theory
15. political left
16. intended effects

MULTIPLE CHOICE:

1.	d - social science	9.	d -	all of the above
2.	c - democracy	10.	b -	Fascists
3.	c - referendum	11.	a -	Thomas Dye
4.	a - initiative	12.	c -	group
5.	b - recall	13.	a -	Harold Lasswell
6.	c - comparative government			
7.	c - language			
8.	a - majoritarian theory			

CHAPTER TWO

CONSTITUTIONAL GOVERNMENT

CHAPTER SUMMARY:

Chapter 2 examines the development of constitutional governments with particular emphasis on the political theories of Jean Jacques Rousseau, Charles de Montesquieu, and John Locke. The development of the United States Constitution begins with the issues leading to the revolution from Great Britain and ends with the Framers in Philadelphia carving an organic law that would guide the newly created nation down the path of democracy.

IDENTIFICATION:

Briefly describe each term.

Articles of Confederation

Constitutionalism

Daniel Shay

Declaration of Independence

Democracy

Good Behavior

Government

Jean Jacques Rousseau

Plato

Republic

Social Contract

TRUE/FALSE:

Indicate whether each statement is true (T) or false (F). The correct answers are given at the end of the chapter.

_____ 1. Some form of government is an absolute necessity for any society whether they are members of a clan, tribe, city, nation state or empire.

_____ 2. Outlined in *The Republic*, Plato designed his just city that would be ruled by the philosopher kings.

_____ 3. The nation's first government called for a unitary system under the Articles of Confederation.

_____ 4. Ruling from 495 BC to 429 BC, Emperor Pericles reigned during Rome's Golden Age.

_____ 5. In 1786, a group of angry farmers under the leadership of John Dickerson launched an ill-fated insurrection against the state of Massachusetts.

_____ 6. Signed in 1215, the Magna Carta was the first legal document to question the authority of a divine right monarch.

_____ 7. Aristotle determined that a tyranny or a rule of one was a sound governing format as long as the monarch ruled for the benefit of his/her people.

_____ 8. In *The Rights of Men*, John Locke drew a direct connection between a constitution, a government, and the concept of the social contract.

_____ 9. At the Constitutional Convention, the delegates believed that the best governing format was to further strengthen state governments and weaken the national government.

_____ 10. Democratic ideology is based on the principles of individualism, liberty, equality, and fraternity.

_____ 11. The Currency Act of 1751 prohibited colonials from issuing their own paper currency as legal tender.

_____ 12. In *Palko v Connecticut*, Justice Louis D. Brandies wrote that the doctrine of separation of powers was adopted by the Convention in 1787 not to promote efficiency but to preclude the exercise of arbitrary government.

_____ 13. The New Jersey Plan called for the revision of the Articles of Confederation and a one-house legislative body.

_____ 14. In the Greek city states, full participatory or pure democracy worked as long as the membership of the governing assembly was manageable.

_____ 15. The 16th Amendment to the United States Constitution calls for the popular or direct election of members to the United States Senate.

_____ 16. According to Article I, Section 9, the importation of slaves would be prohibited by 1808.

_____ 17. It takes a 2/3's vote in both Houses of Congress to call for a national convention to amend the Constitution.

_____ 18. The Three-fifths Compromise called for 3/5's of a state's African-American slaves to be counted as population for apportionment and for direct tax calculations.

_____ 19. The Framers required approval or ratification from all thirteen states for the acceptance of the United States Constitution.

_____ 20. Washington's first Cabinet was composed of Thomas Jefferson as Secretary of State, Alexander Hamilton as Attorney General, Henry Knox as Secretary of the Treasury, and Edmund Randolph as Secretary of War.

_____ 21. The major obstacle against ratification of the United States Constitution was that the document lacked a bill of rights.

_____ 22. Article II of the United States Constitution specifically requires the president to form a Cabinet of key officials to head various government departments.

_____ 23. Supporters of the new Constitution were commonly known as Federalists while the opposition was coined as the Know-Nothings.

FILL IN THE BLANKS:

Write the appropriate word(s) to complete the sentence. The correct answers are given at the end of the chapter.

1. _____is the formal institutional structure and processes of a society by which policies are developed and implemented in the form of law binding on all.

2. The _____ of 1795 required colonists to purchase a stamp for all commercial and legal documents.

3. A _____is a form of government in which sovereign power resides in the electorate and is exercised by elected representatives who are responsible to the people.

4. _____ is the political principle of limited government under a written contract.

5. In his Reflections on the Revolution in France, _____ emphasized that society is indeed a contract.

6. Representative or _____ is a form of governance in which the citizens rule through representatives who are periodically elected in order to keep them accountable.

7. In _____, Justice Brandies wrote that the doctrine of separation of powers was adopted by the Convention in 1787 not to promote efficiency but to preclude the exercise of arbitrary power.

8. _____ is the notion that constitutional devises can prevent any power within a nation from becoming absolute by being balanced against, or checked by, another source of power within that same nation.

9. Greek philosopher _____ believed that "the state is a creation of nature, and that man is a by nature a political animal."

24

10. In _____, James Madison drew a distinction between a democracy and a republic

11. The United States Constitution is the embodiment of the _____ concept of government.

12. In *The Republic*, _____ outlined his concept of a "just city."

13. An _____ is the way of life of a people, reflected in their collectively held ideas and beliefs concerning the nature of the ideal political system, economic order, social goals, and moral values.

14. In *Federalist #5*, _____emphasized that the weaknesses of the confederative system would undermine the viability of the United States.

15. In order to be a meaningful document, a constitution must be regarded as the _____ of its state.

16. _____ is a system of government in which the ultimate political authority rests with the people.

17. John Locke called the relationship between the governed and the governing a _____.

18. In *Federalist #69*, _____ justifies his support of a limited term for the presidency.

19. In his *The Rights of Man*, _____ drew a direct connection between a constitution, a government, and the concept of the social contract.

20. A _____ was a small but autonomous political unit in which all major political, social, and religious activities were carried out at one central location.

21. A _____ is a fundamental or organic law that establishes the framework of a state, assigns the powers and duties of governmental agencies, and establishes the relationship between the people and their government.

22. Under the _____, the traditional executive and legislative functions were merged into the National Assembly, composed of representatives from each state.

23. At the Constitution Convention, James Madison served as the body's secretary while _____ was selected as the president or presiding officer.

MULTIPLE CHOICE:

Circle the correct response. The correct answers are given at the end of the chapter.

1. In his *Confessions*, _____ wrote "I have seen that everything is rooted in politics and that, whatever might be attempted, no people would ever be other than the nature of their government made them."

   a) Charles de Montesquieu
   b) Edmund Burke
   c) John Locke
   d) Jean Jacques Rousseau

2. Under the Articles of Confederation, the National Congress was empowered to _____.

   a) declare war, conduct foreign policy, make treaties and control interstate commerce.
   b) declare war, make treaties, establish a national currency, and conduct foreign policy.
   c) declare war, conduct foreign policy and make treaties.
   d) conduct foreign policy, declare war, collect taxes and make treaties.

3. *Federalist #10* was written by _____.

   a) John Adams
   b) John Jay
   c) Alexander Hamilton
   d) James Madison

4. An amendment to the Constitution must first pass with a majority vote in both Houses of Congress and win the approval of _____ of the states' legislative houses.

   a) 2/3's
   b) 4/5's
   c) 3/5's
   d) 3/4's

5. At the Constitutional Convention, _____ served as the body's secretary.

   a) James Madison
   b) John Hancock
   c) John Adams
   d) Alexander Hamilton

6. _____ of the United States Constitution details its ratification process.

   a) Article V
   b) Article VI
   c) Article VII
   d) Article VIII

7. _____ is the distribution of governing power among the three branches of government and giving them specific duties and responsibilities.

   a) Checks and Balances
   b) Interposition
   c) Intergovernmental Relationships
   d) Separation of Powers

8. *The Politics* was written by _____.

   a) Plato
   b) Pericles
   c) Aristotle
   d) Cicero

9. _____ is the notion that constitutional devices can prevent any power within a nation from becoming absolute by being balanced against, or checked by, another source of power within that same nation.

   a) Checks and Balances
   b) Interposition
   c) Intergovernmental Relationships
   d) Separation of Powers

10. _____ is a form of governance in which the citizens rule through representatives, who are periodically elected in order to keep them accountable.

   a) Representative Democracy
   b) Pure Democracy
   c) Autocratic Government
   d) Oligarchical Government

11. Commonly known as the Great Compromise, the _____ plan consolidated the Virginia and New Jersey plans.

    a) Pennsylvania
    b) Vermont
    c) Connecticut
    d) Massachusetts

12. _____ of the United States Constitution gives the legislative branch the authority to make laws.

    a) Article I
    b) Article II
    c) Article III
    d) Article IV

13. Democracy in America was written by _____.

    a) Alexis de Tocqueville
    b) Thomas Paine
    c) John Locke
    d) John Stuart Mill

14. The _____ Amendment to the United States Constitution calls for the direct or popular election United States Senators.

    a) 16th
    b) 17th
    c) 18th
    d) 19th

15. _____ of the United States Constitution charges the executive branch with the implementation of laws enacted by the legislative branch.

    a) Article I
    b) Article II
    c) Article III
    d) Article IV

16. _____ is a system of government in which the ultimate political authority is vested in the people.

    a) Socialism
    b) Communism
    c) Democracy
    d) Autocracy

17. _____ was the only state not to send a delegation to the Constitution Convention held in Philadelphia.

    a) New Jersey
    b) Vermont
    c) Rhode Island
    d) New Hampshire

18. Introduced at the Constitutional Convention, the _____ called for a bicameral or a two house legislative body.

    a) Maryland Plan
    b) North Carolina Plan
    c) Virginia Plan
    d) New Jersey Plan

19. In *The Republic*, Plato envisioned that his "just city" would consist of three classes:

    a) the philosopher kings, the auxiliaries and slaves.
    b) the legislative body, the auxiliaries and slaves.
    c) the philosopher kings, the auxiliaries, and the productive class.
    d) the philosopher kings, the craftsmen.

20. _____ of the United States Constitution created the nation's federal court and justice system.

    a) Article I
    b) Article II
    c) Article III
    d) Article IV

21. _____ is the aspiration of some group—grounded in some existing sentiment of national or racial identify associated with common territory, language or religion—to form its own sovereign state and to govern itself.

    a) Imperialism
    b) Democracy
    c) Nationalism
    d) Self-Determination

22. The concept of the _____ rests on the premise that when men decided to form societies they gave up their absolute rights to life, liberty and property in exchange for creating a government that would protect the rights to life, liberty and property for all members of the society.

    a) Self-Determination
    b) Social Contract
    c) Imperialism
    d) Nationalism

23. Representing the interests of the small states at the Constitutional Convention, the _____ called for a one house legislature and the revision of the Articles of Confederation.

    a) New Jersey Plan
    b) Virginia Plan
    c) Connecticut Plan
    d) New York Accord

24. _____ served as the nation's first vice president.

    a) Thomas Jefferson
    b) John Adams
    c) Samuel Adams
    d) James Madison

25. The first legislative assembly in the American colonies, the _____ was founded in 1619 in Virginia.

    a) House Assembly
    b) Senate
    c) House of Burgess
    d) House of Representatives

26. A member of Parliament, political philosopher _____ urged the British government to use restraint in dealing with colonial issues.

   a) Harold McMillian
   b) John Stuart Mill
   c) Jeremy Bentham
   d) Edmund Burke

27. _____ wrote in *Federalist No. 51*, "if men were angels, no government would be necessary."

   a) John Adams
   b) Alexander Hamilton
   c) James Madison
   d) John Jay

ESSAY QUESTIONS:

1. What did Aristotle mean by his phrase "man is a political animal"?

2. What are the four main purposes of a constitution?

3. What were the six basic reasons why James Madison wanted to create a strong national government?

ANSWERS TO CHAPTER TWO: CONSTITUTIONAL GOVERNMENT

TRUE/FALSE:

1.	True	6.	True	11.	True	16.	True	21.	True
2.	True	7.	False	12.	False	17.	True	22.	False
3.	False	8.	False	13.	True	18.	True	23.	False
4.	False	9.	False	14.	True	19.	False		
5.	False	10.	True	15.	False	20.	False		

FILL-IN-THE-BLANKS:

1.	Government	13.	Ideology
2.	Stamp Tax	14.	John Jay
3.	Republic	15.	Organic Law
4.	Constitutionalism	16.	Democracy
5.	Edmund Burke	17.	Fiduciary Trust
6.	Indirect Democracy	18.	Alexander Hamilton
7.	*Myers v United States*	19.	Thomas Paine
8.	Checks and Balances	20.	Polis
9.	Aristotle	21.	Constitution
10.	*Federalist #10*	22.	National Congress
11.	Madisonian	23.	George Washington
12.	Plato		

MULTIPLE CHOICE:

1.	d – Jean Jacques Rousseau	15.	b – Article II
2.	c – Declare war, conduct foreign policy and make treaties	16.	c - Democracy
3.	d – James Madison	17.	c – Rhode Island
4.	d – ¾'s	18.	c – Virginia Plan
5.	b – James Madison	19.	c –Philosopher kings, the auxiliaries, and productive class
6.	c – Article VII	20.	c - Article III
7.	d – Separation of Powers	21.	d – Self-Determination
8.	c – Aristotle	22.	b – Social Contract
9.	a – Checks and Balances	23.	a – New Jersey Plan
10.	a –Representative Democracy	24.	b – John Adams
11.	c – Connecticut	25.	c – House of Burgess
12.	a – Article I	26.	d – Edmund Burke
13.	a – Alexis de Tocqueville	27.	c – James Madison
14.	b – 17th		

CHAPTER THREE

FEDERALISM

CHAPTER SUMMARY:

The chapter delves into the establishment of the federal system in the United States within the constitutional framework designed by the Framers. Particular attention is devoted to the ever changing relationship between the states and the national government.

IDENTIFICATION:

Briefly describe each term.

<u>10th Amendment</u>

<u>Compact Theory</u>

<u>Eminent Domain</u>

<u>Full Faith and Credit Clause</u>

<u>*Fullilove v Klutznik*</u>

Grants

Horizontal Federalism

Interstate Rendition

John C. Calhoun

Nullification

TRUE/FALSE:

Indicate whether each statement is true (T) or false (F). The correct answers are given at the end of the chapter.

_____ 1. Intergovernmental relations are the complex network of interrelationships among governments, i.e., political, fiscal, programmatic and administrative process by which higher units of government share revenues and other resources with lower units of government.

_____ 2. The United Nations is basically a federal association of nation states.

_____ 3. The Northwest Land Ordinance gave federal lands for public education in the Western territories.

_____ 4. In _McCullough v Maryland,_ the Supreme Court ruled that the federal government did not have the right of eminent domain to seize state land to build a branch office of the National Bank in Maryland.

_____ 5. Categorical grants are federal payments to states or federal or state payments to local governments for specified purposes.

_____ 6. The Full Faith and Credit Clause of Article V places the individual as a citizen of his/her country above residency in a state.

_____7. Under the formula grant program, Congress allocated money to states and local governments based on a predetermined formula.

_____8. As adopted in 1789, the Constitution created a national government with sovereign powers of its own-powers that one belonged exclusively to the states.

_____9. Federalism is actually a hybrid combination of the unitary and confederative systems.

_____10. According to Article IV, states are required to recognize the public acts, records and judicial proceedings of every other state.

_____11. Federal grant programs may also include cross cutting regulations to include if necessary, an environmental impact statement.

_____12. In *Cohen v Virginia*, the Supreme Court ruled that states do not have the right to secede from the union.

_____13. Article I of the United States Constitution grants Congress the exclusive authority to levy and collect taxes for the national government.

_____14. The Supremacy Clause of Article IV of the United States Constitution makes the constitution the "supreme law of the land."

_____15. The 9th Amendment to the U.S. Constitution gives the states their reserved powers.

_____16. An interstate compact is an agreement between two or more states requiring congressional approval.

_____17. John C. Calhoun believed in the compact theory of government whereby governments were created by and existed for the benefit of the people.

_____18. The Anti-Federalists believed that the necessary and proper clause along with the Supremacy Clause gave the national government too much power and authority over state governments.

_____19. In *Marbury v Madison*, the United States Supreme Court defined interstate commerce as including all navigable waters even those within a state.

_____20. The advantages of the unitary system are uniformity of public policy enforcement and a centralized government.

_____ 21. A confederative system is the mode of political organization that unites separate units within an overarching political system by distributing power among general and con stituent governments in a manner designed to protect the existence and authority of both.

_____ 22. In *Cohen v Virginia* (1821) the Supreme Court upheld a federal court's authority to review judicial decisions rendered by state courts.

_____ 23. In *Texas v White*, the Supreme Court ruled that Congress could tax interest earned from individual savings accounts and dividends on state and locally issued bonds.

_____ 24. Article III, Section 4 of the United States Constitution places certain restrictions on both the national and state governments.

_____ 25. Intrastate commerce is all commerce traveling across state boundary lines.

_____ 26. According to the Constitution, the writ of habeas corpus cannot be suspended except in cases of rebellion and insurrection.

_____ 27. Eminent domain is an example of a government's proprietary function.

_____ 28. In *Plintz v United States*, the Supreme Court ruled unconstitutional a federal law making it a crime to carry a gun within 1,000 feet of a school.

_____ 29. In *Garcia v San Antonio Metropolitan Transit Authority*, the Supreme Court ruled constitutional a federal mandate requiring that all state public employees be paid at least minimum wage and overtime.

_____ 30. Pragmatic federalism is based on the creation of empowerment zones whereby non-federal resources are combined with modest federal cash outlays.

_____ 31. States' rights is defined as the opposition to increasing the national government's power at the expense of the states.

_____ 32. Calhoun's concept of interposition is based on the belief that democratic decisions should be made only with the concurrence of all major segments of society.

_____ 33. The national government has the authority to oversee all commercial activity that crosses any state boundary line.

_____ 34. President George W. Bush retooled Reagan's New Federalism into his own concept entitled Constrained Empathetic Federalism.

_____ 35. According to Calhoun, if the national government failed to fulfill the needs of the people of a particular state, then that state had the right to nullify its compact with the national government and form its own government.

_____ 36. Dual federalism is oftentimes called marble cake federalism.

FILL IN THE BLANKS:

Write the appropriate word(s) to complete the sentence. The correct answers are given at the end of the chapter.

1. _____is the notion that the national, state and local governments are interacting agents, jointly working to solve common problems.

2. Calhoun's concept of _____is based on the belief that democratic decisions should be made only with the concurrence of all major segments of society.

3. A _____ is a form of gift that entails certain obligations on the part of the grantee and expectations on the part of the grantor.

4. _____ of the United States Constitution prohibits state governments from entering into treaties.

5. A _____ occurs when a state or local government fails to establish its own requirements thereby leaving the door open for a federal agency to issue its own mandates.

6. Dual federalism is oftentimes called _____federalism.

7. _____ is all commerce traveling within state boundary lines.

8. _____ are federal payments to states or federal or state payments to local governments for specified purposes.

9. _____federalism is based on the creation of empower-ment zones whereby non-federal resources are combined with modest federal cash outlays.

10. An _____ is one level of government requiring another to offer and pay for a program as a matter of law or as a prerequisite to partial or full funding for either the program in question or other programs.

11. _____ is the opposition to increase the national government's powers at the expense of the states.

12. Cooperative federalism is also known as _____.

13. Created by Ronald Reagan, _____ was designed to reduce the role of the national government in state and local affairs.

14. John C. Calhoun believed in the _____of government whereby governments were created by and existed for the benefit of the people.

15. _____ were used to build the majority of the nation's public housing projects.

16. In _____, the Supreme Court ruled that states cannot secede from the Union.

17. In _____, the Supreme Court ruled that the 10th Amendment to the Constitutional prohibited the national government from setting wages and maximum working hour requirements for all public state government employees.

18. The _____ system is one in which principal power within the political system lies at the level of a national or central government.

19. _____ federalism is state-to-state interactions and relations.

20. _____ of the Constitution places certain restrictions on both the national and state governments.

21. _____ or delegated powers are those rights and responsibilities of the U.S. government specifically provided for and listed in the Constitution.

22. In _____, the Supreme Court ruled that Congress had the authority to use quotas to remedy past discrimination in the hiring, promotion and termination of government public works programs.

23. According to the 10th Amendment, those power not delegated to the United States by the Constitution, or prohibited by it to the states, are _____ to the states, respectively, or to the people.

24. In _____, the Supreme Court ruled that the national government did have the authority to control shipping on the Hudson River.

25. _____ is the governing authority that flows up and down between the national and state governments.

26. A _____ system is the mode of political organization that unites separate polities within an overarching political system by distributing power among general and constituent governments in a manner designed to protect the existence and authority of both.

27. _____ is the return of fugitives from justice by a state upon the demand of the executive authority of the state in which the crime was committed.

28. A _____ is a congressional law or regulation that must be enforced or grant recipients can be held accountable to civil or criminal penalties.

MULTIPLE CHOICE:

Circle the correct response. The correct answers are given at the end of the chapter.

1. The Supremacy Clause is located in _____ of the United States Constitution.

    a) Article III
    b) Article IV
    c) Article V
    d) Article VI

2. A _____ was a federal payment to a state or local government for a specific purpose.

    a) Project Grant
    b) Categorical Grant
    c) Formula Grant Program
    d) Block Grant

3. _____ is the authority to promote and safeguard the health, morals, safety and welfare of the people.

    a) Implied Powers
    b) Inherent Powers
    c) Police Powers
    d) Enumerated Powers

4. _____ are given for prescribed broader activities from health care to education.

   a) Project Grants
   b) Categorical Grants
   c) Formula Grant Programs
   d) Block Grants

5. The _____ is one in which principal power within the political system lies at the level of a national or central government.

   a) Confederative System
   b) Federal System
   c) Multi-Level System
   d) Unitary System

6. Under the General Revenue Fund, _____ was a combination of federal and state money allocated on a formula basis to assist local communities to fund intercity projects.

   a) Revenue Sharing
   b) Categorical Grants
   c) Formula Grant Programs
   d) Block Grants

7. Created by Ronald Reagan, _____ was designed to reduce the role of the national government in state and local affairs.

   a) Dual Federalism
   b) Pragmatic Federalism
   c) Cooperative Federalism
   d) New Federalism

8. Calhoun's concept of _____ placed the states as the middlemen or buffer zones to shield the people living in their states from harmful national mandates.

   a) Compact Theory
   b) Nullification
   c) Interposition
   d) Concurrent Majority

9. In *Federalist #45*, _____ attempted to explain the relationship between the states and the national government.

   a) James Madison
   b) John Adams
   c) John Jay
   d) Alexander Hamilton

10. In _____ (1948), the Supreme Court ruled that any state laws denying women the right to practice certain occupations usually held by men were unconstitutional.

   a) *Goesaert v Cleary*
   b) *Fullilove v Klutznik*
   c) *Gibbons v Ogden*
   d) *McCullough v Maryland*

11. A _____ system is a loose collection of states in which principal power lies at the level of the individual states rather than at the level of the central or national government.

   a) Confederative
   b) Federal
   c) Unitary
   d) Multi-Level

12. In _____, the Supreme Court ruled that Congress could tax interest earned from individual savings accounts and dividends on state and locally issued bonds.

   a) *Goesaert v Cleary*
   b) *South Carolina v Baker*
   c) *National League of Cities v Usery*
   d) *Garcia v San Antonio Metropolitan Transit Authority*

13. In _____, the Supreme Court upheld a federal court's authority to review decisions rendered by state courts.

   a) *Goesaert v Cleary*
   b) *Cohen v Virginia*
   c) *Gibbons v Ogden*
   d) *McCullough v Maryland*

14. The necessary and proper clause of the United States Constitution is located in _____.

   a)   Article I, Section 5
   b)   Article I, Section 8
   c)   Article II, Section 3
   d)   Article III, Section 1

15. _____ of the United States Constitution grants Congress the exclusive authority to levy and collect taxes for the national government.

   a)   Article IV
   b)   Article III
   c)   Article II
   d)   Article I

16. The necessary and proper clause is also known as the _____.

   a)   Concurrent Powers Clause
   b)   Enumeration Decree
   c)   Implied Powers Doctrine
   d)   Inherent Powers Doctrine

17. The power for both the states and the national government to levy and collect taxes is an example of _____.

   a)   Implied Powers
   b)   Concurrent Powers
   c)   Enumerated Powers
   d)   Inherent Powers

18. In _____, the Supreme Court reinforced the equality of the states by ruling that all states are admitted into the union on an equal footing.

   a)   Goesaert v Cleary
   b)   Fullilove v Klutznik
   c)   Gibbons v Ogden
   d)   Coyle v Smith

19. Until 1932, the relationship between the states and the national government was _____ whereby autonomous national, subnational and local governments all pursued their own interests independently of each other.

   a)   Cooperative Federalism
   b)   Dual Federalism
   c)   Creative Federalism
   d)   Pragmatic Federalism

ESSAY QUESTIONS:

1.   What are the strengths and weaknesses of the unitary system?

2. What are the strengths and weaknesses of the confederative system?

3. What are the strengths and weaknesses of the federal system?

4. What were the weaknesses of the Articles of Confederation?

ANSWERS TO CHAPTER THREE: FEDERALISM

TRUE/FALSE:

1.	True	9.	True	17.	True	25.	False	33.	True
2.	False	10.	True	18.	True	26.	True	34.	False
3.	True	11.	True	19.	False	27.	True	35.	True
4.	False	12.	False	20.	True	28.	False	36.	False
5.	False	13.	True	21.	False	29.	True		
6.	False	14.	False	22.	True	30.	False		
7.	True	15.	False	23.	False	31.	True		
8.	True	16.	True	24.	False	32.	False		

FILL IN THE BLANKS:

1. Cooperative Federalism
2. Concurrent Majority
3. Grant
4. Article I, Section 10
5. Partial Mandate
6. Layered Cake
7. Interstate Commerce
8. Grants-in-Aid
9. Constrained Empathetic
10. Unfunded Mandate
11. States' Rights
12. Marble Cake Federalism
13. New Federalism
14. Compact Theory
15. Project Grants
16. *Texas v White*
17. *National League of Cities v Usery*
18. Unitary
19. Horizontal
20. Article, I, Section 9
21. Enumerated
22. *Fullilove v Klutznik*
23. Reserved
24. *Gibbons v Ogden*
25. Vertical Federalism
26. Federal
27. Interstate Rendition
28. Direct Order

MULTIPLE CHOICE:

1. d) Article VI
2. b) Categorical Grant
3. c) Police Powers
4. d) Block Grants
5. d) Unitary System
6. a) Revenue Sharing
7. d) New Federalism
8. c) Interposition
9. a) James Madison
10. a) *Goesaert v Cleary*
11. a) Confederative
12. b) *South Carolina v Baker*
13. b) Cohen v Virginia
14. b) Article I, Section 8
15. d) Article I
16. c) Implied Powers Doctrine
17. b) Concurrent Powers
18. d) *Coyle v Smith*
19. b) Dual Federalism

PUBLIC OPINION, POLITICAL CULTURE, AND POLITICAL SOCIALIZATION

CHAPTER SUMMARY:

Public opinion, political culture, and political socialization are three integrated theories. These theories attempt to explain how individuals and countries come to share a common set of enduring political beliefs and orientations and how these political beliefs and orientations continually shape, and are shaped by, public opinion.

IDENTIFICATION:

Briefly describe each term.

Latent opinion

Public opinion

Political culture

Political socialization

Agents of socialization (Identify term and list them)

Peers

Diffuse support

Alexis de Tocqueville

Mass communication media

The Civic Culture

TRUE/FALSE:

Indicate whether each statement is true (T) or false (F). The correct answers are given at the end of the chapter.

_____ 1. Public opinion is so closely related to political culture and political socialization that it is difficult to talk about only one of the three with reference to the other two.

_____ 2. Unlike his immediate predecessor, Bill Clinton, George W. Bush did not court the women's vote during the presidential campaign.

_____ 3. Public opinion tends to be much more volatile and transitory in nature than political culture.

_____ 4. Political culture is defined as "an aggregate of individual views, attitudes or beliefs shared by a portion of a community."

_____ 5. Of all the aspects of American political culture, Tocqueville seemed to be most struck by the strong emphasis citizens place on money and property.

_____ 6. It was concluded in *The Civic Culture Revisited* that the American political culture had undergone a fundamental change as a result of the Vietnam War and the Watergate experience.

_____ 7. During the 2000 campaign Bush used emotional words in an effort to attract young voters.

_____ 8. Virtually everyone at some point qualifies as an agent of socialization.

_____ 9. Almond and Verba wrote the first major work on the subject of political socialization.

_____ 10. Researchers have found that children idealize the presidential role.

_____ 11. In the 2004 presidential election, Democrat John Kerry won the women's vote by 51 percent to Bush's 48 percent.

_____ 12. Thomas Paine's little pamphlet, *The Social Contract*, swayed public opinion against King George III and toward independence in 1776.

_____ 13. A agent of socialization is any formal or informal group or structure that intentionally sends out a political message.

FILL-IN-THE-BLANKS:

Write the appropriate word(s) to complete the sentence. The correct answers are given at the end of the chapter.

1. The more salient, meaning _____, that poll respondents say that an issue is to them the more likely it is to be listened to by politicians.

2. The affluent, middle-class, suburban women who were said to have re-elected President Clinton in 1996 and who were identified as the "key swing voter[s] in suburban America" in 2000, are referred to in the media as _____ .

3. The first major work on the topic of political socialization was written by_____.

4. Tocqueville, author of _____, wrote about the qualities that distinguish Americans from their European counterparts.

5. _____argued that among the valid reasons for the American colonies to separate from England was its unique national spirit, character and culture.

6. Political socialization is defined in two ways; it is defined as the process by which political _____ are passed down over the generations and as the process by which _____ political outlooks are acquired.

7. According to Herbert H. Hyman, the most important agent of political socialization is _____ .

8. In the late 1960s and early 70s, the United States experienced a _____ that was against the war in Vietnam, deceptive business practices, and racial and sexual inequality.

9. The unequivocal type of support, which the majority of Americans have been socialized to give to the U.S. political system in good times and in bad times, is called _____ support.

10. In the first post-9/11 presidential election, women who voiced concerns about national security issues were coined by the media as _____.

11. The first politician to use scientific public opinion polls was_____ in his unsuccessful bid for the Republican presidential nomination in 1940.

12. Traditionally, the term _____ was used to designate high school courses specifically developed to teach students about citizenship, and American political institutions and processes.

MULTIPLE CHOICE:

Circle the correct response. The correct answers are given at the end of the chapter.

1. Which of the following list of presidents cut his own presidential career short because of unfavorable public opinion ratings?

    a) Gerald Ford
    b) Jimmy Carter
    c) Lyndon Johnson
    d) Dwight Eisenhower

2. The first presidential candidate to actually hire a pollster was

    a) George Washington.
    b) Woodrow Wilson.
    c) Franklin Roosevelt.
    d) John Kennedy.

3. Which of the following statements about political culture is NOT true?

   a) It is enduring.
   b) It does not exist in the United States.
   c) It includes citizens' notions about their political role.
   d) It is referred to by systems analysts as the "domestic environment."

4. In addition to polls, reliable means of measuring public discontent includes:

   a) the frequency of large scale protests, demonstrations and riots.
   b) negative articles and reports about government in the media.
   c) the decline of legitimate political participation.
   d) all of the above.

5. Political socialization occurs

   a) over the entire span of a lifetime.
   b) only in adolescence.
   c) only in adulthood.
   d) only in childhood.

6. The primary political value conveyed by cartoons is

   a) freedom.
   b) equality.
   c) patriotism.
   d) justice.

7. Approximately 50 percent of conservative students at Columbia University during the late 1960s and 1970s reported that they were radicalized by

   a) communications media.
   b) parents/family.
   c) friends/peers.
   d) school/teachers.

8. Political culture and socialization concepts help to answer some of the eternal political questions including those about political participation, regime stability, patriotism, legitimacy, and partisanship. Because they do, these concepts have been described as

    a) beta-concepts.
    b) pro-concepts.
    c) mega-concepts.
    d) un-concepts.

ESSAY QUESTIONS:

1. Fully discuss public opinion in terms of both its limited range and extended range importance. Be sure to define the terms and use specific examples cited in the chapter.

2. In a comprehensive response, explain the relationship that connects public opinion, political culture, and political socialization.

ANSWERS TO CHAPTER FOUR: PUBLIC OPINION

TRUE/FALSE:

1.	True	7.	False
2.	False	8.	True
3.	True	9.	False
4.	False	10.	True
5.	False	11.	True
6.	False	12.	False
		13.	True

FILL-IN-THE-BLANKS:

1. important
2. soccer moms
3. Herbert H. Hyman
4. *Democracy in America*
5. Benjamin Franklin
6. cultures; individual
7. family
8. peer counterculture
9. diffuse
10. security moms
11. Thomas E. Dewey
12. civics

MULTIPLE CHOICE:

1. c - Lyndon Johnson
2. d - John Kennedy
3. b - it does not exist in the United States
4. d – all of the above
5. a - over the entire span of a lifetime
6. c - patriotism
7. c - friends/peers
8. c - mega-concepts

POLITICAL PARTIES

CHAPTER SUMMARY:

This chapter examines the development of the American political party system. It also details the primary functions of the party system as well as the role political parties play in the election process.

IDENTIFICATION:

Briefly describe each term.

Charles de Montesquieu

Consensual Party System

Conservatism

Democratic Party

Edmund Burke

John Locke

Liberalism

Marx-Leninism

Republican Party

Third Party Movements

TRUE/FALSE:

Indicate whether each state is true (T) or false (F). The correct answers are given at the end of the chapter.

_____ 1. An interest group is an organization whose members are sufficiently homogeneous to band together for the overt purpose of winning elections which entitles them to exercise government power.

_____ 2. In its 2012 platform, the Democratic Party pledged that any valued added tax or national sales tax would be tied to the repeal of the 16th Amendment, which established the federal income tax.

_____ 3. Since the election of Abraham Lincoln, the Republican Party follows more liberal viewpoints while the Democrats favor the conservative side of the political spectrum.

_____ 4. Socialism is a doctrine advocating economic collectivism through governmental or industrial group ownership of the means of production and distribution of goods.

_____ 5. Farther to the right, the New Right or the Religious Right places its emphasis more on religious rather than cultural values.

_____ 6. In fulfilling its role as the party in the electorate, political parties must develop a solid political philosophy that attracts individuals to affiliate themselves to the party for the long-term.

_____ 7. In the 1860 presidential election, the Republicans ran Abraham Lincoln while the Democrats split into two factions over slavery running both Stephen A. Douglas and John C. Calhoun as presidential candidates.

_____ 8. The 2012 Republican platform calls for raising the minimum wage and indexing it to inflation.

_____ 9. The majority of the American electorate share political viewpoints that places them in the mainstream of the political spectrum.

_____ 10. On the environment, today's Republican Party support less government regulation while Democrats favor stronger regulatory oversight.

_____ 11. To date, the modern Republican Party is the only third party movement to evolve into a major political party.

_____ 12. Founded in 1948 by Senator Strom Thurmond, the Southern Democratic Party promoted states' rights and anti-civil rights legislations.

_____ 13. A libertarian holds that government is an unnecessary evil and should be replaced by voluntary cooperation among individuals and groups.

_____ 14. Liberalism is based on support for traditional western Judeo-Christian values not just has a matter of comfort ad faith, but out of a firm belief that the secular, the economic, and the political success of the western world is rooted in this value.

_____ 15. The American Socialist Party unsuccessfully ran Eugene Debs as its presidential candidate in 1912.

_____ 16. The New Left believes in freeing people not merely from the constraints of traditional political institutions, but also from inner constraints imposed by their mistaken attribution of power to ineffectual things.

_____ 17. American political parties are more pragmatic and less ideological.

_____ 18. Major positions of the Tea Party Movement include eliminating tax programs, reducing the federal budget deficit, and eliminating all government-sponsored social programs.

_____ 19. In practice, American political parties are highly centralized organizations with the national committee overseeing all party functions.

_____ 20. A faction is a political group or clique that functions within a larger group, such as a government, party or organization.

_____ 21. A third party is usually composed of independents and dissents from the major parties in a two-party system the typically is based on a protest movement.

_____ 22. Alexander Hamilton formed the Democratic/Republican Party while Thomas Jefferson formed the Federalist Party.

_____ 23. The Tea Party Movement is a faction operating within the Democratic Party.

_____ 24. Positive liberty is that tranquility of spirit which comes from the opinion each one has of his security, and in order for him to have this liberty, the government must be such that one citizen cannot fear another citizen.

_____ 25. The Credentials Committee's primary responsibility is to write the party's platform.

FILL IN THE BLANKS:

Write the appropriate word(s) to complete the sentence. The correct answers are given at the end of the chapter.

1. Farther to the right, the _____ places its emphasis more on religious rather than cultural values.

2. A _____ is a statement of principles and objectives espoused by a party or a candidate that is used during a campaign to win support from voters.

3. A major event for both national conventions is the highly anticipated _____ _____ delivered by each party's presidential nominee.

4. The term _____ means that an individual who enjoys some benefit from living in a certain nation consents to obey the law of that country, therefore, giving his/her consent for the existence of that government.

5. The _____ Party promoted the interests of farmers and ranchers to include regulatory laws overseeing railroads, banks, and insurance companies.

6. Formed in the 1960s and 70s, the _____was fueled by the convergence of the unpopularity of the Vietnam War, the Civil Rights movement and woman's liberation movement.

7. A _____ is usually composed of independents and dissents from the major parties in a two-party system the typically is based on a protest movement.

8. A _____ is an organization whose members are sufficiently homogeneous to band together for the overt purpose of winning elections which entitles them to exercise government power.

9. The Federalist Party was founded by _____.

10. The _____ Theory underscores that once absolutely free individuals living apart from each other come together to form a community that out of necessity for public order, subsequently create a governing body that establishes the rules for the exercise of certain basic fundament rights.

11. Democrat _____ is credited with changing the philosophical positions of both the Democrat and Republican Parties.

12. Norway and Sweden follow a _____ whereby the parties commanding most of the legislative seats are not too far apart on policies and have a reasonable amount of trust in each other and in the political system.

13. Currently, the _____ Movement is a faction operating within the Republican Party.

14. _____ is a political doctrine that espouses freedom of the individual from interference by the state, toleration by the state in matters of morality and religion, laissez-faire economic policies, and a belief in natural rights that exist independent of government.

15. According to Montesquieu, _____is forcing one to be free.

16. _____ is the political, economic and social concept that places primary emphasis on the worth, freedom, and well-being of the individual rather than on the group, society or nation.

17. The _____ Party advocated anti-immigration policies and the prohibition of Catholics and foreign-born persons from holding elective office.

18. A _____ or centrist is an individual or political group advocating a moderate approach to the political decision making and to the solution of social programs.

19. British lawmaker _____ defined a political party as a body of men united, for promoting by their joint endeavors the national interest upon some particular principle in which they all agreed.

20. Nations such as North Korea, Cuba and Vietnam use the one-party or _____ system.

21. An _____ is a comprehensive system of political beliefs about the nature or people and society.

22. _____ is based on support for traditional western Judeo-Christian values not just as a matter of comfort and faith, but out of a firm belief that the secular, the economic, and the political success of the western world is rooted in this value.

23. An _____ holds that government is an unnecessary evil and should be replaced by voluntary cooperation among individuals and groups.

24. In his *Spirit of the Laws*, Charles de Montesquieu defines _____ as having the power to do what one should want to do and in no way being constrained to do what one should not want to do.

25. _____ is a doctrine holding that change in a political system occurs only by small steps, each of which should be carefully evaluated before proceeding to the next step.

26. The _____ Party opposed the extension of slavery into the territories and the enactment of homestead laws.

27. _____ is based on the concept of ending formalized structured government with the development of collective societies.

28. A _____ is a political group or clique that functions within a larger group, such as a government party or organization.

MULTIPLE CHOICE:

Circle the correct response. The correct answers are given at the end of the chapter.

1. Political parties consist of three inter-related components:

    a)   Party in the electorate, party in government, and party organization.
    b)   Party in power, party in government, and party organization.
    c)   Party in the electorate, party organization and party in action.
    d)   Party organization, party in government and party in public policy.

2. The _____ favored Alexander Hamilton's pro-business positions particularly on low taxes, a strong central government and opposition to the French Revolution.

    a)   Federalist Party
    b)   Anti-Federalist Movement
    c)   Jefferson Republicans
    d)   Know Nothing Party

3. _____is based on the concept of ending formalized structured government with the development of collective societies.

    a)   Socialism
    b)   Libertarianism
    c)   Communism
    d)   Liberalism

4. A predominately pro-environmental party, the _____ supports peace and disarmament of all nuclear weapons.

    a)   Progressive Party
    b)   Green Party
    c)   Greenpeace Party
    d)   Populist Party

5. The lowest rung of an American political party is the _____.

    a)   County Committee
    b)   Precinct
    c)   Electoral District
    d)   Party Cell

6. The _____'s primary responsibility is to craft a document the embraces the overall political philosophy of the party.

   a) Credentials Committee
   b) Convention Selection Committee
   c) National Committee
   d) Platform Committee

7. In 1891, the United States Supreme Court ruled in _____ that a state's party leadership could not force the DNC's credentials committee to accept a delegation that was selected in violation of DNC rules.

   a) *Democratic Party v Lafollette*
   b) *Cousins v Wigoda*
   c) *Baker v Carr*
   d) *Reynolds v Sims*

8. The Reform Party was founded by _____.

   a) H. Ross Perot
   b) Theodore Roosevelt
   c) John Anderson
   d) George Wallace

9. In *Federalist #14*, _____ warned about the danger factions pose to national unity.

   a) John Jay
   b) Alexander Hamilton
   c) James Madison
   d) Samuel Adams

10. A ____ system develops when the legislature is dominated by parties that are far apart on issues or highly antagonistic toward each other and the political system.

   a) Two-party
   b) Conflictual Party
   c) Consensual Party
   d) Exclusive Governing Party

11. _____ believe in freeing people not merely from the constraints of traditional political institutions, but also from inner constraints imposed by their mistaken attribution of power to ineffectual things.

    a) Conservatives
    b) Socialists
    c) Libertarians
    d) Liberals

12. _____ is the political outlook which springs from a desire to conserve existing things, held to be either good in themselves, are at least safe, familiar and the objects of trust and affection.

    a) Liberalism
    b) Conservatism
    c) Socialism
    d) Communism

13. President _____ defined conservatism as "the policy of to make no change and consult your grandmother when in doubt."

    a) Grover Cleveland
    b) Theodore Roosevelt
    c) Woodrow Wilson
    d) Rutherford Hayes

14. The nation's first third party, the _____ promoted abolition of secret organizations such as the Masons.

    a) American Independent Party
    b) Know Nothings
    c) Anti-Mason Party
    d) Free Soil Party

15. In his *Spirit of the Laws*, _____ defines liberty as having the power to do what one should want to do and in no way being constrained to do what one should not want to do.

    a) John Locke
    b) Jean Jacques Rousseau
    c) Charles de Montesquieu
    d) John Stuart Mill

16. _____ is a doctrine advocating economic collectivism through governmental or industrial group ownership of the means of production and distribution of goods.

    a) Communism
    b) Socialism
    c) Libertarianism
    d) Liberalism

17. The American Independent Party was founded by _____ who made an unsuccessful bid for the White House in 1968.

    a) John Anderson
    b) H. Ross Perot
    c) Henry Cabot Lodge
    d) George Wallace

ESSAY QUESTIONS:

1. What are the advantages and disadvantages of the two-party system?

2. Why are third-party movements discouraged in the American political system?

3. Compare and contrast the differences between liberalism and conservatism.

ANSWERS TO CHAPTER FIVE: POLITICAL PARTIES

TRUE/FALSE:

1. False	6. True	11. True	16. False	21. True
2. False	7. False	12. False	17. True	22. False
3. False	8. False	13. False	18. True	23. False
4. True	9. True	14. False	19. False	24. False
5. True	10. True	15. True	20. True	25. False

FILL IN THE BLANKS:

1. Religious Right
2. Platform
3. Keynote Address
4. Tacit Consent
5. Grange
6. New Left
7. Third Party
8. Political Party
9. Alexander Hamilton
10. Social Contract
11. Woodrow Wilson
12. Consensual Party System
13. Tea Party
14. Liberalism
15. Positive Liberty
16. Individualism
17. Know Nothing
18. Moderate
19. Edmund Burke
20. Exclusive Governing Party
21. Ideology
22. Cultural Conservatism
23. Anarchist
24. Liberty
25. Incrementalism
26. Free Soil
27. Faction

MULTIPLE CHOICE:

1. a – Party in the electorate, party in government, and party organizatio
2. a – Federalist Party
3. c – Communism
4. b -Green Party
5. b – Precinct
6. d – Platform Committee
7. a – *Democratic Party v Lafollette*
8. a – H. Ross Perot
9. c- James Madison
10. b – Conflictual Party
11. c – Libertarians
12. b – Conservatism
13. c – Woodrow Wilson
14. c – Anti-Mason Party
15. c – Charles de Montesquieu
16. b- Socialism
17. d – George Wallace

CHAPTER SIX

CAMPAIGNS AND ELECTIONS

CHAPTER SUMMARY:

Chapter Six looks at how the United States conducts campaigns and elections. It begins with an examination of how candidates for national office are nominated, how they are elected, and how they campaign. Particular attention is focused on the changing nature of campaigns and elections, particularly the increased role of the media and money. Finally, the chapter discusses the declining turnout in elections and the question of what factors determine the vote choice of those who do choose to participate.

IDENTIFICATION:

Briefly describe each term.

<u>Federal Election Campaign Act of 1971</u>

<u>On behalf of spending</u>

<u>Long term forces</u>

<u>Short term forces</u>

<u>Bell weather</u>

Anti-establishment outsiders

Washington insiders

Cumulative voting

"Deliver the Bacon"

Federal Elections Campaign Act of 1974

TRUE/FALSE:

Indicate whether each statement is true (T) or false (F). The correct answers are given at the end of the chapter.

_____ 1. The political parties raise most of the money needed in modern campaigns.

_____ 2. The process for nominating candidates is largely controlled by the U. S. Constitution.

_____ 3. Voting turnout in primary elections tends to be low.

_____ 4. The Jefferson/Republicans were founded by Thomas Jefferson in opposition to Federalist's positions developed by Alexander Hamilton.

_____ 5. In plurality systems, the winning candidate must receive a majority of the votes.

_____ 6. The election of the president entails a two-step process.

_____ 7. The candidate who wins the presidency must receive a majority of the popular vote.

_____ 8. The first state primary law was passed by the Tennessee state legislature in 1903.

_____ 9. Turnout in recent elections has been increasing.

_____ 10. Today, the ties to the political parties seem to be getting stronger.

_____ 11. A 1995 federal law prohibits members of Congress from accepting any gifts from lobbyists valued at more than $50.

_____ 12. The number of a state's electoral votes is determined by the total number of United States representatives and senators from that state.

_____ 13. The United States Constitution mandates that the selection of a state's electoral college representatives rests with each state's legislative house.

_____ 14. In 1876, Rutherford B. Hayes became president even though his opponent Grover Cleveland won the popular vote.

_____ 15. By 1800, both the Federalists under Alexander Hamilton and the Republicans under Thomas Jefferson had established congressional caucuses that would nominate their party's candidates for general elections.

_____ 16. In 1986, the United States Supreme Court ruled that any redistricting plan designed for the political benefit of one group over another group could be challenged on constitutional grounds.

_____ 17. Although a close race, George W. Bush won the 2000 presidential election with both the electoral and popular vote over his opponent Al Gore.

_____ 18. The Hatch Act forbids political contributions from government employees and individuals, and companies receiving government funds.

_____ 19. In 1943, direct political contributions from labor unions were approved by the United States Congress.

_____ 20. The term bundling refers to the practice of corporations and interest groups combining their individual contributions and delivering them together to a candidate or a political party.

_____ 21. In 1990, the United States Supreme Court ruled in *Austin v Michigan State Chamber of Commerce* that both the states and the federal government can limit independent, direct corporate expenditures on behalf of candidates.

_____ 22. The 24th Amendment to the United States Constitution granted women the right to vote while the 19th Amendment outlawed the use of the poll tax.

_____23. Although they were "political enemies," George Washington appointed Alexander Hamilton as his Secretary of the Treasury and Thomas Jefferson as Secretary of State.

_____24. The bundling voting system allows each voter to cast as many votes as candidates running and distribute those votes among the candidates or give all of the votes to one candidate.

_____25. In 1996, the United States Supreme Court ruled in *Colorado Republican Federal Campaign Committee v Federal Election Commission* that political parties, interest groups, and individuals can make independent expenditures to candidates.

_____26. In the 2008 presidential election, Republican John McCain declined public financing for the first time since the system's creation of public funding in 1974.

_____27. In the 2008 election, incumbent power was evident with 95 percent of House and 93 percent of Senate incumbents winning their elections.

_____28. The role of political parties in election campaigns began to diminish as a result of the anti-party reforms enacted during the Progressive Era.

_____29. Plurality election systems can bring victory to the candidate with the most votes even if the candidate falls short of a majority and even if the candidate is the person the majority likes best.

_____30. By requiring that only one half of the Senate seats are up for election every two years, the Framers fulfilled their desires that the Senate should not reflect the temporary passions of the moment.

_____31. Even before the general election campaign had even started, all candidates running for the White House in 2008 had raised and spent more money than in all seven of the last eight presidential elections.

_____32. In the 2008 presidential primaries, it was the Iowa caucus that jump-started Hillary Clinton's campaign with a win while Barack Obama came in second and John Edwards placed a distant third.

_____33. After the 2008 general election, the Republican Party sued the Federal Elections Commission, seeking to overturn prohibitions unregulated corporate and local contributions.

_____34. Currently, 527 organizations do not fall under the regulatory eye of the Federal Elections Commission and are not subject to the same restrictions placed on Political Action Committees.

_____35. In a 2007 decision, the United States Supreme Court ruled that issue ads immediately before federal elections are banned under the provisions of the campaign finance law.

_____36. Recent congressional reform efforts have empowered the Federal Elections Commission to use court injunctions to half illegal campaign activities and to conduct random audits of a candidate's financial books.

_____37. As a result of the 2008 president election, a 19-pont gap now separates Democratic Party affiliation and Republican Party affiliation among voters ages 18-29.

_____38. Joe Biden is the first Roman Catholic to be elected to the vice presidency.

_____39. Overall voter turnout in the 2008 general election was significantly higher than the tallies for the 2004 election.

_____40. The election of 2008 saw the highest percentage of youth turnout since the 1972 president election.

_____41. In *Citizens United v Federal Election Commission,* the United States Supreme Court upheld provisions of the McCain-Feingold campaign finance act prohibiting corporations and unions from making expenditures to influence the outcome of electoral contests.

_____42. During the 2010 mid-term elections, the American Future Fund collected millions from anonymous donors to buy attack ads against incumbent Democratic members of the House of Representatives.

FILL-IN-THE-BLANKS:

1. In response to reform movements seeking to end party controlled selection processes, states began to develop the_____system.

2. The reshuffling of House seats to the states every ten years is called _____

3. The elections for the House of Representatives are called _____ elections.

4. The body that chooses the president is called the _____.

5. In a _____ primary format, voters must declare a party affiliation before casting their ballots.

6. The most important structural feature of a general election is whether a/an _____ is running.

7. The _____ enforces compliance with the requirements of the Federal Election Campaign Act.

8. A loophole in campaign finance laws, referred to as _____, allows individuals and groups to give unlimited amounts of money to the political party organization.

9. A state primary may be _____, _____ or _____.

10. The total amount of money spent in campaigns in an election year is in the _____ of dollars.

11. The _____ Amendment to the United States Constitution mandates that the Electoral College is the official body charged with the selection of the president.

12. A presidential candidate must receive a minimum of _____ electoral votes in order to become president.

13. In 1824, _____ received fewer popular votes but still became president as the United States Congress selected him over Andrew Jackson.

14. In the _____ primary format, each voter receives ballots for all participating political parties and chooses which party's election they want to vote in.

15. The _____ to the United States Constitution gives the District of Columbia or Washington, D.C., three electoral college votes.

16. The term _____ applies to an elector who casts his/her vote for their personal choice, even if the candidate was not on the original ballot.

17. _____ are organized groups that solicit money from their membership in support of political candidates favorable to their group's goals and objectives.

18. An _____ is a campaign expenditure made by business corporations, labor unions, and other interest groups for campaign items such as advertisements, that are not coordinated directly with those of the candidate or his/her political party.

19. The Bipartisan Campaign Reform Act is also known as the _____.

20. The _____ required that potential voters take a literacy test if their grandfathers could not vote before 1867.

21. The _____ Amendment to the United States Constitution lowered the voting age to eighteen.

22. Iowa uses the _____ method to select their parties' candidates.

23. Following a Democrat defeat in the 1952 presidential election, the _____ was organized to reform the delegate selection process.

24. The nation's first political party was organized by _____.

25. A new election system, _____ allows everyone to cast one vote per candidate.

26. The _____ was a fee states charged for the right to vote.

27. Another term for the secret ballot is the _____.

28. Viable third party candidates have included _____ in 1994 and 1996, and Ralph Nader in 2000 and 2004.

29. Known as _____, these independent tax-exempt groups can raise and disburse funds as a means of influencing the nominations, elections, or even appointments of candidates for public office.

30. In 2008, both political parties used local _____ at their party conventions to raise money from corporate sponsors to offset the costs of staging the conventions.

31. A registered political action committee, the _____ sued two Internet advertisements to attack Obama's position on the war in Iraq.

32. _____ are political action committees that can except anonymous donations for their political activities and promotion of political candidates.

33. In _____, the United States Supreme Court ruled that the 1st Amendment protects political speech and money spent in furtherance of promoting and disseminating political speech.

MULTIPLE CHOICE:

Circle the correct response. The answers are given at the end of the chapter.

1. The organization and control of elections is left to

    a) Congress.
    b) the states.
    c) judicial bodies.
    d) the candidates themselves.

2. Before his announcement that he would not seek a second term, Lyndon Johnson's primary challengers included

    a) Hubert Humphrey, Adlai Stevenson and Robert Kennedy.
    b) Eugene McCarthy, Ted Kennedy and Hubert Humphrey.
    c) Harry Truman, Eugene McCarthy, and Adlai Stevenson.
    d) Robert Kennedy and Eugene McCarthy.

3. The drawing of district lines to benefit one group at the expense of another is called

    a) gerrymandering.
    b) reapportionment.
    c) single-member plurality election.
    d) discrimination.

4. The incumbents have an electoral advantage in

    a) House elections.
    b) Senate elections.
    c) only in rare cases.
    d) in both House and Senate elections.

5. The electoral college is a compromise that pleases

    a) states on either coast.
    b) large states.
    c) small states.
    d) both large and small states.

6. According to the Supreme Court case *Buckley v Valeo*

   a) a campaign contribution is not a form of speech.
   b) money spent on behalf of a candidate's campaign is a constitutionally protected form of speech.
   c) people and groups may not use their money to speak on behalf of a candidate.
   d) Congress can never limit the amount of money donated to a campaign.

7. The effects of the campaign finance system include

   a) the selling of access and influence.
   b) the distracting of public officials from the job of governing the country.
   c) the weakening of political parties.
   d) all of the above.

8. A person's vote choice is influenced by

   a) identification with a particular group or political party.
   b) issues.
   c) candidate image.
   d) all of the above.

9. An argument against abolishing the electoral college is that the electoral college

   a) always works to elect the most popular candidate.
   b) encourages third parties to run candidates for the presidency.
   c) represents state interests and thereby reinforces the federal structure.
   d) weakens the electoral mandate given to the new president.

10. The political unrest at the 1968 Democratic national convention led to

    a) the reform of the delegate selection process.
    b) a decline in the number of primaries.
    c) an increase in the number of caucuses.
    d) less emphasis being placed on the demographic characteristics of delegates to national conventions.

11. At the end of the 2008 election, voters reported _____ whereby the touch-screen voting machines actually selected another candidate from the one they selected.

    a) fraudulent tabulation
    b) vote flipping
    c) mechanical problems
    d) software sabotage

12. The primary issue for voters in the 2008 presidential election was:

    a) the Iraq war.
    b) rising health care costs.
    c) the economy.
    d) global warming and energy efficiency.

ESSAY QUESTIONS

1. How does the nomination process affect the way in which candidates campaign for national office?

2. Are there advantages to the executive and legislative branches being controlled by different parties? Explain your answer. Are there disadvantages? Explain your answer.

3. Explain how the electoral college works today within the framework of the Constitution. Do you believe this system is outdated?

4. Have the changes in campaigns worked to make the system more democratic or less democratic?

ANSWERS TO CHAPTER SIX: CAMPAIGNS AND ELECTIONS

TRUE/FALSE:

1.	False	11.	True	21.	True	31.	True
2.	False	12.	True	22.	False	32.	False
3.	True	13.	True	23.	True	33.	True
4.	True	14.	False	24.	False	34.	True
5.	False	15.	True	25.	True	35.	False
6.	True	16.	True	26.	False	36.	False
7.	False	17.	False	27.	True	37.	True
8.	False	18.	True	28.	True	38.	True
9.	False	19.	False	29.	True	39.	False
10.	False	20.	True	30.	False	40.	True
						41.	False
						42.	True

FILL-IN-THE-BLANKS:

1. Primary
2. reapportionment
3. single-member plurality elections
4. electoral college
5. closed
6. incumbent
7. Federal Election Commission
8. soft money
9. open, closed, blanket
10. billions
11. 12th
12. 270
13. John Quincy Adams
14. Open primary
15. 23rd Amendment
16. Faithless elector
17. Political action committees
18. Independent expenditure
19. McCain-Feingold
20. Grandfather clause
21. 26th
22. Caucus
23. McGovern-Frazer Commission
24. Thomas Jefferson
25. Approval voting
26. Poll tax
27. Australian ballot
28. Ross Perot
29. 527s
30. Host Committees
31. Vets for Freedom
32. 501c
33. *Buckley v Valeo*

MULTIPLE CHOICE:

1. b - the states
2. d – Robert Kennedy and Eugene McCarthy
3. a - gerrymandering
4. d - in both House and Senate elections
5. d - both large and small states
6. b - money spent on behalf of a candidate's campaign is a constitutionally protected form of speech
7. d - all of the above
8. d - all of the above
9. c - represents state interests and thereby reinforces the federal structure
10. a - the reform of the delegate selection process
11. b - vote flipping
12. c - the economy

THE MEDIA

CHAPTER SUMMARY:

Chapter Seven looks at how the mass media came to be such an important and autonomous force in American society. It begins with an examination of the structure of the media. It then outlines the historical development of the press. The chapter discusses the content of the news and political advertisements. Finally, the chapter looks at the factors that affect the content of the news and the biases that may result from such factors.

IDENTIFICATION:

Briefly describe each term.

Agenda setting

Efficacy

Fourth-estate

Conglomerate ownership

Social Media

TRUE/FALSE:

Indicate whether each statement is true (T) or false (F). The correct answers are given at the end of the chapter.

_____1. The members of the Federal Communications Commission can be removed by the president.

_____2. The FCC repealed the fairness doctrine because the growth of cable made it unnecessary.

_____3. John Adams once wrote that "our liberty depends on freedom of the press, and that cannot be limited without being lost."

_____4. Most Americans find the televised news credible.

_____5. The early press was partisan.

_____6. Media ownership is becoming less concentrated.

_____7. The news covers the president more than the Congress.

_____8. Increased cynicism, alienation, and declining efficacy may be associated with negative press coverage.

_____9. Journalists need a license to practice in the United States.

_____10. The media's access to classified information is limited by law.

_____11. The Anti-Federalists published their opposition to the new constitution through the _Letters of a Federal Farmer_.

_____12. The media's criticism of Senate Majority Leader Trent Lott's racist statement at the birthday party for the now late Senate Strom Thurmond caused such a political problem for Lott that he had to resign his leadership position.

_____13. The term "Washington insiders" refers to the established journalists assigned to cover the president and other top national officials.

_____14. Alexander Hamilton hired John Fenno, an ardent Federalist, to establish a newspaper favorable to George Washington.

_____ 15. Political scientist Theodore Lowi sees corporate ownership of the mass media as leading journalists to take pro-capitalist and pro-corporate positions.

_____ 16. In 1996, Mario Cuomo created a conservative radio program as a counterpoint to Rush Limbaugh's more liberal program.

_____ 17. During the first Persian Gulf War, the Pentagon required that reporters could only interview military personnel with an official escort present.

_____ 18. Colonial authorities could prosecute a newspaper's owner for seditious libel if the paper printed articles seen as offensive to the government.

_____ 19. In the 1960s, the media participated in adversarial journalism only to switch gear in the 1970s to advocacy journalism.

_____ 20. The Bipartisan Commission on Presidential Debates will allow a third party candidate to participate in the debate only if the candidate scores at least 25 percent in nationwide polls.

_____ 21. The consolidation of media ownership has worked to the advantage of women and minorities.

_____ 22. A Canadian comedy duo prank called vice presidential candidate Joe Biden and convinced him that he was talking to French President Nicolas Sarkozy.

_____ 23. In *Federal Election Commission v Wisconsin Right to Life, Inc.,* the United States Supreme Court ruled that the Bipartisan Campaign Reform Act's provision of limiting the timeframe for airing issue ads during elections was unconstitutional.

_____ 24. In 2007, the Hearst Corporation extended its media empire with the acquisition of *The Wall Street Journal.*

_____ 25. According to a new report, most Americans now get their news from the Internet rather than from newspapers or the radio.

FILL-IN-THE-BLANKS:

Write the appropriate word(s) to complete the sentence. The correct answers are given at the end of the chapter.

1. In 1934, Congress passed the Federal Communications Act, which created the

_____.

2. _____ laws preclude the media's printing or airing of a story that unjustly and falsely damages a person's reputation.

3. The focusing on sensationalism and scandal is referred to as _____.

4. The electronic media's catering to specialized interests is called _____.

5. Politicians may hire _____ to try to influence and shape media coverage.

6. The term _____ refers to the major channels of communication that carry messages to a mass audience.

7. Some call the press the _____ because it has become so independent.

8. Advertisements are becoming increasingly important in campaigns at least partly because they are considered to be _____ activities on which the political parties can spend unlimited amounts of money.

9. When the media cover the competitive, game aspects of a campaign it is called _____ coverage.

10. When the media deals with political matters as stories it is called_____.

11. The United States Congress declared public ownership of the airwaves with the passage of the _____ in 1927.

12. The nation's first continuous newspaper was the _____, which began publication in 1704.

13. Both William Randolph Hearst and _____ openly practiced yellow journalism during their infamous circulation wars.

14. Freedom of the press is directly covered under the _____ Amendment to the United States Constitution.

15. According to the _____, the FCC requires that any station selling time to a political candidate, must make an equal offer of air time availability to all candidates running for that office.

16. Imposed by the British government, the _____ placed a tax on the distribution of newspapers.

17. The _____ theory argued that the press must be allowed to print the truth.

18. In the 1970s, a report issued by the _____
was very critical of how the media reported racially-sensitive news items.

19. In _____, the Third Circuit court chastised
the FCC for ignoring the issue of female and minority ownership of mass media outlets.

20. Former Vice President _____ recently won an Academy
Award for his pro-environmental movie "An Inconvenient Truth."

21. Repealed in 1987, the _____ required that
stations provide opportunities for the expression of conflicting views on issues.

22. In Iraq, approximately 500 reporters are _____ into
military units, enabling them to have greater access to operational combat missions.

23. In Washington, an off-the-cuff remark is known as a _____.

24. _____ means that internet servers must maintain
a neutral, hands-off policy of all information to flow unmolested.

MULTIPLE CHOICE:

Circle the correct response. The correct answers are given at the end of the chapter.

1. Since the 1950s, Congress has moved to

   a) tighten media ownership rules.
   b) completely deregulate media ownership.
   c) increase regulation of the media.
   d) loosen media ownership rules.

2. The First Amendment allows Congress to regulate

   a) newspapers.
   b) radio.
   c) all broadcasting.
   d) only the Internet.

3. The media tend to focus on

   a) infotainment.
   b) negativity.
   c) the incumbent.
   d) all of the above.

4. Advertisements are

   a) increasingly important in modern campaigns.
   b) increasingly less important in modern campaigns.
   c) often negative in content.
   d) a and c.

5. Over the course of history, the press has become

   a) less partisan.
   b) more partisan.
   c) more widely owned.
   d) less interested in making money.

6. The ideological bias of the media

   a) is liberal.
   b) is conservative.
   c) is middle-of-the-road.
   d) has never been clearly documented.

7. The most important factors affecting news decisions are

   a) the personal values of the journalists.
   b) the economic imperatives of the media companies.
   c) the upper middle class backgrounds of journalists.
   d) the ideology of the journalists.

8. The media are playing a

   a) less investigative role in politics.
   b) more investigative role in politics.
   c) less important role in covering politics.
   d) more partisan role in covering politics.

9. The media's coverage of gaffes tends to

   a) paint the politician in a less favorable light.
   b) have no effect on the politician's image.
   c) increase the public's sense of efficacy.
   d) have no effect at all.

10. The content of the news is molded by

   a) the journalists themselves.
   b) the conglomerate ownership.
   c) politicians.
   d) all of the above.

ESSAY QUESTIONS:

1. What are the major functions of the mass media in a democracy? How well do the American mass media fulfill these functions?

2. Why have the media become more important in American politics?

3. Do you think that the press and the media should be reporting on "personal" matters of the president's family? Explain your answer.

ANSWERS TO CHAPTER SEVEN: THE MEDIA

TRUE/FALSE:

1.	False	11.	True	21.	False
2.	True	12.	True	22.	False
3.	False	13.	True	23.	True
4.	True	14.	True	24.	False
5.	True	15.	False	25.	True
6.	False	16.	False		
7.	True	17.	True		
8.	True	18.	True		
9.	False	19.	False		
10.	True	20.	False		

FILL-IN-THE-BLANKS:

1. Federal Communications Commission
2. Libel
3. yellow journalism
4. narrowcasting
5. spin doctors
6. mass media
7. fourth estate
8. party building
9. horserace
10. infotainment
11. Federal Radio Act
12. *Boston Newsletter*
13. Joseph Pultizer
14. 1st
15. Equal time provision
16. Stamp Act
17. Libertarian
18. Kerner Commission
19. Prometheus v FCC
20. Al Gore
21. Fairness doctrine
22. Embedded
23. Gaffe
24. Net neutrality

MULTIPLE CHOICE:

1. d - loosen media ownership rules
2. c - all broadcasting
3. d - all of the above
4. d - a and c
5. a - less partisan
6. d - has never been clearly documented
7. b - the economic imperatives of the media companies
8. b - more investigative role in politics
9. a - paint the politician in a less favorable light
10. d - all of the above

INTEREST GROUPS

CHAPTER SUMMARY:

Chapter Eight defines interest groups and the roles they play in American politics. The various types of interest groups are identified. The chapter then focuses on the sources and effects of the modern proliferation of interest groups. Finally, the methods and strategies employed by interest groups in their attempt to influence the policy making process are discussed.

IDENTIFICATION:

Briefly describe each term.

Citizen groups

Government interest groups

Clientele groups

Direct lobbying

Bribery

Going public

Trade associations

Single issue groups

Buckley v Valeo

United States v Harriss

TRUE/FALSE:

Indicate whether each statement is true (T) or false (F). The correct answers are given at the end of the chapter.

_____1. Political parties usually have narrower issue concerns than interest groups do.

_____2. The most important role performed by interest groups is basically representing the interests of their membership.

_____3. The interests of the nation's small farmers are advocated by the American Farm Bureau while the interests of large farming businesses are pursued by the National Farmers Organization and the National Farmers Union.

_____4. The Democratic Party receives large campaign contributions and candidate endorsements from a woman's organization known as the Susan B's.

_____5. The United Farm Workers Union was founded by Tony Sanchez.

_____6. According to the Federal Regulation of Lobbying Act of 1946, all lobbyists are required to register with the secretary of the United States Senate and the clerk of the House of Representatives.

_____7. The Christian Coalition actively backed Jerry Farwell for the 1988 Republican Party presidential nomination.

_____8. Pluralism is the view that the public policy arena is shaped through the competition, negotiation, and bargaining among multiple centers of power with no one group controlling the entire process.

_____9. The New Politics Movement began in the 1950s as students organized in protest of the Korean War.

_____10. The Human Rights Campaign Fund works to advance the cause of gay and lesbian rights.

_____11. Material incentives involve the pleasure that members get from joining a group.

_____12. Common Cause, the Sierra Club, the Environmental Defense Fund and Greenpeace are examples of single-issue groups.

_____13. Interest groups provide people with an avenue to participate in politics.

_____14. Organized labor's influence has declined in states in the north and northeast where people have been historically hostile to unions.

_____15. The nation's first clientele department was the Department of Defense.

_____16. Postindustrial changes have generated a large number of interest groups focusing in the areas of the fine arts and music.

_____17. According to the 1971 Federal Elections Campaign Act, primary, general, run-off and special elections are all separate elections meaning that PAC can give $5,000 per election, per candidate.

_____18. Generally, PACs contribute more money to challengers than to incumbent candidates.

_____19. According to federal law, lobbyists are required to register and to report twice a year the names of their clients, their income, expenditures, and the issues they have discussed with lawmakers.

_____20. In the heat of the 2008 campaign, Barack Obama was forced to sever ties with his pastor John Hagee, for sermons that were deemed racist and anti-American.

_____21. Signed into law by President Obama, the Dodd-Frank Wall Street Reform and Consumer Protection Act has been successful in reforming the financial and investment businesses.

_____22. Former president of the Federal Reserve Bank of New York Lawrence H. Summers was named Secretary of the Treasury by President Obama.

_____23. Trends indicate that membership in private-sector organizations has grown while public sector unions are losing membership.

_____24. Organized in 2010, the LGBT groups have worked for the repeal of the Defense of Marriage Act and Don't Ask, Don't Tell policy.

_____25. In 2010, Fight Back New York was instrumental in overturning same-sex marriage in New York while the National Organization for Marriage favors gay marriages.

FILL-IN-THE-BLANKS:

Write the appropriate word(s) to complete the sentence. The correct answers are given at the end of the chapter.

1. An organization of people and/or companies with specific policy goals, entering the policy process at several points, is called an _____ .

2. Groups that represent occupations that usually involve extensive training and expertise are called _____ .

3. The most common type of interest group is the _____ group.

4. Citizen groups are often called _____ .

5. To attract members, interest groups can offer three types of incentives: _____ , _____ , _____ .

6. One of the main reasons that people fail to join interest groups is that groups provide what economists call _____ .

7. A person who benefits from a group's activities but who refuses to join the group is called a _____ .

8. Groups whose interests are directly affected or promoted by a government agency are called _____ groups.

9. Pressuring government officials through the provision of information is called_____ .

10. The tight relationship that develops between an interest group, members of a congressional committee, and a bureaucratic department or agency is called an _____ .

11. The _____ is the most powerful important voice of organized labor.

12. The nation's largest women's interest group is the _____ with over 250,000 members.

13. The _____ is the preeminent group representing the "gray lobby."

14. Some interest groups offer their members _____ benefits derived from working for a group whose cause they see as just and right.

15. The major benefits of the New Politics movement were the creation of _____ groups.

16. The _____ is an example of a single issue group.

17. _____ are goods and services that come from belonging to a group.

18. The spread of affluence and education in the United States has led to a society that is capable of thinking of more than mere subsistence issues, a society that some have called _____.

19. The _____ included Alan Cranston, Dennis deConcini, John Glenn, Donald Reigle and John McCain.

20. In _____, the United States Supreme Court ruled that the Federal Regulation of Lobbying Act of 1954 applied to direct contacts with members of Congress.

21. The term _____ means friend of the court.

22. Some groups attract and retain members by using _____ such as stressing passionate feelings about the group's cause.

23. _____ include anything that might make the group financially attractive to a member.

24. _____ attempt to speak for the entire business community.

25. The _____ and the _____ are two prominent examples of professional associations.

26. A liberal interest group, the _____ focuses on a wide range of issues from abortion to censorship of the arts.

27. The_____ is the number of members actually in the group compared to its potential membership.

28. AARP offers its members a wide range of _____ to include cruise and software discounts.

29. A _____ is any person who shall engage him/herself or pay any consideration for the purpose of attempting to influence the passage or defeat of any legislation.

30. In the 1970s, Tong Sun Park was the focal point of a Washington bribery scandal known as _____.

31. _____ is the Christian Coalition's automated telephone bank.

32. In 2007, Congress passed the_____Act that requires registered lobbyists to report lobbying activities quarterly, as opposed to semiannually.

33. In _____, the United States Supreme Court held that the Endangered Species Act made it an unqualified duty for agencies to refrain from taking actions that would harm the threatened or endangered species.

34. _____believed that the only tendency of factions was to impose their will on the greater society in a large republic that encourages a greater diversity of opinion thereby making despotism at the hands of any one group difficult if not impossible.

35. The _____ is the nation's largest business lobbying organization representing over 3 million businesses.

36. The Group of Ten to include the National Wildlife Federation and the Sierra Club are known as _____.

MULTIPLE CHOICE:

Circle the correct response. The correct answers are given at the end of the chapter.

1.   The power of labor unions has

    a) grown greatly in recent years.
    b) grown somewhat in recent years.
    c) not changed over time.
    d) declined in recent years.

2. A business group can be

   a) a peak business association.
   b) a trade association.
   c) an individual company.
   d) all of the above.

3. Interest groups share certain organizational features that include

   a) a leadership.
   b) a financial structure.
   c) members.
   d) all of the above.

4. Groups that attract members on the basis of a clear economic self interest tend to be

   a) smaller.
   b) larger.
   c) the hardest to organize.
   d) the least powerful groups.

5. Interests shared by a large number of people are

   a) easier to get organized.
   b) harder to get organized.
   c) tend to be economic interests.
   d) called peak associations.

6. Noncollective goods, benefits that group members get only if they join the group, are

   a) called ideological benefits.
   b) useless in attracting members.
   c) usually unimportant to people.
   d) called selective benefits.

7. Organizations that solicit campaign contributions from members and channel the funds to candidates' campaigns are called

   a) interest groups.
   b) peak associations.
   c) political action committees.
   d) trade associations.

8.   An example of an iron triangle is the

       a) military industrial complex.
       b) grassroots organization.
       c) labor union.
       d) relationship between big business and environmentalists.

9.   In recent years, many of the early victories of public interest groups have been

       a) reinforced by court decisions.
       b) codified into law.
       c) overturned or weakened by court decisions and laws.
       d) not been affected.

10.   To avoid future scandals like that of the Savings and Loan, people are calling for the

       a) deregulation of banks.
       b) deregulation of the campaign finance system.
       c) reduction in the public funding of campaigns.
       d) increased regulation of soft money.

ESSAY QUESTIONS:

1. What are the major reasons for the formation of political action committees? What effects do they have on the political process?

2. Do you think interest groups have been beneficial to the democratic process in the United States? If so, why? If not, why not?

3. It has been said that the only thing worse than too much money in politics is too little money. What do you think this means?

4. Writing in the nineteenth century, De Tocqueville found that the United States is a country of joiners. What is it about the American constitutional system that may work to increase Americans' enthusiasm for interest groups?

ANSWERS TO CHAPTER EIGHT: INTEREST GROUPS

TRUE/FALSE

1. False	11. False	21. False
2. True	12. False	22. False
3. False	13. True	23. False
4. False	14. False	24. True
5. False	15. False	25. False
6. True	16. False	
7. False	17. True	
8. True	18. False	
9. False	19. True	
10. True	20. False	

FILL-IN-THE-BLANKS:

1. interest group
2. professional associations
3. business
4. public interest groups
5. solidary, material, purposive
6. collective goods
7. free rider
8. clientele
9. lobbying
10. iron triangle
11. AFL-CIO
12. National Organization for Women (NOW)
13. American Association of Retired Persons (AARP)
14. Expressive
15. Public interest
16. National Right to Life Committee
17. Material benefits
18. Post-industrial
19. Keating Five
20. *United States v. Harris*
21. *Amicus Curiae*
22. Purposive incentives
23. Material incentives
24. Peak associations
25. American Medical Association (AMA), American Bar Association (ABA)
26. People for the American War
27. Market share
28. Selective goods
29. Lobbyist
30. Koreagate
31. hypothenuse
32. Lobbying Transparency and Accountability
33. *TV v Hill*
34. James Madison
35. U.S. Chamber of Commerce
36. Non-governmental organization or NGOs

MULTIPLE CHOICE:

1. d - declined in recent years
2. d - all of the above
3. d - all of the above
4. a - smaller
5. b - harder to get organized
6. d - called selective benefits
7. c - political action committees
8. a - military industrial complex
9. c - overturned or weakened by court decisions and laws
10. d - increased regulation of soft money

CONGRESS

CHAPTER SUMMARY:

Chapter Nine reviews the origin and powers of the United States Congress. The factors that affect the quality of representation in Congress are identified. The chapter then focuses on the organizational structure, the committee system, and the legislative process of the House and Senate. Finally, the public's disillusionment with Congress and divided government is discussed.

IDENTIFICATION:

Briefly describe each term.

Casework

Incumbent

Term limits

Committee system

Staff system

Article I, Section 8

Instructed-delegate view of representation

Descriptive representation

Office of Technology Assessment

Congressional Budget Office

Line item veto

Mark-up

Bicameralism

TRUE/FALSE:

Indicate whether each statement is true (T) or false (F). The correct answers are given at the end of the chapter.

_____1. "To impeach" means to convict and remove a federal official from office.

_____2. In 2007, President George W. Bush signed into law the Honest Leadership and Open Government Act, an ethics reform package.

_____3. During the last two years of his administration, George W. Bush had a smoother relationship with Congress since the Republicans were in the majority in both the House and the Senate.

_____4. John Boehner (R-Ohio) founded the Freedom Project, a political action committee to raise campaign money to assist Republican candidates in their election bids.

_____5. In 2006, Rep. John Murtha was able to edge out Rep. Hoyer as the House Majority Leader.

_____6. Standing committees are the most important type of committee in Congress.

_____7. Select committees are permanent features of Congress.

_____8. The filibuster may be used in either the House or Senate to stop a bill from being passed.

_____9. The president's pocket veto cannot be overridden by Congress.

_____10. The two highest-ranking leaders in the Senate are largely ceremonial.

_____11. Presidents Bill Clinton and Andrew Jackson were formally impeached by the House of Representatives.

_____12. Redistricting is the allocation of seats in the House to each state after each census; whereas, reapportionment is the redrawing of the boundaries of the districts within each state.

_____13. The United States Supreme Court has ruled in *U.S. Term Limits v Thornton* that states do not have the power to impose limits on the number of terms their United States Representatives and Senators can serve.

_____14. In the House of Representatives the Democratic forum is commonly known as the Boll Weevils.

_____15. Debate in the United States Senate can be stopped by evoking the rule of cloture.

_____16. The President of the United States can use a line-item veto to overturn an appropriated amount without vetoing the entire bill.

_____17. While Senate members serve only a two-year term and all seats are elected in a two-year election cycle, House members serve a six-year term and only one third- are selected in any two-year election cycle.

_____18. John Kennedy's administration was coined "The New Frontier" as he advocate space missions to the moon.

_____19. As a result of Watergate, Congress increased its budgetary powers through the Budget and Impoundment Control Act of 1974.

_____20. In *Wesberry v Sanders*, the United States Supreme Court held that reapportion- ment must not violate the "one person, one vote" principle.

_____21. The president pro-tempore serves as the presiding officer of the House of Repre- sentatives.

_____22. The only way to remove a bill from a House committee is through a discharge petition.

_____23. The primary task of the Committee on Committees is to assign newly elected House members to committees and deal with requests of incumbent members to transfer from one committee to another.

_____24. The House Ways and Means Committee serves as a gatekeeper by structuring floor action.

_____25. Appropriations legislation originates in a legislative committee and states the maximum amount of money an agency may spend on a given program.

_____26. Article I, Section 10 of the United States Constitution gives Congress the power to establish rules for its own members.

_____27. According to the 11th Amendment to the United States Constitution, Congress has the power to certify the election of the president and the vice president or to choose these officers if no candidate has received a majority of the Electoral Col- lege vote.

_____28. Article I, Section 2 of the United States Constitution gives the House of Repre- sentatives the power to impeach a federal judge.

_____29. Whereas the War of 1812 was planned and directed by Congress, the executive- branch assumed the bulk of war making capabilities beginning with World War I.

_____30. According to the trustee view of representation, member of Congress are delegates with specific instructions from their voters at home on how to vote on critical issues.

_____31. In 1995, the United States Supreme Court ruled that the creation of minority-majority districts is unconstitutional.

_____32. In 1994, Speaker of the House Robert Dole created the "Contract with America," a laundry list of legislative priorities for the Republican Party.

_____33. To veto a bill, the president must return it to the chamber in which it originate within ten days with his objections to the bill.

_____34. A Democrat, President Barack Obama began his term of office with Democratic majorities in both houses of Congress.

_____35. The Select Committee on Energy Independence & Global Warming is tasked with analyzing the nation's energy resources, clean technologies and climate change.

_____36. In the halls of Congress, the conservative Democrats are known as the Congressional Caucus while liberal Democrats are members of the Blue Dog Caucus.

FILL-IN-THE-BLANKS:

Write the appropriate word(s) to complete the sentence. The correct answers are given at the end of the chapter.

1. The Connecticut Compromise created a _____, meaning two chamber, national legislature.

2. Article I of the Constitution specifies the _____ powers of Congress.

3. The _____ has the power to advise the president on appointments.

4. The power of Congress to do anything necessary and proper to carrying into execution the powers given to it in Article I appears in the _____ clause.

5. The three different theories of representation are: _____, _____, _____ .

6. Legislation that delivers pet projects to a Senator's state or House member's district is called _____ .

7. The elected leader of the majority party in the House is called the _____ .

8. The committee that acts as a gatekeeper, structuring floor debate, is the _____.

9. The almost 40,000 people who are employed by the Congress are referred to as the_____.

10. The Senate is presided over by the _____ .

11. The United States Congress conducted a formal investigation known as the _____ Affair during the Reagan administration.

12. A _____ bill grants some kind of relief or special privilege to the person named in the bill.

13. In 1986, the U. S. Supreme Court ruled in _____ that redistricting for the political benefit of one group over other groups can be challenged on constitutional grounds.

14. The _____ is Congress's financial watchdog over the federal bureaucracy.

15. Harry Truman's _____ programs included an executive order mandating the desegregation of the military's officer corps.

16. Lyndon Johnson introduced his War on Poverty program as part of his _____ legislative package.

17. Traditionally congressional committee leadership positions are selected on the_____.

18. A direct form of casework, _____ occurs when a member of Congress runs interference with a federal administrative agency seeking favorable treatment for a constituent.

19. In _____, the United States Supreme Court ruled that reapportionment must not violate the 14th Amendment's principle that no state can deny to any person the equal protection of the laws.

20. All members of the United States Congress have _____to include free mail service.

21. _____refers to the purposeful redrawing of congressional/legislative districts for the benefit of one candidate or one political party.

22. Candidates can put aside unused campaign money into a _____that can be used for future elections.

23. Congressional party _____assist party leaders by transmitting information from the leadership to party members and by getting party members onto the floor for key votes.

24. A _____ is a temporary committee created by Congress to fulfill a certain purpose.

25. A _____ is composed of members from both legislative houses.

26. Senators can prevent a legislative item or a presidential appointment from coming to the floor for vote by using the _____.

27. Congressional _____ enables members of Congress to oversee bureaucratic agencies.

28. The United States Constitution allows the Senate to elect a _____ to preside over the Senate in the vice president's absence.

29. _____ allows Congress to create and empower federal agencies.

30. The term _____ refers to Congress's right to pass on certain federal agency decisions.

31. The most important of the domestic powers granted to Congress by the United States Constitution are the rights to collect taxes, spend money and _____.

32. _____ of the United States Constitution gives Congress the power to over ride presidential vetoes.

33. Edmund Burke saw legislators as _____, to do what they believe to be in the best interests of society.

34. The 107th Congress witnessed the development of the _____, a group of 20 to 30 Democrats willing to work with the Bush administration on key legislative issues.

35. The _____ view of representation is really a combination of the delegate and trustee perspectives of representation.

36. The term _____ applies to when a member of Congress works on his own statewide or district-wide needs.

37. In the 110th Congress, _____ was elected as the Speaker with _____ serving as the majority leader and _____ as the majority whip.

38. In 1998, the Republican controlled House and Senate investigated President Clinton, his wife and several close friends on their heading of the Arkansas_____ land deal.

39. _____ committees are permanent committees that specialize in a particular policy area.

40. If both Houses pass a bill with different provisions, a _____ is formed from members of both Houses to reconcile the differences.

41. _____ are groups of senators or representatives who share certain opinions, interest or social characteristics.

42. If Congress adjourns during the president's ten-day decision period, the president can use the _____ by simply taking no official action on the bill.

43. _____ legislation originates in a legislative committee and states the maximum amount of money an agency may spend on a given program.

44. At the beginning of the 2007 congressional session, _____(D) of California became the nation's first woman to serve as Speaker of the House of Representatives.

45. Currently, _____ (D) is the Senate Majority Leader.

46. _____ is the practice of appropriating or dedicating money for projects within a congressperson's district.

47. The senior committee member from the minority party is called the _____.

48. The 2010 Republican House majority announced _____ as their plan to reduce the nation's deficit.

MULTIPLE CHOICE:

Circle the correct response. The correct answers are given at the end of the chapter.

1. The proportion of seats in the Senate up for election in any two-year election is

   a) two-thirds.
   b) one-fourth.
   c) one-half.
   d) one-third.

2. Congress has

   a) enumerated powers.
   b) elastic powers.
   c) domestic and foreign affairs powers.
   d) all of the above.

3. Treaties must be ratified by

   a) the Senate.
   b) the House.
   c) Congress.
   d) the president.

4. Over time Congress has seen its powers

   a) shrink.
   b) grow.
   c) ebb and flow.
   d) be consistently usurped by the president.

5. When a member of Congress does something for an individual constituent it is called

   a) casework.
   b) patronage.
   c) a private bill.
   d) all of the above.

6. Incumbents are electorally advantaged because they have

   a) the franking privilege.
   b) high visibility.
   c) greater access to campaign contributions.
   d) all of the above.

7. A party vote is a vote on which

   a) 75 percent or more of the members of one party take one position while 75 percent of the other party's members take the opposing position.
   b) 90 percent or more of the members of one party take one position while 90 percent of the other party's members take the opposing position.
   c) the parties split 50-50.
   d) a party unanimously agrees to a position.

8. A bill may be introduced by

   a) a member of Congress.
   b) the president.
   c) an interest group representative.
   d) a congressional staff member.

9. If there are differences between the version of a bill passed by the House and the version passed by the Senate, the bill is sent to

    a) the president.
    b) the courts.
    c) the House Rules Committee.
    d) a conference committee.

10. After a bill is passed by Congress the president has the power to

    a) veto the entire bill.
    b) veto only the funding portions of the bill.
    c) veto the portions he finds troublesome.
    d) veto only the parts Congress has already voted to override.

11. The Senate version of the Emergency Economic Stabilization Act of 2008 contained money for

    a) a plug-in hybrid vehicle tax credit and a suspension of tariffs on wool and wool products.
    b) an exemption from excise tax for wooden arrows designed for use by children.
    c) a tax break for Star-Kist Tuna.
    d) all of the above.

ESSAY QUESTIONS:

1. What are the major structural features of Congress? Do these features suggest that the Founding Fathers were more interested in creating a free country or an orderly one?

2. What are the advantages and disadvantages for a president having a majority in both Houses of Congress from his/her political party?

3. In your opinion, should the Constitution be amended to mandate term limits for members of the House of Representatives and the Senate? If so, what would be the length of and number of terms each could serve? Please defend your response.

4. Under what conditions is a member of Congress more likely to act as a "trustee" and under what conditions is he/she more likely to act as a "delegate"?

ANSWERS TO CHAPTER NINE: THE CONGRESS

TRUE/FALSE:

1.	True	12.	False	23.	True	34.	True
2.	True	13.	True	24.	False	35.	True
3.	False	14.	True	25.	False	36.	False
4.	True	15.	True	26.	False		
5.	False	16.	False	27.	False		
6.	True	17.	False	28.	True		
7.	False	18.	True	29.	True		
8.	False	19.	True	30.	False		
9.	True	20.	True	31.	True		
10.	True	21.	False	32.	False		
11.	False	22.	True	33.	True		

FILL-IN-THE-BLANKS:

1. bicameral
2. enumerated
3. Senate
4. elastic
5. instructed delegate, trustee, politico
6. pork barrel legislation
7. Speaker of the House
8. House Rules Committee
9. staff system
10. vice president
11. Iran-Contra
12. private
13. *Davis v Bandemer*
14. General Accounting Office
15. Fair Deal
16. Great Society
17. seniority system
18. patronage
19. *Baker v Carr*
20. franking privileges
21. gerrymandering
22. war chest
23. whips
24. Select Committee
25. Joint Committee
26. filibuster
27. oversight
28. President pro-tempore
29. enabling legislation
30. committee clearance
31. regulate commerce
32. Article I, Section 7
33. trustee
34. Blue Dog Democrats
35. politico
36. pork barrel
37. Nancy Pelosi, Steny Hoyer, James Clyburn
38. Whitewater
39. standing
40. Conference Committee
41. caucuses
42. pocket veto
43. authorization
44. Nancy Pelosi
45. Harry Reid
46. earmarking
47. Ranking member
48. Pledge to America

MULTIPLE CHOICE:

1. d - one-third
2. d - all of the above
3. a - the Senate
4. c - ebb and flow
5. d - all of the above
6. d - all of the above
7. b - 90 percent or more of the members of one party take one position while 90 percent of the other party's members take the opposing position
8. a - a member of Congress
9. d - a conference committee
10. a - veto the entire bill
11. d - all of the above

CHAPTER TEN

THE BUREAUCRACY

CHAPTER SUMMARY:

Chapter Ten traces the development and expanding functions of the bureaucracy in the United States. The organization of the federal bureaucracy, who the bureaucrats are, and what they do are covered. The issue of accountability is raised, specifically the question of how much control the president and/or Congress can exert over the bureaucracy. Finally, the benefits of the bureaucracy are explored along with the prospects for reform and reorganization.

IDENTIFICATION:

Briefly describe each term.

Clientele services

Spoils system

Pendelton Act

Subgovernments

Issue Networks

TRUE/FALSE:

Indicate whether each statement is true (T) or false (F). The correct answers are given at the end of the chapter.

_____1. There is no one bureaucracy; rather, the federal bureaucracy is a loose collection of departments and agencies.

_____2. The structure of the bureaucracy is specified in the Constitution.

_____3. The bureaucracy grew stronger with the country's embracing of laissez-faire economic theory.

_____4. World War II led to the creation of a permanent bureaucratic state.

_____5. Bureaucrats are usually reluctant to lobby Congress.

_____6. Most of the changes in the size and shape of the bureaucracy come from budget cuts.

_____7. The deregulation of the savings and loan industry is an example of successful deregulation.

_____8. The regulatory agencies are the second most important type of organization within the federal bureaucracy.

_____9. At its highest levels, the bureaucracy reflects the ethnic diversity of the United States.

_____10. Most bureaucrats are employed outside of Washington, D.C.

_____11. The Federal Trade Commission was created in 1914 to protect consumers from unfair business practices in the advertising and labeling of their products.

_____12. President Ronald Reagan was an advocate of broadening the federal bureaucracy's role in regulating the nation's businesses and industries.

_____13. The relationship between congressional committee members, clientele groups, and government agencies is known as an iron triangle.

_____14. President William McKinley was assassinated by a disappointed civil service office seeker.

_____15. The Food and Drug Administration was created in 1906 to regulate the purity and safety of foods and pharmaceutical products.

_____ 16. Several key federal government agencies are empowered with rule adjudication duties commonly known as quasi-judicial functions.

_____ 17. The Freedom of Information Act requires that citizens have the opportunity to be heard concerning proposed rules or regulations to be issued by the executive branch bureaus.

_____ 18. The Federal Advisory Committee Act requires that all meetings involving executive officials and private citizens be open meetings to the general public.

_____ 19. The Clinton administration exerted more control over the federal bureaucracy by requiring that all major regulations be approved by the Office of Management and Budget.

_____ 20. The rational-comprehensive model of bureaucratic decision making is based on a sequence of four steps to include goals, objectives, evaluation and a reliance upon information and analysis.

_____ 21. Congress has the power by law to appoint the heads of agencies and the president has the authority to create new federal agencies.

_____ 22. Ralph Nader, a consumer activist and lawyer, drew the public's attention to the faulty automobile designs that posed a threat to consumers.

_____ 23. Established in 1887, the Bureau of Labor Management was the first independent regulatory commission.

_____ 24. The Bureau of Labor Statistics collects and publishes information about the economy.

_____ 25. All regulatory agencies perform the same basic function: they try to promote the public interest by writing and enforcing rules that regulate a sector of the economy of a specific type of activity.

_____ 26. Division of labor is the core function of the national bureaucracy.

_____ 27. Regulatory bodies are headed by a small number of commissioners appointed by the president for a fixed term with the consent of the House of Representatives.

_____ 28. Regulations issued by federal agencies have the effect of law.

_____ 29. If an individual refuses to testify or appear at a congressional investigation, the individual faces charges of contempt and, if warranted, jail time.

_____ 30. Policymakers tend to stop their analysis of solutions when they find one that is "good enough."

_____ 31. The Exxon *Valdez* oil disaster revealed the inefficient policies and regulatory practices of the Minerals Management Service, the nation's offshore drilling regulatory agency.

_____ 32. An investigation into the tragic coal mining disaster in West Virginia revealed that the Minerals Management Service did not cite the mine operator Massey Energy for numerous violations before the accident.

FILL-IN-THE-BLANKS:

Write the appropriate word(s) to complete the sentence. The correct answers are given at the end of the chapter.

1. A _____ is any large, complex organization with division of labor, a hierarchy of authority, and formal rules.

2. The first three departments created by Congress in 1789 were the Departments of _____, _____, and _____.

3. The early 1900s philosophy of reform that called the laissez-faire theory into question is called _____.

4. Conservatives have championed _____ as a way to limit the role of the federal government in the economy.

5. The fourteen secretaries and the attorney general make up what has become known as the _____.

6. _____ agencies are not part of any executive department.

7. Congress has created a small number of_____ to provide public services that could be provided by the private sector.

8. Congress has given agencies wide latitude to make policy; this is called _____.

9. The agencies that are created specifically to foster and promote the interests of certain groups are called _____.

10. The concept of _____ dictated a minimal role for government in economic management.

11. _____is the bureaucracy's issuance of regulations that govern the operation of all government programs.

12. In 1989, the United States Congress passed the _____, to provide job protection to federal employees who reported fraud, waste, corruption or abuse of agency authority.

13. The Federal Aviation Agency is an example of a _____, a federally created organization charged with overseeing particular behavior of the private business sector.

14. Created by President Carter, the _____ of 1978 created the Senior Executive Service.

15. The _____requires government agencies headed by commissions or boards to be open to the public.

16. Many federal agencies are responsible for determining if the rules they administer have been broken, a process known as _____.

17. In 1983, the United States Supreme Court ruled in the _____ case that the legislative veto was unconstitutional.

18. _____ leads to a form of decision-making best described as "muddling through."

19. The _____ of 1934 was the first federal attempt at an extensive security program.

20. Before he became president, _____was the primary advocate that the national government was too involved in regulation to the point that government was interfering in what should be the natural working practices of the business markets.

21. The mission of the Department of _____is to prevent terrorist attacks within the United States, reduce America's vulnerability to terrorism, and minimize the damage and recover from attacks that do occur.

22. An _____ is the close relationship between a congressional committee, clientele groups and government agencies.

23. Bernie Madoff's _____defrauded thousands of investors of billions of dollars.

MULTIPLE CHOICE:

Circle the correct response. The correct answers are given at the end of the chapter.

1. The seeds of the bureaucracy are found in

   a) Article II, section 2 of the Constitution.
   b) Article I, section 7 of the Constitution.
   c) the Bill of Rights.
   d) Article V of the Constitution.

2. The chief legal adviser for the government is the

   a) president.
   b) attorney general.
   c) postmaster general.
   d) none of the above.

3. The bureaucracy grew in response to

   a) Progressivism's criticism of laissez-faire economic theory.
   b) the economic depression of the 1930s.
   c) the entitlements revolution of the 1960s.
   d) all of the above.

4. The public's dislike of bureaucratic regulation became most apparent during the

   a) 1930s.
   b) 1960s.
   c) 1970s.
   d) 1980s.

5. Modern attempts to reduce the size of the federal bureaucracy have resulted in

   a) a much smaller bureaucracy.
   b) a great number of departments and agencies being dismantled.
   c) very small reductions in the size of the bureaucracy.
   d) an increase in presidential oversight over the bureaucracy.

6. The redistributive efforts of the bureaucracy go to

   a) the less privileged members of society.
   b) the wealthy.
   c) groups such as farmers and defense corporations.
   d) all of the above .

7. The percent of federal employees hired through the civil service system is roughly

   a) 10 percent.
   b) 25 percent.
   c) 50 percent.
   d) 80 percent.

8. Charles Lindblom has argued that the most prevalent model of bureaucratic decision making is the

   a) rational model.
   b) rational-comprehensive model.
   c) incremental model .
   d) rational-incremental model.

9. The institution best equipped to exercise oversight over the bureaucracy is the

   a) Congress.
   b) presidency.
   c) Supreme Court.
   d) office of the attorney general.

10. The bureaucracy has been reformed and reorganized by the

    a) Administrative Procedures Act.
    b) Freedom of Information Act.
    c) Sunshine Act.
    d) all of the above.

ESSAY QUESTIONS:

1. Explain why Americans tend to have a love-hate relationship with the federal bureaucracy.

2. Do you think the federal bureaucracy will grow in the future or be downsized? Explain your reasons for taking either position.

3. Why are independent regulatory agencies called "independent"?

4. Why are some agencies called "clientele" agencies?

5. In light of the recent downturn of the United States economy, should the government assume a more active regulatory role of key business sectors of the economy, i.e., banking? Support your response.

ANSWERS TO CHAPTER TEN: THE BUREAUCRACY

TRUE/FALSE:

1.	True	11.	True	21.	False	31.	False
2.	False	12.	False	22.	True	32.	True
3.	False	13.	True	23.	False		
4.	True	14.	False	24.	True		
5.	False	15.	True	25.	True		
6.	True	16.	True	26.	False		
7.	False	17.	False	27.	False		
8.	True	18.	True	28.	True		
9.	False	19.	False	29.	True		
10.	True	20.	True	30.	True		

FILL-IN-THE-BLANKS:

1. bureaucracy
2. State, War, Treasury
3. Progressivism
4. deregulation
5. cabinet
6. Independent
7. government corporations
8. administrative discretion
9. clientele agencies
10. laissez-faire
11. rule making
12. Whistle Blower Protection Act
13. regulatory agency
14. Civil Service Reform Act
15. Sunshine Act
16. rule adjudication
17. *Chadha*
18. incrementalism
19. Railroad Retirement Act
20. Ronald Reagan
21. Homeland Security
22. iron triangle
23. Ponzi scheme

MULTIPLE CHOICE:

1. a - Article II, section 2 of the Constitution
2. b - attorney general
3. d - all of the above
4. d - 1980s
5. c - very small reductions in the size of the bureaucracy
6. d - all of the above
7. d - 80 percent
8. c - incremental model
9. a - Congress
10. d - all of the above

THE PRESIDENCY AND LEADERSHIP

CHAPTER SUMMARY:

Chapter Eleven looks at the presidency from two perspectives. It begins with an examination of the various roles that a president plays and is followed by a discussion of leadership.

IDENTIFICATION:

Briefly describe each term.

<u>Electoral College</u>

<u>Inherent power</u>

<u>Executive agreement</u>

<u>Veto</u>

<u>Pocket veto</u>

<u>Leadership</u>

TRUE/FALSE:

Indicate whether each statement is true (T) or false (F). The correct answers are given at the end of the chapter.

_____1. It is not possible for a presidential candidate to win an election unless the majority of voters select him.

_____2. The role of chief Executive is an essentially "ceremonial" or "symbolic" one.

_____3. The Constitution makes no mention of a cabinet of advisors to the president.

_____4. Many presidents have used their constitutional power to declare war although Congress was against it.

_____5. Jefferson modeled many of his own diplomatic procedures after those he observed when he was the American Minister to France.

_____6. History has shown that most of the major negotiations that take place among countries occurs at summit meetings.

_____7. A presidential veto is not easily or usually overridden by Congress.

_____8. Not every president provides leadership.

_____9. The ability to make accurate predictions about presidents is enhanced by placing them into a typology.

_____10. Presidential powers have vastly decreased over time.

_____11. By issuing the 1794 Proclamation of Neutrality, James Madison expanded the range of presidential decision making in foreign policy.

_____12. During the American Civil War, President Abraham Lincoln bypassed Congress and the Constitution when he revoked the right of _habeas corpus_.

_____13. Andrew Jackson became the first president to use his veto authority to prevent a bill from becoming law simply because he personally did not like it.

_____14. The ultimate downfall of President Richard Nixon was tied directly to his Chief of Staff H. R. Halderman and John Erlichman, his assistant to the President for Domestic Afffairs.

_____15. The War Powers Act requires the president to submit to Congress a written report detailing his/her decision to use military forces overseas seventy-two hours after the military action has commenced.

_____16. During the waning years of the Vietnam War, President Gerald Ford entered into a secret agreement with the president of South Vietnam pledging full military support if North Vietnam invaded South Vietnam.

_____17. Woodrow Wilson and Franklin Roosevelt are credited with moving the power of the federal government from a congressional to a presidential government.

_____18. The United States Senate attached so many conditions to the Strategic Arms Limitation Treaty that President Carter simply withdrew the treaty from Senate consideration.

_____19. The Federalist philosophy believed that Congress, not the president should be the catalyst for legislative actions.

_____20. The presidential election of 1800 resulted in a tie between Thomas Jefferson and Alexander Hamilton.

_____21. In *Federalist #69*, Alexander Hamilton stressed that while the British monarch can declare war at his/her discretion, the American president has only the "right to command the military and naval forces of the nation."

_____22. Under the authority of the Budget Allocation Act, Congress has the final say on whether a president can delay or withhold spending.

_____23. The Framers created the Electoral College because they considered but rejected the idea that the people would directly elect the president.

_____24. John Adams seized the chance to purchase Louisiana before getting congressional approval.

_____25. Like a treaty, an executive agreement requires Senate approval.

_____26. Inaugurated in 1901, Teddy Roosevelt at forty-two was the nation's youngest president.

_____27. In order to become president, the official Constitutional requirements are that the individual must be a native-born citizen of at least thirty years of age who has resided in the nation for fourteen years prior to his election.

_____28. President George W. Bush used Congressional Resolution 114 to use military force in Iraq without first having to ask Congress for an official declaration of war.

FILL-IN-THE-BLANKS:

Write the appropriate word(s) to complete the sentence. The correct answers are given at the end of the chapter.

1. An elector who follows personal choice rather than the wishes of state voters is called an
    _____ .

2. That the terms "president" and _____ are so often
    used interchangeably indicates how closely a president is identified with that particular role.

3. Presidents usually yield to _____by consulting with Senators of his political
    party prior to announcing nominations of candidates for agency heads and federal judgeships.

4. Presidential powers, such as recognizing foreign governments, which are inferred in the
    Constitution, are referred to as _____ powers.

5. Congress oftentimes attaches a _____, an extraneous amendment
    that the president does not support to a bill he/she does support.

6. _____ refers to the power a president has to refuse to spend
    money appropriated by Congress.

7. As explained in the case study, Jimmy Carter's primary weakness as president was _____.

8. According to James D. Barber's typology, a president is classified according to
    his activity and _____.

9. Of the four types of presidential character identified by Barber, George W. Bush is placed in
    the _____ category.

10. "Headship" is defined as "leadership by _____."

11. The term "Manifest Destiny" was popularized during the presidential administration of
    _____who subsequently declared
    war on Mexico and added nearly a half million square miles to the United States.

12. President Obama had to withdraw _____from
    consideration as the Secretary of Commerce since he was part of an on-going investigation
    into whether he or his advisors exchanged state contracts for political contributions.

13. According to the _____, the president of the U. S. can commit United States military forces to foreign soil for a sixty day period without first obtaining permission from the United States Congress.

14. During his tenure in the White House, _____ sent military forces to the Iraqi border, Haiti, and Kosovo.

15. _____was the first president to submit to Congress a whole legislative program at the start of a congressional session.

16. An _____ is a presidential order that has the force of law.

17. The _____(1972) requires the president to inform Congress of an executive agreement within sixty days of its execution.

18. Presidents can use their _____ powers to address extraordinary domestic and foreign crises situations.

19. During his term of office, President _____ sent troops into Santa Domingo and Cuba.

20. A *writ of* _____ is an order to bring a person before a judge and to explain why that individual is being held.

21. In 1953, Congress tried unsuccessfully to curb the use of executive agreements when the _____ Amendment failed to pass.

22. During the 19th and early 10th centuries, presidents usually followed the_____ belief that presidents should not interfere or take over Congress's legislative powers.

23. Recent presidents rely upon their _____ to give the media favorable interpretations of policy actions.

24. In 1939, Franklin Roosevelt used an executive order to create the _____ .

MULTIPLE CHOICE:

Circle the correct response. The correct answers are given at the end of the chapter.

1.   The Constitution specifies that those seeking the office of the presidency must be

   a)   at least forty years old.
   b)   a male.
   c)   a resident of the U.S. for at least fourteen years.
   d)   all of the above.

2.   An alternative to the winner-take-all rule of the electoral college is the

   a)   direct-vote plan.
   b)   proportional plan.
   c)   both of the above.
   d)   neither of the above.

3.   Which is NOT a part of the Executive Office of the President?

   a)   the Cabinet
   b)   The Office of the Vice President
   c)   Independent Agencies
   d)   Quasi-Official Organizations

4.   Which of the following are among the four U.S. presidents who have been identified as "achieving landmark legislation and giving new direction to national policy."

   a)   George Washington
   b)   Woodrow Wilson
   c)   Richard Nixon
   d)   none of the above

5.   Included among the many roles a president plays today is

   a)   initiating legislation.
   b)   fundraising.
   c)   both of the above.
   d)   neither of the above.

6. Leadership is

   a) headship.
   b) a relationship.
   c) a quality all people possess.
   d) none of the above.

7. To win the presidential election, a candidate must win how many of the 538 electoral votes?

   a) 250
   b) 265
   c) 285
   d) none of the above

8. Taft, Harding and Reagan are characterized in Barber's presidential typology as

   a) active positive.
   b) active negative.
   c) passive positive.
   d) passive negative.

9. According to Barber's presidential typology, presidents who emphasize their civic virtue and who are oriented toward dutiful service to their country are categorized as

   a) active positive.
   b) active negative.
   c) passive positive.
   d) passive negative.

10. According to Barber's presidential typology, which category of presidents is most likely to bring himself down in defeat?

    a) active positive
    b) active negative
    c) passive positive
    d) passive negative

11. The War Powers Resolution requires the president to:

    a) consult with the Congress before introducing U.S. forces into hostilities.
    b) submit a report to Congress within forty-eight hours after introducing forces.
    c) terminate the use of armed forces within sixty days unless Congress either declares war or grants an extension to the sixty-day rule.
    d) all of the above.

ESSAY QUESTIONS:

1.   Although Article II of the Constitution specifies the formal powers of the president, over time presidents have assumed many more. Discuss and explain the presidential powers and duties given and assumed.

2. Discuss presidential leadership in the context of Barber's *Presidential Character* typology and explain its utility in predicting presidential performance.

ANSWERS TO CHAPTER ELEVEN: THE PRESIDENCY

TRUE/FALSE:

1. False	11. False	21. True
2. False	12. True	22. False
3. True	13. True	23. True
4. False	14. True	24. False
5. False	15. False	25. False
6. False	16. False	26. True
7. True	17. True	27. False
8. True	18. True	28. True
9. True	19. False	
10. False	20. False	

FILL-IN-THE-BLANKS:

1. faithless elector	13. War Powers Act
2. chief executive	14. Bill Clinton
3. senatorial courtesy	15. Harry Truman
4. inherent	16. executive order
5. rider	17. Case Act
6. impoundment	18. emergency
7. ideology	19. Teddy Roosevelt
8. affect	20. *Habeas Corpus*
9. passive positive	21. Bricker
10. position	22. Old Whig
11. James K. Polk	23. spin doctors
12. Bill Richardson	24. Executive Office of the President

MULTIPLE CHOICE:

1. c - a resident for at least fourteen years
2. c - all of the above
3. a - the Cabinet
4. b - Woodrow Wilson
5. c - all of the above
6. b - a relationship
7. d - none of the above
8. c - passive positive
9. d - passive negative
10. b - active negative
11. d – all of the above.

CHAPTER TWELVE

THE FEDERAL COURT SYSTEM

CHAPTER SUMMARY:

This chapter examines the development of the legal system with special emphasis on the federal court system. The chapter explores the relationship and interdependency upon the investigative agencies such as the FBI, the federal prosecution arm via United States Attorneys, the federal courts and the federal prison system.

IDENTIFICATION:

Briefly describe each term.

Charging Document

Circuit Judges

Corpus Luris Civilis

Equity Law

Good Faith Exception

<u>Felony</u>

<u>Misdemeanor</u>

<u>Negligence</u>

<u>Warrantless Search</u>

TRUE/FALSE:

Indicate whether each statement is true (T) or false (F). The corrects answers are given at the end of the chapter.

_____ 1. Judges usually base their decisions on procedural due process meaning that they use the decisions handed down by judges involving similar cases.

_____ 2. Federal judges frequently use injunctions to halt a state law or ordinance from taking effect while it is under the Court's review.

_____ 3. An arraignment is a hearing before a court having jurisdiction in a criminal case, in which the identity of the defendant is established, the defendant is informed of his/her rights, and the defendant enters a plea.

_____ 4. An order is a written judicial procedure issued by a court ordering the performance of an act or prohibiting some act.

_____ 5. Judicial self-restraint is the ability of judges to make new public policies through their decisions.

_____ 6. A misdemeanor is a minor criminal offense.

_____ 7. In a criminal case, a conviction is based upon the preponderance of the evidence.

_____ 8. With or without a warrant, evidence seized in plain view of law enforcement officers is a legally conducted search.

_____ 9. The United States Supreme Court has ruled that investigative questioning cannot continue without legal representation present.

_____ 10. Criminal law deals with disagreements between individuals such as a dispute over the ownership of private property.

_____ 11. Law is composed of three basic elements – force, official authority and regularity.

_____ 12. A conviction of criminal charges is based on guilt beyond a reasonable doubt.

_____ 13. The exclusionary rule means that evidence which is otherwise admissible may not be used in a criminal trial if it is a product of an illegal search or illegal police conduct.

_____ 14. The 7th Amendment to the United States Constitution mandates that no person shall be held to answer for a capital, otherwise infamous crime, unless on the presentment or indictment of a grand jury.

_____ 15. The United States Marshals Service was created in 1908 during the Theodore Roosevelt administration by then Attorney General Charles Bonaparte.

_____ 16. Members of the jury pool can be eliminated through a series of preemptory challenges from both the defense and prosecution attorneys.

_____ 17. The primary investigative agencies of the federal government include the Federal Bureau of Investigation, the Drug Enforcement Administration, and the Bureau of Alcohol, Tobacco, Firearms and Explosives.

_____ 18. The position of Attorney General is a presidential appointment subject to approval of the House of Representatives Judicial Committee.

_____ 19. The parties involved in a civil suit are the defendant who initiates the grievance and the plaintiff, the person accused of causing harm to the either the person of or to the property of the defendant.

_____ 20. The Solicitor General is the nation's chief law enforcement officer and lawyer.

_____ 21. Article III, Section 2 of the United States Constitution give the president the power to appoint all federal judges for confirmation by the U.S. Senate.

_____ 22. Original jurisdiction is the authority of a court to hear a case in the first instance.

_____ 23. The United States Supreme Court is the court of last resort on all appellate and constitutionally-related decisions.

_____ 24. Assigned to all federal courts, Deputy U.S. Marshals escort defendants to and from trial, protect judges, prosecutors and witnesses, and oversee courtroom security.

_____ 25. It takes the vote of five justices of the Supreme Court to determine whether or not to hear a case.

_____ 26. The federal appellate and Supreme Court were granted the right of judicial review with the passage of the Judiciary Act of 1789.

_____ 27. Rehabilitation is the notion that punishment is intended to restore offenders to a rejoin society and lead a productive life.

FILL IN THE BLANKS:

Write the appropriate word(s) to complete the sentence. The correct answers are given at the end of the chapter.

1. _____ is the current Chief Justice of the United States Supreme Court.

2. Initially the Supreme Court ruled the death penalty unconstitutional in its 1972 decision in _____, only to reverse its position in 1976 with its ruling in _____.

3. A _____ is an order or writ from a higher court demanding that a lower court send up the record of a case for review.

4. The _____ represents the federal government in all litigation cases heard by the Supreme Court.

5. An _____ is an order issued by a court in an equity proceeding to compel or retrain the performance of an act by an individual or government official.

6. _____ is simply a body of rules enacted by public officials in a legitimate manner and backed by the force of the state.

7. _____ jurisdiction is the authority of a court to review decisions of an inferior court.

8. A judge's decision is based on _____, that is findings from cases similar to the one currently under his/her consideration.

9. _____ law is the compilation of all court rulings on the meaning of the various words, phrases and clauses in the United States Constitution.

10. A _____ is a judge's order that lawyers and witnesses not discuss the trial with outsiders.

11. The French term _____ means that all of the judges in an appellate court participate in the court proceedings.

12. A _____ is an indictment made and endorsed by a grand jury when it finds that there is sufficient evidence to bring a person to trial.

13. _____ is a self-imposed limitation on judicial decision making.

14. The term amicus curaie is Latin for _____.

15. Babylonian King _____ initiated the codification of laws.

16. _____ is a Latin phrase meaning "I will not contest it."

17. _____ is the process through which a defendant pleads guilty to a criminal charge with the expectation of receiving some consideration from the state.

18. _____ is carelessness or the failure to use ordinary care, under the particular circumstances revealed by the evidence in a lawsuit.

19. The _____ is tasked with the chore of reviewing the prosecution's evidence before a trial begins.

20. A _____ is a written document signed by a judge or magistrate authorizing a law enforcement officer to conduct a search.

21. _____ litigation usually involves disputes over contracts, domestic and business relations, destruction of property, medical malpractice, fraud, etc.

22. An _____ is a document issued by a judicial officer directing a law enforcement officer to arrest an identified person who has been accused of a specific crime.

23. A _____ is a serious crime punishable by death or by imprisonment in a penitentiary for a year or more.

24. _____ is another term for ecclesiastical law.

25. The term _____ means let the decision stand.

26. _____ law is that branch of law that creates administrative agencies, establishes their methods of procedures, and determines the scope of judicial review of agency practices and actions.

27. _____ is law developed in England by judges who made legal decisions in absence of written law.

28. A _____ is an order in writing issued by a court ordering the performance of an act or prohibiting some act.

29. _____ is the authority vested in a court to hear and decide a case.

30. _____ deals with disagreements between individuals for example, a dispute over ownership of private property.

31. The term _____ refers to the concept that the punishment for criminal-wrong during should be proportionate to the severity of the offense.

MULTIPLE CHOICE:

Circle the correct response. The correct answers are given at the end of the chapter.

1. Emperor of the Eastern Roman Empire, _____ codified Roman law into the Corpus Luris Civilis.

   a) Hammurabi
   b) Nero
   c) Justinian
   d) Clovis

2. The _____ to the United States Constitution protects one against unreasonable searches and seizures.

   a) 3rd Amendment
   b) 4th Amendment
   c) 5th Amendment
   d) 6th Amendment

3. An _____ is a separate opinion that partly concurs and partly dissents from an opinion of the court.

   a) Majority Opinion
   b) Minority Opinion
   c) Extended Opinion
   d) Advisory Opinion

4. An _____ is a formal request to a higher court to review the actions of a lower court.

   a) Judicial Restraint
   b) Judicial Activism
   c) Appeal
   d) Political Question

5. An _____ is an opinion given by a court, though no actual case or controversy is before it, on the constitutional or legal effect of a law.

   a) Majority Opinion
   b) Minority Opinion
   c) Extended Opinion
   d) Advisory Opinion

6. Judges appointed to _____ federal courts serve fixed terms of office.

   a) Article I
   b) Article II
   c) Article III
   d) Article IV

7. In _____, the Supreme Court ruled that is up to the judge to determine if a plea of guilty was knowingly entered into and absolutely voluntarily granted by the defendant.

   a) *Boykin v Alabama*
   b) *Betts v Brady*
   c) *Douglas v California*
   d) *Morrison v Olson*

8. A _____ is a document prepared by an attorney for presentation to the court containing arguments and data in support of a case.

   a) Brief
   b) Friend of the Court Document
   c) Law Suit
   d) Writ of Certiorari

9. Originally established in 1855, the _____ hears cases filed by private individuals against the federal government.

   a) Court of International Trade
   b) U.S. Customs Court
   c) Court of Federal Claims
   d) Federal Appellate Court.

10. _____ of the United States Constitution states that the "judicial power of the United States shall be vested in one Supreme Court, and in such inferior courts as the Congress may from time to time ordain and establish."

   a) Article III, Section 1
   b) Article III, Section 3
   c) Article II, Section 1
   d) Article I, Section 4

11. A _____ is a judicial doctrine enunciated by the Supreme Court holding that certain constitutional issues cannot be decided by the courts but are to be decided by the executive or legislative branches.

   a) Judicial Restraint
   b) Political Question
   c) Judicial Activism
   d) Judicial Discretion

12. The nation's first attorney general was _____.

   a) Benjamin Franklin
   b) Alexander Hamilton
   c) Edmund Randolph
   d) William Pinkney

13. By definition, _____ is a set of facts and circumstances that would induce a reasonably intelligent prudent person to believe a particular person had committed a specific crime or reasonable grounds to make or to believe an accusation.

    a) Reasonable Doubt
    b) Probable Cause
    c) Due Process
    d) Good Faith Exception

14. A _____is an order of a court, grand jury, legislative body or committee, or any duly authorized administrative agency, compelling the attendance of a person.

    a) Injunction
    b) Writ
    c) Subpoena
    d) Charging Document

15. A _____ is the movement of a case from the jurisdiction of one court to that of another court that has the same subject matter jurisdiction but is in a different geographical location.

    a) Change of Venue
    b) Relocation Order
    c) Injunction
    d) Preemptory Decree

16. In _____, the Supreme Court ruled that juvenile defendants have the constitutional right to counsel under the 6th Amendment.

    a) *Hamilton v Alabama*
    b) *Argersinger v Hamilton*
    c) *In re Gault*
    d) *Jonson v Zerbst*

17. In _____, the United States Supreme Court ruled that the good faith exception did apply to warrantless searches.

    a) *Minnick v Mississippi*
    b) *Miranda v Arizona*
    c) *Illinois v Krull*
    d) *Georgia v Furman*

18. A _____ carries of term of imprisonment that has a specific number of years.

   a) Indeterminate Sentence
   b) Determinate Sentence
   c) Terminal Sentence
   d) Mandate Sentence

19. Founded in 1973 during the Nixon Administration, the _____ is charged with the enforcement of the Controlled Substance Act.

   a) U.S. Parole Commission
   b) U.S. Marshals Service
   c) Federal Bureau of Investigation
   d) U.S. Drug Enforcement Administration

20. _____ is the law of civil wrongs.

   a) Tort Law
   b) Equity Law
   c) Administrative Law
   d) Criminal Law

21. _____ is the embodiment of offenses against the state itself, that is, actions that may be directed against a person but that are deemed to be offensive to society as a whole.

   a) Tort Law
   b) Equity Law
   c) Civil Law
   d) Criminal Law

ESSAY QUESTIONS:

1. What is the difference between judicial self-restraint and judicial activism?

2. What is a political question?

3. What is the difference between the concepts of just desserts and rehabilitation?

4. In your opinion, should Article III federal judges be appointed for life-time terms? Defend your position.

ANSWERS FOR CHAPTER TWELVE: THE FEDERAL COURT SYSTEM

TRUE/FALSE:

1.	False	10.	False	19.	False
2.	True	11.	True	20.	False
3.	True	12.	True	21.	False
4.	False	13.	True	22.	True
5.	False	14.	False	23.	True
6.	True	15.	True	24.	True
7.	False	16.	True	25.	False
8.	True	17.	True	26.	True
9.	False	18.	False	27.	True

FILL IN THE BLANKS:

1.	John Roberts	16.	Nolo Contendere
2.	*Furman v Georgia; Gregg v Georgia*	17.	Plea Bargaining
		18.	Negligence
3.	*Writ of Certiorari*	19.	Grand Jury
4.	Solicitor General	20.	Search Warrant
5.	Injunction	21.	Civil
6.	Law	22.	Arrest Warrant
7.	Appellate	23.	Felony
8.	Precedent	24.	Canon Law
9.	Constitutional Law	25.	*Stare Decisis*
10.	Gag Order	26.	Administrative
11.	*En Banc*	27.	Common Law
12.	True Bill	28.	Writ
13.	Judicial Restraint	29.	Jurisdiction
14.	Friend of the Court	30.	Civil Law
15.	Hammurabi	31.	Just Desserts

MULTIPLE CHOICE:

1.	c – Justinian	12.	c – Edmund Randolph
2.	b – 4th Amendment	13.	b – Probable Cause
3.	c – Extended Opinion	14.	c - Subpoena
4.	c – Appeal	15.	a – Change of Venue
5.	d – Advisory Opinion	16.	c – *In re Gault*
6.	a – Article I	17.	c - *Illinois v Krull*
7.	a – *Boykin v Alabama*	18.	b - Determinate Sentence
8.	a – Brief	19.	d - U.S. Drug Enforcement Admin.
9.	c – Court of Federal Claims	20.	a – Tort Reform

CIVIL LIBERTIES

CHAPTER SUMMARY:

Chapter Thirteen discusses the importance of civil liberties guaranteed to each American citizen through the Bill of Rights. Particular emphasis is focused on the First Amendment rights to the freedoms of religion, speech, press, and assembly and association as well as amendments protecting the rights of the accused, property, and privacy.

IDENTIFICATION:

Briefly describe each term.

Reasonable restrictions

Substantive due process

Writ of *Habeas Corpus*

Eminent domain

Exclusionary rule

Establishment clause

Divine right theory

Lemon test

Child benefit theory

Probable cause

Procedural due process

Gag order

Boyd v United States

Escobedo v Illinois

Aimee's Law

TRUE/FALSE:

Indicate whether each statement is true (T) or false (F). The correct answers are given at the end of the chapter.

_____   1.   The Framers of the Constitution believed that in order to live in a civil society, everyone had to respect the rights of others and subject their activities to reasonable restrictions enacted for the good of society.

_____ 2. In *Engle v Vitale* (1962), the United States Supreme Court ruled that the verbal reading of Biblical versus in a public school classroom was a violation of the First Amendment to the United States Constitution.

_____ 3. The United States Supreme Court reversed a lower court's conviction of Gregory Johnson for burning the American flag at the Republican National Convention in 1984.

_____ 4. The writ of *habeas corpus* is the fundamental instrument of due process for those accused of committing a crime.

_____ 5. In 1968, the United States Supreme Court ruled that testing for drugs or alcohol by penetrating the skin is a legal search under the Fourth Amendment to the United States Constitution.

_____ 6. The Supreme Court has ruled that the police do not need to obtain a search warrant or an arrest warrant if they have a probable cause to believe that a crime has or will be committed.

_____ 7. The Supreme Court has ruled that words that have "no essential value to the content of the speech" and are used to create a danger to public order, are fighting words, which are unconstitutional.

_____ 8. In 1977, the Supreme Court ruled that the American Nazi Party could march through a Jewish neighborhood in *Collins v Skokie*.

_____ 9. In *Barron v Baltimore*, the Court confirmed dual citizenship, meaning that citizens had different statuses and rights in their relationships with state and national governments.

_____ 10. Libel cases must prove that the author of the material knew that the information was false and intentionally used the information with malice in mind.

_____ 11. In *Everson v Board of Education of the Township of Ewing*, the United States Supreme Court ruled that the use of public school funds for the transportation of students to parochial schools was an unconstitutional violation of the First Amendment to the United States Constitution.

_____ 12. The United States Supreme Court ruled that the practice of having a public pre-game prayer at a high school football game violated the First Amendment's protection of religious freedom.

13. In *Skinner v Railway Labor Executive Association* (1989), the United States Supreme Court ruled that routine employer-ordered drug tests were not a violation of constitutionally protected privacy rights.

14. The United States Supreme Court has ruled that the Cleveland School Voucher Program is constitutional since it provides parents of eligible children genuine non-religious options consistent with separation of church and state protections.

15. The Supremacy Clause is located in Article I of the United States Constitution.

16. The United States Supreme Court upheld a Louisiana law providing public funding for instructional equipment for both private and parochial schools in *Mitchell v Helms*.

17. The United States Supreme Court upheld the use of breathalyzer tests on suspected drunken drivers in *Furman v Georgia*.

18. In his *Objections to This Constitution of Government*, George Mason stressed that the absence of a "declaration of rights" made the proposed constitution unacceptable.

19. In *Wallace v Jaffree*, the U. S. Supreme Court ruled that the mandatory reading of biblical verses in the public schools violated the separation of church and state doctrine.

20. In 1997, the United States Supreme Court ruled that the Communications Decency Act was an unconstitutional infringement upon users of the internet.

21. During its 1999 session, the United States Supreme Court ruled that law enforcement agencies can be sued for letting reporters and photographers accompany them on raids in private homes.

22. In 2005, the United States Supreme Court upheld the execution of convicted juveniles.

23. The Framers opted to separate church or religious issues from government by incorporating the separation of church and state doctrine into the 1st Amendment to the United States Constitution.

24. In *Cohen v California*, the United States Supreme Court ruled that the wearing of black arm bands as a silent protest against the Vietnam War by high school students did not present a clear and present danger to others.

_____ 25. In *Roth v United States*, the United States Supreme Court drew a fine line in distinguishing between constitutionally and unconstitutionally protected forms of expression.

_____ 26. The concept of "no prior restraint" means that the government cannot "stop the presses" unless what is being printed poses a viable current threat to national security.

_____ 27. In *Detriot v Musgrave*, the United States Supreme Court ruled that the city's anti-gang ordinance was an unconstitutional violation of the 1st Amendment's right to assembly.

_____ 28. In 2002, the United States Supreme Court ruled that juries, not judges, must determine whether a convicted murderer should receive the death penalty.

_____ 29. In *Boyd v United States*, the United States Supreme Court ruled that the practice of eavesdropping on conversations in private residences through the pipes of a heating system as an unconstitutional breach of the 4th Amendment to the United States Constitution.

FILL-IN-THE-BLANKS:

Write the appropriate word(s) to complete the sentence. The correct answers are given at the end of the chapter.

1. John Locke, John Stuart Mill and Jean J. Rousseau believed that the pursuits of life, liberty and property were_____
that could not be denied to citizens by their government.

2. The United States Supreme Court has used the concept of _____
_____ to gradually apply the Bill of Rights to the states.

3. _____ is a verbal malicious attack against another person.

4. In _____(1971), the United States Supreme Court ruled that the *New York Times* did not breach national security when it printed excerpts from the *Pentagon Papers*.

5. The American judicial system is based on the _____ system whereby the accused is innocent until proven guilty.

6. _____ limit the power of a government to act against its citizens.

7. In 1925, the Supreme Court ruled in _____ that the First Amendment of the U.S. Constitution applied to the states.

8. An unconstitutional speech must present a _____ danger to others.

9. _____ is sexually explicit material that is "patently" offensive to others and has no artistic, scientific or literary value.

10. In _____(1966), the Supreme Court ruled that upon arrest all individuals must be told of their constitutional rights by law enforcement.

11. In 1215, a group of English noblemen forced King John to sign the _____, an agreement guaranteeing the preservation of certain rights and privileges to all Englishmen.

12. In _____ (1992), the United States Supreme Court ruled that clergy-led prayer at public school ceremonies was a violation of the separation of church and state doctrine.

13. In _____ (1961), the United States Supreme Court ruled that illegally obtained evidence can be excluded from a trial.

14. In _____(1937), the United States Supreme Court ruled that the states had to comply with the fundamental rights guaranteed in the Bill of Rights.

15. The _____ made it illegal to organize and knowingly become a member of any organization advocating by force or violence the overthrow of any agency or branch of the United States government.

16. The principal of "no prior restraint" for the print media was established by the United States Supreme Court in _____.

17. In _____ (1971), the United States Supreme Court declared a city ordinance unconstitutional because it did not clearly define what constituted "annoying behavior."

18. The phrase "Congress shall make no laws respecting the establishment of religion" is commonly known as the _____.

19. In _____ (1969), the United States Supreme Court ruled that the mere advocacy of violence is not a justifiable reason to deny a person's right of assembly and association.

20. To ensure a fair trial, judges oftentimes grant a _____ _____ and relocate the trial site to a more neutral location.

21. The Alien and Sedition Acts included the Naturalization Act, the Alien Act, Alien Enemies Act and the most objectionable of the group, the _____.

22. In _____, the United States Supreme Court ruled that burning the American flag as a sign of protest was a constitutionally protected under the 1st Amendment.

23. The United States Supreme Court drew a distinction between acceptable and unacceptable speech in _____ (1919).

24. _____is the use of symbols, rather than words to convey ideas.

25. In _____, the United States Supreme Court established a three-part criteria for determining obscenity.

26. In 1996, the United States Supreme Court ruled that the _____, requiring the FCC to block non-compliant cable stations from airing sexually explicit programs, was an unconstitutional infringement upon the 1st Amendment.

27. In the American judicial system, a defendant can be convicted of a criminal act only if the evidence presented at trial proved his/her guilt _____.

28. In _____, the United States Supreme Court ruled that wiretapping was not a breach of the 4th Amendment's protection against unreasonable searches and seizures.

29. In 1767, the _____ Acts granted colonial courts the power to use general warrants to conduct invasive searches and seizures of colonial residences and businesses.

30. _____ is the condition of being free from restrictions or constraints.

31. _____ enables the Supreme Court and appellate courts to hold unconstitutional any law, any official action based upon a law, and any other action by a public official it deems to be in conflict with the United States Constitution.

MULTIPLE CHOICE:

Circle the correct response. The correct answers are given at the end of the chapter.

1.   The right to legal representation when questioning shifts from investigative to accusatory was guaranteed by the United States Supreme Court by its 1964 ruling in

     a) *Furman v Georgia.*
     b) *Escobedo v Illinois.*
     c) *New York Times v Sullivan.*
     d) *Gitlow v New York.*

2.   This refers to the procedural safeguards guaranteed to those who would be deprived of life, liberty, or property because they are accused of criminal wrong doing.

     a) substantive due process
     b) due process
     c) selective incorporation
     d) procedural due process

3.   The Supreme Court established a three-part test for religious-based issues in its 1971 ruling in

     a) *Coates v Cincinnati.*
     b) *Powell v Alabama.*
     c) *Lemon v Kurtzman.*
     d) *Near v Minnesota.*

4.   Although protesting is a protected right, the United States Supreme Court ruled that the burning of draft cards was an illegal act in

     a) *Barron v Baltimore.*
     b) *United States v O'Brien.*
     c) *Tinker v DesMoines.*
     d) *Mapp v Ohio.*

5.   The United States Supreme Court mandated that those accused of a criminal act must be guaranteed the right to counsel as mandated by the Sixth Amendment to the United States Constitution by its 1932 decision in

     a) *Powell v Alabama.*
     b) *Furman v Georgia.*
     c) *Gideon v Wainwright.*
     d) *Katz v United States.*

6. Article I, Section 10 of the United States Constitution is also known as the

   a) establishment clause.
   b) necessary and proper clause.
   c) contract clause.
   d) due process clause.

7. The Supreme Court settled the question of whether the Bill of Rights applied to the states or only to the national government by ruling that the Bill of Rights was applicable only at the national level in its 1833 ruling in

   a) *New York Times v Sullivan.*
   b) *Schenck v United States.*
   c) *Olmstead v United States.*
   d) *Barron v Baltimore.*

8. The manner in which a law, an ordinance, an administrative practice or judicial task is carried out is known as

   a) substantive due process.
   b) procedural due process.
   c) contractual due process.
   d) inclusive due process.

9. The current guidelines for libel cases were outlined by the Supreme Court's ruling in

   a) *Lemon v Kurtzman.*
   b) *Nixon v Hernon.*
   c) *Smith v Allwright.*
   d) *New York Times v Sullivan.*

10. Speech without any conduct is

   a) symbolic speech.
   b) pure speech.
   c) significant speech.
   d) clear and present danger speech.

11. The United States Supreme Court upheld a Louisiana law allowing the use of public tax dollars to be used for the purchase of equipment for both private and parochial schools in

    a) *Lemon v Kurtzman.*
    b) *Schenck v United States.*
    c) *Tinker v Des Moines School District.*
    d) *Mitchell v Helms.*

12. The United States Supreme Court upheld the use of breathalyzer tests on suspected drunken drivers in

    a) *California v Trombetta.*
    b) *Terry v Ohio.*
    c) *Furman v Georgia.*
    d) *Gitlow v New York.*

13. The United States Supreme Court ruled that all individuals charged with a criminal felony offense had the constitutional right to legal representation in

    a) *Gitlow v New York.*
    b) *Gideon v Wainwright.*
    c) *Miranda v Arizona.*
    d) *Powell v Alabama.*

14. The United States Supreme Court upheld the concept of "no prior restraint" of the print media in

    a) *Miller v California.*
    b) *New York Times v Sullivan.*
    c) *Near v Minnesota.*
    d) *Street v New York.*

15. As a result of the attacks on the World Trade Center and the Pentagon, the United States Congress passed a package of anti-terrorist actions known collectively as

    a) The Smith Act.
    b) The Patriot Act.
    c) Anti-Civil Liberties Legislation.
    d) The World Trade Center Protection Act.

ESSAY QUESTIONS:

1. What were the motivating and historical factors that led the framers to create the establishment clause? Should government assume a more active role in this country's religious activities? Defend your answer.

2. Should men and women have the absolute freedom to pursue their unalienable rights? Defend your answer as defined by the Supreme Court.

3. What is the historical significance of the Writ of *Habeas Corpus*? Why is it referred to as the cornerstone of the American judicial system?

ANSWERS TO CHAPTER THIRTEEN: CIVIL LIBERTIES

TRUE/FALSE:

1. True	9. True	17. False	25. True
2. False	10. True	18. True	26. True
3. True	11. False	19. False	27. False
4. True	12. True	20. True	28. True
5. True	13. True	21. True	29. False
6. True	14. True	22. False	
7. True	15. False	23. True	
8. True	16. True	24. False	

FILL-IN-THE-BLANKS:

1. unalienable rights
2. selective incorporation
3. Slander
4. *New York Times v The United States*
5. adversary system
6. Civil liberties
7. *Gitlow v New York*
8. clear and present danger
9. Obscenity
10. *Miranda v Arizona*
11. Magna Carta
12. *Lee v Weisman*
13. *Mapp v Ohio*
14. *Palko v Connecticut*
15. Smith Act
16. *Near v Minnesota*
17. *Coates v Cincinnati*
18. Establishment clause
19. *Brandenburg v Ohio*
20. Change of venue
21. Sedition Act
22. *Street v New York*
23. *Schenck v United States*
24. Symbolic speech
25. *Miller v California*
26. Telecommunications Act
27. Beyond a reasonable doubt
28. *Olmstead v United States*
29. Townshend
30. Individual liberty
32. Judicial review

MULTIPLE CHOICE:

1. a - *Furman v Georgia*
2. b - due process
3. c - *Lemon v Kurtzman*
4. b - *United States v O'Brien*
5. a - *Powell v Alabama*
6. c - contract clause
7. d - *Barron v Baltimore*
8. b - procedural
9. d - *New York Times v Sullivan*
10. b - pure speech
11. d - *Mitchell v Helms*
12. a - *California v Trombetta*
13. b - *Gideon v Wainwright*
14. c - *Near v Minnesota*
15. b - The Patriot Act

CIVIL RIGHTS

CHAPTER SUMMARY:

Chapter Fourteen focuses on the theories of racism and the quest of minority groups and women in the United States to achieve equal treatment and protection of their civil rights. The role of the United States Supreme Court is discussed with emphasis placed on important court rulings expanding civil rights to those adversely impacted by discriminatory practices.

IDENTIFICATION:

Briefly describe each term.

<u>Discrimination</u>

<u>De jure discrimination</u>

<u>Affirmation action</u>

<u>Assimilation</u>

<u>Host culture</u>

<u>Poll tax</u>

White-only primary

Glass ceiling

Grandfather clause

Integration

Disparate treatment

Indian Removal Act

Second Seminole War

15th Amendment to the United States Constitution

Pink collar jobs

Roe v Wade

Sweatt v Painter

Dream Act

TRUE/FALSE:

Indicate whether each statement is true (T) or false (F). The correct answers are given at the end of the chapter.

_____ 1. Discrimination is an unfavorable attitude towards people because they are members of a particular racial or ethnic group and prejudice is an unfavorable action toward people because they are members of a particular racial or ethnic group.

_____ 2. In *Minor v Happersat* (1875), the United States Supreme Court ruled that the Fourteenth Amendment did give women the right to vote.

_____ 3. In *McLaurin v Oklahoma*, the United States Supreme Court ruled that separate law school facilities and accommodations for African-American students was unconstitutional.

_____ 4. The literacy test was invalidated with the passage of the Voting Rights Act of 1965.

_____ 5. *The Revolution* was founded by Elizabeth Cady Stanton and Susan B. Anthony.

_____ 6. The term glass ceiling is the inability of women to become chief executive officers in the nation's major corporations.

_____ 7. The Civil Rights Act of 1968 created the United States Commission on Civil Rights and the Civil Rights Section of the Justice Department.

_____ 8. The United States Supreme Court ruled that Dred Scott did not have standing to sue because a noncitizen cannot sue the government.

_____ 9. Many southern states implemented rules and regulations designed to deny minorities voting and access to public accommodations that were collectively known as Old Crow Laws.

_____ 10. The forced relocation of the Cherokees, Choctaws, Creeks, Chickasaws, and Seminoles from the East to the West of the Mississippi River was known as the Trail of Tears.

_____ 11. In 1924, the Virginia state legislature passed a bill making it a crime for people to identify themselves as Native Americans or Indians.

_____ 12. President Dwight Eisenhower used an executive order to desegregate the nation's military.

_____ 13. The first woman elected to the United States Senate in her own right was Margaret Chase Smith, a Republican from Maine.

_____ 14. The prevailing problem with crafting hate crimes legislation is to provide a clear-cut definition for what distinguishes a hate crime from other criminal actions.

_____ 15. The term racial profiling is a practice of assuming that criminals possess certain common traits and characteristics that separate them from law-abiding citizens.

_____ 16. The grandfather clause required that all eligible voters had to take and pass a literacy test if their grandfathers could not vote before 1867.

_____ 17. In *Mein Kampf*, Joseph Stalin envisioned a new world order dominated by an Aryan or Germanic race whereby the races would be divided into three main groups: culture-creating, the culture-bearing and the culture-destroying.

_____ 18. In his book *Jim Crow*, Jim Conrad believes that racism is purely a political and social issue.

_____ 19. In 1862, the United States Congress passed the Militia Act, enabling African Americans to join the Union side of the warfront.

_____ 20. Slavery was outlawed with the passage of the 15th Amendment to the U. S. Constitution.

_____ 21. The Separate Car Act mandated that for every rail car set aside for white passengers a separate car had to be reserved for African-American passengers.

_____ 22. State governments gradually outlawed the practice of lynching through the efforts of the Association of Southern Women for the Prevention of Lynching.

_____ 23. The Civil Rights Act of 1964 authorized federal appointed voter referees conduct voter registration drives and to monitor federal elections in areas with historical patterns of voter-related problems.

_____ 24. Lucy Stone founded the American Women Suffrage Association while Elizabeth Stanton and Susan B. Anthony founded the National American Women Suffrage Association.

_____ 25. The federal trust doctrine holds that the federal government and the Indian nations are inextricably bound together as trustee to oblige.

_____ 26. It is estimated that lands granted to Native Americans through treaties hold 40 percent of the nation's coal reserves, 65 percent of the uranium supply, and vast untapped pockets of natural gas and oil.

_____ 27. The leading voices originally opposing woman's suffrage were Harriet Beecher Stowe, her sister Catharine Beecher and Carrie Nation.

_____ 28. The National Origins Act of 1927 limited Asian immigration to 150,000 per year.

_____ 29. Keeping a key campaign promise, President Obama used an executive order to overturn the controversial "Don't Ask, Don't Tell" policy enacted by the Clinton administration.

FILL-IN-THE-BLANKS:

Write the appropriate word(s) to complete the sentence. The correct answers are given at the end of the chapter.

1. _____ are collectively known as the acts of government intended to protect disadvantaged classes of persons or minority groups from arbitrary, unreasonable, or discriminatory treatment.

2. _____ is a feeling or act of any individual or any group in which a prejudgment about someone else or another group is made on the basis of emotion rather than reason.

3. In _____ , the United States Supreme Court ruled the Texas White Primary Law of 1924 as unconstitutional.

4. In_____(1944), the United States Supreme Court ruled that the Texas Democratic Party was not a private club and, therefore, could not discriminate against African Americans with the white only primary system.

5. The late _____ was the founder of the United Farm Workers Union.

6. The _____ of male superiority over women is supported by the myth that women are just too fragile to survive the rigors of life.

7. The Women's Rights Convention held at Seneca Falls, New York, in 1848 was organized by Elizabeth Cady Stanton and _____ .

8. The _____ doctrine was upheld in *Plessy v Ferguson*.

9. The National Association for the Advancement of Colored People was created in 1909 with _____ serving as its first president.

10. A _____is a clause in a house sale contract requiring the buyer to agree not to sell the home later to a member of a minority group.

11. _____was the practice used by financial institutions to deny loans to individuals wanting to purchase property in a racially changing neighborhood.

12. In _____(1915), the United States Supreme Court invalidated Oklahoma's grandfather clause as a direct violation of the Fifteenth Amendment to the United States Constitution.

13. The _____ issue drives home the point that women employed in similar positions continue to earn less than their male counterparts.

14. President George W. Bush successfully appointed Gail Norton to head the Interior Department and former New Jersey Governor _____ to oversee the Environmental Protection Agency.

15. _____ occurs when the standards of employment have the effect of excluding people with disabilities on the basis of standards and tests that are not directly related to determining the skills or experience necessary to perform the job.

16. The federal Justice Department reopened the 1955 murder of 14-year old _____.

17. In 1887, the United States Congress passed the _____ Act as a concerted effort to break up large reservation holdings that bonded Native Americans to their tribes.

18. The nativist movement developed into a third party movement known as the_____ that eventually resulted in the election of Millard Filmore to the presidency.

19. A perspective of racism, many immigrant groups believe in _____ by forming their own confined societies such as Chinatown, within the larger community.

20. The _____ granted former slaves the rights to own property, file lawsuits, and make contractual agreements.

21. The _____ Amendment to the United States Constitution granted citizenship to former slaves as well as guaranteeing them equal protection of the laws.

22. Eventually ruled unconstitutional, the _____ prohibited private discrimination in accommodations, transportation, and public places of amusement.

23. The late _____ is known as the Mother of the Civil Right Movement.

24. The _____ prohibited discrimination in public accommodations and employment practices.

25. The _____ requires state and local governments to provide handicapped accessible mass transportation systems.

26. *Johnson v McIntosh, Cherokee Nation v Georgia* and *Worester v Georgia* are collectively known as the _ _____.

27. Arizona's controversial _____ signed into law by its governor, gives the state's law enforcement the authority to question the immigration status of anyone cited for a traffic violation.

MULTIPLE CHOICE:

Circle the correct response. The correct answers are given at the end of the chapter.

1. The unintentional action producing an adverse impact on a group or groups is known as

   a) de facto discrimination.
   b) prejudice.
   c) redlining.
   d) de jure discrimination.

2. The belief that only those born on their country's soil should reap the benefits of their birthrights is known as

   a) superior/inferior.
   b) prejudice.
   c) nativism.
   d) economic-based segregation.

3. Racism based on the belief that one group or culture is genetically, intellectually, and culturally more superior than any other group is known as

   a) nativism.
   b) separate but equal.
   c) superior/inferior.
   d) separation.

4. At the 1848 Seneca Falls Convention, an audience was told that the ultimate goals of civil rights was to reach the point where right is of no sex, truth is of no color in a speech delivered by

   a) Pontiac.
   b) Frederick Douglass.
   c) Susan B. Anthony.
   d) Alice Paul.

5. The belief that the Anglo-American's destiny was to own all of the land between the Atlantic and Pacific Oceans was known as

   a) nationalism.
   b) globalism.
   c) imperialism.
   d) manifest destiny.

6. In 1960, federally appointed voter referees were authorized to conduct voter registration drives and monitor elections in those areas with historical track records of voter fraud under the provisions of the

    a) Civil Rights Act.
    b) Voting Rights Act.
    c) Affirmative Action Act.
    d) Motor Voter Bill.

7. Farm workers in Texas and California are known as

    a) Mestizos.
    b) Creoles.
    c) Campesinos.
    d) patrons.

8. The feeling of becoming a member of the new minority as the existing minority becomes a majority within the social community is called

    a) paternalistic attitude.
    b) white fear.
    c) separation anxiety.
    d) superior/inferior sentiments.

9. The illegal technique of showing African Americans only available housing in African-American neighborhoods while avoiding housing opportunities in white areas is called

    a) restrictive covenant.
    b) redlining.
    c) steering.
    d) de facto discrimination.

10. The Supreme Court reversed the *Plessy v Ferguson* decision in 1954 with its ruling in

    a) *Brown v Board of Education.*
    b) *Guinn v United States.*
    c) *Roe v Wade.*
    d) *Abington School District v Schempp.*

11. In the 1970s, the Hispanic community formed a third political party movement known as

    a) Mecha.
    b) La Raza Unida.
    c) League of United Latin American Citizens.
    d) La Prensa.

12. The first female presidential candidate to actually receive votes in a presidential election was

    a) Victoria Woodhull.
    b) Lucy Stone.
    c) Belva Lockwood.
    d) Susan B. Anthony.

13. In 1975, the U. S. Supreme Court recognized the right of women to serve on juries by its ruling in

    a) *Taylor v Louisiana.*
    b) *Minor v Happersat.*
    c) *Sweat v Painter.*
    d) *Guinn v United States.*

14. In 1942, the United States government contracted with the Mexican government to bring Mexican nationals into the United States as workers under the

    a) Works Progress Administration Plan.
    b) Bracero Program.
    c) Worker Exchange Program.
    d) Rio Grande Workers Agreement.

15. The first Native American to serve as vice president of the United States was

    a) W. E. B. Dubois.
    b) Lewis Cass.
    c) Alton B. Parker.
    d) Charles Curtis.

ESSAY QUESTIONS:

1.   Define and provide an example in the development of American society for the following theories of racism: nativism, superior/inferior, separation, assimilation, and white fear.

2. Is hate crime legislation necessary if killing someone is already a felony? Would this federal legislation strengthen state laws?

TRUE/FALSE:

1. False	9. False	17. False	25. True
2. False	10. True	18. False	26. True
3. True	11. True	19. True	27. False
4. True	12. False	20. False	28. False
5. True	13. True	21. True	29. False
6. True	14. True	22. True	
7. False	15. True	23. False	
8. True	16. True	24. False	

FILL-IN-THE-BLANKS:

1. Civil rights
2. Prejudice
3. *Nixon v Herndon*
4. *Smith v Allwright*
5. Ceasar Chavez
6. paternalistic attitude
7. Lucretia Mott
8. separate but equal
9. W.E.B. Dubois
10. restrictive covenant
11. Redlining
12. *Guinn v United States*
13. pay equity
14. Christine Whitman
15. Disparate impact
16. Emmitt Till
17. Dawes
18. Know-Nothings
19. Separation
20. Civil Rights Act of 1886
21. 14th
22. Civil Rights Act of 1875
23. Rosa Parks
24. Civil Rights Act of 1964
25. Urban Mass Transportation Act
26. Marshall Trilogy
27. SB 1070

MULTIPLE CHOICE:

1. a - de facto discrimination
2. c - nativism
3. c - superior/inferior
4. b - Frederick Douglass
5. d - manifest destiny
6. a - Civil Rights Act
7. c - Compesinos
8. b - white fear
9. c - steering
10. a - *Brown v Board of Education*
11. b - La Raza Unida
12. c - Belva Lockwood
13. a - *Taylor v Louisiana*
14. b - Bracero Program
15. d - Charles Curtis

PUBLIC POLICY

CHAPTER SUMMARY:

Chapter Fifteen focuses on the public policy process from the inception of the policy concept to the evaluation process. Particular emphasis is placed on the identification of the key actors involved in the development and implementation of public policy initiatives and the role politics plays in the public policy arena.

IDENTIFICATION:

Briefly describe each term.

<u>Public policy</u>

<u>License</u>

<u>Redistributive policies</u>

<u>Fiscal policy</u>

<u>Elasticity</u>

<u>Regulatory policies</u>

Porkbarrel politics

Proportional tax programs

Sanctions

Substantive problems

Strategic defense policy

Earmarked funding

Tax

Tax reliability

Tax yield

Incremental budget process

TRUE/FALSE:

Indicate whether each statement is true (T) or false (F). The correct answers are given at the end of the chapter.

_____ 1. Public policy has an authoritative, potentially legally coercive quality that policies of private organizations do not have.

_____ 2. Public policy initiatives created in a democratic government are the products of conflict and accommodation.

_____ 3. Contractors can lose existing contracts and the right to bid on future contracts if held in noncompliance to contractual mandates.

_____ 4. Governments can indirectly control individual spending habits through its spending, taxing, and pricing functions.

_____ 5. Policy makers must be able to determine whether a situation is a problem or a crisis situation in order to determine the correct response.

_____ 6. The New Deal programs created by Harry Truman were designed as temporary measures to alleviate the suffering of those in hunger during the Great Depression.

_____ 7. Privatization should be used sparingly since some functions cannot be shifted to the private sector due to the sensitivity of the function.

_____ 8. The budgeting process is a nonpolitical activity.

_____ 9. The national government relies heavily on property taxes; whereas, most state, county and city governments use income, property, and corporate taxes to fund their budgets.

_____ 10. The evaluation process must be an honest appraisal of the policy initiative or the evaluation will be meaningless.

_____ 11. In designing public policy options, most lawmakers use a combination of the punitive, alleviative and preventative strategies.

_____ 12. A crisis policy response is oriented toward foreign policy and international politics, and it involves the units and uses of military force, their strength, and their deployment.

_____ 13. The implementation phase of public policy is the most politically heightened step in the process of developing policy initiatives.

_____ 14. A progressive tax program is one that increases the tax burden for upper-income people while reducing it for lower-income people.

_____ 15. Property and income taxes are reliable sources of income because experts can predict with only a small margin of error future revenues.

_____ 16. Policy-making involves the choice of an alternative from among a series of alternatives.

_____ 17. Tax accuracy is the measure of whether given a state's economic situation, it is taxing above or below its capacity to raise revenue.

_____ 18. Both the income and property tax are considered to have low visibility while the sales tax is a high visibility tax.

_____ 19. Public policy is a series of policy outputs and outcomes.

_____ 20. The United States Supreme Court's ruling in _Roe v Wade_ had a ripple effect by overturning forty-six state laws prohibiting elective abortion procedures.

_____ 21. In 2005, the United States Supreme Court ruled unconstitutional the sentencing guidelines mandated by Congress on the grounds that the rules violated a defendant's 7th Amendment right to a jury trial.

_____ 22. An increase in mortgage and consumer loan rates will provide the incentive for individuals to purchase high ticket items to include real estate properties.

_____ 23. User fees enable governments to control the use of a service while at the same time, provide additional revenue for its maintenance.

_____ 24. In many respects, the development of public policy is "analogous to biological natural selection."

_____ 25. President Richard Nixon decided to cancel free wheat shipments to the Soviet Union as a means of punishing them for invading Afghanistan.

_____ 26. When lawmakers treat a problem as a crisis, the problem will never be adequately addressed or solved.

_____ 27. In establishing relations with other nations, the federal government uses a wide range of subsidies to include cash payments, military equipment, and humanitarian aid.

_____ 28. The zero-based budgeting format has a built-in cost benefit analysis feature.

FILL-IN-THE-BLANKS:

Write the appropriate word(s) to complete the sentence. The correct answers are given at the end of the chapter.

1. The term _____ is a proposed course of action of a person, group or government within an environment providing obstacles and opportunities that the policy was proposed to utilize and overcome in an effort to reach a goal or realize an objective or purpose.

2. A _____ is a technical document in the form of a detailed balance sheet that identifies expenditures and revenues for all government activities.

3. Government contracts contain _____ that the recipient must enact or face losing the contract.

4. _____ are those issues such as trade, finance, pollution, energy, terrorism, human rights, etc., which overlap the foreign and domestic policy boundaries.

5. _____ are simply government grants of cash and other commodities.

6. A _____ response is used when the perception of a threat to national security cuts across normal channels of decisions.

7. _____ is a general effort to relieve the disincentives toward efficiency in public organizations by subjecting them to the incentives of the private market.

8. _____ politics is the use of political influence by members of Congress to secure government funds and projects for their constituents.

9. A tax is tagged as _____ when it does not generate increased revenues in proportion to economic growth.

10. A _____ is defined as a condition or situation that produces a human need, deprivation, or dissatisfaction, self-identified or identified by others for which relief is sought.

11. _____ are specified sums that consumers of a government service pay to receive that service.

12. _____ relate to how government is organized and how it conducts its operations and activities.

13. _____ are the strategies used to obtain the desired goal.

14. _____ are governmental actions that convey tangible benefits to individuals, groups, or corporations.

15. _____ is a public policy that concerns taxes, government spending, public debt, and the management of government money.

16. _____ are multi-year or amortized expenses.

17. _____ is those public perspectives or viewpoints on policy issues that public officials consider or take into account in making decisions.

18. Initially, President _____ wanted to eliminate the majority of the Great Society programs but retreated when his staff could not decide upon the appropriate approach to take with Congress.

19. The modern civil rights era actually began in 1954 with the United States Supreme Court's decision in _____.

20. The _____ administration tried to encourage Americans to save money by increasing the interest rates on savings and checking accounts.

21. Basically, public policy problems fall into two broad categories: _____ and _____.

22. _____ must contain well defined goals and objectives to ensure that all parties have a clear understanding of the intent of the policy directive.

23. The belief that poverty is self-inflicted is guided by the concepts of _____ _____ and the free market theory.

24. The _____ strategy avoids actually curing the problem by just preventing it from getting worse.

25. Redistributive programs are also known as _____ programs.

26. Lawmakers can ensure that appropriate money is actually used for its intended purpose by _____ the money to that budget item.

27. The _____ is based on the principle that those who reap more benefits from the government should shoulder more of the tax burden.

28. The fairness of a tax is known as _____.

MULTIPLE CHOICE:

Circle the correct response. The correct answers are given at the end of the chapter.

1. The tangible manifestations of public policies, the things actually done in pursuance of policy decisions and statements, are known as policy

    a) outcomes.
    b) outputs.
    c) inputs.
    d) policy factors.

2. The choice of an alternative from among a series of alternatives is commonly known as

    a) decision-making.
    b) crisis management.
    c) policy-making.
    d) response modules.

3. How government is organized, and how it conducts its operations and activities involve

    a) substantive problems.
    b) crisis problems.
    c) procedural problems.
    d) reactionary problems.

4. Relieving the suffering caused by the problem without addressing the problem itself is known as the

    a) alleviative approach.
    b) preventive approach.
    c) curative approach.
    d) punitive approach.

5. Curing the policy problem is the ultimate goal of the

    a) alleviative approach.
    b) preventive approach.
    c) curative approach.
    d) punitive approach.

6. Governmental actions that convey tangible benefits to individuals, groups, or corporations are known as

    a) redistributive policies.
    b) distributive policies.
    c) privatization policies.
    d) reallocative policies.

7. Oriented towards foreign policy and international politics, policies involving decisions about the procurement, allocation, and organization of men, money, and material that constitute the military forces are known as

    a) strategic defense policies.
    b) intermestic issue policies.
    c) nuclear defense policies.
    d) structural defense policies.

8. The amount of money a tax produces is known as the

    a) tax yield.
    b) tax effort.
    c) tax visibility.
    d) tax elasticity.

9. Yearly expenses needed to run governments are known as

   a) operating expenses.
   b) capital expenses.
   c) tangible expenses.
   d) cost-overrun allocations.

10. A tax program that increases the tax burden for lower-income people while reducing it for upper-income persons is a

    a) flat tax program.
    b) progressive tax program.
    c) regressive tax program.
    d) value added tax program.

11. The end result of an action is the definition of a

    a) objective.
    b) goal.
    c) strategy.
    d) action step.

12. A foreign policy decision option involving the perception of a threat to national security that cuts across normal channels is known as:

    a) structural defense policy.
    b) crisis policy response.
    c) strategic defense policy.
    d) detente defense policy.

13. The ability of a tax to generate increased revenue as economic growth or inflation increases is known as:

    a) tax yield.
    b) elasticity.
    c) tax visibility.
    d) tax effort.

14. Denying the poor food stamps because they use them for inappropriate purchases is an example of the:

   a) curative policy approach.
   b) alleviative policy approach.
   c) preventive policy approach.
   d) punitive policy approach.

15. The consequences for society, intended or unintended, that flow from the action or inaction of government are known as

   a) policy outputs.
   b) policy decisions.
   c) policy inputs.
   d) policy outcomes.

ESSAY QUESTIONS:

1. What are the pros and cons to privatization of governmental functions? In your opinion, what functions would be successfully handed over to private contractors?

2. As the mayor of a local community, you are confronted with the worst drought in fifty years. The city's supply of drinking water is dwindling fast as each day goes by. The heat has adversely effected the city's elderly and poor who can not afford to pay their electrical bills. The death toll is rising as the temperatures continue to increase. In addressing this issue, in what ways would you apply the alleviative, preventive, curative and punitive options to handle both the current and future problems related to droughts?

3. In your opinion, what is the future for affirmation action programs? In what ways have they both helped and hindered the advancement of minorities and women in America?

ANSWERS FOR CHAPTER FIFTEEN: PUBLIC POLICY

TRUE/FALSE:

1. True	9. False	17. False	25. False
2. True	10. True	18. False	26. True
3. True	11. True	19. True	27. True
4. True	12. False	20. True	28. False
5. True	13. False	21. False	
6. False	14. True	22. False	
7. True	15. True	23. True	
8. False	16. False	24. True	

FILL-IN-THE-BLANKS:

1. policy
2. budget
3. mandates
4. Intermestic issues
5. Subsidies
6. crisis policy
7. Privatization
8. Porkbarrel
9. inelastic
10. problem
11. user fees
12. Procedural problems
13. objectives
14. Distributive policies
15. Fiscal policy
16. Capital expenses
17. Public opinion
18. Richard Nixon
19. *Brown v Board of Education of Topeka, Kansas*
20. Carter
21. Foreign, domestic
22. action plans
23. Social Darwinism
24. preventive
25. Robin Hood
26. dedicating
27. Benefit principle system
28. tax equity

MULTIPLE CHOICE:

1. b - outputs
2. a - decision-making
3. c - procedural
4. a - alleviative
5. c - curative
6. b - distributive
7. d - structural defense
8. a - tax yield
9. a - operating expenses
10. c - regressive
11. b - goal
12. b - crisis policy response
13. b - elasticity
14. d - punitive policy approach
15. d - policy outcomes

SOCIAL SERVICES

CHAPTER SUMMARY:

Chapter Sixteen explores the issue of poverty and the public policy initiatives traditionally taken to address this concern to include AFDC, food stamps, and welfare reform efforts. The vocabulary of poverty reveals that there are several distinct groups that experience economic reversals. A complete demographic profile of the nation's impoverished is provided. In addition, the chapter contains a detailed discussion of health-care issues.

IDENTIFICATION:

Briefly describe each term.

Cash transfers

Persistent poverty

Safety net

Supplemental Security Income

Culture of poverty

Absolute poverty

Great Society

Nonworking poor

Special Supplemental Program for Women, Infants and Children

Employment Opportunity Act of 1965

Doughnut hole

Independent practice association

Binding Out

TRUE/FALSE:

Indicate whether each statement is true (T) or false (F). The correct answers are given at the end of the chapter.

_____1. Welfare reform legislation now requires that able-bodied adults without children must be full time employees in order to qualify for food stamps.

_____2. The United States Congress recently passed legislation removing the earnings limit for Social Security recipients.

_____3. The 1996 Democratic Party openly advocated the traditional conservative belief that economic deprivation is the inevitable result of an individual's failure to avail one's self of the free market's promise of economic viability and riches.

_____4. The safety net has been successful in shielding diverse segments of the population from falling into the poverty level.

_____5. The states cannot set their own eligibility standards for federally funded social service programs.

_____6. Social Security is funded through payroll taxes paid by both employers and employees.

_____7. The United States is the only highly industrialized nation in the world without a universal health-care coverage system.

_____8. America's welfare programs, such as Social Security, drain productivity from the economy.

_____9. Americans have distinguished between the deserving and undeserving poor and tried to help the former.

_____10. Women and children are the fastest growing segment of the homeless.

_____11. The number of the nation's homeless does not include those individuals living with relatives due to their own inability to afford shelter.

_____12. The majority of the nation's social service programs do not distinguish between the needs of the permanently poor and the temporarily poor, opting instead for a "one size fits all" approach.

_____ 13. Over the past four years, the percentage of aggregated income shared by lower- and middle-income earners has actually increased while upper income earners have seen their aggregate income slightly decrease due to the decline of profitable stock investments.

_____ 14. An early assessment of welfare reform indicates a significant decline in the number of single-parent women on public assistance.

_____ 15. According to the Census Bureau, the 2007 poverty level for a family of three is $16,530 and for a family of four $21,203.

_____ 16. As of 2003, the number of Americans living in poverty equals the entire population of Canada or Morocco.

_____ 17. In colonial America, the French poor laws served as the foundation for the colonial response to poverty and homelessness.

_____ 18. The Roosevelt administration created the Civilian Conservation Corps, the Works Progress Administration, the Emergency Relief Administration, the National Youth Corps and the National Food Distribution Association as a means of putting Americans back to work.

_____ 19. Many needy Americans simply do not apply for assistance because of the stigmatized image associated with welfare.

_____ 20. In general, federal assistance programs tend to be more generous in states with wealth, strong labor unions, high voter turnout by low-income people, and liberal political beliefs.

_____ 21. The least generous states in welfare benefits are found in the Northeast, Midwest, and Pacific regions.

_____ 22. The Social Security system is facing rising gaps between revenues and promised benefits starting in 2017 and an exhaustion of the trust fund assets by 2041.

_____ 23. A provision of the welfare reform package adopted in 1996 places a ten- year lifetime limit on welfare benefits.

FILL-IN-THE-BLANKS:

Write the appropriate word(s) to complete the sentence. The correct answers are given at the end of the chapter.

1. _____ is the state of condition of being poor by lacking the means of providing material needs or comforts.

2. The _____ is based on the assumption that poor families spend one-third of their income on food.

3. The poorhouse was also known as the _____.

4. _____ are benefits provided by government to which recipients have a legally enforceable right.

5. _____ eligibility is based upon the applicant's documented inability to provide for his/herself the desired benefit because of depressed income levels.

6. Passed in 1996, the_____ mandated welfare reform.

7. The increase in the number of poverty families headed by a female head of household is called the _____ of poverty.

8. In 1964, Congress implemented the _____ program that provides the needy with coupons to purchase food items.

9. Lyndon Johnson's programs to help the poor and all Americans to achieve a better quality of life were collectively packaged as the_____program.

10. The concept of putting all welfare recipients to work is known as_____.

11. Designed in 1977, the _____is a free federally sponsored health-care program for children whose parents earn too much money to qualify for Medicaid but lack the income to afford their own insurance coverage for their children.

12. The _____ perspective of poverty rests on the belief that those who are living in poverty are not individually responsible for their economic deprivation any more than those who are prosperous have individually produced their own wealth.

13. _____ is a temporary entitlement benefit for temporarily displaced workers.

14. The Democratic Party became the standard bearer for the liberal perspective of poverty with the election of _____ to the White House.

15. The federally-funded _____ program is designed to provide health care to the nation's poor.

16. _____ is the inability to recognize a problem in the face of compelling evidence.

17. The federal government encouraged cities to construct low-income housing through the _____ program

18. The _____ of 1935 resulted in the creation of the Old Age Assistance, the Aid to Blind and the Aid Dependent Children programs.

19. A comprehensive Medicare reform package, the _____ _____ was signed into law by President Bush in 2003.

20. The _____ poor are usually undereducated individuals who are either employed full time or part-time in minimum or below minimum wage jobs.

21. As the governor of Texas, Bush first introduced his _____ _____ package of educational reforms.

22. The _____ created by Franklin Roosevelt was designed to prevent extreme deprivation among the most disadvantaged while at the same time, cushioning the future impact of an economic reversal.

23. _____ were community centers located in the poor districts of major cities.

24. In announcing his War on Poverty plan, President Lyndon Johnson defined his _____ as a place where every child can find knowledge to enrich his/her mind and to enlarge his/her talents.

25. In _____, the United States Supreme Court ruled that Society Security is not a guaranteed right.

MULTIPLE CHOICE:

Circle the correct response. The correct answers are given at the end of the chapter.

1. Comparing an individual's income to the nation's overall standard of living is known as

    a) absolute poverty.
    b) hyper poverty.
    c) relative poverty.
    d) temporary poverty.

2 . Individuals whose annual incomes are less than half of the official poverty level are collectively known as the

    a) hyperpoor.
    b) persistently poor.
    c) absolutely poor.
    d) temporarily poor.

3. The Democratic Party became the standard bearer for the liberal version of poverty and the need for social programs with the election of

    a) Lyndon Johnson.
    b) John Kennedy.
    c) Harry Truman.
    d) Woodrow Wilson.

4. Means-tested programs that provide non-cash assistance are called

    a) workfare programs.
    b) means-tested programs.
    c) in-kind programs.
    d) comprehensive assistance plans.

5. This 1998 law mandated that social service benefits be extended to qualifying two parent families for at least six months out of a year if the principal wage earner was unemployed.

    a) Welfare Reform Act.
    b) Family Support Act.
    c) Workfare Program Act.
    d) AFDC Retention Act.

6. Those who experience poverty for one to two years in a ten year period of time are living in

   a) absolute poverty.
   b) persistent poverty.
   c) temporary poverty.
   d) hyper-poverty.

7. The nation's medical insurance plan offered to the elderly is called

   a) Medicare.
   b) Medicaid.
   c) Patient Provider Organization.
   d) Universal Coverage Health Plan.

8. In 1935, Franklin Roosevelt's administration passed the country's first national social welfare program as part of the

   a) Workfare Act.
   b) National Recovery Act.
   c) Social Security Act.
   d) Civilian Conservation Corps Act.

9. Reforms for the welfare system include

   a) working requirements for recipients.
   b) gradual weaning period from welfare payments.
   c) increased efforts to collect child support payments.
   d) all of the above.

10. The leading interest group representing the concerns of the nation's senior citizens is the

    a) American Medical Association.
    b) American Hospital Association.
    c) American Association of Retired Persons.
    d) United Gray Power League.

11. After the Revolutionary War, the practice of requiring able-bodied indigent men to work to offset costs of their support was called

    a) binding out.
    b) farming out.
    c) slavery.
    d) indentured servitude.

12. Jane Addams founded one of the nation's first settlement houses known as

    a) Henry Street Settlement.
    b) South End House.
    c) Hull House.
    d) Neighborhood Guild.

13. The Social Security Act of 1935 resulted in the creation of the

    a) Old Age Assistance Program.
    b) Aid to the Blind Program.
    c) Aid to Dependent Children Program.
    d) all of the above.

14. To offset the rising costs of out-of-pocket health-care expenses, many of the nation's elderly are purchasing their own policies commonly known as

    a) Medigap Insurance Programs.
    b) Health Maintenance Prescription Drug Plans.
    c) Point of Service Plans.
    d) Preferred Provider Organizations.

15. Proposals to save Social Security include:

    a) elimination of the mandatory retirement age.
    b) reductions in the annual cost-of-living adjustments.
    c) increasing the Social Security tax paid by workers.
    d) all of the above.

ESSAY QUESTIONS:

1.   In what specific provisions does the newly enacted welfare reform package use the alleviative, preventive, and punitive public policy approaches? In your opinion, do you believe that this legislation will actually, not just statistically, reduce the number of Americans living below the poverty level? Support your answer.

2. What types of government programs are needed to address the following categories of the impoverished:

   a) Homeless
   b) Temporarily Poor
   c) Persistently Poor

3. What are the pros and cons to requiring welfare recipients to work in order to receive benefits?

ANSWERS TO CHAPTER SIXTEEN: SOCIAL SERVICES

TRUE/FALSE:

1. False	9. True	17. False
2. True	10. True	18. False
3. False	11. True	19. True
4. True	12. True	20. True
5. False	13. False	21. False
6. True	14. False	22. True
7. True	15. True	23. False
8. False	16. True	

FILL-IN-THE-BLANKS:

1. Poverty
2. poverty level
3. almshouse
4. Entitlements
5. Means-tested
6. Personal Responsibility & Work Opportunity Act
7. feminization
8. Food Stamp
9. War on Poverty
10. workfare
11. Children's Health Insurance
12. liberal
13. Unemployment Compensation
14. Woodrow Wilson
15. medicaid
16. denial
17. model cities
18. Social Security Act
19. Medicare Prescription Drug Improvement and Modernization Act
20. working
21. No Child Left Behind
22. Safety net
23. Settlement houses
24. Great Society
25. *Flemming v Nestor*

MULTIPLE CHOICE:

1. c - relative poverty
2. a - hyperpoor
3. d - Woodrow Wilson
4. c - in-kind
5. b - Family Support Act
6. c - temporary
7. a - Medicare
8. c - Social Security
9. d - all of the above
10. c - American Association of Retired Persons
11. b - farming out
12. c - Hull House
13. d - all of the above
14. a - Medigap
15. d - all of the above.

CHAPTER SEVENTEEN

THE ENVIRONMENT

CHAPTER SUMMARY:

The primary focus of this chapter is the condition of the nation's environment and actions government has taken to address these concerns. Topics discussed include air and water pollution, incidences of oil spills, the disposal of toxic waste substances, forest and wetland conservation efforts, and the plight of endangered species. Public policy issues focus on the historical development of environmental policy initiatives at both the state and national levels.

IDENTIFICATION:

Briefly describe each term.

Smog

Non-point source pollution

Biochemical oxygen demand

Global warming

Municipal solid waste

Mandates

Silent Spring

National ambient air quality standards

Community Right-to-Know-More Act (1991)

General Revision Act (1891)

Wilderness

Migratory Bird Conservation Act (1972)

TRUE/FALSE:

Indicate whether each statement is true (T) or false (F). The correct answers are given at the end of the chapter.

_____1.   The United States Forestry Service was founded by Franklin Roosevelt in 1905.

_____2.   Air is basically a mixture of nitrogen, oxygen, argon, carbon dioxide, and traces of neon, helium, krypton, hydrogen, xenon, methane, and vitreous oxide.

_____3.   The Pitman-Robertson Act (1937) allocated revenue for state wildlife conservation efforts from the collection of excise taxes on rifles, shotguns, ammunition, and archery equipment.

4. The polluting effects of acid rain from the United States was crossing into Mexico destroying crops and deteriorating buildings and national monuments.

5. Exposure to neon can cause severe brain damage and mental retardation.

6. Former United States Senator Lloyd Bentsen introduced legislation requiring triple hulling of oil tankers as a means to preventing oil spills.

7. The EPA's enforcement track-record has been described as mired in lengthy and costly litigation resulting in lenient cleanup schedules and few fines.

8. The Toxic Substance Control Act established the process for the disposal of hazardous wastes.

9. It is estimated that 75 percent of American garbage still ends up in landfills, with half the remainder incinerated and half recycled.

10. The Comprehensive Environmental Response, Compensation, and Liability Act of 1980 required that all pesticides used in any interstate commerce action be officially approved and certified as harmless to humans, animal life, and so on prior to use.

11. The United States Supreme Court has upheld the EPA's tougher air quality standards set by the Clinton administration.

12. The Army Corps of Engineers believes that the answer to reducing flood damage is to continue its efforts to dam up the nation's largest rivers.

13. President George W. Bush reversed his 2000 campaign promise to set regulations on carbon dioxide emissions from power plants.

14. Exxon is currently paying all of the criminal and civil fines plus the punitive damage awards caused by the *Valdez* oil spill.

15. *Silent Spring* was written by Rachel Carson.

16. The Air Pollution Control Act of 1955 enabled the federal government to provide funding to those states conducting air pollution research.

17. The Wilderness Act provides cash incentives to property owners as a means of encouraging preservation efforts.

18. A threatened species is one likely to become endangered in the foreseeable future.

_____19. The cost of construction materials in the United States has dramatically increased because the emerging middle-class in Japan is demanding higher-end goods and services to include American-style homes.

_____20. In the 1970s it was discovered that migrant farm workers were becoming the victims of deadly skin cancers due to their exposure to fruits and vegetables heavily sprayed with pesticides.

_____21. A friend of Teddy Roosevelt, George Grinnell led an impassioned campaign against poachers and women who favored feathered hats.

_____22. As a result of Carson's *The Jungle*, the federal government enacted a series of laws placing controls and bans on the use of DDT's, other pesticides, and herbicides.

_____23. President Richard Nixon played an instrumental role in the passage of the Clean Air Act, National Environmental Policy Act, the Federal Water Pollution Control Act, and the Endangered Species Act.

_____24. The Air Pollution Control Act created the Office of Ocean and Coastal Resource Management to provide federal grants for the development of state coastal preservation projects.

_____25. Safety standards for the transportation of natural and other gases by pipelines were established with the passage of the Federal Hazardous Liquid Pipeline Safety Act.

_____26. The El Nino and El Nina weather cycles are the primary cause of prolonged drought conditions followed by short-lived monsoon-like flooding.

_____27. Since Clinton's presidency, Congress and environmentalists have been battling over drilling for oil in the pristine Aransas Pass area of the Gulf of Mexico.

_____28. In Corpus Christi, the city's largest employers are six major oil refineries located all in a row on a 109-mile corridor commonly known as Refinery Row.

_____29. The EPA has determined that the primary causes of water quality problems in the nation's rivers and streams come from farm fertilizers, animal waste, pesticides, and suspended solids.

_____30. Passed in 1986, the Emergency Planning and Community Right-to-Know Act requires local businesses to notify communities about the types of hazardous substances they use in producing their products.

_____31. The Wetlands Reserve Program requires farmers and ranchers receiving Department of Agriculture benefits and subsidies to protect any wetlands located on their property.

_____32. President Obama's environmental plan includes the goal of renewable energy generating 25 percent of the nation's electricity by 2025; and having at least 60 billion gallons of biofuels in the nation's supply by 2030.

_____33. With approximately 1.5 million acres, the Big Bend Natural Preserve is the nation's third largest national park.

FILL-IN-THE-BLANKS:

Write the appropriate word(s) to complete the sentence. The correct answers are given at the end of the chapter.

1. _____ is defined as a group of chemical compounds that are in the wrong place or in the wrong concentration at the wrong time.

2. _____ refers to a wide-scale, low-level pollution that obstructs visibility.

3. The _____ (1963) provided a $95 million grant-in-aid program to assist state governments in setting their own air quality standards.

4. Global warming or the_____ occurs when methane, carbon dioxide, and certain other air pollutants increase, trapping heat in the earth's atmosphere and gradually warming it.

5. _____ is refuse materials composed primarily of solids at normal ambient temperatures.

6. Signed by 125 nations in 1987, the _____ froze the production of CFCs.

7. _____ are areas that are inundated or saturated by surface or ground water often enough or for a long enough period to support vegetation adapted for saturated soils.

8. The EPA requires that all federal agencies file_____ detailing any potential harm a project might cause to the environment as well as the measures to be taken to avoid environmental damage.

9. President Clinton used the _____ of 1906 to federally protect over 58 million acres of land from logging and development.

10. The nation's first national park was _____.

11. The _____ (1899) required that all potential dumpers of waste materials into navigable rivers had to obtain a permit from the Army Corps of Engineers prior to dumping.

12. A river is considered to be _____ when it cannot support aquatic life or is unsafe for fishing and swimming.

13. In 1864, the eventual founder of the American Forestry Service Association, _____ wrote *Man and Nature*.

14. An area declared as _____ has met federal guidelines under the Clean Air Act.

15. _____ are permanently flooded lands lying below the deepwater boundary of wetlands.

16. The _____ Act requires the EPA to conduct inspections and if required, removal of all asbestos-containing materials from public school buildings.

17. The Energy Policy and Conservation Act created the nation's _____ to offset future oil and gas shortages in emergency situations.

18. In 1889, approximately 2,200 residents of _____ were killed by rising flood waters and the collapse of an earthen dam.

19. George Marsh was instrumental in forming the _____, originally an interest group of bird watchers concerned about the conservation of the nation's forests.

20. _____ include ash, smoke, dust, soot, and liquid droplets.

21. The _____ (1916) allowed the federal government to set aside park lands for public use without impairment.

22. The nation's first wildlife sanctuary was _____.

23. Linked directly to air pollution, _____are a family of inert, nontoxic chemicals used in refrigeration, air conditioning, packaging, and insulation.

24. The _____ provided incentives for bike lanes and trails as well as mass transportation projects.

25. _____ describes the rise in the earth's temperature caused by an increase in the concentration of certain gases, especially carbon dioxide.

26. Eventually blocked by federal courts, Congress approved a project to build a low-level radioactive waste disposal complex in _____, a small town located near the Texas-Mexico border.

27. _____ is solid waste resulting from or incidental to municipal, community, commercial, institutional, and recreational activities including garbage, rubbish, ashes, street clearings, and all other solid waste other than industrial.

28. Former Vice President _____ won an Academy Award for his short-subject film entitled *An Inconvenient Truth*.

29. In 2001, the Bush administration withdrew the United States from the _____ _____, an international agreement setting binding reduction targets and emissions caps to help eliminate greenhouse gas emissions.

30. _____ is a pollution course that has a precise, identifiable location, such as a pipe or smokestack.

MULTIPLE CHOICE:

Circle the correct response. The correct answers are given at the end of the chapter.

1. The _____passed in 1900 outlawed both the interstate exportation and importation of wildlife harvested or possessed in violation of federal laws.

    a) Migratory Bird Treaty Act
    b) Pitman-Robertson Act
    c) Lacey Act
    d) Pollution Prevention Act

2. A complex chemical and atmospheric phenomenon that occurs when emissions of sulfur and nitrogen compounds and other substances are transformed by chemical processes in the atmosphere, often far from the original source, and then deposited on earth in either a wet or dry form is commonly known as

    a) air pollution.
    b) acid rain.
    c) haze.
    d) smog.

3. Billions over a six-year period for highway and public transportation projects was authorized with the passage of the

    a) Fish Conservation Act.
    b) Federal Highway Act.
    c) Surface Transportation Act.
    d) Public Transportation Enhancement Act.

4. Federal standards for all suppliers of drinking water serving more than 25 people were established with the passage of the

    a) Safe Water Drinking Act.
    b) Clean Water Act.
    c) Water Pollution Control Act.
    d) Drinking Water Standards Act.

5. The guidelines for the identification, monitoring and disposal of solid and industrial waste products were established through the

    a) National Ambient Air Quality Standards Act.
    b) Nuclear Dumping Act.
    c) Pollution Prevention Act.
    d) Toxic Substances Control Act.

6. Guidelines for the protection of endangered plant, wildlife, and marine life were developed with the passage of the

    a) Animal Protection Act.
    b) Endangered Species Act.
    c) Migratory Bird Treaty Act.
    d) Pitman-Robertson Conservation Act.

7. The primary ingredient of smog is

    a) ozone.
    b) haze.
    c) particulate matter.
    d) acid rain.

8. In 1978, 235 families were evacuated from the residential development near Niagara Falls known as

a) Mohawk Valley.
b) St. Lawrence Hills.
c) Love Canal.
d) Green Aces Estates.

9. National guidelines for water pollution standards were established with the passage of the 1972

a) Clean Water Act.
b) Safe Water Drinking Act.
c) Water Pollution Control Act.
d) Lacey Act.

10. Ozone pollution causes respiratory ailments to include

a) shortness of breath.
b) premature aging of the lungs.
c) nasal congestion and eye irritation.
d) all of the above.

11. Environmentalist John Muir founded the

a) Sierra Club.
b) American Forestry Association.
c) Greenpeace.
d) The National Conservation Conservatory.

12. Hunting in the nation's national park system was outlawed by the

a) General Revision Act (1891).
b) Park Protection Act (1894).
c) Wilderness Act (1964).
d) National Park Act (1916).

13. The Superfund was created by the

a) Emergency Planning and Community Right-to-Know-Act (1986).
b) Pollution Prevention Act (1990).
c) Community-Right-to-Know Act (1991).
d) Comprehensive Environmental Response Compensation and Liability Act (1980).

14. The Environmental Protection Agency shares its responsibilities for the environment with the

   a) Fish and Wildlife Service.
   b) Interior Department.
   c) National Park Service.
   d) all of the above.

15. Federal guidelines for the transportation of hazardous liquids through pipelines was established by the

   a) Resource Conservation and Recovery Act (1976).
   b) Federal Hazardous Liquid Pipeline Safety Act (1979).
   c) Refuse Act (1899).
   d) Federal Water Pollution Control Act (1948).

ESSAY QUESTIONS:

1. Why should Americans be concerned about the deforestation of the Brazilian rain forests? What is the ecological value of the rain forests?

2. Why are environmentalists so concerned about preserving the wetlands?

3. In your opinion, should business and industry bear the total responsibility for the air and water pollution problems in this country? If not, who should shoulder the responsibility? Defend your response.

ANSWERS FOR CHAPTER SEVENTEEN: THE ENVIRONMENT

TRUE/FALSE:

1. False	11. True	21. True	31. False
2. True	12. False	22. False	32. True
3. True	13. True	23. True	33. False
4. False	14. False	24. False	
5. False	15. True	25. False	
6. True	16. True	26. True	
7. True	17. False	27. False	
8. False	18. True	28. True	
9. True	19. False	29. True	
10. False	20. True	30. True	

FILL-IN-THE-BLANKS:

1. Air pollution
2. Haze
3. Clear Air Act
4. greenhouse effect
5. Solid waste
6. Montreal Protocal
7. Wetlands
8. impact statement
9. Antiquities Act
10. Yellowstone National Park
11. Refuse Act
12. impaired
13. George Perkins Marsh
14. Attainment
15. Deepwater habitats
16. Asbestos Hazard Emergency Response
17. Strategic Petroleum Reserve
18. Johnstown
19. American Forestry Association
20. Suspended particulates
21. National Park Act
22. Pelican Island
23. Chlorofluorocarbons (CFCs)
24. Intermodal Surface Transportation Efficiency Act
25. Climate change
26. Sierra Blanca
27. Municipal solid waste
28. Al Gore
29. Kyoto Protocol
30. Point source pollution

MULTIPLE CHOICE:

1. c - Lacey Act
2. b - acid rain
3. c - Surface Transportation Act
4. a - Safe Water Drinking Act
5. d - Toxic Substance Control Act
6. b - Endangered Species Act
7. a - ozone
8. c - Love Canal
9. c - Water Pollution Control Act
10. d - all of the above
11. a - Sierra Club
12. b - Park Protection Act (1894)
13. d - Comprehensive Environmental Response Compensation and Liability Act (1980)
14. d - all of the above
15. b - Federal Hazardous Pipeline Safety Act (1979)

CHAPTER EIGHTEEN

FOREIGN POLICY

CHAPTER SUMMARY:

Chapter 18 details the complex nature of foreign policy to include the process employed by the president and Congress in weighing and ultimately developing a policy response to an international concern. The chapter also explores the constitutional authority granted to both the legislative and executive branches in foreign affairs. The chapter concludes with a regional overview of some of the existing and potential problems the Obama administration will be called upon to address.

IDENTIFICATION:

Briefly describe each term.

Protectionism

Self-Determination

Internal Sovereignty

Psychological Warfare

Nation State

First World Power Nation States

Alliance

Multilateral Agreements

Balance of Terror

Glasnost

Internationalism

Deterrence

Détente

Bilateral Agreements

Vietnamization Plan

Case-Zablocki Act

<u>National Security Council</u>

<u>War Guilt Clause</u>

<u>Iron Curtain</u>

<u>Marshall Plan</u>

<u>Domino Theory</u>

TRUE/FALSE:

Indicate whether each statement is true (T) or false (F). The correct answers are given at the end of the chapter.

_____ 1. Since nation states cannot focus on all of their national interests, they tend to concentrate on a selective handful of objectives known as vital interests.

_____ 2. The majority of the world's former colonial possessions did not receive their independence from their mother countries until the late 17th and early 18th centuries.

_____ 3. Since obtaining its independence through the Peace of Westphalia in 1648, Iceland has pursued a policy of neutrality.

_____ 4. In 1784, the United States sent the _Empress of China_ to Canton, China, for ginseng, a highly prized herb used for medicinal purposes.

_____ 5. The Gore-McLemore Tariff Act imposed extremely high tariffs on agricultural and industrial imports.

_____ 6. A neutral state takes no part in war and agrees not to defend its territory against attacks.

_____ 7. By 1854, the United States government annexed Hawaii, formally known as the Marshall Islands primarily for its sandalwood and strategic location as a fuel station for American cargo ships.

_____ 8. Today, the international community is closely monitoring the South Korean government's launching of short-range nuclear weapons and Iran's development of its own nuclear program.

_____ 9. The Cold War was a struggle over economic philosophies because the Soviet Union wanted to expand its socialist system throughout the Eastern bloc and the United States desired to see more nation states adopt a capitalist system.

_____ 10. Economic sanctions used as a means of punishing a state nation for unacceptable behavior have proven to be very effective long-term options to bring the rogue state into line.

_____ 11. The last two groups in Europe to form into nation states were Italy and Austria.

_____ 12. Initially, the United Nations imposed strict sanctions against the Iraqi government for its supposed program of producing weapons of mass destruction.

_____ 13. The three major factions or cultural groups in Iraq are the Kurds, Sunni and Shiites.

_____ 14. A state of war exists in the legal sense when two or more states officially declare that a condition of hostilities exists between them.

_____ 15. In second world power nation states, industry and agriculture are basically equal economic partners while, in third world power nation states agriculture dominates with industry playing a second or marginal role.

_____ 16. A most-favored-nation clause added to a trade agreement extends tariff concessions to a nation or nations as a means of reversing an unfavorable trade deficit.

_____ 17. At the Constitutional Convention, the Framers agreed that the sole responsibility for all foreign policy initiatives belonged exclusively with the executive branch with the legislative branch having no authority over foreign policy decisions.

_____ 18. In 2009, the United Nations joined by the United States imposed heavy sanctions on North Korea in hopes of dismantling their nuclear power program.

_____ 19. President Harry Truman's containment policy was designed to prevent the Soviet Union from expanding its influence over other European nations.

_____ 20. The United States government used the Open Door Policy to establish trade agreements with both China and Japan.

_____ 21. In pre-World War II Europe, the rise of Hitler's totalitarian government of Fascism and Italy's implementation of Nazism marked the beginning of hostilies with the British and French.

_____ 22. During World War II, Nationalist Chinese Leader Mao Zedong was fighting Japanese aggression in the Southern area of China while Chaing Kai-shek was forming the Red Army composed of peasants from the Northern area.

_____ 23. The term commander-in-chief was first used by Charles I of England in 1639 during the first Bishops War.

_____ 24. In 1936, the Japanese and Germans signed the Anti-Comintern Pact, a collective security agreement offering military support to each other in case of an attack.

_____ 25. Cold War politics created two Koreas with North Korea as an anti-socialist/communist state and South Korea as a pro-socialist/communist nation.

_____ 26. President Franklin Roosevelt initiated the Berlin Airlift to bring needed food and supplies to the Eastern sector of Berlin after the Soviets closed it off.

_____ 27. The first executive agreement was the Rush-Bagot Agreement signed by President Monroe in 1817.

_____ 28. Article I, Section 7 of the United States Constitution prohibits the individual states from entering into any treaty, alliance or confederation.

_____ 29. The Geneva Conventions of 1864 and 1906 mandate the humane treatment of military personnel wounded in battle.

_____ 30. In the Iran/Contra Conflict, the United States government supported the Sandinistas and the Contras were funded by the Soviets through the Cuban government.

_____ 31. In _Federalist #69_, John Jay clarified the role the president would have as the Nation's commander-in-chief.

_____ 32. The United States Senate rejected Woodrow Wilson's Treaty of Versailles particularly its provision for the United States to join the League of Nations.

_____ 33. Interventionism is the coercive interference in the affairs of a state by another group of states to affect the internal and external policies of that state.

_____ 34. With the Camp David Accords, Syria became the first Arab nation to officially recognize Israel.

_____ 35. One of the world's first collective security agreements, the Paris League was signed in the 15th Century by merchants throughout Europe to guard against unfair trade practices.

_____ 36. A provision of the War Powers Act enables Congress to pass a concurrent resolution at any time to end the president's commitment of troops overseas.

_____ 37. The Obama administration has signaled its willingness to work with the Cuban government by lifting barriers for family members in the states to visit and send money to their relatives in Cuba.

_____ 38. Al Qaeda is a world-wide organization composed of ideologically joined by operationally separate independent "cell" organizations.

_____ 39. The United States Congress has officially declared war five times: the War of 1812, the Mexican War, the Spanish-American War, World War I and World War II.

_____ 40. The Monroe Doctrine was actually written by President's Monroe's Secretary of State James Madison.

FILL IN THE BLANKS:

Write the appropriate word (s) to complete the sentence. The correct answers are given at the end of the chapter.

1. _____ is the policy of curtailing as much as possible a nation's international relations so one's country can exist in peace and harmony by itself in the world.

2. A nation's _____ is its annual net trade surplus or deficit, based on the difference in the value of its total imports and exports.

3. _____means that those nation states falling into the third-, fourth- and fifth world categories have significantly high infant mortality rates, extreme poverty, a heavy dependence upon subsistence agriculture, and a rigid social structure that severely restricts social mobility.

4. _____ is the independent legal authority over a population in a particular territory, based on the recognized right to self-determination.

5. Through the _____ program, the Roosevelt administration was able to lend much needed military equipment, airplanes, and weapons to the British during the initial stages of World War II.

6. _____ is the right of a nation state to conclude binding agreements or treaties with other states without interference from the international community.

7. _____ is defined as the hostilities between states or within a state or territory undertaken by means of armed force.

8. _____ is a strategy or planned course of action developed by the decision makers of a state vis a vis other states or international entities aimed at achieving specific goals defined in terms of national interests.

9. A _____ is a limited but powerful military maneuver designed to scare the other side away from hostile action.

10. _____ is the spirit of belonging together or the corporate will that seeks to preserve the identity of the group by institutionalizing it in the form of a state.

11. The _____ is an agreement between Mexico, Canada and the United States to develop transparency in trade between the three nations.

12. _____ is the extension by one state of preponderant influence or control over another state or region.

13. A _____ involves the participation of the entire populations in the war effort and an unconditional surrender of the enemy.

14. Beginning with Marco Polo's journey to China, merchants established a series of trade routes known collectively as the _____.

15. Article I, Section 8 of the United States Constitution is known as the_____.

16. _____ is the domination of one state by another, usually for exploitative purposes.

17. _____ of the United States Constitution names the president as commander-in-chief of the army and navy of the United States, and of the militia of the several states.

18. In 1955, the Soviet Union signed the _____,
    a collective security agreement between the Eastern bloc nations and the Soviet Union.

19. During the American Civil War, President Abraham suspended the writ of_____.

20. A _____ is a first-strike nuclear attack under
    taken on the assumption that an enemy state is planning an imminent nuclear attack.

21. A _____ is a formal agreement entered into between two
    or more countries.

22. In 1973, Congress reigned in the president's war making powers with the passage of the
    _____.

23. An _____is an international agreement
    reached by the president with foreign heads of state that does not require senatorial approval.

24. Lyndon Johnson was given the power to take all necessary measures to repel any armed
    attack against the United States in Vietnam through the _____
    _____.

25. A _____ response calls upon the president to
    exercise his/her emergency powers to act quickly to address a perceived or actual threat to
    national security.

26. The sinking of the British ship _____ as well as
    American vessels drew the United States into World War I.

27. In 1793, President George Washington issued the _____
    _____ indicating the United States desired to refrain from involvement
    in international affairs.

28. A _____ is an armed conflict fought
    for objectives less than the total destruction of the enemy and its unconditional surrender.

29. The _____
    was formed in 1949 by the West for the sole purpose of blocking the threat of Soviet
    military aggression in Europe.

30. The Treaty of Versailles contained President Wilson's _____
    advocating open relations for all nations as a means of avoiding wars.

31. Announced in 1947, the _____ pledged the full support of the United States to any "free" nation resisting invasion.

32. The United States government pledged economic support to Latin American countries through the _____, and to Britain, France, Belgium, the Netherlands and Luxembourg with the _____.

33. The father of modern China is _____.

34. The _____ separates North from South Korea.

MULTIPLE CHOICE:

Circle the correct response. The correct answers are given at the end of the chapter.

1.　Basically, the national interest of the United States are to:

    a)　protect our physical security and that of our neighbors and major democratic allies.
    b)　protect our economic security and extend our sphere of influence.
    c)　only a.
    d)　a and b.

2.　In order for a nation state to maintain its neutrality, it must

    a)　refrain from aiding any belligerent.
    b)　not have a armed military, navy or air force.
    c)　agree not be involved in any international organizations.
    d)　refrain from entering into any trade agreements with other nation states.

3.　The Holy Alliance agreement was between:

    a)　Russia, Italy and Austria.
    b)　Russia, Prussia and Austria.
    c)　Great Britain, France and Russia.
    d)　Prussia, Italy, and France.

4.　The 1945 Yalta Agreement was signed by:

    a)　Harry Truman, Joseph Stalin and Winston Churchill.
    b)　Harry Truman, I.V. Lenin and Winston Churchill.
    c)　Franklin Roosevelt, Joseph Stalin and Neville Chamberlain.
    d)　Franklin Roosevelt, Joseph Stalin and Winston Churchill.

5. The Quadruple Alliance formed in 1815 was between the governments of:

   a) Austria, France, Great Britain and Italy.
   b) Great Britain, Austria, Prussia and Germany.
   c) Great Britain, Austria, Prussia and Russia.
   d) France, Russia, Italy, and Germany.

6. World War I was fought between the Triple Alliance of Germany, Austria-Hungary and Italy and the Triple Entente of:

   a) Great Britain, France and Denmark.
   b) Great Britain, France and Russia.
   c) Great Britain, Russia and Spain.
   d) Great Britain, Spain and Portugal.

ESSAY QUESTIONS

1. In your opinion, should nation states on the losing side of a war such as Germany and Japan for World War II, apologize to the international community for their actions and compensate the victims of their enemies? Defend your response.

2. What were the provisions of the Monroe Doctrine?

3. In your opinion, should the United States have joined the League of Nations? Would its participation in the League have prevented World War II?

ANSWERS TO CHAPTER EIGHTEEN: FOREIGN POLICY

TRUE/FALSE:

1.	True	11.	False	21.	False	31.	False
2.	False	12.	True	22.	False	32.	True
3.	False	13.	True	23.	True	33.	True
4.	True	14.	True	24.	True	34.	False
5.	False	15.	True	25.	False	35.	False
6.	False	16.	True	26.	False	36.	True
7.	False	17.	False	27.	True	37.	True
8.	False	18.	True	28.	False	38.	True
9.	True	19.	True	29.	True	39.	True
10.	False	20.	True	30.	False	40.	False

FILL-IN-THE-BLANKS:

1. Isolationism
2. balance of trade
3. Underdevelopment
4. Sovereignty
5. Lend-Lease
6. External sovereignty
7. War
8. Foreign policy
9. Preventive war
10. Nationalism
11. North American Free Trade Agreement
12. Hegemony
13. total war
14. Silk Road
15. war clause
16. Imperialism
17. Article II, Section 2
18. Warsaw Pact
19. Habeas Corpus
20. preemptive strike
21. treaty
22. War Powers Resolution
23. executive agreement
24. Gulf of Tonkin Resolution
25. crisis policy
26. The Lusitania
27. Proclamation of Neutrality
28. limited war
29. North Atlantic Treaty Organization
30. Fourteen Points
31. Truman Doctrine
32. Rio Pact; Brussels Pact
33. Dr. Sun Yat-Sen
34. 38th parallel

MULTIPLE CHOICE:

1. d – a and b.
2. a – refrain from aiding any belligerent.
3. b – Russia, Prussia and Austria.
4. d – Roosevelt, Stalin and Churchill.
5. c – Great Britain, Austria, Prussia and Russia
6. b – Great Britain, France and Russia.

PART I

Foundations of Government

WILLIAM BRADFORD ON SAMOSET, SQUANTO, MASSASOIT, AND THE PILGRIMS, 1620

The arrival of the Pilgrims to Plymouth Rock in Massachusetts in 1620 began the shaky relationship between the "white man" and the "red man." Colonist William Bradford recalls his encounters with his new neighbors.

... All this while the Indians came skulking about them, and would sometimes show them selves aloofe of, but when any aproached near them, they would rune away. And once they stoale away their tools wher they had been at worke, & were gone to diner. But about the 16. *of March* a certaine Indian came bouldly amongst them, and spoke to them in broken English, which they could well understand, but marvelled at it. At length they understood by discourse with him, that he was not of these parts, but belonged to the eastrene parts, wher some English-ships came to fhish, with whom he was aquainted, & could name sundrie of them by their names, amongst whom he had gott his language. He became profitable to them in aquainting them with many things concerning the state of the cuntry in the east-parts wher he lived, which was afterwards profitable unto them; as also of the people hear, of their names, number, & strenggth; of their situation & distance from this place, and who was cheefe amongst them. His name was *Samaset*; he tould them also of another Indian whos name was *Squanto*, a native of this place, who had been in England & could speake better English then him selfe. Being, after some time of entertainments & gifts, dismist, a while after he came againe, & 5. more with him, & they brought againe all the tooles that were stolen away before, and made way for the coming of their great Sachem, called *Massasoyt*; who, about 4. or 5. *days after*, came with the cheefe of his friends & other attendance, with the aforesaid *Squanto*. With whom, after frendly entertainment, & some gifts given him, they made a peace with him (which hath now continued this 24. years) in these terms.

1. That neither he nor any of his, should injurie or doe hurte to any of their peopl.
2. That if any of his did any hurte to any of theirs, he should send the offender, that they might punish him.
3. That if any thing were taken away from any of theirs, he should cause it to be restored; and they should doe the like to his.
4. If any did unjustly warr against him, they would aide him; if any did warr against them, he should aide them.
5. He should send to his neighbours confederats, to certifie them of this, that they might not wrong them, but might be likewise comprised in the conditions of peace.
6. That when ther men came to them, they should leave their bows & arrows behind them.

After these things he returned to his place caled *Sowams*, some 40. mile from this place, but *Squanto* continued with them, and was their interpreter, and was a spetiall instrument sent of God for their good beyond their expectation. He directed them how to set their corne, wher to take fish, and to procure other comodities, and was also their pilott to bring them to unknowne places for their profitt, and never left them till he dyed. He was a *native of this place*, & scarce any left alive besids him self. He was caried away with diverce others by one *Hunt*, a Mr. of a ship, who thought to sell them for slaves in Spaine; but he got away for England, and was entertained by a marchante in London, & imployed to New-found-land & other parts, & lastly brought hither into these parts by one Mr. *Dermer*, a gentle-man imployed by Sr. Ferdinando Gorges & others, for discovery, & other designes in these parts....

HOW WELL DID YOU UNDERSTAND THIS SELECTION?

In your opinion, were Squanto's terms with the white settlers reasonable? Provide specific examples to support your response.

The Virginia slave statutes served as the basis for similar laws passed in the other British colonies and eventually became the foundation for the gradual growth and institutionalization of slavery in the United States. However, slavery never developed equally throughout the colonies and consequently divided them along geo-economic lines. Slavery ultimately became the basis for one of the most hotly debated issues at the Constitutional Convention in 1787. Although many compromises were made at this convention, they were done so to secure a union of states. The compromises made among the states over slavery were done at the expense of the freedom of African Americans. In so doing, the Constitution drafted in Philadelphia legitimized the already established construction of race in North America. The Constitution, the supreme law of the land, legitimized slavery in the newly formed United States of America.

Africans arrived in Jamestown, Virginia in 1619, and their introduction significantly altered the labor force in the colony. A Dutch ship dropped anchor off the coast of Virginia. The captain and the crew of the frigate were starving. The only commodity the captain had to trade with the colonists for food were twenty Africans whom they had stolen from a Spanish ship. The Dutch captain exchanged the Africans for food and quickly set sail. These Africans maintained a very different status than those that followed because the early colonists had a very different concept of race than did subsequent generations. According to one theory, "the first white settlers were organized around concepts of class, religion, and nationality, and they apparently had little or no understanding of the concepts of race and slavery."

In 1619, English law forbade the enslavement of baptized Christians. Since the Africans from the Dutch frigate had been baptized, they could not be sold as slaves. Instead, they became indentured servants. The first Africans were bought by the shareholders of the Virginia Company and were not the property of any individual. They were considered servants of the state. Their services were used in the homes of high-ranking officials within the colony. In this regard, the indentured Africans held a higher status than did the white indentured servants. After fulfilling the terms of their contracts, the Africans achieved the status of free blacks within the colony capable of owning land and their own indentured servants. Records indicate that the socioeconomic status of the first generation of black indentured servants in Virginia approximated that of whites.

Although the first black indentured servants in Jamestown maintained the same status as their white counterparts, evidence indicates that this did not last long. As the tobacco industry in Virginia expanded, the need for labor increased. White indentured servants could not provide enough labor for the settlement, and the Virginia colonists began to give serious thought to the "perpetual servitude" of blacks. Using the neighboring Caribbean islands as models, the colonists soon recognized that blacks could not easily escape without being identified. It was then easier to keep black servants in a state of perpetual servitude than whites, and it wasn't long before black and white servants were being treated differently.

The Virginia legislature then began to pass laws that changed the status of blacks in the colony. The legislature clearly defined servitude in terms of race. The following slave codes are some of the laws that were passed that gradually institutionalized slavery.

At the time these statutes were written, spelling was not standardized, as we know it today. Therefore, be patient with the language of the following documents.

MARCH, 1642-3—18th CHARLES 1st. ACT XXII. 1: 254.

WHEREAS there are divers loytering runaways in the collony who very often absent themselves from their masters service, And sometimes in two or three monthes cannot be found, whereby their said masters are at great charge in finding them, And many times even to the losse of their year's labour before they be had, *Be it therefore enacted and confirmed* that all runaways that shall absent themselves from their said masters service shall be lyable to make satisfaction by service at the end of their tymes by indenture (vizt.) double the tyme of service soe neglected, And in some cases more if the comissioners for the place appointed shall find it requisite and convenient. And if such runnaways shall be found to transgresse the second time or oftener (if it shall be duely proved against them) that then they shall be branded in the cheek with the letter R. and passe under the statute of incorrigible rogues, Provided notwithstanding that where any servants shall have just cause of complaint against their masters or mistrises by harsh or unchristianlike usage or otherways for want of diet, or convenient necessaryes that then it shall be lawfull for any such servant or servants to repaire to the next comissioner to make his or their complaint, And if the said commissioner shall find by good and sufficient proofes, that the said servant's cause of complaint is just, The said comissioner is hereby required to give order for the warning of any such master or mistris before the comissioners in their seuerall county courts, where the matter in difference shall be decided as they in their discretions shall think fitt, And that care be had that no such servant or servants be misused by their masters or mistrises, where they shall find the cause of complaint to be just. Be it further also enacted that if any servant running away as aforesaid shall carrie either peice, powder and shott, And leave either all or any of them with the Indians, And being thereof lawfully convicted shall suffer death as in case of felony.

MARCH, 1642-3 ACT XXVI , 1:257.

WHEREAS divers controversies have risen between masters and sevants being brought into the colony without indentures or covenants to testifie their agreements whereby both masters and servants have been often prejudiced, *Be it therefore enacted and confirmed* for prevention of future controversies of the like nature, that such servants as shall be imported haveing no indentures or covenants either men or women if they be above twenty year old to serve fowre year, if they shall be above twelve and under twenty to serve five years, And if under twelve to serve seaven years.

MARCH, 1654-55 - 6th of Commonwealth, ACT VI, 1:411.

BE it enacted by this Grand Assembly, That all Irish servants that from the first of September, 1653, have bin brought into this collony without indenture (notwithstanding the for servants without indentures it being only the benefitt of our own nation) shall serve as followeth, (vizt.) all above sixteen yeares old to serve six years, and all under to serve till they be twenty-four years old and in case of dispute in that behalfe the court shall be judge of their age.

MARCH, 1659-60, 11th of Commonwealth, ACT XIV, 1:538

An Act for repealing an Act for Irish Servants.

WHEREAS the act for Irish servants comeing in without indentures enjoyning them to serve six yeeres, carried with it both rigour and inconvenience, many by the length of time they have to serve being discouraged from comeing into the country, And by that meanes the peopling of the country retarded, And these inconveniences augmented by the addition of the last clause in that act, That all aliens should be included, *Bee it therefore enacted and confirmed,* That the whole act be repealed and made void and null, And that for the future no servant comeing into the country without indentures, of what christian nation soever, shall serve longer then those of our own contry, of the like age: *And it is furtherenacted,* That what alien soever arrive here before that clause was inserted and that hath been by vertue of that last clause inforced to serve any time longer then the custom of the countrey did oblige them to shall be allowed competent wages by their severall masters for the time they have overserved, Any act, order of court or judgment to the contrary notwithstanding, *Provided alwaies* that all such aliens as came in servants during the time that the said clause was in force shall serve according to the tenor of that act.

William Waller Henning - Vol II, MARCH, 1660-1, 13th Charles II, ACT XXII, 2:26.

English running away with negroes.

BEE itt enacted That in case any English servant shall run away in company with any negroes who are incapable of makeing satisfaction by addition of time, *Bee itt enacted* that the English so running away in company with them shall serve for the time of the said negroes absence as they are to do for their owne by a former act.

MARCH, 1661-2, ACT CII, 14th Charles II, 2:116.

Run-aways.

WHEREAS there are diverse loytering runaways in this country who very often absent themselves from their masters service and sometimes in a long time cannot be found, that losse of the time and the charge in the seeking them often exceeding the value of their labor: *Bee it therefore enacted* that all runaways that shall absent themselves from their said masters shalbe lyable to make satisfaction by service after the times by custome or indenture is expired (vizt.) double their times of service soe neglected, and if the time of their running away was in the crop or the charge of recovering them extraordinary the court shall lymitt a longer time of service proportionable to the damage the master shall make appeare he hath susteyned, and because the adjudging the time they should serve is often referred untill the time by indenture is expired, when the proofe of what is due is very uncertaine, *it is enacted* that the master of any runaway that intends to take the benefitt of this act, shall as soone as he hath recovered him carry him to the next commissioner and there declare and prove the time of his absence, and the charge he hath bin at in his recovery, which commissioner thereupon shall grant his certificate, and the court on that certificate passe judgment for the time he shall serve for his absence; and in case any English servant shall run away in *enacted* that the English soe running away in the company with them shall at the time of service to their owne masters expired, serve the masters of the said negroes for their absence soe long as they should have done by this act if they had not beene slaves, every christian in company serving his proportion; and if the negroes be lost or dye in such time of their being run away, the christian servants in company with them shall by proportion among them, either pay fower thousand five hundred pounds of tobacco and caske or fower yeares service for every negroe soe lost or dead.

December 1662 - 14th Charles II, 2:170, Act XII.

Negro womens children to serve according to the condition of the mother.

WHEREAS some doubts have arrisen whether children got by any Englishman upon a negro woman should be slave or ffree, *Be it therefore enacted and declared by this present grand assembly,* that all children borne in this country shalbe held bond or free only according to the condition of the mother, *And* that if any christian shall committ ffornication with a negro man or woman, hee or shee so offending shall pay double the ffines imposed by the former act.

September 1667 - 19th Charles II, ACT III, 2:260.

An act declaring that baptisme of slaves doth not exempt them from bondage.

WHEREAS some doubts have risen whether children that are slaves by birth, and by the charity and piety of their owners made pertakers of the blessed sacrament of baptisme, should by vertue of their baptisme be made ffree; *It is enacted and declared by this grand assembly, and the authority thereof,* that the conferring of baptisme doth not alter the condition of the person as to his bondage or freedome; that diverse masters, ffreed from this doubt, may more carefully endeavour the propagation of christianity by permitting children, though slaves, or those of growth if capable to be admitted to that sacrament

September 1668 - 20th Charles II, Act VII (1668), 2:267.

Negro women not exempted from tax.

WHEREAS some doubts, have arisen whether negro women set free were still to be accompted tithable according to a former act, *It is declared by this grand assembly* that negro women, though permitted to enjoy their freedome yet ought not in all respects to be admitted to a full fruition of the exemptions and impunities of the English, and are still lyable to payment of taxes.

October 1669 - 21st Charles II, 2:270, Act I.

An act about the casuall killing of slaves.

WHEREAS the only law in force for the punishment of refreactory servants (*a*) resisting their master, mistris or overseer cannot be inflicted upon negroes, nor the obstinacy of many of them by other then violent meanes supprest, *Be it enacted and declared by this grand assembly,* if any slave resist his master (or othe by his masters order correcting him) and by ffelony, but the master (or that other person appointed by the master to punish him) be acquit from molestation, since it cannot be presumed that prepensed malice (which alone makes murther ffelony) should induce any man to destroy his owne estate.

October 1670 - 22nd Charles II, Act V, 1670,2:280.

Noe Negroes nor Indians to buy christian servants.

Whereas it hath beene questioned whither Indians or negroes manumited, or otherwise free, could be capable of purchasing christian servants, *It is enacted* that noe negro or Indian though baptised and enjoyned their

224

owne freedome shall be capable of any such purchase of christians, but yet not debarred from buying any of their owne nation.

June 1680 - 32nd Charles II, Act X, 2.481.

An act for preventing Negroes Insurrections.

WHEREAS the frequent meeting of considerable numbers of negroe slaves under pretence of feasts and burialls is judged of dangerous consequence; for prevention whereof for the future, *Bee it enacted by the kings most excellent majestie by and with the consent of the generall assembly, and it is hereby enacted by the authority aforesaid,* that from and after the publication of this law, it shall not be lawfull for any negroe or other slave to carry or arme himselfe with any club, staffe, gunn, sword or any other weapon of defence or offence, nor to goe or depart from of his masters ground without a certificate from his master, mistris or overseer, and such permission not to be granted but upon perticuler and necessary occasions; and every negroe or slave soe offending not haveing a certificate as aforesaid shalbe sent to the next constable, who is hereby enjoyned and required to give the said negroe twenty lashes on his bare back well layd on, and soe sent home to his said master, mistris or overseer. *And it is further enacted by the authority aforesaid* that if any negroe or other slave shall presume or lift up his hand in opposition against any christian, shall for every such offence, upon due proofe made thereof by the oath of the party before a magistrate, have and receive thirty lashed on his bare back well laid on. *And it is hereby further enacted by the authority aforesaid* that if any negroe or other slave shall absent himself from his masters service and lye hid and lurking in obscure places, comitting injuries to the inhabitants, and shall resist any person or persons that shalby any lawfull authority be imployed to apprehend and take the said negroe, that then in case of such resistance, it shalbe lawfull for such person or persons to kill the said negroe or slave soe lying out and resisting, and that this law be once every six months published at the respective county courts and parish churches within this colony.

William Waller Henning - Vol. III, April 1692 - 4th William and Mary,Act III, 3.102

An act for the more speedy prosecution of slaves comitting Capitall Crimes

WHEREAS a speedy prosecution of negroes and other slaves for capital offences is absolutely necessarie, that others being detered by the condign punishment inflicted on such offenders, may vigorously proceed in their labours and be affrighted to commit the like crimes and offences, and whereas such prosecution has been hitherto obstructed by reason of the charge and delay attending the same

Be it therefore enacted by their Majesties Lieutenant Governour, Councell and Burgesses of this present Generall Assembly and the authority therof, and it is hereby enacted. That every negro or other slave which shall after this present session of Assembly commit or perpetrate any cappitall offence which the law of England requires to be satisfyed with the death of the offender or loss of member, after his commiting of the said offence, shall be forthwith committed to the common gaol of the county within which such offence shall be committed, there to be safely continued, well laden with irons, and that the sheriff of the said county doe forthwith signify the same to the governoar for the time being, who is desired and impowered to issue out a commission of oyer and terminer directed to such persons of the said county as he shall think fitt, which persons forthwith after the receipt of the said commission are required and commanded publicly at the courthouse of the said county to cause the offender to be arraigned and indicted, and to take for evidence the confession of the party or the oaths of two witnesss or of one with pregnant circumstances, without the sollemnitie of jury, and the offender being found guilty as aforesaid, to pass judgment as the law of England provides in the like case, and on such judgment to award execution.

And be it enacted by the authority aforesaid, and it is herby enacted, That all horses, cattle and hoggs marked of any negro or other slaves marke, or by any slave kept, and which shall not by the last day of December next, be converted by the owner of such slave to the use and marke of the said owner, shall be forfeited to the use of the poore of the parish wherein such horse, beast, or hogg shall be kept, seizable by the church wardens thereof.

And be it enacted by the authority aforesaid, and it is hereby enacted that where it shall happen that any damage shall be hereafter commited by any negro or other slave living at a quarter, where there is noe christian overseer, the same damage shall be recompenced by the owner of such slave to the party injured.

October 1705 - 4th Anne, Chap XXIII, 3.333.

An act declaring the Negro, Mulatto, and Indian slaves within this dominion, to be real estate.

I. FOR the better settling and preservation of estates within this dominion,

II. *Be it enacted, by the governor, council and burgesses of this present general assembly, and it is hereby enacted by the authority of the same;* That from and after the passing of this act, all negro, mulatto, and Indian slaves, in all courts of judicature, and other places, within this dominion, shall be held, taken, and adjudged, to be real estate (and not chattels;) and shall descend unto the heirs and widows of persons departing this life, according to the manner and custom of land of inheritance, held in fee simple.

III. *Provided always,* That nothing in this act contained, shall be taken to extend to any merchant or factor, bringing any slaves into this dominion, or having any consignments thereof, unto them, for sale: But that such slaves, whilst they remain unsold, in the posession of such merchant, or factor, or of their executors, administrators, or assigns, shall, to all intents and purposes, be taken, held, and adjudged, to be personal estate, in the same condition they should have been in, if this act had never been made.

IV. *Provided also,* That all such slaves shall be liable to the paiment of debts, and may be taken by execution, for that end, as other chattels or personal estate may be.

V. *Provided also,* That no such slaves shall be liable to be escheated, by reason of the decease of the proprietor of the same, without lawful heirs: But all such slaves shall, in that case, be accounted and go as chattels, and other estate personal.

VI. *Provided also,* That no person, selling or alienating any such slave, shall be obliged to cause such sale or alienation to be recorded, as is required by law to be done, upon the alienation of other real estate: But that the said sale or alienation may be made in the same manner as might have been done before the making of this act.

VII. *Provided also,* That this act, or any thing therein contained, shall not extend, nor be construed to extend, to give any person, being owner of any slave or slaves, and not seized of other real estate, the right or privilege as a freeholder, meant, mentioned, and intended, by one act of this present session of assembly, intituled, *An act for regulating the elections of Burgesses, for settling their privileges, and for ascertaining their allowances.*

VIII. *Provided also,* That it shall and may be lawful, for any person, to sue for, and recover, any slave, or damage, for the detainer, trover, or conversion therof, by action personal, as might have been done if this act had never been made.

IX. *Provided always,* That where the nature of the case shall require it, any writ *De Partitione facienda,* or of dower, may be sued forth and prosecuted, to recover the right and possession of any such slave or slaves.

X. *Provided, and be it enacted,* That when any person dies intestate, leaving several children, in that case all the slaves of such person, (except the widow's dower, which is to be first set apart) shall be inventoried and appraised; and the value therof shall be equally divided amongst all the said children; and the several proportions, according to such valuation and appraisement, shall be paid by the heir (to whom the said slaves shall descend, by virtue of this act) unto all and every the other said children. And thereupon, it shall and may be lawful for the said other children, and every of them, and their executors or administrators, as the case shall be, to commence and prosecute an action upon the case, at the common law, against such heir, his heirs, executors and administrators, for the recovery of their said several proportions, respectively.

XI. *And be it further enacted by the authorityaforesaid,* That if any widow, seised of any such slave or slaves, as aforesaid, as of the dower of her husband, shall send, or voluntarily permit to be sent out of this colony and dominion, such slave or slaves, or any of their increase, without the lawful consent of him or her in revesion, such widow shall forfeit all and every such slave or slaves, and all other the dower which she holds of the endowment of her husband's estate, unto the person or persons that shall have the reversion thereof; any law, usage or custom to the contrary notwithstanding. And if any widow, seized as aforesaid, shall be married to an husband, who shall send, or voluntary permit to be sent out of this colony and dominion, any such slave or slaves, or any of their increase, without the consent of him or her in reversion; in such case, it shall be lawful for him or her in reversion, to enter into, possess and enjoy all the state which such husband holdeth, in right of his wife's dower, for and during the life of the said husband.

October 1705 - 4th Anne. CHAP. KLIX. 3.447.

An act concerning Servants and Slaves.

I. *Be it enacted, by the governor, council, and burgesses, of this present general assembly, and it is hereby enacted by the authority of the same,* That all servants brought into this country without indenture, if the said servants be christians, and of christian parentage, and above nineteen years of age, shall serve but five years; and if under nineteen years of age, 'till they shall become twenty-four years of age, and no longer.

II. *Provided always,* That every such servant be carried to the country court, within six months after his or her arrival into this colony, to have his or her age adjudged by the court, otherwise shall be a servant no longer than the accustomary five years, although much under the age of nineteen years; and the age of such servant being adjudged by the court, within the limitation aforesaid, shall be entered upon the records of the said court, and be accounted, deemed, and taken, for the true age of the said servant, in relation to the time of service aforesaid.

III. *And also be it enacted, by the authority aforesaid, and it is herby enacted,* That when any servant sold for the custom, shall pretend to have indentures, the master or owner of such servant, for discovery of the truth thereof, may bring the said servant before a justice of the peace; and if the said servant cannot produce the indenture then, but shall still pretend to have one, the said jsutice shall assign two months time for the doing thereof, in which time, if the said servant shall not produce his or her indenture, it shall be taken for granted that there never was one, and shall be a bar to his or her claim of making use of one afterwards, or taking any advantage by one.

IV. *And also be it enacted, by the authority aforesiad, and it is hereby enacted,* That all servants imported and brought into this country, by sea or land, who were not christians in their native country, (except Turks and Moors in amity with her majesty, and others that can make due proof of their being free in England, or any other christian country, before they were shipped, in order to transporation hither) shall be accounted and be slaves, and as such be here bought and sold notwithtanding a conversion to christianity afterwards.

V. *And be it enacted, by the authority aforesaid, and it is hereby enacted,* That if any person or persons shall hereafter import into this colony, and here sell as a slave, any person or persons that shall have been a freeman in any christian country, island, or plantation, such importer and seller as aforesaid, shall forfeit and pay, to the party from whom the said freeman shall recover his freedom, double the sum for which the said freeman was sold. To be recovered, in any court of record within this colony, according to the course of the common law, wherein the defendant shall not be admitted to plead in bar, any act or statute for limitation of actions.

VI. *Provided always,* That a slave's being in England, shall not be sufficient to discharge him of his slavery, without other proof of his being manumitted there.

VII. *And also be it enacted, by the authority aforesaid, and it is hereby enacted,* That all masters and owners of servants, shall find and provide for their servants, wholesome and competent diet, clothing, and lodging, by the discretion of the county court; and shall not, at any time, give immoderate correction; neither shall, at any time, whip a christian white servant naked, without an order from a justice of the peace: And if any, notwithstanding this act, shall presume to whip a christian white servant naked, without such order, the person so offendmg, shall forfeit and pay for the same, forty shillings sterling, to the party injured: To be recovered, with costs, upon petition, without the formal process of an action, as in and by this act is provided for servants complaints to be heard; provided complaint be made within six monts after such whipping.

VIII. *And also be it enacted, by the authority aforesaid, and it is herby enacted,* That all servants, (not being slaves,) whether imported, or become servants of their own accord here, or bound by any court or churchwardens, shall have their complaints received by a justice of the peace, who, if he find cause, shall bind the master over to answer the complaint at court; and it shall be there determined: And all complaints of servants, shall and may, by virtue hereof, be received at any time, upon petition, in the court of the county wherein they reside, without the formal process of an action; and also full power and authority is hereby given to the said court, by their discretion, (having first summoned the masters or owners to justify themselves, if they think fit,) to adjudge, order, and appoint what shall be necessary, as to diet, odging, clothing, and correction: And if any master or owner shall not thereupon comply with the said court's order, the said court is hereby authorised and impowered, upon a second just complaint, to order such servant to be immediately sold at an outcry, by the sheriff, and after charges deducted, the remainder of what the said servant shall be sold for, to be paid and satisfied to such owner.

IX. *Provided always, and be it enacted,* That if such servant be so sick or lame, or otherwise rendered so uncapable, that he or she cannot be sold for such a value, at least, as shall satisfy the fees, and other incident charges accrued, the said court shall then order the churchwardens of the parish to take care of and provide for the said servant, until such servant's time, due by law to the said master, or owner, shall be expired, or until such servant, shall be so recovered, as to be sold for defraying the said fees and charges: And further, the said court, from time to time, shall order the charges of keeping the said servant, to be levied upon the goods and chattels of the master or owner of the said servant, by distress.

X. *And be it also enacted,* That all servants, whether, by importation, indenture, or hire here, as well feme coverts, as others, shall, in like manner, as is provided, upon complaints of misusage, have their petitions received in court, for their wages and freedom, without the formal process of an action; and proceedings, and judgment, shall, in like manner, also, be had thereupon.

XI. And for a further christian care and usage of all christian servants, *Be it also enacted, by the authority aforesaid, and it is hereby enacted,* That no negros, mulattos, or Indians, although christians, or Jews, Moors, Mahometans, or other infidels, shall, at any time, purchase any christian servant, nor any other, except of their own complexion, or such as are declared slaves by this act: And if any negro, mulatto, or Indian, Jew, Moor, Mahometan, or other infidel, or such as are declared slaves by this act, shall, notwithstanding, purchase any christian white servant, the said servant shall, *ipso facto,* become free and acquit from any service then due, and shall be so held, deemed, and taken: And if any person, having such christian servant, shall intermarry with any such negro, mulatto, or Indian, Jew, Moor, Mahometan, or other infidel, every Christian white servant of every such person so intermarrying, shall, *ipso facto,* become free and acquit from any service then due to such master or mistress so intermarrying, as aforesaid.

XII. *And also be it enacted, by the authority aforesaid, and it is hereby enacted,* That no master or owner of any servant shall during the time of such servant's servitude, make any bargain with his or her said servant for further service, or other matter or thing relating to liberty, or personal profit, unless the same be made in the presence, and with the approbation, of the court of that county where the master or owner resides: And if any servants shall, at any time bring in goods or money, or during the time of their service, by gift, or any other lawful ways or means, come to have any goods or money, they shall enjoy the propriety thereof, and have the sole use and benefit thereof to themselves. And if any servant shall happen to fall sick or lame, during the time of service, so that he or she becomes of little or no use to his or her master or owner, but rather a charge, the said master or owner shall not put away the said servant, but shall maintain him or her, during the whole time he or she was before obliged to serve, by indenture, custom, or order of court: And if any master or owner, shall put away any such sick or lame servant, upon pretence of freedom, and that servant shall become chargeable to the parish, the said master or owner shall forfeit and pay ten pounds current money of Virginia, to the church-wardens of the parish where such offence shall be committed, for the use of the said parish: To be recovered by action of debt, in any court of record in this her majesty's colony and dominion, in which no essoin, protection, or wager of law, shall be allowed.

XIII. And whereas there has been a good and laundable custom of allowing servants corn and cloaths for their present support, upon their freedom; but nothing in that nature ever made certain, *Be it also enacted, by the authority aforesaid, and it is hereby enacted,* That there shall be paid and allowed to every imported servant, not having yearly wages, at the time of service ended, by the master or owner of such servant, viz: To every male servant, ten bushels of indian corn, thirty shillings in money, or the value thereof, in goods, and one well fixed musket or fuzee, of the value of twenty shillings, at least: and to every woman servant, fifteen bushels of indian corn, and forty shillings in money, or the value thereof, in goods: Which, upon refusal, shall be ordered, with costs, upon petition to the county court, in manner as is herein before directed, for servants complaints to be heard.

XIV. *And also be it enacted, by the authority aforesaid, and it is hereby enacted,* That all servants shall faithfully and obediently, all the whole time of their service, do all thir masters or owners just and lawful commands. And if any servant shall resist the master, or mistress, or overseer, of offer violence to any of them, the said servant shall, for every such offence, be adjudged to serve his or her said master or owner, one whole year after the time, by indenture, custom, or former order of court, shall be expired.

XV. *And also be it enacted, by the authority aforesaid, and it is hereby enacted,* That no person whatsoever shall buy, sell, or receive of, to, or from, any servant, or slave, any coin or commodity whatsoever, without the leave, licence, or consent of the master or owner of the said servant, or slave: And if any person shall, contrary hereunto, without the leave or licence aforesaid, deal with any servant, or slave, he or she so offending, shall be imprisoned one calender month, without bail or main-prize; and then, also continue in prison, until he or she shall find good security, in the sum of ten pounds current money of Virginia, for the good behaviour for one year following; wherein, a second offence shall be a breach of the bond and moreover shall forfeit and pay four times the value of the things so bought, sold, or received, to the master or owner of such servant, or slave: To be recovered, with costs, by action upon the case, in any court of record in this her majesty's colony and dominion, wherein no essoin, protection, or wager of law, or other than one imparlance, shall be allowed.

XVI. *Provided always, and be it enacted,* That when any person or persons convict for dealing with a servant, or slave, contrary to his act shall not immediately give good and sufficient security for his or her good behaviour, as aforesaid: then, in such case, the court shall order thirty-nine lashes, well laid on, upon the bare back of such offender, at the common whipping-post of the county, and the said offender to be thence discharged of giving such bond and security.

XVII. *And also be it enacted, by the authority aforesaid, and it is hereby enacted, and declared,* That in all cases of penal laws, whereby persons free are punishable by fine, servants shall be punished by whipping, after the rate of twenty lashes for every five hundred pounds of tobacco, or fifty shillings current money, unless the servant so culpable, can and will procure some person or persons to pay the fine; in which case, the said servant shall be adjudged to serve such benefactor, after the time by indenture, custom, or order of court, to his or her then present master or owner, shall be expired, after the rate of one month and a half for every hundred pounds of tobacco; any thing in this act contained, to the contrary, in any-wise, notwithstanding.

XVIII. And if any women servant shall be delivered of a bastard child within the time of her service aforesaid, *Be it enacted, by the authority aforesaid, and it is hereby enacted,* That in recompence of the loss and trouble occasioned her master or mistress thereby, she shall for every such offence, serve her said master or owner one whole year after her time by indenture, custom, and former order of court shall be expired; or pay her said master or owner, one thousand pounds of tobacco; and the reputed father, if free, shall give security to the church-wardens of the parish where that child shall be, to maintain the child, and keep the parish indemnified; or be compelled thereto by order of the county court, upon the said church-wardens complaint: But if a servant, he shall make satisfaction of the parish, for keeping the said child, after his time by indenture, custom, or order of court, to his then present master or owner, shall be expired; or be compelled thereto, by order of the county court, upon complaint of the church wardens of the said parish, for the time being.

And if any woman servant shall be got with child by her master, neither the said master, nor his executors administrators, nor assigns, shall have any claim of service against her, for or by reason of such child; but she shall, when her time due to her said master, by indenture, custom or order of court, shall be expired, be sold by the church-wardens, for the time being, of the parish wherein such child shall be born, for one year, or pay one thousand pounds of tobacco; and the said one thousand pounds of tobacco, or whatever she shall be sold for, shall be emploied, by the vestry, to the use of the said parish. And if any woman servant shall have a bastard child by a negro, or mulatto, over and above the years service due to her master or owner, she shall immediately, upon the expiration of her time to her then present master or owner, pay down to the church-wardens of the parish wherein such child shall be born, for the use of the said parish fifteen pounds current money of Virginia, or be by them sold for five years to the use aforesaid: And if a free christian white woman shall have such bastard child, by a negro, or mulatto, for every such offence, she shall, within one month after her delivery of such bastard child, pay to the church-wardens for the time being, of the parish wherein such child shall be born, for the use of the said parish fifteen pounds current money of Virginia, or be by them sold for five years to the use aforesaid: And in both the said cases, the church-wardens shall bind the said child to be a servant, until it shall be of thirty one years of age.

XIX.   And for a further prevention of that abominable mixture and spurious issue, which hereafter may increase in this her majesty's colony and dominion, as well by English, and other white men and women intermarrying with negros or mulattos, as by their unlawful whatsoever English, or other white man or woman, being free, shall intemarry with a negro or mulatto man or woman, bond or free, shall, by judgtment of the county court, be committed to prison, and there remain, during the space of six months, without bail or mainprize; and shall forfeit and pay ten pounds current money of Virginia, to the use of the parish, as aforesaid.

XX. *And be further enacted,* That no minister of the church of England, or other minister,or person whatsoever, within this colony and dominion, shall hereafter wittingly presume to marry a white man with a negro or mulatto woman; or to marry a white woman with a negro or mulatto man, upon pain of forfeiting and paying, for every such marriage the sum of ten thousand pounds of tobacco; one half to our sovereign lady the Queen, her heirs and successors, for and towards the support of the government, and the contingent charges thereof; and the othe half to the informer, To be recovered, with costs, by action of debt, bill, plaint, or information, in any court of record within this her majesty's colony and dominion, wherein no essoin, protection, or wager of law, shall be allowed.

XXI. And because poor people may not be destitute of emploiment, upon suspicion of being servants, and servants also kept from running away, *Be it enacted, by the authority aforesaid, and it is hereby enacted,* That every servant, when his or her time of service shall be expired, shall repair to the court of the county where he or she served the last of his or her time, and there, upon sufficient testimony, have his or her freedom entered; and a certificate thereof from the clerk of the said court, shall be sufficient to authorise any person to entertain or hire such servant, without any danger of this law. And if it shall at any time happen, that such certificate is won out, or lost, the said clerk shall grant a new one, and therein also recite the accident happened to the old one. And whoever shall hire such servant, shall take his or her certificate, and keep it, 'till the contracted time shall be expired. And if any person whatsoever, shall harbour or entertain any servant by importation, or by contract, or indenture made here, not having such certificate, he or she so offending, shall pay to the master or owner of such servant, sixty pounds of tobacco for every natural day he or she shall so harbour or entertain such runaway: To be recovered, with costs, by action of debt, in any court of record withint this her majesty's colony and dominion, wherein no essoin, protection, or wager of law, shall be allowed. And also, if any runaway shall make use of a forged certificate, or after the same shall be delivered to any master or mistress, upon being hired, shall steal the same away, and thereby procure entertainment, the person entertaining such servant, upon such forged or stolen certificate, shall not be culpable by this law: But the said runaway, besides making reparation for the loss of time, and charges in recovery, and other penalties by this law directed, shall, for making use of such forged or stolen certificate, or for such theft aforesaid, stand two hours in the pillory, upon a court day: And the person forging such certificate, shall forfeit and pay ten pounds current money; one half thereof to be to her majesty, her heirs and successors, for and towards the support of this government, and the contingent charges thereof; and the other half to the master or owner of such servant, if he or she will inform or sue for the same, otherwise to the informer: To be recovered, with costs, by action of debt, bill, plaint or information, in any court of record in this her majesty's colony and dominion, wherein no essoin, protection, or wager of law, shall be allowed. And if any person or persons convict of forging such certificate, shall not immediately pay the said ten pounds, and costs, or give security to do the same within six months, he or she so convict, shall receive, on his or her bare back, thirty-nine lashes, well laid on, at the common whipping post of the county; and shall be thence discharged of paying the said ten pounds, and costs, and either of them,

XXII. *Provided,* That when any master or mistress shall happen to hire a runaway, upon a forged certificate, and a servant deny that he delivered any such certificate, the *Onus Probandi* shall lie upon the person hiring, who upon failure therein, shall be liable to the fines and penalties, for entertaining runaway servants, without certificate.

XXIII. And for encouragement of all persons to take up runaways, *Be it enacted, by the authority aforesaid, and it is hereby enacted,* That for the taking up of every servant, or slave, if ten miles, or above, from the house or quarter where such servant, or slave was kept, there shall be allowed by the public, as a reward to the taker-up, two hundred pounds of tobacco; and if above five miles, and under ten, one hundred pounds of tobacco: Which said several rewards of two hundred, and one hundred pounds of tobacco, shall also be paid in the county where such taker-up shall reside, and shall be again levied by the public upon the master or owner of such runaway, for re-imbursement of the same to the public. And for the greater certainty in paying the said rewards and re-imbursement of the public, every justice of the peace before whom such runaway shall be brought, upon the taking up, shall mention the proper-name and sur-name of the taker-up, and the county of his or her residence, together with the time and place of taking up the said runaway; and shall also mention the name of the said runaway, and the proper-name and sur-name of the master or owner of such runaway, and the county of his or her residence, together with the distance of miles, in the said justice's judgment, from the place of taking up the said runaway, to the house or quarter where such runaway was kept.

XXIV. *Provided,* That when any negro, or other runaway, that doth not speak English, and cannot, or through obstinacy will not, declare the name of his or her masters or owner, that then it shall be sufficient for the said justice to certify the same, instead of the name of such runaway, and the proper name and sur-name of his or her master or owner, and the county of his or her residence and distance of miles, as aforesaid; and in such case, shall, by his warrant, order the said runaway to be conveyed to the public gaol, of this country, there to be continued prisoner until the master or owner shall be known; who, upon paying the charges of the imprisonment, or give caution to the prison-keeper for the same, together with the reward of two hundred or one hundred pounds of tobacco, as the case shall be, shall have the said runaway restored.

XXV.   And further, the said justice of the peace, when such runaway shall be brought before him, shall, by his warrant commit the said runaway to the next constable, and therein also order him to give the said runaway so many lashes as the said justice shall think fit, not exceeding the number of thirty-nine; and then to be conveyed from constable to constable, until the said runaway shall be carried home, or to the country gaol, as aforesaid, every constable through whose hands the said runaway shall pass, giving a receipt at the delivery; and every constable failing to execute such warrant according to the tenor thereof, or refusing to give such receipt, shall forfeit and pay two hundred pounds of tobacco to the church-wardens of the parish wherein such failure shall be, for the use of the poor of the said parish: To be recovered, with costs, by action of debt, in any court of record in this her majesty's colony and dominion, wherein no essoin, protection or wager of law, shall be allowed, And such corporal punishment shall not deprive the master or owner of such runaway of the other satisfaction herre in this act appointed to be made upon such servant's running away.

XXVI. *Provided always, and be it further enacted,* That when any servant or slave, in his or before a justice of the peace, the said justice shall, instead of committing such runaway to the constable, commit him or her to the sheriff, who is hereby required to receive every such runaway, according to such warrant, and to cause him, her, or them, to be transported again across the bay, and delivered to a constable there; and shall have, for all his trouble and charge herein, for every such servant or slave, five hundred pounds of tobacco, paid by the public; which shall be re-imbursed again by the master or owner of such runaway, as aforesaid, in manner aforesaid.

XXVII. *Provided also,* That when any runaway servant that shall have crossed the said bay, shall get up into the country, in any county distant from the bay, that then, in such case, the said runaway shall be committed to a constable, to be conveyed from constable to constable, until he shall be brought to a sheriff of some county adjoining to the said bay of Chesapeak, which sheriff is also hereby required, upon such warrant, to receive such runaway, under the rules and conditions aforesaid; and cause him or her to be conveyed as aforesaid; and shall have the reward, as aforesaid.

XXVIII.   And for the better preventing of delays in returning of such runaways, *Be it enacted,* That if any sheriff, under sheriff, or other officer of, or belonging to the sheriffs, shall cause or suffer any such runaway (so committed for passage over the bay) to work, the said sheriff, to whom such runaway shall be so committed, shall forfeit and pay to the master or owner, of every such servant or slave, so put to work, one thousand pounds of tobacco; To be recovered, with costs, by action of debt, bill, plaint, or information, in any court of record withint this her majesty's colony and dominion, wherein no essoin, protection, or wager of law, shall be allowed.

XXIX. And be it enacted, by the authority aforesaid, and it is hereby enacted, *That if constable, or sheriff, into whose hands a runaway servant or slave shall be committed, by virtue of this act, shall suffer such runaway to escape, the said constable or sheriff shall be liable to the action of the party grieved, for recovery of his damages, at the common law with costs.*

XXX.   *And also be it enacted, by the authority aforesaid, and it is hereby enacted,* That every runaway servant, upon whose account, either of the rewards aforementioned shall be paid, for taking up, shall for every hundred pounds of tobacco so paid by the master or owner, serve his or her said master or owner, after his or her time by indenture, custom, or former order of court, shall be expired, one calendar month and an half, and moreover, shall serve double the time such servant shall be absent in such running away; and shall also make reparation, by service, to the said master or owner, for all necessary disbursements and charges, in pursuit and recovery of the said runaway; to be adjudged and allowed in the county court, after the rate of one year for eight hundred pounds of tobacco, and so proportionably for a greater or lesser quantity.

XXXI. *Provided,* That the masters or owners of such runaways, shall carry them to court the next court held for the said county, after the recovery of such runaway, othewise it shall be in the breast of the court to consider the occasion of delay, and to hear, or refuse the claim, according to their discretion, without appeal, for the refusal.

XXXII. *And also be it enacted by the authority aforesaid, and it is hereby enacted,* That no master, mistress, or overseer of a family, shall knowingly permit any slave, not belonging to without the leave of such slave's master, mistress, or overseer, on penalty of one hundred and fifty pounds of tobacco to the informer; cognizable by a justice of the peace of the county wherein such offence shall be committed.

XXXIII. *Provided also,* That if any runaway servant, adjudged to serve for the charges of his or her pursuit and recovery, shall, at the time, he or she is so adjudged, repay and satisfy, or give good security before the court, for repaiment and satisfaction of the same, to his or her master or owner, within six months after, such master or owner shall be obliged to accept thereof, in lieu of the service given and allowed for such charges and disbursements.

XXXIV. And if any slave resist his master, or owner, or other person, by his or her order, correcting such slave, and shall happen to be killed in such correction, it shall not be accounted felony; but the master, owner, and every such other person so giving correction, shall be free and acquit of all punishment and accusation for the same, as if such accident had never happened: And also, if any negro, mulatto, or Indian, bond or free, shall at any time, lift his or her hand, in opposition against any christian, not being negro, mulatto, or Indian, he or she so offending, shall, for every such offence, proved by the oath of the party, receive on his or her bare back, thirty lashes, well laid on; cognizable by a justice of the peace for that county wherein such offence shall be committed.

XXXV. *And also be it enacted, by the authority aforesaid, and it is hereby enacted,* That no slave go armed with gun, sword, club, staff, or other weapon, nor go from off the plantation and seat of land where such slave shall be appointed to live, without a certificate of leave in writing, for so doing, from his or her master, mistress, or overseer: And if any slave shall be found offending herein, it shall be lawful for any person or persons to apprehend and deliver such slave to the next constable or head-borough, who is hereby enjoined and required, without further order or warrant, to give such slave twenty lashes on his or her bare back, well laid on, and so send him or her home: And all horses, cattle, and hogs, now belonging, or that hereafter shall belong to any slave, or of any slaves mark in this her majestys colony and dominion, shall be seised and sold by the church-wardens of the parish, wherein such horses, cattle, or hogs shall be, and the profit thereof applied to the use of the poor of the said parish: And also, if any damage shall be hereafter committed by any slave living at a quarter where there is no christian overseer, the master or owner of such slave shall be liable to action for the trespass and damage, as if the same had been done by him or herself.

XXXVI. *And also it is hereby enacted and declared,* That baptism of slaves doth not exempt them from bondage; and that all children shall be bond or free, according to the condition of their mothers, and the particular directions of this act.

XXXVII. And whereas, many times, slaves run away and lie out, hid and lurking in swamps, woods, and other obscure places, killing hogs, and committing other injuries to the inhabitants of this her majesty's colony and dominion, *Be it therefore enacted, by the authority aforesaid, and it is hereby enacted,* That in all such cases, upon intelligence given of any slaves lying out, as aforesaid, any two justices *(Quorum unus)* of the peace of the county wherein such slave is supposed to lurk or do mischief, shall be and are impowered and required to issue proclamation against all such slaves, reciting their names, and owners names, if they are known, and thereby requiring them, and every of them, forthwith to surrender themselves; and also impowering the sheriff of the said county, to take such power with him, as he shall think fit and necessary, for the effectual apprehending such out-lying Sabbath day, at the door of every church and chapel, in the said county, by the parish clerk, or reader, of the church, immediately after divine worship: And in case any slave, against whom proclamation hath been thus issued, and once published at any church or chapel, as aforesaid, stay out, and do not immediately return home, it shall be lawful for any person or persons whatsoever, to kill and destroy such slaves by such ways and means as he, she, or they shall think fit, without accusation or impeachment of any crime for the same: And if any slave, that hath run away and lain out as aforesaid, shall be apprehended by the sheriff, or any other person, upon the applicaiton of the owner of the said slave, it shall and may be lawful for the county court, to order such punishment to the said slave, either by dismembring, or any other way, not touching his life, as they in their discretion shall think fit, for the reclaiming any such incorrigible slave, and terrifying others from the like practices.

XXXVIII. *Provided always, and it is further enacted,* That for every slave killed, in pursuance of this act, or put to death by law, the master or owner of such slave shall be paid by the public:

XXXIX. And to the end, the true value of every slave killed, or put to death, as aforesaid, may be the better known; and by that means, the assembly the better enabled to make a suitable allowance thereupon, *Be it enacted,* That upon application of the master or owner of any such slave, to the court appointed for proof of public claims, the said court shall value the slave in money, and the clerk of the court shall return a certificate thereof to the assembly, with the rest of the public claims.

A Compilation of Virginia State Statutes at Large Regarding the Status of Forced Labor; Being a Collection of all the Laws of Virginia, from the First Session of the Legislature in the Year beginning in1619, Compiled by William Waller Hening *in 1823.*

HOW WELL DID YOU UNDERSTAND THIS SELECTION?

1. When and how did Africans arrive in the colony of Virginia?

2. What was the original status of Africans in the colony?

3. How and why was this status altered?

4. How do the Virginia slave codes distinguish between white and black indentured servants?

5. Give three examples of how the slave codes gradually institutionalized slavery in Virginia.

THOMAS PAINE: Why the Colonies Must Severe Their Ties with the Mother Country

The relationship between the thirteen colonies and their mother country was never a "marriage made in heaven." As the colonists learned to be more self-sufficient, they demanded more authority to govern themselves. Initially, very few colonists wanted to completely severe their ties with Great Britain. However, the British government did not want to relinquish any of its governing authority. The British government took the position that the colonists were being disrespectful of their mother country. In retaliation, the British government decided to punish the disobedient colonials with a series of repressive laws. The colonists "were not amused." Once a lone voice, Thomas Paine began to gain supporters among his fellow colonials to advocate a divorce from their mother country. The following article details Paine's concerns about the abusive actions taken by the British government against the thirteen American colonies.

Some writers have so confounded society with government, as to leave little or no distinction between them; whereas they are not only different, but have different origins. Society is produced by our wants, and government by our wickedness; the former promotes our happiness *positively* by uniting our affections, the latter *negatively* by restraining our vices. The one encourages intercourse, the other creates distinctions. The first is a patron, the last a punisher.

Society in every state is a blessing, but Government, even in its best state, is but a necessary evil; in its worst state an intolerable one: for when we suffer, or are exposed to the same miseries *by a Government,* which we might expect in a country *without Government,* our calamity is heightened by reflecting that we furnish the means by which we suffer. Government, like dress, is the badge of lost innocence; the palaces of kings are built upon the ruins of the bowers of paradise. For were the impulses of conscience clear, uniform and irresistibly obeyed, man would need no other lawgiver; but that not being the case, he finds it necessary to surrender up a part of his property to furnish means for the protection of the rest; and this he is induced to do by the same prudence which in every other case advises him, out of two evils to choose the least . . .

I draw my idea of the form of government from a principle in nature which no art can overturn, viz. that the more simple any thing is, the less liable it is to be disordered, and the easier repaired when disordered; and with this maxim in view I offer a few remarks on the so much boasted constitution of England. That it was noble for the dark and slavish times in which it was erected, is granted. When the world was overrun with tyranny the least remove therefrom was a glorious rescue. But that it is imperfect, subject to convulsions, and incapable of producing what it seems to promise, is easily demonstrated.

Absolute governments, (tho' the disgrace of human nature) have this advantage with them, they are simple; if the people suffer, they know the head from which their suffering springs; know likewise the remedy; and are not bewildered by a variety of causes and cures. But the constitution of England is so exceedingly complex, that the nation may suffer for years together without being able to discover in which part the fault lies; some will say in one and some in another, and every political physician will advise a different medicine.

I know it is difficult to get over local or long standing prejudices, yet if we will suffer ourselves to examine the component parts of the English constitution, we shall find them to be the base remains of two ancient tyrannies, compounded with some new Republican materials.

First. — The remains of Monarchical tyranny in the person of the King.

Secondly. — The remains of Aristocratical tyranny in the persons of the Peers.

Thirdly. — The new Republican materials, in the persons of the Commons, on whose virtue depends the freedom of England.

The two first, by being hereditary, are independent of the People; wherefore in a *constitutional sense* they contribute nothing towards the freedom of the State.

To say that the constitution of England is an *union* of three powers, reciprocally *checking* each other, is farcical; either the words have no meaning, or they are flat contradictions.

To say that the Commons is a check upon the King, presupposes two things.

First. — That the King is not to be trusted without being looked after; or in other words, that a thirst for absolute power is the natural disease of monarchy.

Secondly. — That the Commons, by being appointed for that purpose, are either wiser or more worthy of confidence than the Crown.

But as the same constitution which gives the Commons a power to check the King by withholding the supplies, gives afterwards the King a power to check the Commons, by empowering him to reject their other bills; it again supposes that the King is wiser than those whom it has already supposed to be wiser than him. A mere absurdity!

There is something exceedingly ridiculous in the composition of Monarchy; it first excludes a man from the means of information, yet empowers him to act in cases where the highest judgment is required. The state of a king shuts him from the World, yet the business of a king requires him to know it thoroughly; wherefore the different parts, by unnaturally opposing and destroying each other, prove the whole character to be absurd and useless.

Some writers have explained the English constitution thus: the King, say they, is one, the people another; the Peers are a house in behalf of the King, the commons in behalf of the people; but this hath all the distinctions of a house divided against itself; and though the expressions be pleasantly arranged, yet when examined they appear idle and ambiguous; and it will always happen, that the nicest construction that words are capable of, when applied to the description of something which either cannot exist, or is too incomprehensible to be within the compass of description, will be words of sound only, and though they may amuse the ear, they cannot inform the mind: for this explanation includes a previous question, viz. *how came the king by a power which the people are afraid to trust, and always obliged to check?* Such a power could not be the gift of a wise people, neither can any power, *which needs checking*, be from God; yet the provision which the constitution makes supposes such a power to exist.

But the provision is unequal to the task; the means either cannot or will not accomplish the end, and the whole affair is a *Felo de se:* for as the greater weight will always carry up the less, and as all the wheels of a machine are put in motion by one, it only remains to know which power in the constitution has the most weight, for that will govern: and tho' the others, or a part of them, may clog, or, as the phrase is, check the rapidity of its motion, yet so long as they cannot stop it, their endeavours will be ineffectual: The first moving power will at last have its way, and what it wants in speed is supplied by time.

That the crown is this overbearing part in the English constitution needs not be mentioned, and that it derives its whole consequence merely from being the giver of places and pensions is self-evident; wherefore, though we have been wise enough to shut and lock a door against absolute Monarchy, we at the same time have been foolish enough to put the Crown in possession of the key.

The prejudice of Englishmen, in favour of their own government, by King, Lords and Commons, arises as much or more from national pride than reason. Individuals are undoubtedly safer in England than in some other countries: but the will of the king is as much the law of the land in Britain as in France, with this difference, that instead of proceeding directly from his mouth, it is handed to the people under the formidable shape of an act of parliament. For the fate of Charles the First hath only made kings more subtle—not more just.

Wherefore, laying aside all national pride and prejudice in favour of modes and forms, the plain truth is that *it is wholly owing to the constitution of the people, and not to the constitution of the government* that the crown is not as oppressive in England as in Turkey.

An inquiry into the *constitutional errors* in the English form of government, is at this time highly necessary; for as we are never in a proper condition of doing justice to others, while we continue under the influence of some leading partiality, so neither are we capable of doing it to ourselves while we remain fettered by any obstinate prejudice ...

As much hath been said of the advantages of reconciliation, which, like an agreeable dream, hath passed away and left us as we were, it is but right that we should examine the contrary side of the argument, and enquire into some of the many material injuries which these Colonies sustain, and always will sustain, by being connected with and dependent on Great Britain. To examine that connection and dependance, on the principles of nature and common sense, to see what we have to trust to, if separated, and what we are to expect, if dependent.

I have heard it asserted by some, that as America has flourished under her former connection with Great Britain, the same connection is necessary towards her future happiness, and will always have the same effect. Nothing can be more fallacious than this kind of argument. We may as well assert that because a child has thrived upon milk, that it is never to have meat, or that the first twenty years of our lives is to become a precedent for the next twenty. But even this is admitting more than is true; for I answer roundly that America would have flourished as much, and probably much more, had no European power taken any notice of her. The commerce by which she hath enriched herself are the necessaries of life, and will always have a market while eating is the custom of Europe.

But she has protected us, say some. That she hath engrossed us is true, and defended the Continent at our expense as well as her own, is admitted; and she would have defended Turkey from the same motive, *viz.* for the sake of trade and dominion.

Alas! we have been long led away by ancient prejudices and made large sacrifices to superstition. We have boasted the protection of Great Britain, without considering, that her motive was *interest* not *attachment;* and that she did not protect us from *our enemies* on *our account;* but from *her enemies* on *her own account,* from those who had no quarrel with us on any *other account,* and who will always be our enemies on the *same account.* Let Britain waive her pretensions to the Continent, or the Continent throw off the dependance, and we should be at peace with France and Spain, were they at war with Britain. The miseries of Hanover last war ought to warn us against connections.

It hath lately been asserted in parliament, that the Colonies have no relation to each other but through the Parent Country, *i.e.* that Pennsylvania and the Jerseys and so on for the rest, are sister Colonies by the way of England; this is certainly a very roundabout way of proving relationship, but it is the nearest and only true way of proving enmity (or enemyship, if I may so call it). France and Spain never were, nor perhaps ever will be, our enemies as *Americans,* but as our being the *subjects of Great Britain.*

But Britain is the parent country, say some. Then the more shame upon her conduct. Even brutes do not devour their young, nor savages make war upon their families …

To conclude, however strange it may appear to some, or however unwilling they may be to think so, matters not, but many strong and striking reasons may be given to show that nothing can settle our affairs so expeditiously as an open and determined declaration for independence. Some of which are,

First — It is the custom of Nations, when any two are at war, for some other powers, not engaged in the quarrel, to step in as mediators, and bring about the preliminaries of a peace; But while America calls herself the subject of Great Britain, no power, however well disposed she may be, can offer her mediation. Wherefore, in our present state we may quarrel on for ever.

Secondly — It is unreasonable to suppose that France or Spain will give us any kind of assistance, if we mean only to make use of that assistance for the purpose of repairing the breach, and strengthening the connection between Britain and America; because, those powers would be sufferers by the consequences.

Thirdly — While we profess ourselves the subjects of Britain, we must, in the eyes of foreign nations, be considered as Rebels. The precedent is somewhat dangerous to their peace, for men to be in arms under the name of subjects; we, on the spot, can solve the paradox; but to unite resistance and subjection requires an idea much too refined for common understanding.

Fourthly — Were a manifesto to be published, and despatched to foreign Courts, setting forth the miseries we have endured, and the peaceful methods which we have ineffectually used for redress; declaring at the same time that not being able longer to live happily or safely under the cruel disposition of the British Court, we had been driven to the necessity of breaking off all connections with her; at the same time, assuring all such Courts of our peaceable disposition towards them, and of our desire of entering into trade with them; such a memorial would produce more good effects to this Continent than if a ship were freighted with petitions to Britain.

Under our present denomination of British subjects, we can neither be received nor heard abroad; the custom of all Courts is against us, and will be so, until by an independence we take rank with other nations.

These proceedings may at first seem strange and difficult, but like all other steps which we have already passed over, will in a little time become familiar and agreeable; and until an independence is declared, the Continent will feel itself like a man who continues putting off some unpleasant business from day to day, yet knows it must be done, hates to set about it, wishes it over, and is continually haunted with the thoughts of its necessity.

HOW WELL DID YOU UNDERSTAND THIS SELECTION?

1. What did Paine mean by the statement that "her (Great Britain) motive was interest not attachment; and that she (Great Britain) did not protect us from our enemies on our account but from her enemies on her own account"?

2. What specific charges of misgovernment did Paine levy against the British government?

3. What remedy did Paine seek from the British government to address the above mentioned concerns?

JAMES MADISON PROMOTES RELIGIOUS FREEDOM

The First Amendment to the United States Constitution grants to every citizen freedom of religion. The underlying rationale of the Framers was to ensure that government did not in any way endorse, promote, advocate, or advance any form of religion or religious practice over other religions and religious practices. The members of the Constitutional Convention wanted to avoid the pitfalls so often witnessed in other countries that tried to force religious preferences upon their citizens. In 1785, James Madison address the General Assembly of the Commonwealth of Virginia on the necessity of preserving the right to religious preferences and practices. The following is an excerpt of his address to this assembly.

To the Honorable the General Assembly of the Commonwealth of Virginia

We, the subscribers, citizens of the said Commonwealth, having taken into serious consideration, a Bill printed by order of the last Session of General Assembly, entitled "A Bill establishing a provision for Teachers of the Christian Religion," and conceiving that the same, if finally armed with the sanctions of a law, will be a dangerous abuse of power, are bound as faithful members of a free State, to remonstrate against it, and to declare the reasons by which we are determined. We remonstrate against the said Bill,

1. Because we hold it for a fundamental and undeniable truth, "that Religion or the duty which we owe to our Creator and the Manner of discharging it, can be directed only by reason and conviction, not by force or violence." The Religion then of every man must be left to the conviction and conscience of every man; and it is the right of every man to exercise it as these may dictate. This right is in its nature an unalienable right. It is unalienable; because the opinions of men, depending only on the evidence contemplated by their own minds, cannot follow the dictates of other men: It is unalienable also, because what is here a right towards men, is a duty towards the Creator. It is the duty of every man to render to the Creator such homage, and such only, as he believes to be acceptable to him. This duty is precedent both in order of time and degree of obligation, to the claims of Civil Society. Before any man can be considered as a member of Civil Society, he must be considered as a subject of the Governor of the Universe: And if a member of Civil Society, who enters into any subordinate Association, must always do it with a reservation of his duty to the general authority; much more must every man who becomes a member of any particular Civil Society, do it with a saving of his allegiance to the Universal Sovereign. We maintain therefore that in matters of Religion, no man's right is abridged by the institution of Civil Society, and that Religion is wholly exempt from its cognizance. True it is, that no other rule exists, by which any question which may divide a Society, can be ultimately determined, but the will of the majority; but it is also true, that the majority may trespass on the rights of the minority.

2. Because if religion be exempt from the authority of the Society at large, still less can it be subject to that of the Legislative Body. The latter are but the creatures and vicegerents of the former. Their jurisdiction is both derivative and limited: it is limited with regard to the coordinate departments, more necessarily is it limited with regard to the constituents ...

3. Because, it is proper to take alarm at the first experiment on our liberties. We hold this prudent jealousy to be the first duty of citizens, and one of [the] noblest characteristics of the late Revolution. The freemen of America did not wait till usurped power had strengthened itself by exercise, and entangled the

question in precedents. They saw all the consequences in the principle, and they avoided the consequences by denying the principle …

4. Because, the bill violates that equality which ought to be the basis of every law, and which is more indispensable, in proportion as the validity or expediency of any law is more liable to be impeached. If "all men are by nature equally free and independent," all men are to be considered as entering into Society on equal conditions; as relinquishing no more, and therefore retaining no less, one than another, of their natural rights. Above all are they to be considered as retaining an *"equal* title to the free exercise of Religion according to the dictates of conscience." Whilst we assert for ourselves a freedom to embrace, to profess and to observe the Religion which we believe to be of divine origin, we cannot deny an equal freedom to those whose minds have not yet yielded to the evidence which has convinced us. If this freedom be abused, it is an offence against God, not against man: To God, therefore, not to men, must an account of it be rendered....

5. Because the bill implies either that the Civil Magistrate is a competent Judge of Religious truth; or that he may employ Religion as an engine of Civil policy. The first is an arrogant pretension falsified by the contradictory opinions of Rulers in all ages, and throughout the world: The second an unhallowed perversion of the means of salvation.

6. Because the establishment proposed by the Bill is not requisite for the support of the Christian Religion. To say that it is, is a contradiction to the Christian Religion itself; for every page of it disavows a dependence on the powers of this world: it is a contradiction to fact; for it is known that this Religion both existed and flourished, not only without the support of human laws, but in spite of every opposition from them; and not only during the period of miraculous aid, but long after it had been left to its own evidence, and the ordinary care of Providence: Nay, it is a contradiction in terms; for a Religion not invented by human policy, must have pre-existed and been supported, before it was established by human policy. It is moreover to weaken in those who profess this Religion a pious confidence in its innate excellence, and the patronage of its Author; and to foster in those who still reject it, a suspicion that its friends are too conscious of its fallacies, to trust it to its own merits.

7. Because experience witnesseth that ecclesiastical establishments, instead of maintaining the purity and efficacy of Religion, have had a contrary operation....

8. Because the establishment in question is not necessary for the support of Civil Government. If it be urged as necessary for the support of Civil Government only as it is a means of supporting Religion, and it be not necessary for the latter purpose, it cannot be necessary for the former.... A just government, instituted to secure & perpetuate it, needs them not. Such a government will be best supported by protecting every citizen in the enjoyment of his Religion with the same equal hand which protects his person and his property; by neither invading the equal rights of any Sect, nor suffering any Sect to invade those of another.

9. Because the proposed establishment is a departure from that generous policy, which, offering an asylum to the persecuted and oppressed of every Nation and Religion, promised a lustre to our country, and an accession to the number of its citizens. What a melancholy mark is the Bill of sudden degeneracy? Instead of holding forth an asylum to the persecuted, it is itself a signal of persecution. It degrades from the equal rank of Citizens all those whose opinions in Religion do not bend to those of the Legislative authority....

10. Because, it will have a likely tendency to banish our Citizens. The allurements presented by other situations are every day thinning their number. To superadd a fresh motive to emigration, by revoking the liberty which they now enjoy, would be the same species of folly which has dishonoured and depopulated flourishing kingdoms.

11. Because, it will destroy that moderation and harmony which the forbearance of our laws to intermeddle with Religion, has produced amongst its several sects. Torrents of blood have been spilt in the old world, by vain attempts of the secular arm to extinguish Religious discord, by proscribing

all difference in Religious opinions. Time has at length revealed the true remedy. Every relaxation of narrow and rigorous policy, wherever it has been tried, has been found to assuage the disease....

12. Because, the policy of the bill is adverse to the diffusion of the light of Christianity. The first wish of those who enjoy this precious gift, ought to be that it may be imparted to the whole race of mankind. Compare the number of those who have as yet received it with the number still remaining under the dominion of false Religions; and how small is the former! Does the policy of the Bill tend to lessen the disproportion? No; it at once discourages those who are strangers to the light of [revelation] from coming into the Region of it; and countenances, by example the nations who continue in darkness, in shutting out those who might convey it to them. Instead of levelling as far as possible, every obstacle to the victorious progress of truth, the Bill with an ignoble and unchristian timidity would circumscribe it, with a wall of defence, against the encroachments of error.

13. Because attempts to enforce by legal sanctions, acts obnoxious to so great a proportion of Citizens, tend to enervate the laws in general, and to slacken the bands of Society....

14. Because a measure of such singular magnitude and delicacy ought not to be imposed, without the clearest evidence that it is called for by a majority of citizens: and no satisfactory method is yet proposed by which the voice of the majority in this case may be determined, or its influence secured....

15. Because, finally, "the equal right of every citizen to the free exercise of his Religion according to the dictates of conscience" is held by the same tenure with all our other rights. If we recur to its origin, it is equally the gift of nature; if we weigh its importance, it cannot be less dear to us; if we consult the Declaration of those rights which pertain to the good people of Virginia, as the "basis and foundation of Government," it is enumerated with equal solemnity, or rather studied emphasis. . . . We the subscribers say, that the General Assembly of this Commonwealth have no such authority: And that no effort may be omitted on our part against so dangerous an usurpation, we oppose to it, this remonstrance; earnestly praying, as we are in duty bound, that the Supreme Lawgiver of the Universe, by illuminating those to whom it is addressed, may on the one hand, turn their councils from every act which would affront his holy prerogative, or violate the trust committed to them: and on the other, guide them into every measure which may be worthy of his [blessing, may re]dound to their own praise, and may establish more firmly the liberties, the prosperity, and the Happiness of the Commonwealth.

HOW WELL DID YOU UNDERSTAND THIS SELECTION?

1. Why did Madison believe that religious freedom was a "fundamental and undeniable truth"?

2. Why did Madison believe that civil society should not determine the religious preference of its citizens?

3. What problems did Madison foresee for the citizens of the United States if the government did indeed mandate that citizens could only practice one religion over all forms of religion?

At the Constitutional Convention, one of the major obstacles confronting the delegates was how to design a new national government that would be beneficial to the interests of all of the states. Several different proposals were introduced. The Virginia or Randolph Plan proposed a national government benefitting the interests of the most populous states. The smaller or less populated states countered with the New Jersey or Patterson Plan. The delegates weighed both plans carefully. Through their wisdom, the wishes of the smaller and larger states were combined under the Connecticut Compromise.

The Virginia, or Randolph, Plan, May 29, 1787

1. Resolved that the Articles of Confederation ought to be so corrected and enlarged as to accomplish the objects proposed by their institution; namely "common defence, security of liberty and general welfare."

2. Resolved therefore that the rights of suffrage in the National Legislature ought to be proportioned to the Quotas of contribution, or to the number of free inhabitants, as the one or the other rule may seem best in different cases.

3. Resolved that the National Legislature ought to consist of two branches.

4. Resolved that the members of the first branch of the National Legislature ought to be elected by the people of the several States every for the terms of; to be of the age of years at least, to receive liberal stipends by which they may be compensated for the devotion of their time to public service, to be ineligible to any office established by a particular State, or under the authority of the United States, except those peculiarly belonging to the functions of the first branch, during the term of service, and for the spare of after its expiration; to be incapable of reelection for the space of after the expiration of their term of service, and to be subject to recall.

5. Resolved that the members of the second branch of the National Legislature ought to be elected by those of the first, out of a proper number of persons nominated by the individual Legislatures, to be of the age of years at least; to hold their offices for a term sufficient to ensure their independency; to receive liberal stipends, by which they may be compensated for the devotion of their time to public service; and to be ineligible to any office established by a particular State, or under the authority of the United States, except those peculiarly belonging to the functions of the second branch, during the term of service, and for the space of after the expiration thereof.

6. Resolved that each branch ought to possess the right of originating Acts; that the National Legislature ought to be empowered to enjoy the Legislative Rights vested in Congress by the Confederation and moreover to legislate in all cases to which the separate States are incompetent, or in which the harmony of the United States may be interrupted by the exercise of individual Legislation; to negative all laws passed by the several States, contravening in the opinion of the National Legislature the articles of Union; and to call forth the force of the Union against any member of the Union failing in its duty under the articles thereof.

7. Resolved that a National Executive be instituted; to be chosen by the National Legislature for the term of years; to receive punctually, at stated times, a fixed compensation for the services rendered, in which no increase or diminution shall be made so as to affect the Magistracy, existing at the time of the increase or diminution, and to be ineligible a second time; and that besides a general authority to execute the National laws, it ought to enjoy the Executive rights vested in Congress by the Confederation.

8. Resolved that the Executive and a convenient number of the National Judiciary, ought to compose a Council or revision with authority to examine every act of the National Legislature before it shall operate, and every act of a particular Legislature before a Negative thereon shall be final; and that the dissent of the said Council shall amount to a rejection, unless the Act of the National Legislature be passed again, or that of a particular Legislature be again negatived by of the members of each branch.

9. Resolved that a National Judiciary be established to consist of one or more supreme tribunals, and of inferior tribunals to be chosen by the National Legislature, to hold their offices during good behaviour; and to receive punctually at stated times fixed compensation for their services, in which no increase or diminution shall be made so as to affect the persons actually in office at the time of such increase or diminution. That the jurisdiction of the inferior tribunals shall be to hear and determine in the first instance, and of the supreme tribunal to hear and determine in the dernier resort, all piracies and felonies on the high seas, captures from an enemy; cases in which foreigners or citizens of other States applying to such jurisdictions may be interested, or which respect the collection of the National revenue; impeachments of any National officers, and questions which may involve the national peace and harmony.

10. Resolved that provision ought to be made for the admission of States lawfully arising within the limits of the United States, whether from a voluntary junction of Government and Territory or otherwise, with the consent of a number of voices in the National legislature less than the whole.

11. Resolved that a Republican Government and the territory of each State, except in the instance of a voluntary junction of Government and territory, ought to be guaranteed by the United States to each State.

12. Resolved that provision ought to be made for the continuance of Congress and their authorities and privileges, until a given day after the reform of the articles of Union shall be adopted, and for the completion of all their engagements.

13. Resolved that provision ought to be made for the amendment of the Articles of Union whensoever it shall seem necessary, and that the assent of the National Legislature ought not to be required thereto.

14. Resolved that the Legislative, Executive, and Judiciary powers within the several States ought to be bound by oath to support the articles of Union.

15. Resolved that the amendments which shall be offered to the Confederation, by the Convention ought at a proper time, or times, after the approbation of Congress to be submitted to an assembly or assemblies of Representatives, recommended by the several Legislatures to be expressly chosen by the people, to consider and decide thereon.

The New Jersey, or Paterson Plan, June 15, 1787

1. Resolved that the Articles of Confederation ought to be so revised, corrected, and enlarged as to render the federal Constitution adequate to the exigencies of Government, and the preservation of the Union.

2. Resolved that in addition to the powers vested in the United States in Congress, by the present existing articles of Confederation, they be authorized to pass acts for raising a revenue, by levying a duty or duties on all goods or merchandizes of foreign growth or manufacture, imported into any part of the United States, by Stamps on paper, vellum or parchment, and by a postage on all letters or packages passing through the general post office, to be applied to such federal purposes as they shall deem proper and expedient; to make rules and regulations for the collection thereof; and the same from time to time, to alter and amend in such manner as they shall think proper: to pass Acts for the regulation of trade and commerce as well with foreign nations as with each other; provided that all punishments, fines, forfeitures and penalties to be incurred for contravening such acts rules and regulations shall be adjudged by the Common law Judiciaries of the State

in which any offence contrary to the true intent and meaning of such Acts rules and regulations shall have been committed or perpetrated, with liberty of commencing in the first instance all suits and prosecutions for that purpose, in the superior common law Judiciary in such state, subject nevertheless, for the correction of errors, both in law and fact in rendering Judgement, to an appeal to the Judiciary of the United States.

3. Resolved that whenever requisitions shall be necessary, instead of the rule for making requisitions mentioned in the articles of Confederation, the United States in Congress be authorized to make such requisitions in proportion to the whole number of white and other free citizens and inhabitants of every age sex and condition including those bound to servitude for a term of years and three fifths of all other persons not comprehended in the foregoing description, except Indians not paying taxes; that if such requisitions be not complied with, in the time specified therein, to direct the collection thereof in the non-complying States and for that purpose to devise and pass acts directing and authorizing the same; provided that none of the powers hereby vested in the United States in Congress shall be exercised without the consent of at least States, and in that proportion if the number of Confederated States should hereafter be increased or diminished.

4. Resolved that the United States in Congress be authorized to elect a federal Executive to consist of persons, to continue in office for the term of years, to receive punctually at stated times a fixed compensation for their services, in which no increase or diminution shall be made so as to affect the persons composing the Executive at the time of such increase or diminution, to be paid out of the federal treasury; to be incapable of holding any other office or appointment during their time of service and for years thereafter; to be ineligible a second time, and removeable by Congress on application by a majority of the Executives of the several States; that the Executives besides their general authority to execute the federal acts ought to appoint all federal officers not otherwise provided for, and to direct all military operations; provided that none of the persons composing the federal Executive shall on any occasion take command of any troops so as personally to conduct any enterprise as General or in other capacity.

5. Resolved that a federal Judiciary be established to consist of a supreme tribunal the Judges of which to be appointed by the Executive, and to hold their offices during good behaviour, to receive punctually at stated times a fixed compensation for their services in which no increase or diminution shall be made so as to affect persons actually in office at the time of such increase or diminution; that the Judiciary so established shall have authority to hear and determine in the first instance on all impeachments of federal officers, and by way of appeal in the dernier resort in all cases touching the rights of Ambassadors, in all cases of captures from an enemy, in all cases of piracies and felonies on the high Seas, in all cases in which foreigners may be interested, in the construction of any treaty or treaties, or which may arise on any of the Acts for regulation of trade, or the collection of the federal Revenue: that none of the Judiciary shall during the time they remain in office be capable of receiving or holding any other office or appointment during the time of service, or for thereafter.

6. Resolved that all Acts of the United States in Congress made by virtue and in pursuance of the powers hereby and by the articles of Confederation vested in them, and all Treaties made and ratified under the authority of the United States, shall be the supreme law of the respective States so far forth as those Acts or Treaties shall relate to the said States or their Citizens, and that the Judiciary of the several States shall be bound thereby in their decisions, any thing in the respective laws of the Individual States to the contrary notwithstanding; and that if any State, or any body of men in any State shall oppose or prevent carrying into execution such acts or treaties, the federal Executive shall be authorized to call forth the power of the Confederated States, or so much thereof as may be necessary to enforce and compel an obedience to such Acts or an observance of such Treaties.

7. Resolved that provision be made for the admission of new States into the Union.

8. Resolved the rule for naturalization ought to be the same in every State.

9. Resolved that a Citizen of one State committing an offence in another State of the Union, shall be deemed guilty of the same offence as if it had been committed by a Citizen of the State in which the offence was committed.

HOW WELL DID YOU UNDERSTAND THIS SELECTION?

1. What were the major features of the Virginia Plan?

2. What were the major features of the New Jersey Plan?

3. Compare these two proposals to the United States Constitution. What provisions were taken from which proposals? Provide specific examples.

The emerging battle over the ratification of the newly drafted United States Constitution resulted in two competing camps. The Federalists were strongly behind the new document. Their leading spokespersons were James Madison, Alexander Hamilton, and John Jay. **The Federalist Papers** *is a collection of articles primarily penned by Madison and Hamilton in response to the opposing group known as the Anti-Federalists. George Mason was one of those individuals who voiced concern that the Constitution was a flawed document detrimental to the survival of the newly formed government. This article expresses some of his objections.*

There is no Declaration of Rights; and the Laws of the general Government being paramount to the Laws and Constitutions of the several States, the Declaration of Rights in the separate States are no Security. Nor are the people secured even in the Enjoyment of the Benefits of the common-Law: which stands here upon no other Foundation than its having been adopted by the respective Acts forming the Constitutions of the several States.

In the House of Representatives there is not the Substance, but the Shadow only of Representation; which can never produce proper Information in the Legislature, or inspire Confidence in the People: the Laws will therefore be generally made by Men little concern'd in, and unacquainted with their Effects and Consequences.

The Senate have the Power of altering all Money-Bills, and of originating Appropriations of Money and the Sallerys of the Officers of their own Appointment in Conjunction with the President of the United States; altho' they are not the Representatives of the People, or amenable to them.

These with their other great Powers (vizt. their Power in the Appointment of Ambassadors and all public Officers, in making Treaties, and in trying all Impeachments) their Influence upon and Connection with the supreme Executive from these Causes, their Duration of Office, and their being a constant existing Body almost continually sitting, joined with their being one compleat Branch of the Legislature, will destroy any Balance in the Government, and enable them to accomplish what Usurpations they please upon the Rights and Libertys of the People.

The Judiciary of the United States is so constructed and extended, as to absorb and destroy the Judiciarys of the several States; thereby rendering Law as tedious[,] intricate and expensive, and Justice as unattainable, by a great part of the Community, as in England, and enabling the Rich to oppress and ruin the Poor.

The President of the United States has no constitutional Council (a thing unknown in any safe and regular Government) he will therefore be unsupported by proper Information and Advice; and will generally be directed by Minions and Favourites—or He will become a Tool to the Senate—or a Council of State will grow out of the principal Officers of the great Departments; the worst and most dangerous of all Ingredients for such a Council, in a free Country; for they may be induced to join in any dangerous or oppressive Measures, to shelter themselves, and prevent an Inquiry into their own Misconduct in Office; whereas had a constitutional Council been formed (as was proposed) of six Members; vizt. two from the Eastern, two from the Middle, and two from the Southern States, to be appointed by Vote of the States in the House of Representatives, with the same Duration and Rotation of Office as the Senate, the Executive wou'd always have had safe and proper Information and Advice, the President of such a Council might have acted as Vice President of the United States, pro tempore, upon any Vacancy or Disability of the chief Magistrate; and long continued Sessions of the Senate wou'd in a great Measure have been prevented.

From this fatal Defect of a constitutional Council has arisen the improper Power of the Senate, in the Appointment of public Officers, and the alarming Dependence and Connection between that Branch of the Legislature, and the supreme Executive.

Hence also sprung that unnecessary and dangerous Officer, the Vice President; who for want of other Employment, is made President of the Senate; thereby dangerously blending the executive and legislative Powers; besides always giving to some one of the States an unnecessary and unjust Preeminence over the others.

The President of the United States has the unrestrained Power of granting Pardon for Treason; which may be sometimes exercised to screen from Punishment those whom he had secretly instigated to commit the Crime, and thereby prevent a Discovery of his own Guilt.

By declaring all Treaties supreme Laws of the Land, the Executive and the Senate have in many Cases, an exclusive Power of Legislation; which might have been avoided by proper Distinctions with Respect to Treaties, and requiring the Assent of the House of Representatives, where it cou'd be done with Safety.

By requiring only a Majority to make all commercial and navigation Laws, the five Southern States (whose Produce and Circumstances are totally different from that of the eight Northern and Eastern States) will be ruined; for such rigid and premature Regulations may be made, as will enable the Merchants of the Northern and Eastern States not only to demand an exorbitant Freight, but to monopolize the Purchase of the Commodities at their own Price, for many years: to the great Injury of the landed Interest, and Impoverishment of the People: and the Danger is the greater, as the Gain on one Side will be in Proportion to the Loss on the other. Whereas requiring two thirds of the members present in both Houses wou'd have produced mutual moderation, promoted the general Interest, and removed an insuperable Objection to the Adoption of the Government.

Under their own Construction of the general Clause at the End of the enumerated powers the Congress may grant Monopolies in Trade and Commerce, constitute new Crimes, inflict unusual and severe Punishments, and extend their Power as far as they shall think proper; so that the State Legislatures have no Security for the Powers now presumed to remain to them; or the People for their Rights.

There is no Declaration of any kind for preserving the Liberty of the Press, the Tryal by Jury in civil Causes; nor against the Danger of standing Armys in time of Peace. The State Legislatures are restrained from laying Export Duties on their own Produce.

The general Legislature is restrained from prohibiting the futher Importation of Slaves for twenty odd Years; tho' such Importations render the United States weaker, more vulnerable, and less capable of Defence.

Both the general Legislature and the State Legislatures are expressly prohibited [from] making ex post facto Laws; tho' there never was, or can be a Legislature but must and will make such Laws, when necessity and the public Safety require them; which will hereafter be a Breach of all the Constitutions in the Union, and afford precedents for other Innovations.

This Government will commence in a moderate Aristocracy; it is at present impossible to foresee whether it will, in its Operation, produce a Monarchy, or a corrupt oppressive Aristocracy; it will most probably vibrate some Years between the two, and then terminate in the one or the other.

HOW WELL DID YOU UNDERSTAND THIS SELECTION?

1. As a Southerner, what provisions in the Constitution did Mason see as potentially harmful to the southern states?

2. Why did Mason feel that the Constitution should mandate that the executive form a cabinet or council of advisors?

3. What were Mason's primary concerns about the duties and responsibilities assigned to the Senate and House of Representatives?

4. Why did Mason believe that the Supreme Court would enable "the Rich to oppress and ruin the Poor"?

*After the Constitution was written, it had to be ratified by the state conventions of two-thirds of the thirteen states. Many state leaders, however, felt reluctant about accepting the new Constitution, and they expressed their misgivings. During a heated debate over ratification in New York State, three of the most prominent proponents of the Constitution, John Jay, James Madison, and Alexander Hamilton, began to write essays explaining the philosophy behind the Constitution. These essays appeared as newspaper columns and finally totaled eighty-five in number. **The Federalist Papers**, as the essays have come to be called, are recognized today as the definitive statement of the Federalists' views on the Constitution. They are essential primary sources considered by judges and academicians when analyzing the intent of the American Constitution.*

Federalist No. 10

Madison, writing under the pseudonym Publius, identifies an inimical problem found in all free societies: factions inevitably arise and try to force their will on others, thereby annihilating freedom itself. By faction, Madison means any group less than the whole, united by a common interest, adverse to the interests of other citizens and even to the public interest. These factions develop in societies in which people are free to think for themselves and free to differ in religious, political, and economic areas of their lives. The problem of factions, according to Madison, is that groups will seek to enforce their will on others through control of the government. In short, a faction with a government on its side becomes the very definition of tyranny. Majoritarian democracies, insulated from such despotism in cases where the faction is only a minority interest, can find no such relief when the faction is a majority, for then, by controlling the votes, it will control the government.

*Madison seeks a solution to the evils of factions. One solution would be to do away with freedom itself. In a country where all have the same religion, property, and political views, there will be no conflicts, and, therefore, no factions. Madison adamantly rejects this solution because he values the freedom that the early colonists fought so hard to win in the Revolutionary War against Britain. The only other way to prevent the potential for tyranny at the hands of the majority, as well as the minority, is to design a constitutional system that actually **encourages** factions. A representative government covering a large area will ensure that government represents many diverse interests and that no one faction will be able to dominate.*

Federalist Nos. 47-48, 51

If factions can threaten liberty, so can government. According to Madison, it is human nature to be ambitious and power hungry, especially so when the human is a politician. Only dividing power among ambitious people and making them compete will protect liberty. In Federalist No. 47, James Madison argues that no institution, no one set of government officials, should control the entirety of governmental power. Rather, the legislative, executive, and judicial branches must each have some power exercised independently from the other branches.

Madison, does not go so far as to say that the three branches should be completely separate. In fact in No. 48, he argues that the separation of powers requires that the three departments be connected, giving each some control over the others. A free society has much to fear from despotic legislation and so the law-making power must surely be shared across the three branches. Consequently, the legislative branch is the law-maker, the executive the law-executor, the judicial the law-adjudicator. In Federalist No. 51, Madison more fully articulates the sharing of power that will produce the checks and balances so essential to the protection of liberty.

Among the numerous advantages promised by a well-constructed Union, none needs to be more accurately developed than its tendency to break and control the violence of faction. The friend of popular governments never finds himself so much alarmed for their character and fate as when he contemplates their propensity to this dangerous vice. He will not fail, therefore, to set a due value on any plan which, without violating the principles to which he is attached, provides a proper cure for it. The instability, injustice, and confusion introduced into the public councils have, in truth, been the mortal diseases under which popular governments have everywhere perished, as they continue to be the favorite and fruitful topics from which the adversaries to liberty derive their most specious declamations. The valuable improvements made by the American constitutions on the popular models, both ancient and modern, cannot certainly be too much admired; but it would be an unwarrantable partiality to contend that they have as effectually obviated the danger on this side, as was wished and expected. Complaints are everywhere heard from our most considerate and virtuous citizens, equally the friends of public and private faith and of public and personal liberty, that our governments are too unstable, that the public good is disregarded in the conflicts of rival parties, and that measures are too often decided, not according to the rules of justice and the rights of the minor party, but by the superior force of an interested and overbearing majority. However anxiously we may wish that these complaints had no foundation, the evidence of known facts will not permit us to deny that they are in some degree true. It will be found, indeed, on a candid review of our situation, that some of the distresses under which we labor have been erroneously charged top the operation of our governments; but it will be found, at the same time, that other causes will not alone account for many of our heavier misfortunes; and, particularly, for that prevailing and increasing distrust of public engagements and alarm for private rights which are echoed from one end of the continent to the other. These must be chiefly, if not wholly, effects of the unsteadiness and injustice with which a factious spirit has tainted our public administration.

By a faction I understand a number of citizens, whether amounting to a majority or minority of the whole, who are united and actuated by some common impulse or passion, or of interests, adverse to the rights of other citizens, or to the permanent and aggregate interests of the community.

There are two methods of curing the mischiefs of faction: the one, by removing its causes; the other, by controlling its effects.

There are again two methods of removing the causes of faction: the one, by destroying the liberty which is essential to its existence; the other, by giving to every citizen the same opinions, the same passions, and the same interests.

It could never be more fully said than of the first remedy that it is worse than the disease. Liberty is to faction what air is to fire, an ailment without which it instantly expires. But it could not be less folly to abolish liberty, which is essential to political life, because it nourished faction than it would be to wish the annihilation of air, which is essential to animal life, because it imparts to fire its destructive agency.

The second expedient is as impractical as the first would be unwise. As long as the reason of man continues fallible, and he is at liberty to exercise it, different opinions will be formed. As long as the connection subsists between his reason and his self-love, his opinions and his passions will have a reciprocal influence on each other; and the former will be objects to which the latter will attach themselves. The diversity in the faculties of men, from which the rights of property originate, is not less an insuperable obstacle to a uniformity of interests. The protection of these faculties is the first object of government. From the protection of different and unequal faculties of acquiring property, the possession of different degrees and kinds of property immediately results; and from the influence of these on the sentiments and views of the respective proprietors ensues a division into different interests and parties.

The latent causes of faction are thus sown in the nature of man; and we see them everywhere brought into different degrees of activity, according to the different circumstances of civil society. A zeal for different opinions concerning religion, concerning government, and many other points, as well of speculation as of practice; an attachment to different leaders ambitiously contending for preeminence and power; or to persons of other descriptions whose fortunes have been interesting to the human passions, have in turn, divided mankind into parties, inflamed them with mutual animosity, and rendered them much more disposed to vex and oppress each other than to cooperate for their common good. So strong is this propensity of mankind to fall into mutual animosities that where no substantial occasion presents itself the most frivolous and fanciful distinctions have been sufficient to kindle their unfriendly passions and excite their most violent conflicts. But the most common and durable source of factions has been the various and unequal distribution of property. Those who hold and those who are without property have ever formed distinct interests in society. Those who are creditors, and those who are debtors, fall under a like discrimination. A landed interest, a manufacturing interest, a mercantile interest, a moneyed interest, with many lesser interests, grow up of necessity in civilized nations, and divide them into different classes, actuated by different sentiments and views. The regulation of these various and interfering interests forms the principal task of modern legislation and involves the spirit of party and faction in the necessary and ordinary operations of government.

No man is allowed to be a judge in his own cause, because his interest would certainly bias his judgement, and, not improbably, corrupt his integrity. With equal, nay with greater reason, a body of men are unfit to be both judges and parties at the same time; yet what are many of the most important acts of legislation but so many judicial determinations, not indeed concerning the rights of single persons, but concerning the rights of large bodies of citizens? And what are the different classes of legislators but advocates and parties to the causes which they determine? Is a law proposed concerning private debts? It is a question to which the creditors are parties on one side and the debtors on the other. Justice ought to hold the balance between them. Yet the parties are, and must be, themselves the judges; and the most numerous party, or in other words, the most powerful faction must be expected to prevail. Shall domestic manufacturers be encouraged, and in what degree, by restrictions on foreign manufacturers? are questions which would be differently decided by the landed and the manufacturing classes, and probably be neither with a sole regard to justice and the public good. The appointment of taxes on the various descriptions of property is an act which seems to require the most exact impartiality; yet there is, perhaps, no legislative act in which greater opportunity and temptation are given to a predominant party to trample on the rules of justice. Every shilling with which they overburden the inferior number is a shilling saved to their own pockets.

It is vain to say that enlightened statesmen will be able to adjust these clashing interests and render them all subservient to the public good. Enlightened statesmen will not always be at the helm. Nor, in many cases, can such an adjustment be made at all without taking into view indirect and remote considerations, which will rarely prevail over the immediate interest which one party may find in disregarding the rights of another or the good of the whole.

The inference to which we are brought is that the *causes* of faction cannot be removed and that relief is only to be sought in the means of controlling its *effects*.

If a faction consists of less than a majority, relief is supplied by the republican principle, which enables the majority to defeat its sinister views by regular vote. It may clog the administration, it may convulse the society; but it will be unable to execute and mask its violence under the forms of the Constitution. When a majority is included in a faction, the form of popular government, on the other hand, enables it to sacrifice to its ruling passion or interest both the public good and the rights of other citizens. To secure the public good and private rights against the danger of such a faction, and at the same time to preserve the spirit and the forms of popular government, is then the great object to which or inquiries are directed. Let me add that it is the great desideratum by which alone this form of government can be rescued from the opprobrium under which it has so long labored and be recommended to the esteem and adoption of mankind.

By what means is this object attainable? Evidently by one of two only. Either the existence of the same passion or interest in a majority at the same time must be prevented, or the majority, having such coexistent passion or interest, must be rendered, by their number and local situation, unable to concert and carry into effect schemes of oppression. If the impulse and the opportunity be suffered to coincide, we well know that neither moral nor religious motives can be relied on as an adequate control. They are not found to be such on the injustice and violence of individuals, and lose their efficacy in proportion to the number combined together, that is, in proportion as their efficacy becomes needful.

From this view of the subject it may be concluded that a pure democracy, by which I mean a society consisting of a small number of citizens, who assemble and administer the government in person, can admit of no cure for the mischiefs of faction. A common passion or interest will, in almost every case, be felt by a majority of the whole; a communication and concert results from the form of government itself; and there is nothing to check the inducements to sacrifice the weaker party or an obnoxious individual. Hence it is that such democracies have ever been spectacles of turbulence and contention; have ever been found incompatible with personal security or the rights of property; and in general have been as short in their lives as they have been violent in their deaths. Theoretic politicians, who have patronized this species of government, have erroneously supposed that by reducing mankind to a perfect equality in their political rights, they would at the same time be perfectly equalized and assimilated in their possessions, their opinions, and their passions.

A republic, by which I mean a government in which the scheme of representation takes place, opens a different prospect and promises the cure for which we are seeking. Let us examine the points in which it varies from pure democracy, and shall comprehend both the nature of the cure and the efficacy which it must derive from the Union.

The two great points of difference between a democracy and a republic are: first, the delegation of the government, in the latter, to a small number of citizens elected by the rest; secondly, the greater number of citizens and greater sphere of country over which the latter may be extended.

The effect of the first difference is, on the one hand, to refine and enlarge the public views by passing them through the medium of a chosen body of citizens, whose wisdom may best discern the true interest of their country and whose patriotism and love of justice will be least likely to sacrifice it to temporary or partial considerations. Under such a regulation it may well happen that the public voice, pronounced by the representatives of the people, will be more consonant to the public good than if pronounced by the people themselves, convened for the purpose. On the other hand, the effect may be inverted. Men of factious tempers, of local prejudices, or of sinister designs, may, by intrigue, by corruption, or by other means, first obtain the suffrages, and then betray the interests of the people. The question resulting is, whether small or extensive republics are most favorable to the election of proper guardians of the public weal; and it is clearly decided in favor of the latter by two obvious considerations.

In the first place it is to be remarked that however small the republic may be the representatives must be raised to a certain number in order to guard against the cabals of a few; and that however large it may be they must be limited to a certain number in order to guard against the confusion of multitude. Hence, the number of representatives in the two cases not being in proportion to that of the constituents, and being proportionally greatest in the small republic, it follows that if the proportion of fit characters be not less in the large than in the small republic, the former will present a greater option, and consequently a greater probability of a fit choice.

In the next place, as each representative will be chosen by a greater number of citizens in the large than in the small republic, it will be more difficult for unworthy candidates to practice with success the various arts by which elections are too often carried; and the suffrages of the people being more free, will be more likely to center on men who possess the most attractive merit and the most diffusive and established characters.

It must be confessed that in this, as in most other cases, there is a mean, on both sides of which inconveniences will be found to lie. By enlarging too much the number of electors, you render the representative too little acquainted with all their local circumstances and lesser interests; as by reducing it too much, you render him unduly attached to these, and too little fit to comprehend and pursue great and national objects. The federal Constitution forms a happy combination in this respect; the great and aggregate interests referred to the national , the local and particular to the State legislatures

The other point of difference is the greater number of citizens and extent of territory which may be brought within the compass of republican than of democratic government; and it is this circumstance principally which renders factious combinations less to be dreaded in the former than in the latter. The smaller the society, the fewer probably will be the distinct parties and interests composing it; the fewer the distinct parties and interests, the more frequently will a majority be found of the same party; and the smaller the number of individuals composing a majority, and the smaller the compass within which they are placed, the more easily will they concert and execute their plans of oppression. Extend the sphere and you take in a greater variety of parties and interests; you make it less probable that a majority of a whole will have a common motive to invade the rights of other citizens; or if such a common motive exists, it will be more difficult for all who feel it to discover their own strength and to act in unison with each other. Besides other impediments, it may be remarked that, when there is a consciousness of unjust or dishonorable purposes, communication is always checked by distrust in proportion to the number whose concurrence is necessary.

Hence, it clearly appears that the same advantage which a republic has over a democracy in controlling the effects of faction is enjoyed by a large over a small republic—is enjoyed by the Union over the States composing it. Does this advantage consist in the substitution of representatives whose enlightened views and virtuous sentiments render them superior to local prejudices and to schemes of injustice? It will not be denied that the representation of the Union will be most likely to possess the requisite endowments. Does it consist in the greater security afforded by a greater variety of parties, against the event of any one party being able to outnumber and oppress the rest? In an equal degree does the increased variety of parties comprised within the Union increase this insecurity. Does it, in fine, consist in the greater obstacles to the concert and accomplishment of the secret wishes of an unjust and interested majority? Here again the extent of the Union gives it the most palpable advantage.

The influence of factious leaders may kindle a flame within their particular States but will be unable to spread a general conflagration through the other States. A religious sect may degenerate into a political faction in a part of the Confederacy; but the variety of sects dispersed over the entire face of it must secure the national councils against any danger from that source. A rage for paper money, for an abolition of debts, for an equal division of property, or for any other improper or wicked project, will be less apt to pervade the whole body of the Union than a particular member of it, in the same proportion as such a malady is more likely to taint a particular county or district than an entire State.

In the extent and proper structure of the Union, therefore, we behold a republican remedy for the diseases most incident to republican government. And according to the degree of pleasure and pride we feel in being republican ought to be our zeal in cherishing the spirit and supporting the character of federalists.

…One of the principal objections inculcated by the most respectable adversaries to the constitution is its supposed violation of the political maxim that the legislative, executive, and judiciary departments ought to be separate and distinct. In the structure of the federal government no regard, it is said, seems to have been paid to this essential precaution in favor of liberty. The several departments of power are distributed and blended in such a manner as at once to destroy all symmetry and beauty of form, and to expose some of the essential parts of the edifice to the danger of being crushed by the disproportionate weight of other parts.

No political truth is certainly of greater intrinsic value, or is stamped with the authority of more enlightened patrons of liberty that that on which the objection is founded. The accumulation of all powers, legislative, executive, and judiciary, in the same hands, whether of one, a few, or many, and whether hereditary, self-appointed, or elective, may justly be pronounced the very definition of tyranny. Were the federal Constitution, therefore, really chargeable with this accumulation of power, or with a mixture of powers, having a dangerous tendency to such an accumulation, no further arguments would be necessary to inspire a universal reprobation of the system. I persuade myself, however, that it will be made apparent to everyone that the charge cannot be supported, and that the maxim on which it relies has been totally misconceived and misapplied. In order to form correct ideas on this important subject it will be proper to investigate the sense in which the preservation of liberty requires that the three great departments of power should be separate and distinct.

The oracle who is always consulted and cited on this subject is the celebrated Montesquieu. If he be not the author of this invaluable precept in the science of politics, he has the merit at least of displaying and recommending it most effectually to the attention of mankind. Let us endeavor, in the first place, to ascertain his meaning on this point.

The British Constitution was to Montesquieu what Homer has been to the didactic writers of epic poetry. As the latter have considered the work of the immortal bard as the perfect model from which the principles and rules of the epic art were to be drawn, and by which all similar works were to be judged, so this great political critic appears to have viewed the Constitution of England as the standard, or to use his own expression, as the mirror of political liberty; and to have delivered, in the form of elementary truths, the several characteristic principles of that particular system. That we may be sure, then, not to mistake his meaning in this case, let us recur to the source from which the maxim was drawn.

On the slightest view of the British Constitution, we must perceive that the legislative, executive, and judiciary departments are by no means totally separate and distinct from each other. The executive magistrate forms an integral part of the legislative authority. He alone has the prerogative of making treaties with foreign sovereigns which, when made, have, under certain limitations, the force of legislative acts. Al the members of the judiciary department are appointed by him, and removed by him on the address of the two houses of Parliament, and form, when he pleases to consult them, one of his constitutional councils. One branch of the legislative department forms also a great constitutional council to the executive chief, as, on the other hand, it is the sole depositary of judicial power in cases of impeachment, and is invested with the supreme appellate jurisdiction in al other cases. The judges, again, are so far connected with the legislative department as often to attend and participate in its deliberations, though not admitting to a legislative vote.

From these facts, by which Montesquieu was guided, it may clearly be inferred that in saying "There can be no liberty where the legislative and executive powers are united in the same person, or body of magistrates," or "if the power of judging be not separated from the legislative and executive powers," he did not mean that these departments ought to have no *partial agency* in, or no *control* over, the acts of each other. His meaning, as his own words import, and still more conclusively as illustrated by the example in his eye, can amount to no more than this, that where the *whole* power of one department is exercised by the same hands which possess the *whole* power of another department, the fundamental principles of a free country are subverted. This would have been the case in the constitution examined by him, if the king, who is the sole executive magistrate, had possessed also the complete legislative power, or the supreme administration of justice; or if the entire legislative body had possessed the supreme judiciary, or the supreme executive authority. This, however, is not among the vices of that constitution. The magistrate in whom the whole executive power resides cannot of himself make a law, though he can put a negative on every law; nor administer justice in person, although he has the appointment of those who do administer it. The judges can exercise no executive prerogative, though hey are shoots from the executive stock; nor any legislative function, though they may be advised by the legislative councils. The entire legislature can perform no judiciary act, though by the joint act of two of its branches the judges may be removed from their offices, and though one of its branches is possessed of the judicial power of the last resort. The entire legislature, again, can exercise no executive prerogative, though one of its branched constitutes the supreme executive magistracy, and another, on the impeachment of a third, can try and condemn al the subordinate officers in the executive department.

The reasons on which Montesquieu grounds his maxim are a further demonstration of his meaning "When the legislative and executive powers are united in the same person or body," says he, "there can be no liberty, because apprehensions may arise lest *the same* monarch or senate should *enact* tyrannical laws to *execute* them in a tyrannical manner." Again: "Were the power of judging joined with the legislative, the life and liberty of the subject would be exposed to arbitrary control, for the *judge* would then be *the legislator*. Were it joined to the executive department, the *judge* might behave with al the violence of *an oppressor*." Some of these reasons are more fully explained in other passages; but briefly stated as they are here they sufficiently establish the meaning which we have put on this celebrated maxim of this celebrated author.

If we look into the constitutions of the several States we find that, notwithstanding the emphatical and, in some instances, the unqualified terms in which this axiom has been laid down, there is not a single instance in which the several departments of power have been kept absolutely separate and distinct. New Hampshire, whose constitution was the last formed, seems to have been fully aware of the impossibility and inexpediency of avoiding any mixture whatever of these departments, and has qualified the doctrine by declaring "that the legislative, executive, and judiciary powers ought to be kept as separate from, and independent of, each other *as the nature of a free government will admit; or as is consistent with that chain of connection that binds the whole fabric of the constitution in one indissoluble bond of unity and amity.*" Her constitution accordingly mixes these departments in several respects. The Senate, which is a branch of the legislative department, is also a judicial tribunal for the trial of impeachments, The President, who is the head of the executive department, is the presiding member also of the Senate; and besides an equal vote in all cases, has a casting vote in case of a tie. The executive head is himself eventually elective every year by the legislative department, and his council is every year chosen by and from the members of the same department. Several of the officers of the state are also appointed by the legislature. And the members of the judiciary department are appointed by the executive department.

The constitution of Massachusetts has observed a sufficient though less pointed caution in expressing this fundamental article of liberty. It declares "that the legislative department shall never exercise the executive and judicial powers, or either of them; the executive shall never exercise the legislative and judicial powers, or either of them; the judicial shall never exercise the legislative and executive powers, or either of them." The declaration corresponds precisely with the doctrine of Montesquieu, as it has been explained, and is not a in a single point violated by the plan of the convention. It goes no farther than to prohibit any one of the entire departments from exercising the powers of another department. In the very Constitution to which it is prefixed, a partial mixture of powers has been admitted. The executive magistrate has a qualified negative on the legislative body, and the Senate, which is part of the legislature, is a court of impeachment for members both of the executive and judiciary departments. The members of the judiciary department, again, are appointed by the executive department, and removable by the same authority on the address of the two legislative branches. Lastly, a number of the officers of government are annually appointed by the legislative department. As the appointment to offices, particularly executive offices, is in its nature an executive function, the compilers of the Constitution have, in this last point at east, violated the rue established by themselves...[Publius next reviews other state constitutions.],

In citing these cases, in which the legislative, executive, and judiciary departments have not been kept totally separate and distinct, I wish not to be regarded as an advocate for the particular organizations of the several State governments. I am fully aware that among the many excellent principles which they exemplify they carry strong marks of the haste, and still stronger of the inexperience, under which they were framed. It is but too obvious that in some instances the fundamental principle under consideration has been violated by too great a mixture, and even an actual consolidation of the different powers; and in no instance has a competent provision been made for maintaining in practice the separation delineated on paper. What I have wished to evince is that the charge brought against the proposed Constitution of violating the sacred maxim of free government is warranted neither by the real meaning annexed to that maxim by its author, nor by the sense in which it has hitherto been understood in America. This interesting subject will be resumed in the ensuing paper.

Federalist No. 48

It was shown in the last paper that the political apothegm there examined does not require that the legislative, executive, and judiciary departments should be wholly unconnected with each other. I shall undertake, in the next place, to show that unless these departments be so far connected and blended as to give to each a constitutional control over the others, the degree of separation which the maxim requires, as essential to free government, can never in practice be duly maintained.

It is agreed on all sides that the powers belonging to one of the departments ought not to be directly and completely administered by either of the other departments. It is equally evident that none of them ought to possess, directly or indirectly, an overruling influence over the others in the administration of their respective powers. It will not be denied that power is of an encroaching nature and that it ought to be effectually restrained from passing the limits assigned to it. After discriminating, therefore, in theory, the several classes of power, as they may in their nature be legislative, executive, or judiciary, the next and most difficult task is to provide some practical security for each, against the invasion of the others. What this security ought to be is the great problem to be solved.

Will it be sufficient to mark, with precision, the boundaries of these departments in the constitution of the government, and to trust to these parchment barriers against the encroaching spirit of power? This is the security which appears to have been principally relied on by the compilers of most of the American constitutions. But experience assures us that the efficacy of the provision has been greatly overrated; and that some adequate defense is indispensably necessary for the more feeble against the more powerful members of the government. The legislative department is everywhere extending the sphere of its activity and drawing all power into its impetuous vortex.

The founders of our republics have so much merit for the wisdom which they have displayed that no task can be less pleasing than that of pointing out the errors into which they have fallen. A respect for truth, however, obliges us to remark that they seem never for a moment to have turned their eyes from the danger, to liberty, from the overgrown and all-grasping prerogative of an hereditary magistrate, supported and fortified by an hereditary branch of the legislative authority. They seem never to have recollected the danger from legislative usurpations, which, by assembling all power in the same hands, must lead to the same tyranny as is threatened by executive usurpations.

In a government where numerous and extensive prerogatives are placed in the hands of an hereditary monarch, the executive department is very justly regarded as the source of danger, and watched with all the jealousy which a zeal for liberty ought to inspire. In a democracy, where a multitude of people exercise in person the legislative functions and are continually exposed, by their incapacity for regular deliberation and concerted measures, to the ambitious intrigues of their executive magistrates, tyranny may well be apprehended, on some favorable emergency, to start up in the same quarter. But in a representative republic where the executive magistracy is carefully limited, both in the extent and duration of its power; and where the legislative power is exercised by an assembly, which is inspired by a supposed influence over the people with an intrepid confidence in its own strength; which is sufficiently numerous to feel all the passions which actuate a multitude, yet not so numerous as to be incapable of pursuing the objects of its passions by means which reason prescribes; it is against the enterprising ambition of this department that the people ought to indulge all their jealousy and exhaust their precautions.

The legislative department derives a superiority in our governments from other circumstances. Its constitutional powers being at once more extensive, and less susceptible of precise limits, it can, with the greater facility, mask, under complicated and indirect measures, the encroachments which it makes on the coordinate departments. It is not unfrequently a question of real nicety in legislative bodies whether the operation of a particular measure will, or will not, extend beyond the legislative sphere. On the other side, the executive power being restrained within a narrower compass and being more simple in its nature, and the judiciary being described by landmarks still less uncertain, projects of usurpation by either of these departments would immediately betray and defeat themselves. Nor is this all; as the legislative department alone has access to the pockets of the people, and has in some constitutions full discretion, and in all a prevailing influence, over the pecuniary rewards of those who fill the other departments, a dependence is thus created in the latter, which gives still greater facility to encroachments of the former...

The conclusion which I am warranted in drawing from these observations is that a mere demarcation on parchment of the constitutional limits of the several departments is not a sufficient guard against those encroachments which lead to a tyrannical concentration of all powers of government in the same hands.

Federalist No. 51

To what expedient, then, shall we finally resort, for maintaining in practice the necessary partition of power among the several departments as laid down in the constitution? The only answer that can be given is that as all those exterior provisions are found to be inadequate the defect must be supplied by so contriving the interior structure of the government as that its several constituent parts may, by their mutual relations, be the means of keeping each other in their proper places. Without presuming to undertake a full development of this important idea I will hazard a few general observations which may perhaps place it in a clearer light, and enable us to form a more correct judgment of the principles and structure of the government planned by the convention.

In order to lay a due foundation for that separate and distinct exercise of the different powers of government, which to a certain extent is admitted on all hands to be essential to the preservation of liberty, it is evident that each department should have a will of its own; and consequently should be so constituted that the members of each should have as little agency as possible in the appointment of the member of the others. Were this principle rigorously adhered to, it would require that all the appointments for the supreme executive, legislative, and judiciary magistracies should be drawn from the same fountain of authority, the people, through channels having no communication whatever with one another. Perhaps such a plan of constructing the several departments would be less difficult in practice than it may in contemplation appear. Some difficulties, however, and some additional expense would attend the execution of it. Some deviations, therefore, from the principle must be admitted. In the constitution of the judiciary department in particular, it might be inexpedient to insist rigorously on the principle: first, because peculiar qualifications being essential in the members, the primary consideration ought to be to select that mode of choice which best secures these qualifications; second, because the permanent tenure by which the appointments are held in that department must soon destroy all sense of dependence on the authority conferring them.

It is equally evident that the members of each department should be as little dependent as possible on those of the others for the emoluments annexed to their offices. Were the executive magistrate, or the judges, not independent of the legislature in this particular, their independence in every other would be merely nominal.

But the great security against a gradual concentration of the several powers in the same department consists in giving to those who administer each department the necessary constitutional means and personal motives to resist encroachments of the others. The provision for defense must in this, as in all other cases, be made commensurate to the danger of the attack. Ambition must be made to counteract ambition. The interest of the man must be connected with the constitutional rights of the place. It may be a reflection of human nature that such devices should be necessary to control the abuses of government. But what is government itself but the greatest of all reflections on human nature? If men were angels, no government would be necessary. If angels were to govern men, neither external nor internal controls on government would be necessary. In framing a government which is to be administered by men over men, the great difficulty lies in this: you must first enable the government to control the governed; and in the next place oblige it to control itself. A dependence on the people is, no doubt, the primary control on the government; but experience has taught mankind the necessity of auxiliary precautions.

The policy of supplying, by opposite and rival interests, the defect of better motives, might be traced through the whole system of human affairs, private as well as public. We see it particularly displayed in all the subordinate distributions of power, where the constant aim is to divide and arrange the several offices in such a manner as that each may be a check on the other—that the private interest of every individual may be sentinel over the public rights. These inventions of prudence cannot be less requisite in the distribution of the supreme powers of the State.

But it is not possible to give each department an equal power of self-defense. In republican government, the legislative authority necessarily predominates. The remedy for this inconveniency is to divide the legislature into different branches and to render them, by different modes of election and different principles of action, as little concerned with each other as the nature of their common functions and their common dependence on the society will admit. It may even be necessary to guard against dangerous encroachments by still further precautions. As the weight of the legislative authority requires that it should be thus divided, the weakness of the executive may require, on the other hand, that it should be fortified. An absolute negative on the legislature appears, at first view, to be the natural defense with which the executive magistrate should be armed. But perhaps it would be neither altogether safe nor alone sufficient. On ordinary occasions it might not be exerted with the requisite firmness, and on extraordinary occasions it might be perfidiously abused. May not this defect of an absolute negative be supplied by some qualified connection between this weaker department and the weaker branch of the stronger department, by which the latter may be led to support the constitutional rights of the former, without being too much detached from the rights of its own department?

If the principles on which these observations are founded be just, as I persuade myself they are, and they be applied as a criterion to the several State constitutions, and to the federal Constitution, it will be found that if the latter does not perfectly correspond with them, the former are infinitely less able to bear such a test.

There are, moreover, two considerations particularly applicable to the federal system of America, which place that system in a very interesting point of view.

First. In a single republic, all the power surrendered by the people is submitted to the administration of a single government; and the usurpations are guarded against by a division of the government into distinct and separate departments. In the compound republic of America, the power surrendered by the people is first divided between two distinct governments, and then the portion allotted to each subdivided among distinct and separate departments. Hence a double security arises to the rights of the people. The different governments will control each other, at the same time that each will be controlled by itself.

Second. It is of great importance in a republic not only to guard the society against the oppression of its rulers, but to guard one part of the society against the injustices of the other part. Different interests necessarily exist in different classes of citizens. If a majority be united by a common interests, the rights of the minority will be insecure. There are but two methods of providing against this evil: the one by creating a will in the community independent of the majority—that is, of the society itself; the other, by comprehending in the society so many separate descriptions of citizens as will render an unjust combination of a majority of the whole very improbably, if not impracticable. The first method prevails in all governments possessing an hereditary or self-appointed authority. This, at best, is but a precarious security; because a power independent of the society may as well espouse the unjust views of the major as the rightful interests of the minor party, and may possible be turned against both parties. The second method will be exemplified in the federal republic of the United States. Whilst all authority in it will be derived from and dependent on the society, the society itself will be broken into so many parts, interests and classes of citizens, that the rights of individuals, or of the minority, will be in little danger from interested combinations of the majority. In a free government the security for civil rights must be the same as that for religious rights. It consists in the one case in the multiplicity of interests; and in the other the multiplicity of sects. The degree of security in both cases will depend on the number of interests and sects; and this may be presumed to depend on the extent of country and number of people comprehended under the same government. This view of the subject must particularly recommend a proper federal system to all the sincere and considerate friends of republican government, since it shows that in exact proportion as the territory of the Union may be formed into more circumscribed Confederacies, or States, oppressive combinations of a majority will be facilitated; the best security, under the republican forms, for the rights of every class of citizen, will be diminished; and consequently the stability and independence of some member of the government, the only other security, must be proportionally increased. Justice is the end of government. It is the end of civil society. It ever has been and ever will be pursued until it be obtained, or until liberty be lost in the pursuit. In a society under the forms of which the stronger faction can readily unite and oppress the weaker, anarchy may as truly be said to reign as in a state of nature, where the weaker individual is not secured against the violence of the stronger; and as, in the latter state, even the stronger individuals are prompted, by the uncertainty of theor condition, to submit to a government which may protect the weak as well as themselves; so, in the former state, will the more powerful factions or parties be gradually induced, by a like motive, to wish for a government which will protect all parties, the weaker as well as the more powerful. It can be little doubted that if the State of Rhode Island was separated from the Confederacy and left to itself, the insecurity of rights under the popular form of government within such narrow limits would be displayed by such reiterated oppressions of factious majorities that some power altogether independent of the people would soon be called for by the voice of the very factions whose misrule had proved the necessity of it. In the extended republic of the United States, and among the great variety of interests, parties, and sects which it embraces, a coalition of a majority of the whole society could seldom take place on any other principle than those of justice and the general good; whilst there being thus less danger to a minor from the will of a major party, there must be less pretext, also, to provide for the security of the former, by introducing into the government a will not dependent on the latter, or, in other words, a will independent of the society itself. It is no less certain than it is important, notwithstanding the contrary opinions which have been entertained, that the larger the society, provided it lie within a practicable sphere, the more duly capable it will be of self-government. And happily for the *republican cause*, the practicable sphere may be carried to a very great extent by a judicious modification and mixture of the *federal principle*.

HOW WELL DID YOU UNDERSTAND THIS SELECTION?

1. *Federalist No. 10* discusses the "problem" of factions. What are factions and why do they pose a problem for the nation?

2. According to Madison in *Federalist No. 10*, what are the essential differences between a democracy and a republic?

3. Employing the reasoning of *Federalist Papers Numbers 47, 48, and 49*, explain why a free nation requires that the institutions of government have both separate and shared powers.

DEMOCRACY IN AMERICA
ALEXIS de TOCQUEVILLE

According to official records, the French aristocrat and lawyer Alexis de Tocqueville came to America in May 1831 in order to study its penal system. However, he examined much more. During his nine-month visit Tocqueville traveled throughout the country visiting virtually every major city. In these cities he talked with both ordinary citizens and a long list of prominent Americans including John Quincy Adams, Nicholas Biddle (president of the Bank of New York), Supreme Court Justices Salmon P. Chase and John McLean, Sam Houston, Andrew Jackson, and Daniel Webster. All of what Tocqueville learned about democracy in America from his conversations with these people was recorded in journals, which were published in 1835. The two-volume publication provided, among other things, insights into "equality" and the lack thereof for certain Americans.

EXCERPTS FROM DEMOCRACY IN AMERICA

I. Equality

Amongst the novel objects that attracted my attention during my stay in the United States, nothing struck me more forcibly than the general equality of condition among the people. I readily discovered the prodigious influence which this primary fact exercises on the whole course of society; it gives a peculiar direction to public opinion, and a peculiar tenor to the laws; it imparts new maxims to the governing authorities, and peculiar habits to the governed.

I soon perceived that the influence of this fact extends far beyond the political character and the laws of the country, and that it has no less empire over civil society than over the government; it creates opinion, gives birth to new sentiments, founds novel customs, and modifies whatever it does not produce. The more I advanced in the study of American society, the more I perceived that this equality of condition is the fundamental fact from which all others seem to derived, and the central point at which all my observations constantly terminated.

"Introduction," 3.

II. Slaves, Servants and Paupers

It is not always feasible to consult the whole people, either directly or indirectly, in the formation of the law; but it cannot be denied that, when this is possible, the authority of the law is much augmented....

In the United States, except slaves, servants, and paupers supported by the townships, there is no class of persons, who do not exercise the elective franchise, and who do not indirectly contribute to make the laws.

"What Are the Real Advantages Which American
Society Derives from Democratic Government?" 83-84.

I said one day to an inhabitant of Pennsylvania, "Be so good as to explain to me how it happens, that in a State founded by Quakers, and celebrated for its toleration, free Blacks are not allowed to exercise civil rights. They pay taxes; is it not fair that they should vote?"

"You insult us," replied my informant, "if you imagine that our legislators could have committed so gross an act of injustice and intolerance."

"Then the Blacks possess the right of voting in this country?"

"Without doubt."

"How comes it, then, that at the polling-booth, this morning, I did not perceive a single Negro in the meeting?"

"This is not the fault of the law: the Negroes have an undisputed right of voting; but they voluntarily abstain from making their appearance."

"A very pretty piece of modesty on their part!" rejoined I.

"Why, the truth is, that they are not disinclined to vote, but they are afraid of being maltreated; in this country, the law is sometimes unable to maintain its authority, without the support of the majority. But in this case, the majority entertains very strong prejudices against the Blacks, and the magistrates are unable to protect them in the exercise of their legal rights."

"Unlimited Power of the Majority in the United
States and Its Consequences," 94-95.

III. Women

Long before an American girl arrives at the marriageable age, her emancipation from maternal control begins: she has scarcely ceased to be a child, when she already thinks for herself, speaks with freedom, and acts on her own impulse. The great scene of the world is constantly open to her view: far from seeking to conceal it from her, it is every day disclosed more completely, and she is taught to survey it with a firm and calm gaze....

I have been frequently surprised, and almost frightened, at the singular address and happy boldness with which young women in America contrive to manage their thoughts and their language, amidst all the difficulties of free conversation; a philosopher would have stumbled at every step along the narrow path which they trod without accident and, without effort ....

As it is neither possible not desirable to keep a young woman in perpetual and complete ignorance, they [Americans] hasten to give her a precocious knowledge on all subjects. Far from hiding the corruptions of the world from her, they prefer that she should see them at once, and train herself to shun them; and they hold it of more importance to protect her conduct, than to be overscrupulous of the innocence of her thoughts.

"Education of Young Women in the United States," 236-238.

In America, the independence of woman is irrecoverably lost in the bonds of matrimony.

"The Young Woman in the Character of a Wife," 239.

Source: Tocqueville, Alexis de. *Democracy in America*, edited by Andrew Hacker. New York: Washington Square Press, Inc., 1964.

HOW WELL DID YOU UNDERSTAND THIS SELECTION?

1. According to official records, why did Tocqueville come to America?

2. What contradiction did Tocqueville observe about the freedom and independence of American women?

3.   A citizen interviewed by Tocqueville gave what explanation for why "free Blacks" did not vote in Pennsylvania?

DECLARATION OF SENTIMENTS AND RESOLUTIONS:
ADOPTED BY THE SENECA FALLS Convention
July 19-20, 1848

Paternalistic attitudes toward women in the United States effectively kept them out of the political process for many years. With a few exceptions, it was not until the abolitionist movement of the 1830s that women became involved in the political process in any significant numbers. Many women found it easy to identify with the plight of the slaves since both were the victims of male tyranny. Women engaged in the abolitionist movement believed that in abolishing slavery they could also set themselves free from the paternalistic attitudes that held them in bondage. A feminist ideology began to develop within the abolitionist movement that espoused gender equity.

Although the antislavery societies served as a vehicle for feminist ideology, they did not openly embrace or offer leadership roles to women. Male abolitionists were divided over the issue of women's rights and what role women should play in the movement. At the World Anti-Slavery Convention held in London in 1840, the delegates refused to let women participate. Two New Yorkers, Elizabeth Cady Stanton and Lucretia Mott, were forced to sit behind curtains so that they would not be seen let alone heard. In 1848, as a direct response to their treatment at the abolitionist's convention, Stanton and Mott organized a convention in Seneca Falls, New York that specifically focused on the rights of women. The convention produced the "Declaration of Sentiments" that was modeled on the Declaration of Independence. It proclaimed that "all men and women are created equal" and that men had usurped women's freedom and dignity. It protested against double standards and asked for women's rights to property, children, and the vote. It argued that "because women do feel themselves aggrieved, oppressed, and fraudulently deprived of their most sacred rights, we insist that they have immediate admission to all the rights and privileges which belong to them as citizens of the United States."

The Seneca Falls Convention established the groundwork for the women's rights movement. It was the first time that women had made a public statement regarding their struggle for equality. The women at the convention not only called for educational and professional opportunities for women but also demanded the right to vote.

The Declaration of Sentiments adopted at the Seneca Falls convention officially stated the intent of the women's movement; however, the struggle for equal political and economic rights for women continues today. Although women were constitutionally granted the right to vote in 1920, it was many years before their voice was heard in the political arena.

When, in the course of human events, it becomes necessary for one portion of the family of man to assume among the people of the earth a position different from that which they have hitherto occupied, but one to which the laws of nature and of nature's God entitle them, a decent respect to the opinions of mankind requires that they should declare the causes that impel them to such a course.

We hold these truths to be self-evident: that all men and women are created equal; that they are endowed by their Creator with certain inalienable rights; that among these are life, liberty, and the pursuit of happiness; that to secure these rights governments are instituted, deriving their just powers from the consent of the governed. Whenever any form of government becomes destructive of these ends, it is the right of those who suffer from it to refuse allegiance to it, and to insist upon the institution of a new government, laying its foundation on such principles, and organizing its powers in such form, as to them shall seem most likely to effect their safety and happiness. Prudence, indeed, will dictate that governments long established should not be changed for light and transient causes; and accordingly all experience hath shown that mankind are more disposed to suffer, while evils are sufferable, than to right themselves by abolishing the forms to which they were accustomed. But when a long train of abuses and usurpations, pursuing invariably the same object, evinces a design to reduce them under absolute despotism, it is their duty to throw off such government, and to provide new guards for their future security. Such has been the patient sufferance of the women under this government, and such is now the necessity which constrains them to demand the equal station to which they are entitled.

The history of mankind is a history of repeated injuries and usurpations on the part of man toward woman, having in direct object the establishment of an absolute tyranny over her. To prove this, let facts be submitted to a candid world.

He has never permitted her to exercise her inalienable right to the elective franchise.

He has compelled her to submit to laws, in the formation of which she had no voice.

He has withheld from her rights which are given to the most ignorant and degraded men—both natives and foreigners.

Having deprived her of this first right of a citizen, the elective franchise, thereby leaving her without representation in the halls of legislation, he has oppressed her on all sides.

He has made her, if married, in the eye of the law, civilly dead.

He has taken from her all right in property, even to the wages she earns.

He has made her, morally, an irresponsible being, as she can commit many crimes with impunity, provided they be done in the presence of her husband. In the covenant of marriage, she is compelled to promise obedience to her husband, he becoming to all intents and purposes, her master — the law giving him power to deprive her of her liberty, and to administer chastisement.

He has so framed the laws of divorce, as to what shall be the proper causes, and in case of separation, to whom the guardianship of the children shall be given, as to be wholly regardless of the happiness of women—the law, in all cases, going upon a false supposition of the supremacy of man, and giving all power into his hands.

After depriving her of all rights as a married woman, if single, and the owner of property, he has taxed her to support a government which recognizes her only when her property can be made profitable to it.

He has monopolized nearly all the profitable employments, and from those she is permitted to follow, she receives but a scanty remuneration. He closes against her all the avenues to wealth and distinction which he considers most honorable to himself. As a teacher of theology, medicine, or law, she is not known.

He has denied her the facilities for obtaining a thorough education, all colleges being closed against her.

He allows her in Church, as well as State, but a subordinate position, claiming Apostolic authority for her exclusion from the ministry, and, with some exceptions, from any public participation in the affairs of the Church.

He has created a false public sentiment by giving to the world a different code of morals for men and women, by which moral delinquencies which exclude women from society, are not only tolerated, but deemed of little account in man.

He has usurped the prerogative to Jehovah himself, claiming it as his right to assign for her a sphere of action, when that belongs to her conscience and to her God.

He has endeavored, in every way that he could, to destroy her confidence in her own powers, to lessen her self-respect, and to make her willing to lead a dependent and abject life.

Now, in view of this entire disfranchisement of one-half the people of this country, their social and religious degradation — in view of the unjust laws above mentioned, and because women do feel themselves aggrieved, oppressed, and fraudulently deprived of their most sacred rights, we insist that they have immediate admission to all the rights and privileges which belong to them as citizens of the United States.

In entering upon the great work before us, we anticipate no small amount of misconception, misrepresentation, and ridicule; but we shall use every instrumentality within our power to effect our object. We shall employ agents, circulate tracts, petition the State and National legislatures, and endeavor to enlist the pulpit and the press in our behalf. We hope this Convention will be followed by a series of Conventions embracing every part of the country.

[The following resolutions were discussed by Lucretia Mott, Thomas and Mary Ann McClintock, Amy Post, Catharine A. F. Stebbins, and others, and were adopted:]

WHEREAS, The great precept of nature is conceded to be, that "man shall pursue his own true and substantial happiness." Blackstone in his Commentaries remarks, that this law of Nature being coeval with mankind, and dictated by God himself, is of course superior in obligation to any other. It is binding over all the globe, in all countries and at all times; no human laws are of any validity if contrary to this, and such of them as are valid, derive all their force, and all their validity, and all their authority, mediately and immediately, from this original; therefore,

Resolved, That such laws as conflict, in any way, with the true and substantial happiness of woman, are contrary to the great precept of nature and of no validity, for this is "superior in obligation to any other."

Resolved, That all laws which prevent woman from occupying such a station in society as her conscience shall dictate, or which place her in a position inferior to that of man, are contrary to the great precept of nature, and therefore of no force or authority.

Resolved, That woman is man's equal — was intended to be so by the Creator, and the highest good of the race demands that she should be recognized as such.

Resolved, That the women of this country ought to be enlightened in regard to the laws under which they live, that they may no longer publish their degradation by declaring themselves satisfied with their present position, nor their ignorance, by asserting that they have all the rights they want.

Resolved, That inasmuch as man, while claiming for himself intellectual superiority, does accord to woman moral superiority, it is preeminently his duty to encourage her to speak and teach, as she has an opportunity, in all religious assemblies.

Resolved, That the same amount of virtue, delicacy, and refinement of behavior that is required of woman in the social state, should also be required of man, and the same transgressions should be visited with equal severity on both man and woman.

Resolved, That the objection of indelicacy and impropriety, which is so often brought against woman when she addresses a public audience, comes with a very ill-grace from those who encourage, by their attendance, her appearance on the stage, in the concert, or in feats of the circus.

Resolved, That woman has too long rested satisfied in the circumscribed limits which corrupt customs and a perverted application of the Scriptures have marked out for her, and that it is time she should move in the enlarged sphere which her great Creator has assigned her.

Resolved, That it is the duty of the women of this country to secure to themselves their sacred right to the elective franchise.

Resolved, That the equality of human rights results necessarily from the fact of the identity of the race in capabilities and responsibilities.

Resolved, therefore, That, being invested by the Creator with the same capabilities, and the same consciousness of responsibility for their exercise, it is demonstrably the right and duty of woman, equally with man, to promote every righteous cause by every righteous means; and especially in regard to the great subjects of morals and religion, it is self-evidently her right to participate with her brother in teaching them, both in private and in public, by writing and by speaking, by any instrumentalities proper to be used, and in any assemblies proper to be held; and this being a self-evident truth growing out of the divinely implanted principles of human nature, any custom or authority adverse to it, whether modern or wearing the hoary sanction of antiquity, is to be regarded as a self-evident falsehood, and at war with mankind.

HOW WELL DID YOU UNDERSTAND THIS SELECTION?

1. What events and actions lead to the gathering at Seneca Falls?

2. What were the major complaints the women at Seneca Falls expressed against their male counterparts?

3. What remedy(ies) do the attendees at the convention offer to address their concerns?

4. In what specific ways were women denied property, legal, parental, and political rights?

PART II

The Political Process

DRED SCOTT: Does Crossing a State Boundary Line Make A Man Free?

*The anti-slavery movement was dealt a near fatal blow when the United States Supreme Court heard arguments in the **Dred Scott v Sandford** case in 1857. Dred Scott was a African-American slave residing in a slave state. Dred Scott's owner died. The slaves were willed to another member of the family. In this case, Dred Scott and his owner moved to Missouri, a free state. The anti-slavery movement seized upon this opportunity to press for Scott's freedom. The questions before the Court were a) was Scott a citizen of the United States; b) if a citizen, did Scott have the right to sue; and c) if a slave was relocated from a slave to a free state, was this person now free from the bondage of slavery. The following article is a partial excerpt of the Court's 7-2 ruling against Scott. It was written by Chief Justice Taney.*

Mr. Chief Justice Taney Delivered the Opinion of the Court. The question is simply this: Can a negro [African American], whose ancestors were imported into this country, and sold as slaves, become a member of the political community formed and brought into existence by the constitution of the United States, and as such become entitled to all the rights, and privileges, and immunities, guaranteed by that instrument to the citizen? One of which rights is the privilege of suing in a court of the United States in the cases specified in the constitution.

It will be observed, that the plea applies to that class of persons only whose ancestors were negroes [African American] of the African race, and imported into this country, and sold and held as slaves. The only matter in issue before the court, therefore, is, whether the descendants of such slaves, when they shall be emancipated, or who are born of parents who had become free before their birth, are citizens of a State, in the sense in which the word citizen is used in the constitution of the United States. And this being the only matter in dispute on the pleadings, the court must be understood as speaking in this opinion of that class only, that is, of those persons who are the descendants of Africans who were imported into this country, and sold as slaves.

The words "people of the United States" and "citizens" are synonymous terms, and mean the same thing. They both describe the political body who, according to our republican institutions, form the sovereignty, and who hold the power and conduct the government through their representatives. They are what we familiarly call the "sovereign people," and every citizen is one of this people, and a constituent member of this sovereignty. The question before us is, whether the class of persons described in the plea in abatement compose a portion of this people, and are constituent members of this sovereignty? We think they are not, and that they are not included, and were not intended to be included, under the word "citizens" in the constitution, and can therefore claim none of the rights and privileges which that instrument provides for and secures to citizens of the United States. On the contrary, they were at that time considered as a subordinate and inferior class of beings, who had been subjugated by the dominant race, and, whether emancipated or not, yet remained subject to their authority, and had no rights or privileges but such as those who held the power and the government might choose to grant them.

In discussing this question, we must not confound the rights of citizenship which a State may confer within its own limits, and the rights of citizenship as a member of the Union. It does not by any means follow, because he has all the rights and privileges of a citizen of a State, that he must be a citizen of the United States. He may have all of the rights and privileges of the citizen of a State, and yet not be entitled to the rights and privileges of a citizen in any other State. For, previous to the adoption of the constitution of the United States, every State had the undoubted right to confer on whomsoever it pleased the character of citizen, and to endow him with all its rights. But this character of course was confined to the boundaries of the State, and gave him no rights or privileges in other States beyond those secured to him by the laws of nations and the comity of States. Nor have the several States surrendered the power of conferring these rights and privileges by adopting the constitution of the United States.

It is very clear, therefore, that no State can, by any act or law of its own, passed since the adoption of the constitution, introduce a new member into the political community created by the constitution of the United States. It cannot make him a member of this community by making him a member of its own. And for the same reason it cannot introduce any person, or description of persons, who were not intended to be embraced in this new political family, which the constitution brought into existence, but were intended to be excluded from it.

The question then arises, whether the provisions of the constitution, in relation to the personal rights and privileges to which the citizen of a State should be entitled, embraced the negro [African American] race, at that time in this country, or who might afterwards be imported, who had then or should afterwards be made free in any State; and to put it in the power of a single State to make him a citizen of the United States, and endue him with the full rights of citizenship in every other State without their consent? Does the constitution of the United States act upon him whenever he shall be made free under the laws of a State, and raised there to the rank of a citizen, and immediately clothe him with all the privileges of a citizen in every other State, and in its own courts?

The court think the affirmative of these propositions cannot be maintained. And if it cannot, the plaintiff in error could not be a citizen of the State of Missouri, within the meaning of the constitution of the United States, and, consequently, was not entitled to sue in its courts.

It is true, every person, and every class and description of persons, who were at the time of the adoption of the constitution recognized as citizens in the several States, became also citizens of this new political body; but none other; it was formed by them, and for them and their posterity, but for no one else. And the personal rights and privileges guaranteed to citizens of this new sovereignty were intended to embrace those only who were then members of the several State communities, or who should afterwards by birthright or otherwise become members, according to the provisions of the constitution and the principles on which it was founded. It was the union of those who were at that time members of distinct and separate political communities into one political family, whose power, for certain specified purposes, was to extend over the whole territory of the United States. And it gave to each citizen rights and privileges outside of his State which he did not before possess, and placed him in every other State upon a perfect equality with its own citizens as to rights of person and rights of property; it made him a citizen of the United States.

In the opinion of the court, the legislation and histories of the times, and the language used in the declaration of independence, show, that neither the class of persons who had been imported as slaves, nor their descendants, whether they had become free or not, were then acknowledged as a part of the people.

They had for more than a century before been regarded as beings of an inferior order, and altogether unfit to associate with the white race, either in social or political relations; and so far inferior, that they had no rights which the white man was bound to respect...

But there are two clauses in the constitution which point directly and specifically to the negro [African American] race as a separate class of persons, and show clearly that they were not regarded as a portion of the people or citizens of the government then formed.

One of these clauses reserves to each of the thirteen States the right to import slaves until the year 1808, if it thinks proper.... And by the other provision the States pledge themselves to each other to maintain the right of property of the master, by delivering up to him any slave who may have escaped from his service, and be found within their respective territories....

The only two provisions which point to them and include them, treat them as property, and make it the duty of the government to protect it; no other power, in relation to this race, is to be found in the constitution; and as it is a government of special, delegated, powers, no authority beyond these two provisions can be constitutionally exercised. The government of the United States had no right to interfere for any other purpose but that of protecting the rights of the owner, leaving it altogether with the several States to deal with this race, whether emancipated or not, as each State may think justice, humanity, and the interests and safety of society, require. The States evidently intended to reserve this power exclusively to themselves....

[U]pon a full and careful consideration of the subject, the court is of opinion, that, upon the facts stated ...., Dred Scott was not a citizen of Missouri within the meaning of the constitution of the United States, and not entitled as such to sue in its courts.

The act of Congress, upon which the plaintiff relies, declares that slavery and involuntary servitude, except as a punishment for crime, shall be forever prohibited in all that part of the territory ceded by France, under the name of Louisiana, which lies north of thirty-six degrees thirty minutes north latitude and not included within the limits of Missouri. And the difficulty which meets us at the threshold of this part of the inquiry is whether Congress was authorized to pass this law under any of the powers granted to it by the Constitution; for, if the authority is not given by that instrument, it is the duty of this Court to declare it void and inoperative and incapable of conferring freedom upon anyone who is held as a slave under the laws of any one of the states.

The counsel for the plaintiff has laid much stress upon that article in the Constitution which confers on Congress the power "to dispose of and make all needful rules and regulations respecting the territory or other property belonging to the United States"; but, in the judgment of the Court, that provision has no bearing on the present controversy, and the power there given, whatever it may be, is confined, and was intended to be confined, to the territory which at that time belonged to, or was claimed by, the United States and was within their boundaries as settled by the treaty with Great Britain and can have no influence upon a territory afterward acquired from a foreign government.

We do not mean, however, to question the power of Congress in this respect. The power to expand the territory of the United States by the admission of new states is plainly given; and in the construction of this power by all the departments of the government, it has been held to authorize the acquisition of territory, not fit for admission at the time, but to be admitted as soon as its population and situation would entitle it to admission. It is acquired to become a state and not to be held as a colony and governed by Congress with absolute authority; and, as the propriety of admitting a new state is committed to the sound discretion of Congress, the power to acquire territory for that purpose, to be held by the United States until it is in a suitable condition to become a state upon an equal footing with the other states, must rest upon the same discretion. It is a question for the political department of the government, and not the judicial; and whatever the political department of the government shall recognize as within the limits of the United States, the judicial department is also bound to recognize, and to administer in it the laws of the United States, so far as they apply, and to maintain in the territory the authority and rights of the government, and also the personal rights and rights of property of individual citizens, as secured by the Constitution. All we mean to say on this point is that, as there is no express regulation in the Constitution defining the power which the general government may exercise over the person or property of a citizen in a territory thus acquired, the Court must necessarily look to the provisions and principles of the Constitution, and its distribution of powers, for the rules and principles by which its decision must be governed.

Taking this rule to guide us, it may be safely assumed that citizens of the United States who migrate to a territory belonging to the people of the United States cannot be ruled as mere colonists, dependent upon the will of the general government, and to be governed by any laws it may think proper to impose. The principle upon which our governments rest, and upon which alone they continue to exist, is the union of states, sovereign and independent within their own limits in their internal and domestic concerns, and bound together as one people by a general government, possessing certain enumerated and restricted powers, delegated to it by the people of the several states, and exercising supreme authority within the scope of the powers granted to it, throughout the dominion of the United States. A power, therefore, in the general government to obtain and hold colonies and dependent territories, over which they might legislate without restriction, would be inconsistent with its own existence in its present form. Whatever it acquires, it acquires for the benefit of the people of the several states who created it.

But the power of Congress over the person or property of a citizen can never be a mere discretionary power under our Constitution and form of government. The powers of the government and the rights and privileges of the citizen are regulated and plainly defined by the Constitution itself. And, when the territory becomes a part of the United States, the federal government enters into possession in the character impressed upon it by those who created it. It enters upon it with its powers over the citizen strictly defined and limited by the Constitution, from which it derives its own existence, and by virtue of which alone it continues to exist and act as a government and sovereignty. It has no power of any kind beyond it; and it cannot, when it enters a territory of the United States, put off its character and assume discretionary or despotic powers which the Constitution has denied to it. It cannot create for itself a new character separated from the citizens of the United States and the duties it owes them under the provisions of the Constitution. The territory, being a part of the United States, the government and the citizen both enter it under the authority of the Constitution, with their respective rights defined and marked out; and the federal government can exercise no power over his person or property, beyond what that instrument confers, nor lawfully deny any right which it has reserved....

But, in considering the question before us, it must be borne in mind that there is no law of nations standing between the people of the United States and their government and interfering with their relation to each other. The powers of the government and the rights of the citizen under it are positive and practical regulations plainly written down. The people of the United States have delegated to it certain enumerated powers and forbidden it to exercise others. It has no power over the person or property of a citizen but what the citizens of the United States have granted. And no laws or usages of other nations, or reasoning of statesmen or jurists upon the relations of master and slave, can enlarge the powers of the government or take from the citizens the rights they have reserved. And if the Constitution recognizes the right of property of the master in a slave, and makes no distinction between that description of property and other property owned by a citizen, no tribunal, acting under the authority of the United States, whether it be legislative, executive, or judicial, has a right to draw such a distinction or deny to it the benefit of the provisions and guarantees which have been provided for the protection of private property against the encroachments of the government.

Now, as we have already said in an earlier part of this opinion, upon a different point, the right of property in a slave is distinctly and expressly affirmed in the Constitution. The right to traffic in it, like an ordinary article of merchandise and property, was guaranteed to the citizens of the United States, in every state that might desire it, for twenty years. And the government in express terms is pledged to protect it in all future time if the slave escapes from his owner. That is done in plain words—too plain to be misunderstood. And no word can be found in the Constitution which gives Congress a greater power over slave property or which entities property of that kind to less protection than property of any other description. The only power conferred is the power coupled with the duty of guarding and protecting the owner in his rights.

Upon these considerations it is the opinion of the Court that the act of Congress which prohibited a citizen from holding and owning property of this kind in the territory of the United States north of the line therein mentioned is not warranted by the Constitution and is therefore void; and that neither Dred Scott himself, nor any of his family, were made free by being carried into this territory; even if they had been carried there by the owner with the intention of becoming a permanent resident...

HOW WELL DID YOU UNDERSTAND THIS SELECTION?

1. What was the basis of the Court's ruling that Mr. Scott was not a citizen of the United States?

2. What was the basis of the Court's ruling that Mr. Scott did not possess the right to sue in a court of law?

3. What was the Court's rationale in determining that Mr. Scott was still a slave although he currently resided in a state that did not recognize slavery?

The election of 1860 revealed a Democratic Party sharply divided over slavery and the actions the southern states should take if slavery was indeed abolished. Subsequently, three separate candidates ran from the ranks of the Democratic Party. Abraham Lincoln was the sole candidate representing the Republican Party. With the split in the Democratic Party, Abraham Lincoln became president with less than 40 percent of the popular vote. He did not win with a clear mandate from the American people. Delivered in 1861, his first Inaugural Address focused on whether states could legally succeed from the union. The following is an excerpt from his speech.

Fellow-Citizens of the United States:

—In compliance with a custom as old as the Government itself, I appear before you to address you briefly, and to take in your presence the oath prescribed by the Constitution of the United States to be taken by the President . . .

Apprehension seems to exist among the people of the Southern States that by the accession of a Republican administration their property and their peace and personal security are to be endangered. There has never been any reasonable cause for such apprehension. Indeed, the most ample evidence to the contrary has all the while existed and been open to their inspection. It is found in nearly all the published speeches of him who now addresses you. I do but quote from one of those speeches when I declare that "I have no purpose, directly or indirectly, to interfere with the institution of slavery in the States where it exists. I believe I have no lawful right to do so, and I have no inclination to do so. " . . .

I now reiterate these sentiments; and, in doing so, I only press upon the public attention the most conclusive evidence of which the case is susceptible, that the property, peace and security of no section are to be in any wise endangered by the now incoming administration . . .

I take the official oath to-day with no mental reservations, and with no purpose to construe the Constitution or laws by any hypercritical rules. And, while I do not choose now to specify particular acts of Congress as proper to be enforced, I do suggest that it will be much safer for all, both in official and private stations, to conform to and abide by all those acts which stand unrepealed, than to violate any of them, trusting to find impunity in having them held to be unconstitutional....

A disruption of the Federal Union, heretofore only menaced, is now formidably attempted.

I hold that, in contemplation of universal law and of the Constitution, the Union of these States is perpetual. Perpetuity is implied, if not expressed, in the fundamental law of all national governments. It is safe to assert that no government proper ever had a provision in its organic law for its own termination. Continue to execute all the express provisions of our national Constitution, and the Union will endure forever — it being impossible to destroy it except by some action not provided for in the instrument itself.

Again, if the United States be not a government proper, but an association of States in the nature of contract merely, can it as a contract be peaceably unmade by less than all the parties who made it? One party to a contract may violate it — break it, so to speak; but does it not require all to lawfully rescind it?

Descending from these general principles, we find the proposition that in legal contemplation the Union is perpetual confirmed by the history of the Union itself . . .

But if the destruction of the Union by one or by a part only of the States be lawfully possible, the Union is less perfect than before the Constitution, having lost the vital element of perpetuity.

It follows from these views that no State upon its own mere motion can lawfully get out of the Union; that resolves and ordinances to that effect are legally void; and that acts of violence, within any State or States, against the authority of the United States, are insurrectionary or revolutionary, according to circumstances.

I therefore consider that, in view of the Constitution and the laws, the Union is unbroken; and to the extent of my ability I shall take care, as the Constitution itself expressly enjoins upon me, that the laws of the Union be faithfully executed in all the States. Doing this I deem to be only a simple duty on my part; and I shall perform it so far as practicable, unless my rightful masters, the American people, shall withhold the requisite means, or in some authoritative manner direct the contrary. I trust this will not be regarded as a menace, but only as the declared purpose of the Union that it will constitutionally defend and maintain itself.

In doing this there needs to be no bloodshed or violence; and there shall be none, unless it be forced upon the national authority. The power confided to me will be used to hold, occupy, and possess the property and places belonging to the Government, and to collect the duties and imposts; but beyond what may be necessary for these objects, there will be no invasion, no using of force against or among the people anywhere. Where hostility to the United States, in any interior locality, shall be so great and universal as to prevent competent resident citizens from holding the Federal offices, there will be no attempt to force obnoxious strangers among the people for that object. While the strict legal right may exist in the government to enforce the exercise of these offices, the attempt to do so would be so irritating, and so nearly impracticable withal, that I deem it better to forego for the time the uses of such offices ...

If a minority in such case will secede rather than acquiesce, they make a precedent which in turn will divide and ruin them; for a minority of their own will secede from them whenever a majority refuses to be controlled by such minority. For instance, why may not any portion of a new confederacy a year or two hence arbitrarily secede again, precisely as portions of the present Union now claim to secede from it? All who cherish disunion sentiments are now being educated to the exact temper of doing this.

Is there such perfect identity of interests among the States to compose a new Union as to produce harmony only, and prevent renewed secession? ...

One section of our country believes slavery is right, and ought to be extended, while the other believes it is wrong, and ought not to be extended. This is the only substantial dispute. The fugitive slave clause of the Constitution and the law for the suppression of the foreign slave trade are each as well enforced, perhaps, as any law can ever be in a community where the moral sense of the people imperfectly supports the law itself. The great body of the people abide by the dry legal obligation in both cases, and a few break over in each. This, I think, cannot be perfectly cured; and it would be worse in both cases after the separation of the sections than before. The foreign slave trade, now imperfectly suppressed, would be ultimately revived, without restriction, in one section, while fugitive slaves, now only partially surrendered, would not be surrendered at all by the other.

Physically speaking, we cannot separate. We cannot remove our respective sections from each other, nor build an impassable wall between them. A husband and wife may be divorced and go out of the presence and beyond the reach of each other; but the different parts of our country cannot do this. They cannot but remain face to face, and intercourse, either amicable or hostile, must continue between them. Is it possible, then, to make that intercourse more advantageous or more satisfactory after separation than before? Can aliens make treaties easier than friends can make laws? Can treaties be more faithfully enforced between aliens than laws can among friends? Suppose you go to war, you cannot fight always; and when, after much loss on both sides, and no gain on either, you cease fighting, the identical old questions as to terms of intercourse are again upon you.

This country, with its institutions, belongs to the people who inhabit it. Whenever they shall grow weary of the existing government, they can exercise their constitutional right of amending it, or their revolutionary right to dismember or overthrow it. I cannot be ignorant of the fact that many worthy and patriotic citizens are desirous of having the national Constitution amended. While I make no recommendation of amendments, I fully recognize the rightful authority of the people over the whole subject, to be exercised in either of the modes prescribed in the instrument itself, and I should, under existing circumstances, favor rather than oppose a fair opportunity being afforded the people to act upon it. I will venture to add that to me the convention mode seems preferable, in that it allows amendments to originate with the people themselves, instead of only permitting them to take or reject propositions originated by others not especially chosen for the purpose, and, which might not be precisely such as they would wish to either accept or refuse. I understand a proposed amendment to the Constitution — which amendment, however, I have not seen — has passed Congress, to the effect that the Federal Government shall never interfere with the domestic institutions of the States, including that of persons held to service ...

My countrymen, one and all, think calmly and well upon this whole subject. Nothing valuable can be lost by taking time. If there be an object to hurry any of you in hot haste to a step which you would never take deliberately, that object will be frustrated by taking time; but no good object can be frustrated by it. Such of you as are now dissatisfied still have the old Constitution unimpaired, and, on the sensitive point, the laws of your own framing under it; while the new administration will have no immediate power, if it would, to change either. If it were admitted that you who are dissatisfied hold the right side in the dispute, there still is no single good reason for precipitate action. Intelligence, patriotism, Christianity, and a firm reliance on Him who has never yet forsaken this favored land, are still competent to adjust in the best way all our present difficulty.

In your hands, my dissatisfied fellow-countrymen, and not in mine, is the momentous issue of civil war. The government will not assail you. You can have no conflict without being yourselves the aggressors. You have no oath registered in heaven to destroy the government, while I shall have the most solemn one to "preserve, protect, and defend" it.

I am loath to close. We are not enemies, but friends. We must not be enemies. Though passion may have strained, it must not break, our bonds of affection. The mystic chords of memory, stretching from every battlefield and patriot grave to every living heart and hearthstone all over this broad land, will yet swell the chorus of the Union when again touched, as surely they will be, by the better angels of our nature.

HOW WELL DID YOU UNDERSTAND THIS SELECTION?

1. Why did Lincoln believe that the succession of any state from the union would be detrimental to the survival of the country?

2. From the context of his speech, what was Lincoln's official policy regarding the slave system?

3. In what ways did his message help to calm the growing discontent of the southern states regarding their fears that the national government would ban slavery?

*Yes, the United States Supreme Court can and has reversed its positions particularly over the legality of the "separate but equal" doctrine. In 1896, the Court decided in an 8-1 vote that a Louisiana law mandating separate public accommodations for white and African Americans was constitutional, as long as the facility or mode of transportation was equal in quality. The case arose after Mr. Plessy, an African American, was requested to move from the white-only car to the designated "colored" or African-American car. Plessy was arrested after he refused to relocate. However, the Court reversed its favorable opinion on separate but equal when it heard arguments in the 1954 case of **Brown v the Board of Education of Topeka, Kansas.** The Court's unanimous decision was the fuel to the growing fire of the civil rights era. The following article highlights both decisions of the Court.*

Plessy v Ferguson (1896)

Mr. Justice Brown ... delivered the opinion of the court.

This case turns upon the constitutionality of an act of the General Assembly of the State of Louisiana, passed in 1890, providing for separate railway carriages for the white and colored [African American] races....

The first section of the statute enacts "that all railway companies carrying passengers in their coaches in this State, shall provide equal but separate accommodations for the white, and colored races, by providing two or more passenger coaches for each passenger train, or by dividing the passenger coaches by a partition so as to secure separate accommodations: *Provided,* That this section shall not be construed to apply to street railroads. No person or persons, shall be admitted to occupy seats in coaches, other than, the ones, assigned, to them on account of the race they belong to." . . .

The information filed in the criminal District Court charged in substance that Plessy, being a passenger between two stations within the State of Louisiana, was assigned by officers of the company to the coach used for the race to which he belonged, but he insisted upon going into a coach used by the race to which he did not belong.

The petition for the writ of prohibition averred that petitioner was seven eighths Caucasian and one eighth African blood; that the mixture of colored blood was not discernible in him, and that he was entitled to every right, privilege and immunity secured to citizens of the United States of the white race; and that, upon such theory, he took possession of a vacant seat in a coach where passengers of the white race were accommodated, and was ordered by the conductor to vacate said coach and take a seat in another assigned to persons of the colored race, and having refused to comply with such demand he was forcibly ejected with the aid of a police officer, and imprisoned in the parish jail to answer a charge of having violated the above act.

The constitutionality of this act is attacked upon the ground that it conflicts both with the Thirteenth Amendment of the Constitution, abolishing slavery, and the Fourteenth Amendment, which prohibits certain restrictive legislation on the part of the States.

1. That it does not conflict with the Thirteenth Amendment, which abolished slavery and involuntary servitude, except as a punishment for crime, is too clear for argument. Slavery implies involuntary servitude—a state of bondage; the ownership of mankind as a chattel, or at least the control of the labor and services of one man for the benefit of another, and the absence of a legal right to the disposal of his own person, property and services....

A statute which implies merely a legal distinction between the white and colored races [African American]—a distinction which is founded in the color of the two races, and which must always exist so long as white men are distinguished from the other race by color—has no tendency to destroy the legal equality of the two races, or reestablish a state of involuntary servitude. Indeed, we do not understand that the Thirteenth Amendment is strenuously relied upon by the plaintiff in error in this connection.

2. By the Fourteenth Amendment, all persons born or naturalized in the United States, and subject to the jurisdiction thereof, are made citizens of the United States and of the State wherein they reside; and the States are forbidden from making or enforcing any law which shall abridge the privileges or immunities of citizens of the United States, or shall deprive any person of life, liberty or property without due process of law, or deny to any person within their jurisdiction the equal protection of the laws.

The object of the amendment was undoubtedly to enforce the absolute equality of the two races before the law, but in the nature of things it could not have been intended to abolish distinctions based upon color, or to enforce social, as distinguished from political equality, or a commingling of the two races upon terms unsatisfactory to either. Laws permitting, and even requiring, their separation in places where they are liable to be brought into contact do not necessarily imply the inferiority of either race to the other, and have been generally, if not universally, recognized as within the competency of the state legislatures in the exercise of their police power. The most common instance of this is connected with the establishment of separate schools for white and colored children, which has been held to be a valid exercise of the legislative power even by courts of States where the political rights of the colored race have been longest and most earnestly enforced....

While we think the enforced separation of the races, as applied to the internal commerce of the State, neither abridges the privileges or immunities of the colored [African American] man, deprives him of his property without due process of law, nor denies him the equal protection of the laws, within the meaning of the Fourteenth Amendment, we are not prepared to say that the conductor, in assigning passengers to the coaches according to their race, does not act at his peril, or that the provision of the second section of the act, that denies to the passenger compensation in damages for a refusal to receive him into the coach in which he properly belongs, is a valid exercise of the legislative power....

So far, then, as a conflict with the Fourteenth Amendment is concerned, the case reduces itself to the question whether the statute of Louisiana is a reasonable regulation, and with respect to this there must necessarily be a large discretion on the part of the legislature. In determining the question of reasonableness it is at liberty to act with reference to the established usages, customs and traditions of the people, and with a view to the promotion of their comfort, and the preservation of the public peace and good order. Gauged by this standard, we cannot say that a law which authorizes or even requires the separation of the two races in public conveyances is unreasonable, or more obnoxious to the Fourteenth Amendment than the acts of Congress requiring separate schools for colored children in the District of Columbia, the constitutionality of which does not seem to have been questioned, or the corresponding acts of state legislatures.

We consider the underlying fallacy of the plaintiff's argument to consist in the assumption that the enforced separation of the two races stamps the colored [African American] race with a badge of inferiority. If this be so, it is not by reason of anything found in the act, but solely because the colored race chooses to put that construction upon it. The argument necessarily assumes that if, as has been more than once the case, and is not unlikely to be so again, the colored race should become the dominant power in the state legislature, and should enact a law in precisely similar terms, it would thereby relegate the white race to an inferior position. We imagine that the white, race, at least, would not acquiesce in this assumption. The argument also assumes that social prejudices may be overcome by legislation, and that equal rights cannot be secured to the negro [African American] except by an enforced commingling of the two races. We cannot accept this proposition. If the two races are to meet upon terms of social equality, it must be the result of natural affinities, a mutual appreciation of each other's merits and a voluntary consent of individuals.... Legislation is powerless to eradicate racial instincts, or to abolish distinctions based upon physical differences, and the attempt to do so can only result in accentuating the difficulties of the present situation. If the civil and political rights of both races be equal one cannot be inferior to the other civilly or politically. If one race be inferior to the other socially, the Constitution of the United States cannot put them upon the same plane.

It is true that the question of the proportion of colored blood necessary to constitute a colored person, as distinguished from a white person, is one upon which there is a difference of opinion in the different States, some holding that any visible admixture of black blood stamps the person as belonging to the colored [African American] race ... ; others that it depends upon the preponderance of blood ... ; and still others that the predominance of white blood must only be in the proportion of three fourths. . . . But these are questions to be determined under the laws of each State and are not properly put in issue in this case. Under the allegations of his petition it may undoubtedly become a question of importance whether, under the laws of Louisiana, the petitioner belongs to the white or colored race.

The judgment of the court below is, therefore, *Affirmed.*

Brown v Board of Education of Topeka, Kansas (1954)

Mr. Chief Justice Warren delivered the opinion of the Court.

These cases come to us from the States of Kansas, South Carolina, Virginia, and Delaware. They are premised on different facts and different local conditions, but a common legal question justifies their consideration together in this consolidated opinion.

In each of the cases, minors of the Negro [African American] race, through their legal representatives, seek the aid of the courts in obtaining admission to the public schools of their community on a nonsegregated basis. In each instance, they had been denied admission to schools attended by white children under laws requiring or permitting segregation according to race. This segregation was alleged to deprive the plaintiffs of the equal protection of the laws under the Fourteenth Amendment. In each of the cases other than the Delaware case, a three-judge federal district court denied relief to the plaintiffs on the so-called "separate but equal" doctrine announced by this Court in *Plessy v. Ferguson*. . . . Under that doctrine, equality of treatment is accorded when the races are provided substantially equal facilities, even though these facilities be separate. In the Delaware case, the Supreme Court of Delaware adhered to that doctrine, but ordered that the plaintiffs be admitted to the white schools because of their superiority to the Negro [African American] schools.

The plaintiffs contend that segregated public schools are not "equal" and cannot be made "equal," and that hence they are deprived of the equal protection of the laws. Because of the obvious importance of the question presented, the Court took jurisdiction. Argument was heard in the 1952 Term, and reargument was heard this Term on certain questions propounded by the Court.

Reargument was largely devoted to the circumstances surrounding the adoption of the Fourteenth Amendment in 1868. It covered exhaustively consideration of the Amendment in Congress, ratification by the states, then existing practices in racial segregation, and the views of proponents and opponents of the Amendment. This discussion and our own investigation convince us that, although these sources cast some light, it is not enough to resolve the problem with which we are faced. At best, they are inconclusive. The most avid proponents of the post-War Amendments undoubtedly intended them to remove all legal distinctions among "all persons born or naturalized in the United States." Their opponents, just as certainly, were antagonistic to both the letter and the spirit of the Amendments and wished them to have the most limited effect. What others in Congress and the state legislatures had in mind cannot be determined with any degree of certainty.

An additional reason for the inconclusive nature of the Amendment's history, with respect to segregated schools, is the status of public education at that time. In the South, the movement toward free common schools, supported by general taxation, had not yet taken hold. Education of white children was largely in the hands of private groups. Education of Negroes [African American] was almost nonexistent, and practically all of the race were illiterate. In fact, any education of Negroes [African American] was forbidden by law in some states. Today, in contrast, many Negroes [African American] have achieved outstanding success in the arts and sciences as well as in the business and professional world. It is true that public school education at the time of the Amendment had advanced further in the North, but the effect of the Amendment on Northern States was generally ignored in the congressional debates. Even in the North, the conditions of public education did not approximate those existing today. The curriculum was usually rudimentary; ungraded schools were common in rural areas; the school term was but three months a year in many states; and compulsory school attendance was virtually unknown. As a consequence, it is not surprising that there should be so little in the history of the Fourteenth Amendment relating to its intended effect on public education.

In approaching this problem, we cannot turn the clock back to 1868 when the Amendment was adopted, or even to 1896 when *Plessy v. Ferguson* was written. We must consider public education in the light of its full development and its present place in American life throughout the Nation. Only in this way can it be determined if segregation in public schools deprives these plaintiffs of the equal protection of the laws.

Today, education is perhaps the most important function of state and local governments. Compulsory school attendance laws and the great expenditures for education both demonstrate our recognition of the importance of education to our democratic society. It is required in the performance of our most basic public responsibilities, even service in the armed forces. It is the very foundation of good citizenship. Today it is a principal instrument in awakening the child to cultural values, in preparing him for later professional training, and in helping him to adjust normally to his environment. In these days, it is doubtful that any child may reasonably be expected to succeed in life if he is denied the opportunity of an education. Such an opportunity, where the state has undertaken to provide it, is a right which must be made available to all on equal terms.

We come then to the question presented: Does segregation of children in public schools solely on the basis of race, even though the physical facilities and other "tangible" factors may be equal, deprive the children of the minority group of equal educational opportunities? We believe that it does.

In *Sweatt v. Painter* ... , in finding that a segregated law school for Negroes [African American] could not provide them equal educational opportunities, this Court relied in large part on "those qualities which are incapable of objective measurement but which make for greatness in a law school." In *McLaurin v. Oklahoma State Regents* ..., the Court, in requiring that a Negro [African American] admitted to a white graduate school be treated like all other students, again resorted to intangible considerations: "... his ability to study, to engage in discussions and exchange views with other students, and, in general, to learn his profession." Such considerations apply with added force to children in grade and high schools. To separate them from others of similar age and qualifications solely because of their race generates a feeling of inferiority as to their status in the community that may affect their hearts and minds in a way unlikely ever to be undone. The effect of this separation on their educational opportunities was well stated by a finding in the Kansas case by a court which nevertheless felt compelled to rule against the Negro [African American] plaintiffs:

> Segregation of white and colored [African American] children in public schools has a detrimental effect upon the colored [African American] children. The impact is greater when it has the sanction of the law; for the policy of separating the races is usually interpreted as denoting the inferiority of the negro [African American] group. A sense of inferiority affects the motivation of a child to learn. Segregation with the sanction of law, therefore, has a tendency to [retard] the educational and mental development of negro [African American] children and to deprive them of some of the benefits they would receive in a racial[ly] integrated school system.

Whatever may have been the extent of psychological knowledge at the time of *Plessy v. Ferguson*, this finding is amply supported by modern authority. Any language in *Plessy v. Ferguson* contrary to this finding is rejected.

We conclude that in the field of public education the doctrine of "separate but equal" has no place. Separate educational facilities are inherently unequal. Therefore, we hold that the plaintiffs and others similarly situated for whom the actions have been brought are, by reason of the segregation complained of, deprived of the equal protection of the laws guaranteed by the Fourteenth Amendment. This disposition makes unnecessary any discussion whether such segregation also violates the Due Process Clause of the Fourteenth Amendment.

HOW WELL DID YOU UNDERSTAND THIS SELECTION?

1. In the *Plessy* case, what rationale did the Court use to justify its decision to uphold the "separate but equal" doctrine?

2. Why did the Court feel that Plessy's argument that separation of the two races rendered the African American inferior to his/her Anglo counterpart was not a valid argument?

3. Why did the Court believe that it was not the duty of legislatures to mandate equality among the two races?

4. In the *Brown* ruling, why did the justices believe that "separate educational facilities are inherently unequal"?

5. In your opinion, was the "separate but equal" doctrine as applied in the *Brown* case a violation of the 14th Amendment's due process clause?

The Vietnam conflict was a direct result of the Cold War. The United States pursued a policy of containment of the Soviet Union. This not only meant the physical containment of the Soviet Union but the ideology of Communism as well. This policy and the Soviet's action and reaction to it created a political, economic and military power struggle based on ideological superiority that affected virtually every country in the world. Vietnam was a textbook example of the Cold War philosophy at its worst.

North and South Vietnam were engaged in a ferocious civil war. In the North, the Communist forces were led by Ho Chi Minh; in the South, the government was under the leadership of the American-backed regime of Premier Ngo Dinh Diem. The bipolar Cold War mentality of the United States at that time reinforced the concept of zero-sum politics, whatever you lose, I gain and vice-versa. Therefore, if Ho Chi Minh and his forces won in Vietnam, the Soviet Union would have prevailed. It was, therefore, in the global strategic interests of the United States to support the anti-Communist government in Vietnam no matter what its internal interests or policies.

Early in his presidency, Kennedy supported the Diem regime and its policies. The following letter demonstrates that support. However, as time wore on, Kennedy became disillusioned with Diem. He began to demand that Diem resolve some of the economic and social problems of South Vietnam, particularly the mounting religious conflict between Catholics and Buddhists, in return for American support. By 1963, internal support for Diem had begun to erode. Dissident generals staged a coup d'etat and Diem was killed in the governmental takeover. Senator Frank Church, chairperson of the Senate Foreign Relations Committee, held hearings during the 1970s that exposed many of the U.S. foreign policy dealings, particularly during the Vietnam conflict. These hearings exposed the fact that the U.S. sanctioned the coup d'etat that overthrew Premier Diem.

December 14, 1961

Dear Mr. President:

I have received your recent letter in which you described so cogently the dangerous condition caused by North Vietnam's efforts to take over your country. The situation in your embattled country is well known to me and to the American people. We have been deeply disturbed by the assault on your country. Our indignation has mounted as the deliberate savagery of the Communist program of assassination, kidnapping and wanton violence became clear.

Your letter underlines what our own information has convincingly shown—that the campaign of force and terror now being waged against your people and your Government is supported and directed from the outside by the authorities at Hanoi. They have thus violated the provisions of the Geneva Accords designed to ensure peace in Vietnam and to which they bound themselves in 1954.

At that time, the United States, although not a party to the Accords, declared that it "would view any renewal of the aggression in violation of the Agreements with grave concern and as seriously threatening international peace and security." We continue to maintain that view.

In accordance with that declaration, and in response to your request, we are prepared to help the Republic of Vietnam to protect its people and to preserve its independence. We shall promptly increase our assistance to your defense effort as well as help relieve the destruction of the floods which you describe. I have already given the orders to get these programs underway.

The United States, like the Republic of Vietnam, remains devoted to the cause of peace and our primary purpose is to help your people maintain their independence. If the Communist authorities in North Vietnam will stop their campaign to destroy the Republic of Vietnam, the measures we are taking to assist your defense efforts will no longer be necessary. We shall seek to persuade the Communists to give up their attempts of force and subversion. In any case, we are confident that the Vietnamese people will preserve their independence and gain the peace and prosperity for which they have sought so hard and so long.

Sources: *Department of Slate Bulletin.* XXXVII (Washington, D.C. Government Printing Office, January 1, 1962), pp. 13-14.

HOW WELL DID YOU UNDERSTAND THIS SELECTION?

1. In his letter, President Kennedy makes several arguments in defense of U.S. intervention in Vietnam. What are they and are they convincing?

2. What is the relationship between the Cold War and the Vietnam conflict?

*On August 4, 1964, two U.S. naval destroyers were engaged in an incident that changed the course of the Vietnam conflict. The **U.S.S. Maddox,** which had been involved in covert electronic espionage in the Gulf of Tonkin off North Vietnam, wired Washington that they were under attack. A novice sonar operator aboard the **U.S.S. Maddox** reported to his captain that he had seen enemy torpedoes on the radar screen. Based on that information the captain ordered the **Maddox** to fire its torpedoes and begin evasive action.*

Navy flyers were given orders to search the surrounding waters for North Vietnamese ships. They found none. Subsequent reports sent by naval commanders to the Secretary of Defense Robert McNamara in Washington advised that caution be exercised in our reaction to the incident. There was great concern by the commanders in the field that the initial incident and report may have been in error. Nevertheless, President Johnson ordered retaliatory air attacks against North Vietnamese torpedo boat bases and oil storage depots.

President Johnson had decided to use this incident to gain support from the American people and Congress to escalate military involvement in Vietnam. He had stated that he was not going to be the "first American president to lose a war," and he believed that Congress was becoming an impediment to ensuring military success. Johnson believed he needed unlimited power to wage war to ensure victory. This incident provided that opportunity.

President Johnson went on national television and proclaimed to the American public that "they" had been attacked. Armed with public support, Johnson went to Congress to ask it to grant the executive branch the unconditional right to wage war against North Vietnam without further authorization or without a formal declaration of war. Senator William Fulbright of Arkansas, Chairman of the Senate Foreign Affairs Committee, steered the Tonkin Resolution through Congress.

Due in large part to Fulbright's efforts, on August 7, 1964, Congress approved The Gulf of Tonkin Resolution. It was virtually unanimous. The resolution passed by a vote of 416-0 in the House of Representatives and by 88-2 in the Senate. Democratic Senators Wayne Morse of Oregon and Ernest Gruening of Alaska voted against the resolution. Both had grave concerns as to the accuracy of the information presented by the Johnson administration.

Later events would prove that Morse's and Gruening's concerns were justified. Congressional hearings held in 1968 revealed that Johnson and the U.S. Department of Defense had misstated the facts in order to gain congressional support to escalate U.S. military involvement in Vietnam. These hearings revealed that there were never any North Vietnamese ships nor was there ever an attack against the two U.S. destroyers. The congressional resolution essentially transferred Congress's constitutional power to declare war to the president and conferred upon him virtually unlimited war making power. By this time over 500,000 American ground troops had been sent to Vietnam. By the end of the conflict over 58,000 American soldiers had died in Vietnam.

The Gulf of Tonkin Resolution was repealed in 1970; however, congressional funding for the Vietnam conflict continued until 1973.

Resolved by the Senate and House of Representatives of the United States of America in Congress assembled,

That the Congress approves and supports the determination of the President, as Commander in Chief, to take all necessary measures to repel any armed attack against the forces of the United States and to prevent further aggression.

Section 2. The United States regards as vital to its national interest and to world peace the maintenance of international peace and security in southeast Asia. Consonant with the Constitution of the United States and the Charter of the United Nations and in accordance with its obligations under the Southeast Asia Collective Defense Treaty, the United States is, therefore, prepared, as the President determines, to take all necessary steps, including the use of armed force, to assist any member or protocol state of the Southeast Asia Collective Defense Treaty requesting assistance in defense of its freedom.

Section 3. This resolution shall expire when the President shall determine that the peace and security of the area is reasonably assured by international conditions created by action of the United Nations or otherwise, except that it may be terminated earlier by concurrent resolution of the Congress.

Source: Joint Resolution of Congress, H.J. RES 1145 August 7, 1964.

HOW WELL DID YOU UNDERSTAND THIS SELECTION?

1. To what extent did Congress surrender its constitutional authority to declare war when it passed the Gulf of Tonkin Resolution?

2. Did this resolution alter the separation of power and checks and balances that existed between the executive and legislative branches?

THE NEW YORK TIMES COMPANY V. SULLIVAN (1964)
United States Supreme Court

*Sullivan was one of three city commissioners of Montgomery, Alabama. He took exception to a paid advertisement soliciting contributions for civil rights groups, signed by a large number of prominent men and women, and published in **The New York Times**. The advertisement alleged that certain public officials had initiated a campaign of terror against civil rights workers. Some of the allegations in the advertisement were false, and Sullivan sued the newspaper for libel. Although the Alabama court found in favor of Sullivan, the United States Supreme Court overturned their decision.*

Mr. Justice Brennan delivered the opinion of the Court.

Respondent's complaint alleged that he had been libeled by statements in a full-page advertisement that was carried in the New York Times on March 29, 1960. Entitled "Heed Their Rising Voices," the advertisement began by stating that "As the whole world knows by now, thousands of Southern Negro students are engaged in widespread non-violent demonstrations in positive affirmation of the right to live in human dignity as guaranteed by the U.S. Constitution and the Bill of Rights." It went on to charge that "in their efforts to uphold these guarantees, they are being met by an unprecedented wave of terror by those who would deny or negate that document which the whole world looks upon as setting the pattern for modern freedom..." Succeeding paragraphs purported to illustrate the "wave of terror" by describing certain alleged events. The text concluded with an appeal for funds for three purposes: support of the student movement, "the struggle for the right-to-vote," and the legal defense of Dr. martin Luther King, Jr., leader of the movement, against a perjury indictment then pending in Montgomery.

Of the 10 paragraphs of text in the advertisement, the third and a portion of the sixth were the basis of respondent's claim of libel...

It is uncontroverted that some of the statements contained in the two paragraphs were not accurate descriptions of events which occurred in Montgomery. Although Negro students staged a demonstration on the State Capitol steps, they sang the National Anthem and not "My Country, 'Tis of Thee." Although nine students were expelled by the State Board of education, this was not for leading the demonstration at the Capitol, but for demandi9ng service at a lunch counter in the Montgomery County Courthouse on another day. Not the entire student body, but most of it, had protested the expulsion, not by refusing to register, but by boycotting classes on a single day; virtually all the students did register for the ensuing semester. The campus dining hall was not padlocked on any occasion, and the only students who may have been barred from eating there were the few who had neither signed a pre-registration application nor requested temporary meal tickets. Although the police were deployed near the campus in large numbers on three occasions, they did not at any time "ring" the campus, and they were not called to the campus in connection with the demonstration on the State Capitol steps, as the third paragraph implied. Dr. King had not been arrested seven times, but only four; and though he claimed to have been assaulted some years earlier in connection with his arrest for loitering outside a courtroom, one of the officers who made the arrest denied that there was such an assault.

On the premise that the charges in the sixth paragraph could be read as referring to him, respondent was allowed to prove that he had not participated in the events described...

Respondent made no effort to prove he suffered actual pecuniary loss as a result of the alleged libel...

The cost of the advertisement was approximately $4800, and it was published by the Times upon an order from a New York advertising agency acting for the signatory Committee...The Manager of the Advertising Acceptability Department testified that he had approved the advertisement for publication because he knew nothing to cause him to believe that anything in it was false, and because it bore the endorsement of "a number of people who are well known and whose reputation" he "had no reason to question."...

Alabama law denies a public officer recovery of punitive damages in a libel action brought on account of a publication concerning his official conduct unless he first makes a written demand for a public retraction and the defendant fails or refuses to comply. Alabama Code, Tit. 7, 914. Respondent served such a demand upon each of the petitioners. None of the individual petitioners responded to the demand, primarily because each took the position that he had not authorized the use of his name on the advertisement and therefore had not published the statements that respondent alleged had libeled him. The Times did not publish a retraction in response to the demand, but wrote respondent a letter stating, among other things, that "we...are somewhat puzzled as to how you think the statements in the advertisement reflect on you." Respondent filed this suit a few days later without answering the letter...

The trial judge submitted the case to the jury under instructions that the statements in the advertisement were "libelous per se" and were not privileged, so that petitioners might be held liable if the jury found that they had published the advertisement and that the statements were made "of and concerning" respondent...An award of punitive damages—as distinguished from "general" damages, which are compensatory in nature—apparently requires proof of actual malice under Alabama law, and the judge charged that "mere negligence or carelessness is not evidence of actual malice or malice in fact, and does not justify an award of exemplary or punitive damages." He refused to charge, however, that the jury must be "convinced" of malice, in the sense of "actual intent" to harm or "gross negligence and recklessness," to make such an award...

In affirming the judgment, The Supreme Court of Alabama sustained the trial judge's rulings and instructions in all respects...

Because of the importance of the constitutional issues involved, we granted the separate petitions for certiorari of the individual petitioners and of the Times. 371 U.S. 946. We reverse the judgment. We hold that the rule of law applied by the Alabama courts is constitutionally deficient for failure to provide the safeguards for freedom of speech and of the press that are required by the first and Fourteenth Amendments in a libel action brought by a public official against critics of his official conduct.

Respondent relies heavily, as did the Alabama courts, on statements of this Court to the effect that the Constitution does not protect libelous publications. Those statements do not foreclose our inquiry here. None of the cases sustained the use of libel laws to impose sanctions upon expression critical of the official conduct of public officials...In *Beauharnais* v. *Illinois*, the Court sustained an Illinois criminal libel statute as applied to a publication held to be both defamatory of a racial group and "liable to cause violence and disorder." But the Court was careful to note that it "retains and exercises authority to nullify action which encroaches on freedom of utterance under the guise of punishing libel"; for "public men are, as it were, public property," and "discussion cannot be denied and the right, as well as the duty, of criticism must not be stifled."

Thus we consider this case against the background of a profound national commitment to the principle that debate on public issues should be uninhibited, robust, and wide-open, and that it may well include vehement, caustic, and sometimes unpleasantly sharp attacks on government and public officials...The present advertisement, as an expression of grievance and protest on one of the major public issues of our time, would seem clearly to qualify for the constitutional protection. The question is whether it forfeits that protection by the falsity of some of its factual statements and by the alleged defamation of respondent.

Authoritative interpretations of the First Amendment guarantees have consistently refused to recognize an exception for nay test of truth, whether administered by judges, juries, or administrative officials—and especially not one that puts the burden of proving truth on the speaker...The constitutional protection does not turn upon "the truth, popularity, or social utility of the ideas and beliefs which are offered."...As

Madison said, "Some degree of abuse is inseparable from the proper use of every thing; and in no instance is this more true than in that of the press."

Just as factual error affords no warrant for refusing speech that would otherwise be free, the same is true of injury to official reputation. Where judicial officers are involved, the court had held that concern for the dignity and reputation of the courts does not justify the punishment as criminal contempt of criticism of the judge or his decision…This is true even though the utterance contains "half-truths" and "misinformation."…Such repression can be justified, if at all, only by a clear and present danger of the obstruction of justice…

If neither factual error nor defamatory content suffices to remove the constitutional shield from criticism of official conduct, the combination of the two elements is no less inadequate. This is the lesson to be drawn from the great controversy over the Sedition Act of 1798…which first crystallized a national awareness of the central meaning of the First Amendment…

Although the Sedition Act was never tested in this court, the attack upon its validity has carried the day in the court of history. Fines levied in its prosecution were repaid by Act of Congress on the ground that it was unconstitutional…

There is no force in resp0ondent's argument that the constitutional limitations implicit in the history of the Sedition Act apply only to Congress and not to the States…[T}his distinction was eliminated with the adoption of the fourteenth Amendment and the application to the States of the First Amendment's restrictions…

…A rule compelling the critic of official conduct to guarantee the truth of all his factual assertions—and to do so on pain of libel judgments virtually unlimited in amount—leads to comparable "self-censorship." Allowance of the defense of truth, with the burden of proving it on the defendant, does not mean that only false speech will be deterred…

The constitutional guarantees require, we think, a federal rule that prohibits a public official from recovering damages for a defamatory falsehood relating to his official conduct unless he proves that the statement was made with "actual malice"—that is, with knowledge that it was false or with reckless disregard of whether it was false or not.

Such a privilege for criticism of official conduct is appropriately analogous to the protection accorded a public official when *he* is sued for libel by a private citizen. In *Barr* v. *Matteo*, this Court held the utterance of a federal official to be absolutely privileged if made "within the outer perimeter" of his duties. The States accord the same immunity to statements of their highest officers and qualify the privilege they enjoy. But all hold that all officials are protected unless actual malice can be proved…

We hold today that the Constitution delimits a State's power to award damages for libel actions brought by public officials against critics of their official conduct. Since this is such an action, the rule requiring proof of actual malice is applicable…

Applying these standards, we consider that the proof presented to show actual malice lacks the convincing clarity which the constitutional standard demands, and hence that it would not constitutionally sustain the judgment for respondent under the proper rule of law…

…There is no legal alchemy by which a State may thus create the cause of action that would otherwise be denied for a publication which, as respondent himself said of the advertisement, "reflects not only on me but on the other Commissioners and the community." Raising as it does the possibility that a goodfaith critic of government will be penalized for his criticism, the proposition relied on by the Alabama courts strikes at the very center of the Constitutionally protected area of free expression. We hold that such a proposition may not constitutionally be utilized to establish that an otherwise impersonal attack on governmental operations was a libel of an official responsible for those operations…

Reversed and remanded.

HOW WELL DID YOU UNDERSTAND THIS SELECTION?

1. According to the Court, is there a difference between libel of a private citizen and libel of a public official? Why or why not?

2. Must criticism of a public official be true to be protected by the First Amendment?

THE CIVIL RIGHTS MOVEMENT: Fraud, Sham, and Hoax (1964)
George C. Wallace

In the early 1960s, a Southerner, George C. Wallace, began his political career as an economic populist, championing the common people against the powerful special interests. He also appealed to the racial hatred shared by many white Southerners of the early 1960s. At his inauguration in 1963, Governors Wallace called for "Segregation now! Segregation tomorrow! Segregation forever!" He claimed to be the defender of average white Americans, appealing to their fears by attacking the federal government, civil rights activists, student protesters, college intellectuals, and reformers in general. Here, Wallace particularly addresses what he sees as the abuses and wrong-headedness of the Civil Rights Movement.

We come here today in deference to the memory of those stalwart patriots who on July 4, 1776, pledged their lives, their fortunes, and their sacred honor to establish and defend the proposition that governments are created by the people, empowered by the people, derive their just powers from the consent of the people, and must forever remain subservient to the will of the people.

Today, 188 years later, we celebrate that occasion and find inspiration and determination and courage to preserve and protect the great principles of freedom enunciated in the Declaration of Independence.

It is therefore a cruel irony that the President of the United States has only yesterday signed into law the most monstrous piece of legislation ever enacted by the United States Congress.

It is a fraud, a sham, and a hoax...

To illustrate the fraud—it is not a civil Rights Bill. It is a Federal Penal Code. It creates Federal crimes which would take volumes to list and years to tabulate because it affects the lives of 192 million American citizens. Every person in every walk and station of life and every aspect of our daily lives becomes subject to the criminal provisions of this bill...

Today, 188 years later, we have actually witnessed the invasion of the State of Arkansas, Mississippi, and Alabama by the armed forces of the United States and maintained in the state against the will of the people and without consent of state legislatures.

It is a form of tyranny worse than that of King George III who had sent mercenaries against the colonies because today the Federal Judicial tyrants have sanctioned the use of brother against brother and father against son by federalizing the National Guard.

In 1776 the colonists also complained that the monarch "...Has incited domestic insurrections among us..."

Today, we have absolute proof that the Federal Department of Justice has planned, supervised, financed and protected acts of insurrection in the southern states, resulting in vandalism, property damage, personal injury, and staggering expense to the states.

In 1776 it was charged that the monarchy had asserted power to "...Dissolve representative houses and to punish...For opposing with manly firmness his invasions of the rights of the people..."

Today, the Federal judiciary asserts the power not only to dissolve state legislatures but to create them and to dissolve all state laws and state judicial decrees, and to punish a state governor by trial without jury "...For opposing with manly firmness his invasions of the rights of the people..."

The colonists also listed as acts of tyranny: "…The erection of a multitude of new offices and sent hither swarms of officers to harass our people and to eat out their substance…:"

"…Suspending our own legislatures and declaring themselves invested with the power to legislate for us in all cases whatsoever;"

"…Abolishing the free system of the English laws…:"

—it had "abdicated government here;"

—refusing to assent to the laws enacted by the people,

"…Laws considered most wholesome and necessary for the public good;"

—and "…For depriving us in many cases, of the benefit of trial by jury…; For taking away our charters, abolishing our most valuable laws, and altering fundamentally form of our government; for suspending our own legislatures and declaring themselves invested with the power to legislate for us in all cases whatsoever."

The United States Supreme Court is guilty of each and every one of these acts of tyranny.

Let us look at the record further with respect to the court's contribution to the destruction of the concept of God and the abolition of religion.

The Federal court rules that your children shall not be permitted to read the Bible in our public school systems.

Let me tell you this, though. We still read the bible in Alabama schools and as long as I am governor we will continue to read the Bible no matter what the Supreme Court says.

Federal courts will not convict a "demonstrator" invading and destroying private property. But the Federal courts rule you cannot say a simple "God is great, God is good, we thank Thee for our food," in kindergartens supported by public funds.

Now, let us examine the manner in which the Court has continuously chipped away at the concept of private property.

It is contended by the left-wing liberals that private property is merely a legal fiction. That one has no inherent right to own or possess property. The courts have restricted and limited the right of acquisition of property in life and have decreed its disposition in death and have ruthlessly set aside the wills of the dead in order to attain social ends decreed by the court. The court has substituted its judgment for that of the testator based on social theory.

The courts assert authority even in decree the use of private cemeteries.

They assert the right to convert a private place of business into a public place of business without the consent of the owner and without compensation to him.

One justice asserts that the mere licensing of a business by the state is sufficient to convert it into control by the Federal judiciary as to its use and disposition.

Another asserts that the guarantees of equal protection and due process of law cannot be extended to a corporation.

In one instance, following the edicts of the United States Supreme Court, a state Supreme Courts has ordered and directed a private citizen to sell his home to an individual contrary to the wishes of the owner.

In California we witnessed a state Supreme Court taking under advisement the question as to whether or not to compel a bank to make a loan to an applicant on the basis of his race.

We have witnessed the sanction by the courts of confiscatory taxation.

302

Let us take a lokk at the attitude of the court with respect to the control of the private resources of the nation and the allocation of the productive capacity of the nation.

The Supreme Court decisions have sanctioned enactment of the civil rights bill.

What this bill actually does is to empower the United States government to reallocate the entire productive capacity of the agricultural economy covered by quotas and acreage allotments of various types on the basis of race, creed, color and national origin.

It, in effect, places in the hands of the Federal government the right of a farmer to earn a living, making the right dependent upon the consent of the Federal government precisely as is the case in Russia.

The power is there. I am not in the least impressed by the protestations that the government will use this power with benevolent discretion.

We know that the bill authorizes the President of the United States to allocate all defense productive capacity of this country on the basis of race, creed, or color.

It does not matter in the least that he will make such allocations with restraint. The fact is that it is possible with a politically dominated agency to punish and bankrupt and destroy any business that deals with the Federal government if it does not bow to the wishes and demands of the president of the United States.

All of us know what the court has done to capture the minds of our children.

The Federal judiciary has asserted the authority to prescribe regulations with respect to the management, operation, and control of our local schools. The second Brown decision in the infamous school segregation case authorized Federal district courts to supervise such matters as teaching, hiring, firing, promotion, the expenditure of local funds, both administratively and for capital improvements, additions, and renovations, the location of new schools, the drawing of school boundaries, busing and transportation of school children, and, believe it or not, it has asserted the right in the Federal judiciary to pass judgment upon the curricula adopted in local public schools.

A comparatively recent Federal court decision in a Florida case actually entered an order embracing each and every one of these assertions of Federal supervision.

In ruling after ruling, the Supreme Court has overstepped its constitutional authority. While appearing to protect the people's interest, it has in reality become a judicial tyrant...

Certainly I am a candidate for President of the United States.

If the left-wingers do not think I am serious—let them consider this.

I am going to take our fight to the people—the court of public opinion—where truth and common sense will eventually prevail.

At this time, I have definite, concrete plans to get presidential electors pledged to me on the ballots in the following states: Florida, Georgia, South Carolina, North Carolina, Virginia, New York, Indiana, Illinois, Wisconsin, Missouri, Kentucky, Arkansas, Tennessee, and of course Alabama, Mississippi and Louisiana.

Other states are under serious consideration.

A candidate for President must receive 270 electoral votes to win.

The states I am definitely going to enter represent 218 electoral votes.

Conservatives of this nation constitute the balance of power in presidential elections.

I am a conservative.

I intend to give the American people a clear choice. I welcome a fight between our philosophy and the liberal left-wing dogma which now threatens to engulf every man, woman, and child in the United States.

I am in this race because I believe the American people have been pushed around long enough and that they, like you and I, are fed up with the continuing trend toward a socialist state which now subjects the individual to the dictates of an all-powerful central government.

HOW WELL DID YOU UNDERSTAND THIS SELECTION?

1. Why does Wallace see himself in agreement with the founders of the American Constitution?

2. Which decisions of the Federal court system does Wallace find particularly alarming? Why?

SAM ERVIN'S PERSPECTIVE ON WATERGATE AND THE FUTURE OF THE PRESIDENCY

Senator Sam Ervin was appointed chairperson of a special Senate committee to investigate the allegations that the Re-elect Nixon campaign participated in the illegal solicitation of campaign donations. Ervin's investigation, however, took an onymous turn for the worst as his committee uncovered the illegal break in into Democratic Headquarters at the Watergate Hotel. The unfolding drama of Watergate resulted in a lengthy investigation culminating in the resignation of President Nixon and the conviction of several members of his administration. Senator Ervin expresses his own perceptions of the Watergate episode.

Since the Senate Select Committee on Presidential Campaign Activities is filing with the Senate its final report concerning the investigation that body authorized and directed it to make, I deem it appropriate to state as succinctly as possible some of my personal observations respecting the tragic events known collectively as the Watergate, which disgraced the Presidential election of 1972.

In doing this, I ask and endeavor to answer these questions: What was Watergate? Why was Watergate? Is there an antidote which will prevent future Watergates? If so, what is that antidote?

Before attempting to answer these questions, I wish to make these things plain:

1. I am not undertaking to usurp and exercise the power of impeachment, which the Constitution confers upon the House of Representatives alone. As a consequence, nothing I say should be construed as an expression of an opinion in respect to the question of whether or not President Nixon is impeachable in connection with the Watergate or any other matter.

2. Inasmuch as its Committee on the Judiciary is now studying whether or not it ought to recommend to the House the impeachment of the President, I shall also refrain from making any comment on the question of whether or not the President has performed in an acceptable manner his paramount constitutional obligation "to take care that the laws be faithfully executed."

3. Watergate was not invented by enemies of the Nixon administration or even by the news media. On the contrary, Watergate was perpetrated upon America by White House and political aides, whom President Nixon himself had entrusted with the management of his campaign for reelection to the Presidency, a campaign which was divorced to a marked degree from the campaigns of other Republicans who sought election to public office in 1972. I note at this point without elaboration that these White House and political aides were virtually without experience in either Government or politics apart from their association with President Nixon.

4. Life had not subjected these White House and political aides to the disadvantaged conditions which are glibly cited as the causes of wrongdoing. On the contrary, fortune had smiled upon them. They came from substantial homes, possessed extraordinary talents, had had unusual educational opportunities, and occupied high social positions.

5. Watergate was unprecedented in the political annals of America in respect to the scope and intensity of its unethical and illegal actions. To be sure, there had been previous milder political scandals in American history. That fact does not excuse Watergate. Murder and stealing have occurred in every generation since Earth began, but that fact has not made murder meritorious or larceny legal.

What Was Watergate?

President Nixon entrusted the management of his campaign for reelection and his campaign finances to the Committee for the Re-Election of the President, which was headed by former Attorney General John N. Mitchell, and the Finance Committee To Re-Elect the President, which was headed by former Secretary of Commerce, Maurice Stans. Since the two committees occupied offices in the same office building in Washington and worked in close conjunction, it seems proper to call them for ease of expression the Nixon reelection committees.

Watergate was a conglomerate of various illegal and unethical activities in which various officers and employees of the Nixon reelection committees and various White House aides of President Nixon participated in varying ways and degrees to accomplish these successive objectives:

1. To destroy, insofar as the Presidential election of 1972 was concerned, the integrity of the process by which the President of the United States is nominated and elected.

2. To hide from law enforcement officers, prosecutors, grand jurors, courts, the news media, and the American people the identities and wrong-doing of those officers and employees of the Nixon reelection committees, and those White House aides who had undertaken to destroy the integrity of the process by which the President of the United States is nominated and elected.

To accomplish the first of these objectives, the participating officers and employees of the reelection committees and the participating White House aides of President Nixon engaged in one or more of these things:

1. They exacted enormous contributions — usually in cash — from corporate executives by impliedly implanting in their minds the impressions that the making of the contributions was necessary to insure that the corporations would receive governmental favors, or avoid governmental disfavors, while President Nixon remained in the White House. A substantial portion of the contributions were made out of corporate funds in violation of a law enacted by Congress a generation ago.

2. They hid substantial parts of these contributions in cash in safes and secret deposits to conceal their sources and the identities of those who had made them.

3. They disbursed substantial portions of these hidden contributions in a surreptitious manner to finance the bugging and the burglary of the offices of the Democratic National Committee in the Watergate complex in Washington for the purpose of obtaining political intelligence; and to sabotage by dirty tricks, espionage, and scurrilous and false libels and slanders the campaigns and the reputations of honorable men, whose only offenses were that they sought the nomination of the Democratic Party for President and the opportunity to run against President Nixon for that office in the Presidential election of 1972.

4. They deemed the departments and agencies of the Federal Government to be the political playthings of the Nixon administration rather than impartial instruments for serving the people, and undertook to induce them to channel Federal contracts, grants, and loans to areas, groups, or individuals so as to promote the reelection of the President rather than to further the welfare of the people.

5. They branded as enemies of the President individuals and members of the news media who dissented from the President's policies and opposed his reelection, and conspired to urge the Department of Justice, the Federal Bureau of Investigation, the Internal Revenue Service, and the Federal Communications Commission to pervert the use of their legal powers to harass them for so doing.

6. They borrowed from the Central Intelligence Agency disguises which E. Howard Hunt used in political espionage operations, and photographic equipment which White House employees known as the "Plumbers" and their hired confederates used in connection with burglarizing the office of a psychiatrist which they believed contained information concerning Daniel Ellsberg which the White House was anxious to secure.

7. They assigned to E. Howard Hunt, who was at the time a White House consultant occupying an office in the Executive Office Building, the gruesome task of falsifying State Department documents which they contemplated using in their altered state to discredit the Democratic Party by defaming the memory of former President John Fitzgerald Kennedy, who as the hapless victim of an assassin's bullet had been sleeping in the tongueless silence of the dreamless dust for 9 years.

8. They used campaign funds to hire saboteurs to forge and disseminate false and scurrilous libels of honorable men running for the Democratic Presidential nomination in Democratic Party primaries.

During the darkness of the early morning of June 17, 1972, James W. McCord, the security chief of the John Mitchell committee, and four residents of Miami, Fla., were arrested by Washington police while they were burglarizing the offices of the Democratic National Committee in the Watergate complex to obtain political intelligence. At the same time, the four residents of Miami had in their possession more than fifty $100 bills which were subsequently shown to be a part of campaign contributions made to the Nixon reelection committees.

On September 15, 1972, these five burglars, E. Howard Hunt, and Gordon Liddy, general counsel of the Stans committee, were indicted by the grand jury on charges arising out of the bugging and burglary of the Watergate.

They were placed on trial upon these charges before Judge John Sirica, and a petit jury in the U.S. District Court for the District of Columbia in January 1973. At that time, Hunt and the four residents of Miami pleaded guilty, and McCord and Liddy were found guilty by the petit jury. None of them took the witness stand during the trial.

The arrest of McCord and the four residents of Miami created consternation in the Nixon reelection committees and the White House. Thereupon, various officers and employees of the Nixon reelection committees and various White House aides undertook to conceal from law-enforcement officers, prosecutors, grand jurors, courts, the news media, and the American people the identities and activities of those officers and employees of the Nixon reelection committees and those White House aides who had participated in any way in the Watergate affair.

Various officers and employees of the Nixon reelection committees and various White House aides engaged in one or more of these acts to make the concealment effective and thus obstruct the due administration of justice:

1. They destroyed the records of the Nixon reelection committees antedating the bugging and the burglary.

2. They induced the Acting Director of the FBI, who was a Nixon appointee, to destroy the State Department documents which E. Howard Hunt had been falsifying.

3. They obtained from the Acting Director of the FBI copies of scores of interviews conducted by FBI agents in connection with their investigation of the bugging and the burglary, and were enabled thereby to coach their confederates to give false and misleading statements to the FBI.

4. They sought to persuade the FBI to refrain from investigating the sources of the campaign funds which were used to finance the bugging and the burglary.

5. They intimidated employees of the Nixon reelection committees and employees of the White House by having their lawyers present when these employees were being questioned by agents of the FBI, and thus deterred these employees from making full disclosures to the FBI.

6. They lied to agents of the FBI, prosecutors, and grand jurors who undertook to investigate the bugging and the burglary, and to Judge Sirica and the petit jurors who tried the seven original Watergate defendants in January 1973.

7. They persuaded the Department of Justice and the prosecutors to take out-of-court statements from Maurice Stans, President Nixon's chief campaign fundraiser, and Charles Colson, Egil Krogh, and David

Young, White House aides, and Charles Colson's secretary, instead of requiring them to testify before the grand jury investigating the bugging and the burglary in conformity with the established procedures governing such matters, and thus denied the grand jurors the opportunity to question them.

8. They persuaded the Department of Justice and the prosecutors to refrain from asking Donald Segretti, their chief hired saboteur, any questions involving Herbert W. Kalmbach, the President's personal attorney, who was known by them to have paid Segretti for dirty tricks he perpetrated upon honorable men seeking the Democratic Presidential nomination, and who was subsequently identified before the Senate Select Committee as one who played a major role in the secret delivery of hush money to the seven original Watergate defendants.

9. They made cash payments totaling hundreds of thousands of dollars out of campaign funds in surreptitious ways to the seven original Watergate defendants as hush money to buy their silence and keep them from revealing their knowledge of the identities of the officers and employees of the Nixon reelection committees and the White House aides who had participated in the Watergate.

10. They gave assurances to some of the original seven defendants that they would receive Presidential clemency after serving short portions of their sentences if they refrained from divulging the identities and activities of the officers and employees of the Nixon reelection committees and the White House aides who had participated in the Watergate affair.

11. They made arrangements by which the attorneys who represented the seven original Watergate defendants received their fees in cash from moneys which had been collected to finance President Nixon's reelection campaign.

12. They induced the Department of Justice and the prosecutors of the seven original Watergate defendants to assure the news media and the general public that there was no evidence that any persons other than the seven original Watergate defendants were implicated in any way in any Watergate-related crimes.

13. They inspired massive efforts on the part of segments of the news media friendly to the administration to persuade the American people that most of the members of the Select Committee named by the Senate to investigate the Watergate were biased and irresponsible men motivated solely by desires to exploit the matters they investigated for personal or partisan advantage, and that the allegations in the press that Presidential aides had been involved in the Watergate were venomous machinations of a hostile and unreliable press bent on destroying the country's confidence in a great and good President.

One shudders to think that the Watergate conspiracies might have been effectively concealed and their most dramatic episode might have been dismissed as a "third-rate" burglary conceived and committed solely by the seven original Watergate defendants had it not been for the courage and penetrating understanding of Judge Sirica, the thoroughness of the investigative reporting of Carl Bernstein, Bob Woodward, and other representatives of a free press, the labors of the Senate Select Committee and its excellent staff, and the dedication and diligence of Special Prosecutors Archibald Cox and Leon Jaworski and their associates.

Why Was Watergate?

Unlike the men who were responsible for Teapot Dome, the Presidential aides who perpetrated Watergate were not seduced by the love of money, which is sometimes thought to be the root of all evil. On the contrary, they were instigated by a lust for political power, which is at least as corrupting as political power itself.

They gave their allegiance to the President and his policies. They had stood for a time near to him, and had been entrusted by him with great governmental and political power. They enjoyed exercising such power, and longed for its continuance.

They knew that the power they enjoyed would be lost and the policies to which they adhered would be frustrated if the President should be defeated.

As a consequence of these things, they believed the President's reelection to be a most worthy objective, and succumbed to an age-old temptation. They resorted to evil means to promote what they conceived to be a good end.

Their lust for political power blinded them to ethical considerations and legal requirements; to Aristotle's aphorism that the good of man must be the end of politics; and to Grover Cleveland's conviction that a public office is a public trust.

They had forgotten, if they ever knew, that the Constitution is designed to be a law for rulers and people alike at all times and under all circumstances; and that no doctrine involving more pernicious consequences to the commonwealth has ever been invented by the wit of man than the notion that any of its provisions can be suspended by the President for any reason whatsoever.

On the contrary, they apparently believed that the President is above the Constitution, and has the autocratic power to suspend its provisions if he decides in his own unreviewable judgment that his action in so doing promotes his own political interests or the welfare of the Nation. As one of them testified before the Senate Select Committee, they believed that the President has the autocratic power to suspend the fourth amendment whenever he imagines that some indefinable aspect of national security is involved.

I digress to reject this doctrine of the constitutional omnipotence of the President. As long as I have a mind to think, a tongue to speak, and a heart to love my country, I shall deny that the Constitution confers any autocratic power on the President, or authorizes him to convert George Washington's America into Gaius Caesar's Rome.

The lust for political power of the Presidential aides who perpetrated Watergate on America blinded them to the laws of God as well as to the laws and ethics of man.

As a consequence, they violated the spiritual law which forbids men to do evil even when they think good will result from it, and ignored these warnings of the King James version of the Bible:

> There is nothing covered, that shall not be revealed; neither hid, that shall not be known. Be not deceived; God is not mocked: For whatsoever a man soweth, that shall he also reap.

I find corroboration for my conclusion that lust for political power produced Watergate in words uttered by the most eloquent and learned of all the Romans, Marcus Tullius Cicero, about 2100 years ago. He said:

> Most men, however, are inclined to forget justice altogether, when once the craving for military power or political honors and glory has taken possession of them. Remember the saying of Ennius, "When crowns are at stake, no friendship is sacred, no faith shall be kept."

As one after another of the individuals who participated in Watergate goes to prison, we see in action an inexorable spiritual law which Rudyard Kipling phrased in this fashion in his poem about Tomlinson's Ghost:

> For the sin ye do by two and two,
> You must pay for one by one.

As we contemplate the motives that inspired their misdeeds, we acquire a new awareness of the significance of Cardinal Wolsey's poignant lament:

Had I but serv'd my God with half
The zeal I serv'd my King,
He would not in mine age have left me
Naked to mine enemies.

The Antidote for Future Watergates

Is there an antidote which will prevent future Watergates? If so, what is it?

The Senate Select Committee is recommending the enactment of new laws which it believes will minimize the danger of future Watergates and make more adequate and certain the punishment of those who attempt to perpetrate them upon our country.

Candor compels the confession, however, that law alone will not suffice to prevent future Watergates. In saying this, I do not disparage the essential role which law plays in the life of our Nation. As one who has labored as a practicing lawyer, a judge, and a legislator all of my adult years, I venerate the law as an instrument of service to society. At the same time, however, I know the weakness of the law as well as its strength.

Law is not self-executing. Unfortunately, at times its execution rests in the hands of those who are faithless to it. And even when its enforcement is committed to those who revere it, law merely deters some human beings from offending, and punishes other human beings for offending. It does not make men good. This task can be performed only by ethics or religion or morality.

Since politics is the art or science of government, no man is fit to participate in politics or to seek or hold public office unless he has two characteristics.

The first of these characteristics is that he must understand and be dedicated to the true purpose of government, which is to promote the good of the people, and entertain the abiding conviction that a public office is a public trust, which must never be abused to secure private advantage.

The second characteristic is that he must possess that intellectual and moral integrity, which is the priceless ingredient in good character.

When all is said, the only sure antidote for future Watergates is understanding of fundamental principles and intellectual and moral integrity in the men and women who achieve or are entrusted with governmental or political power.

Josiah Gilbert Holland, a poet of a bygone generation, recognized this truth in a poem which he called "The Day's Demand," and which I like to call "America's Prayer." I quote his words:

God give us men! A time like this demands
Strong minds, great hearts, true faith and ready hands;
Men whom the lust of office does not kill;
Men whom the spoils of office cannot buy;
Men who possess opinions and a will;
Men who have honor — men who will not lie;
Men who can stand before a demagogue
And damn his treacherous flatteries without winking;
Tall men, sun-crowned, who live above the fog
In public duty, and in private thinking.

HOW WELL DID YOU UNDERSTAND THIS SELECTION?

1. According to Ervin's investigation, what were the charges of misconduct levied against the Nixon Administration?

2. What was Ervin's viewpoint on why members of the Nixon team decided to break into Democratic Headquarters?

3. Did Senator Ervin believe that President Nixon should have been tried and ultimately impeached for his actions in the Watergate Scandal? Support your response.

4. What solutions did Senator Ervin make to ensure that presidents would not be able to abuse their governing authority?

In Article I, Section 8 of the Constitution, Congress is granted the power to declare war. However, histori-cally Congress has had little success in either exercising this power or curtailing the ever-increasing president's predominant role in controlling our military forces and ultimately our foreign policy. Presidents have often engaged in military actions without a formal congressional declaration of war. The ultimate modern example of "hostilities" was the Vietnam "conflict" in which over 50,000 American soldiers lost their lives. Presidents Eisenhower, Kennedy, Johnson, and Nixon ordered U.S. forces into Vietnam to protect U.S. economic and political interests. The troops were always explained to the American public in terms of the protection of freedom and democracy for the Vietnamese people. Based on a non-incident in the Gulf of Tonkin, President Johnson asked for and received from Congress virtually unlimited war-making powers. Scholars have argued that this transference of power was virtually unconstitutional.

The debacle of Vietnam prompted Congress to re-evaluate the war-making balance that existed between it and the president. Congress believed that the balance of power had tipped too much in favor of the executive branch and desired to restore a more effective check and balance of power in the area of foreign policy making. Thus, in 1973, Congress passed the War Powers Act over President Nixon's veto. The legislation stipulated that presidents must consult with Congress whenever possible prior to using military force and to withdraw forces after sixty days unless Congress declares war or grants an extension.

*There have been many problems with the War Powers Act, not the least of which is that subsequent presidents have considered this resolution to be unconstitutional. Their position was given validity when in 1983, the Supreme Court in **INS v Chadha**, ruled that legislative vetoes were unconstitutional. The War Powers Act could be considered to be a legislative veto since Congress is actually vetoing a presidential act after he has already deployed troops. Besides the constitutional problem presented by the War Powers Act, several presidents have simply been unwilling to adhere to the reporting requirements and fine print of the law. This occurred when President Reagan sent troops into Lebanon and President Bush sent them to Saudi Arabia.*

Text of the war powers resolution enacted into law by Congress, Nov. 7, 1973, over President Nixon's veto:

SECTION 1. This joint resolution may be cited as the "War Powers Resolution".

Purpose and Policy

SEC. 2. (a) It is the purpose of this joint resolution to fulfill the intent of the framers of the Constitution of the United States and insure that the collective judgment of both the Congress and the President will apply to the introduction of United States Armed Forces into hostilities, or into situations where imminent involvement in hostilities is clearly indicated by the circumstances, and to the continued use of such forces in hostilities or in such situations.
(b) Under article 1, section 8, of the Constitution, it is specifically provided that the Congress shall have the power to make all laws necessary and proper for carrying into execution, not only its own powers but also all other powers vested by the Constitution in the Government of the United States, or in any department or officer thereof.

(c) The constitutional powers of the President as Commander-in-Chief to introduce United States Armed Forces into hostilities, or into situations where imminent involvement in hostilities is clearly indicated by the circumstances, are exercised only pursuant to (1) a declaration of war, (2) specific statutory authorization, or (3) a national emergency created by attack upon the United States, its territories or possessions, or its armed forces.

Consultation

SEC. 3. The President in every possible instance shall consult with Congress before introducing United States Armed Forces into hostilities or into situations where imminent involvement in hostilities is clearly indicated by the circumstances and after every such introduction shall consult regularly with the Congress until United States

Armed Forces are no longer engaged in hostilities or have been removed from such situations.

Reporting

SEC. 4. (a) In the absence of a declaration of war, in any case in which United States Armed Forces are introduced-

(1) into hostilities or into situations where imminent involvement in hostilities is clearly indicated by the circumstances;

(2) into the territory, airspace or waters of a foreign nation, while equipped for combat, except for deployments which relate solely to supply, replacement, relate or training of such forces; or

(3) in numbers which substantially enlarge United States Armed Forces equipped for combat already located in a foreign nation: the President shall submit within 48 hours to the Speaker of the House of Representatives and to the President pro tempore of the Senate a report, in writing, setting forth-

(A) the circumstances necessitating the introduction of United States Armed Forces;

(B) the constitutional and legislative authority under which such introduction took place; and

(C) the estimated scope and duration of the hostilities or involvement.

(b) The President shall provide such other information as the Congress may request in the fulfillment of its constitutional responsibilities with respect to committing the Nation to war and to the use of United States Armed Forces abroad.

(c) Whenever United States Armed Forces are introduced into hostilities or into any situation described in subsection (a) of this section, the President shall, so long as such armed forces continue to be engaged in such hostilities or situation, report to the Congress periodically on the status of such hostilities or situation as well as on the scope and duration of such hostilities or situation, but in no event shall he report to the Congress less often than once every six months.

Congressional Action

SEC. 5. (a) Each report submitted pursuant to section 4(a)(1) shall be transmitted to the Speaker of the House of Representatives and to the President pro tempore of the Senate on the same calendar day. Each report so transmitted shall be referred to the Committee on Foreign Affairs of the House of Representatives and to the Committee on Foreign Relations of the Senate for appropriate action. If, when the report is transmitted, the Congress has adjourned sine die or has adjourned for any period in excess of three calendar days, the Speaker of the House of Representatives and the President pro tempore of the Senate, if they deem it advisable (or if petitioned by at least 30 percent of the membership of their respective Houses) shall jointly request the President to convene Congress in order that it may consider the report and take appropriate action pursuant to this section.

(b) Within sixty calendar days after a report is submitted or is required to be submitted pursuant to section 4(a)(1), whichever is earlier, the President shall terminate any use of United States Armed Forces with respect to which such report was submitted (or required to be submitted), unless the Congress (1) has declared war or has enacted a specific authorization for such use of United States Armed Forces, (2) has extended by law such sixty-day period, or (3) is physically unable to meet as a result of an armed attack upon the United States. Such sixty-day period shall be extended for not more than an additional thirty days if the President determines and certifies to the Congress in writing that unavoidable military necessity respecting the safety of United States Armed Forces requires the continued use of such armed forces in the course of bringing about a prompt removal of such forces.

(c) Notwithstanding subsection (b), at any time that United States Armed Forces are engaged in hostilities outside the territory of the United States, its possessions and territories without a declaration of war or specific statutory authorization, such forces shall be removed by the President if the Congress so directs by concurrent resolution.

Source: Public Law 93-148, 93rd Congress, H. J. Res. 542, Nov. 7, 1973.

HOW WELL DID YOU UNDERSTAND THIS SELECTION?

1. Why did Congress pass the War Powers Act of 1973?

2. What power does the Constitution grant the president to declare war? the Congress?

3. How does the Constitution define the relationship between the Congress and the president with regards to the power to declare war?

4. Did the War Powers Act of 1973 support and/or alter the separation of power and checks and balances between these two branches of government as it related to the power to declare war?

In 1970 an unmarried Texas woman who wanted to terminate her pregnancy filed a lawsuit against District Attorney Henry Wade. Wade's job was to enforce the law in Dallas County and under that law (Arts. 1191-1194 and 1196 of the State's Penal Code) abortion, with the exception of instances where it was necessary to save the mother's life, was a crime. The woman had several options: she could get an illegal abortion in Mexico; she could try to meet the residency requirements needed to get a legal abortion in a nearby state such as Colorado or California; or she could forgo the abortion but challenge the law that prevented the termination. The pregnant woman, Norma McCorvey, who used the pseudonym "Jane Roe" in order to protect her privacy, chose the last option.

The case was first heard in a Texas federal court and then was brought, on appeal, to the United States Supreme Court. On January 22, 1973, the Supreme Court released its written opinion in the case of **Roe v. Wade**. *The Court, in a 7-2 ruling, found that a woman has a constitutional right to terminate a pregnancy. Below are excerpts from the majority decision, which was written by Justice Harry Blackmun, from Justice Potter Stewart's concurring opinion and from the two dissenting opinions of Justices William Rehnquist and Byron White.*

ROE v. WADE, 410 U.S. 113 (1973)

Mr. Justice Blackmun

We forthwith acknowledge our awareness of the sensitive and emotional nature of the abortion controversy, of the vigorous opposing views, even among physicians, and of the deep and seemingly absolute convictions that the subject inspires. One's philosophy, one's religious training, one's attitudes toward life and family and their values, and the moral standards one establishes and seeks to observe, are all likely to influence and to color one's thinking and conclusions about abortion.

In addition, population growth, pollution, poverty, and racial overtones tend to complicate and not to simplify the problem.

Our task, of course, is to resolve the issue by constitutional measurement, free of emotion and of predilection. We seek earnestly to do this ....

The Constitution does not explicitly mention any right of privacy. In a line of decisions, however,...the Court has recognized that a right of personal privacy, or a guarantee of certain areas or zones of privacy, does exist under the Constitution. In varying contexts, the Court or individual Justices have, indeed, found at least the roots of that right in the First Amendment ... in the Fourth and Fifth Amendments ... in the Ninth Amendment ... or in the concept of liberty guaranteed by the first section of the Fourteenth Amendment ....

This right of privacy... is broad enough to encompass a woman's decision whether or not to terminate her pregnancy. The detriment that the State would impose upon the pregnant woman by denying this choice altogether is apparent. Specific and direct harm medically diagnosable even in early pregnancy may be involved. Maternity, or additional offspring, may force upon the woman a distressful life and future. Psychological harm may be imminent. Mental and physical health may be taxed by child care. There is also the distress, for all concerned, associated with the unwanted child, and there is the problem of bringing a child into a family already unable, psychologically and otherwise, to care for it. In other cases, as in this one, the additional difficulties and continuing stigma of unwed motherhood may be involved. All these are factors the woman and her responsible physician necessarily will consider in consultation.

On the basis of elements such as these, appellant and some amici argue that the woman's right is absolute and that she is entitled to terminate her pregnancy at whatever time, in whatever way, and for whatever reason she alone chooses. With this we do not agree .... The Court's decisions recognizing a right of privacy also acknowledge that some state regulation in areas protected by that right - is appropriate. As noted above, a State may properly assert important interests in safe-guarding health, in maintaining medical standards, and protecting potential life. At some point in pregnancy, these respective interests become sufficiently compelling to sustain regulation of the factors that govern the abortion decision. The privacy right involved, therefore, cannot be said to be absolute ....

We, therefore, conclude that the right of personal privacy includes the abortion decision, but that this right is not unqualified and must be considered against important state interests in regulation....

Our conclusion that Art. 1196 is unconstitutional means, of course, that the Texas abortion statutes, as a unit, must fall.

Mr. Justice Stewart, concurring.

Several decisions of this court make clear that freedom of personal choice in matters of marriage and family life is one of the liberties protected by the Due Process Clause of the Fourteenth Amendment. *Loving v. Virginia*, 388U.S.1,12; *Griswold v. Connecticut*, (381U.S.4791; *Pierce v. Society of Sisters* (268U.S.510,534-5351; *Meyer v. Nebraska*, [262U.S.390,399-4001 .... As recently as last Term, in *Eisenstadt v. Baird*, 405U.S.438,453, we recognized "the right of the **individual**, married or single, to be free from unwarranted governmental intrusion into matters so fundamentally affecting a person as the decision whether to bear or beget a child." That right necessarily includes the right of a woman to decide whether or not to terminate her pregnancy. "Certainly the interests of a woman in giving of her physical and emotional self during the pregnancy and the interests that will be affected throughout her life by the birth and raising of a child are of a far greater degree of significance and personal intimacy than the right to send a child to private school protected in *Pierce v. Society of Sisters*, 268U.S.510(1925), or the right to teach a foreign language protected in *Meyer v. Nebraska*, 262U. S. 390 (1923). *Abele v. Markle*, 351F. Supp. 224,227 (Conn. 1972).

Clearly, therefore, the Court today is correct in holding that the right asserted by Jane Roe is embraced within the personal liberty protected by the Due Process Clause of the Fourteenth Amendment ....

Mr. Justice Rehnquist, dissenting.

The Court's opinion brings to the decision of this troubling question both extensive historical fact and a wealth of legal scholarship. While the opinion thus commands my respect, I find myself nonetheless in fundamental disagreement with those parts of it that invalidate the Texas statute in question, and therefore dissent ....

Even if there were a plaintiff in this case capable of litigating the issue which the Court decides, I would reach a conclusion opposite to that reached by the Court. I have difficulty in concluding, as the Court does, that the right of privacy is involved in this case. Texas, by the statute here challenged, bars the performance of a medical abortion by a licensed physician on a plaintiff such as Roe. A transaction resulting in an operation such as this is not "private" in the ordinary usage of the word. Nor is the "privacy" that the Court finds here even a distant relative of the freedom from searches and seizures protected by the Fourth Amendment to the Constitution, which the court has referred to as embodying a right to privacy....

The Due Process Clause of the Fourteenth Amendment undoubtedly does place a limit, albeit a broad one, on legislative power to enact laws such as this. If the Texas statute were to prohibit an abortion even where the mother's life is in jeopardy, I have little doubt that such a statute would lack a rational relation to a valid state objective under the test stated in [*Williamson v. Lee Optical Co.,* 348 U.S. 483, 491 (1955)]. But the Court's sweeping invalidation of any restrictions on abortion during the first trimester is impossible to justify under that standard ....

To reach its result, the Court necessarily has had to find within the scope of the Fourteenth Amendment a right that was apparently completely unknown to the drafters of the Amendment .... By the time of the adoption of the Fourteenth Amendment in 1868, there were at least 36 laws enacted by state or territorial legislatures limiting abortion .... The only conclusion possible from this history is that the drafters did not intend to have the Fourteenth Amendment withdraw from the States the power to legislate with respect to this matter ....

For all of the foregoing reasons, I respectfully dissent.

Mr. Justice White, dissenting.

....With all due respect, I dissent. I find nothing in the language or history of the Constitution to support the Court's judgment. The Court simply fashions and announces a new constitutional right for pregnant mothers and, with scarcely any reason or authority for its action, invests that right with sufficient substance to override most existing state abortion statutes. The upshot is that the people and the legislatures of the 50 States are constitutionally disentitled to weigh the relative importance of the continued existence and development of the fetus, on the one hand, against a spectrum of possible impacts on the mother, on the other hand. As an exercise of raw judicial power, the Court perhaps has authority to do what it does today; but in my view its judgment is an improvident and extravagant exercise of the power of judicial review that the Constitution extends to this Court.

The Court apparently values the convenience of the pregnant mother more than the continued existence and development of the life or potential life that she carries. Whether or not I might agree with that marshaling of values, I can in no event join the Court's judgment because I find no constitutional warrant for imposing such an order of priorities on the people and legislatures of the States.

[*Roe v. Wade*: United States Supreme Court, Annotated by Bo Schambelan. Philadelphia, PA.: Running Press, 1992.]

319

HOW WELL DID YOU UNDERSTAND THIS SELECTION?

1. What was the majority opinion in the case of *Roe v. Wade*?

2. Which constitutional "right," according to Justice Blackmun, justifies the opinion in this case?

*In **Federalist 10** James Madison argued that in a free society factions are inevitable and cannot be destroyed without destroying liberty as well. Madison and the other Framers, all of whom were heavily influenced by the writings of the British philosopher John Locke, saw liberty as a natural right. These rights were to be more explicitly addressed in the First Amendment added to the Constitution in 1791. The First Amendment's freedoms of speech, press, assembly, and its right to petition government for a redress of grievances all protect political parties and interest groups, as well as individuals. These rights, however, are not absolute and the courts have always held that governments may interfere with them if to do so is reasonable. The First Amendment shifts the burden of proof to the government, requiring the government to prove that the interference serves the greater needs of the society and is, therefore, reasonable.*

Congress, as well as state legislatures, have attempted, throughout American history, to regulate interest group and political party behavior. During the 1970s, when it became apparent that candidates and their political parties were raising huge sums of campaign money from special interests, Congress moved to tighten the campaign finance laws. The Federal Election Campaign Act of 1971, amended in 1974, limited contributions made by individuals and interest group political action committees (PACs). The law also placed limits on spending that was done on behalf of a candidate's campaign. The law created the Federal Election Commission (FEC), a regulatory body to oversee the complex provisions of the law. Political candidates and interest group PACs must register with the Commission and file detailed reports on their contributions and spending.

In the following opinion the Supreme Court held that political spending by a candidate or party is a form of speech and is protected by the First Amendment. The Court also held that there is a sufficient public interest to justify some limits on campaign contributions and their disclosure.

Buckley v. Valeo
424 U.S. 1 (1976)

Per Curiam

A. Contribution and Expenditure Limitations

The intricate statutory scheme adopted by Congress to regulate federal election campaigns includes restrictions on political contributions and expenditures that apply broadly to all phases and all participants in the election process. The major contribution and expenditure limitations in the Act prohibit individuals from contributing more than $25,000 in a single year or more than $1,000 to any single candidate for an election campaign and from spending more than $1,000 a year "relative to a clearly identified candidate." Other provisions restrict a candidate's use of personal and family resources in his campaign and limit the overall amount that can be spent by a candidate in campaigning for federal office...

A. General Principles

The Act's contribution and expenditure limitations operate in an area of the most fundamental First Amendment activities. Discussion of public issues and debate on the qualifications of candidates are integral to the operation of the system of government established by our Constitution...

The First Amendment protects political association as well as political expression...

It is with these principles in mind that we consider the primary contentions of the parties with respect to the Act's limitations upon the giving and spending of money in political campaigns. Those conflicting contentions could not more sharply define the basic issues before us. Appellees contend that what the Act regulates is conduct, and that its effect on speech and association is incidental at most. Appellants respond that contributions and expenditures are at the very core of political speech, and that the Act's limitations thus constitute restraints on First Amendment liberty that are both gross and direct...

A restriction on the amount of money a person or groups can spend on political communication during a campaign necessarily reduces the quantity of expression by restricting the number of issues discussed, the depth of their exploration, and the size of the audience reached. This is because virtually every means of communicating ideas in today's mass society requires the expenditure of money...

The expenditure limitations contained in the Act represent substantial rather than merely theoretical restraints on the quantity and diversity of political speech. The $1,000 ceiling on spending "relative to a clearly identified candidate," 18 U.S.C. 608(e)(1)...would appear to exclude all citizens and groups except candidates, political parties and the institutional press from any significant use of the most effective modes of communication. Although the Act's limitations on expenditures by campaign organizations and political parties provide substantially greater room for discussion and debate, they would have required restrictions in the scope of a number of past congressional and Presidential campaigns and would operate to constrain campaigning by candidates who raise sums in excess of the spending ceiling.

By contrast with a limitation upon expenditures for political expression, a limitation upon the amount that any one person or group may contribute to a candidate or political committee entails only a marginal restriction upon the contributor's ability to engage in free communication. A contribution serves as a general expression of support for the candidate and his views, but does not communicate the underlying basis for the support...While contributions may result in political expression if spent by a candidate or an association to present views to the voters, the transformation of contributions into political debate involves speech by someone other than the contributor.

Given the important role of contributions in financing political campaigns, contribution restrictions could have a severe impact on political dialogue if the limitations prevented candidates and political committees from amassing the resources necessary for effective advocacy. There is no indication, however, that the contribution limitations imposed by the Act would have any dramatic adverse effect on the funding of campaigns and political associations. The overall effect of the Act's contribution ceilings is merely to require candidates and political committees to raise funds from a greater number of persons and to compel people who would otherwise contribute amounts greater than the statutory limits to expend such funds on direct political expression, rather than to reduce the total amount of money potentially available to promote political expression.

The Act's contribution and expenditure limitations also impinge on protected associational freedoms. Making a contribution, like joining a political party, serves to affiliate a person with a candidate. In addition, it enables like-minded persons to pool their resources in furtherance of common political goals. The Act's contribution ceilings thus limit one important means of associating with a candidate or committee, but leave the contributor free to become a member of any political association and to assist personally in the association's efforts on behalf of candidates. And the Act's contribution limitations permit associations and candidates to aggregate large sums of money to promote effective advocacy. By contrast, the Act's $1,000 limitation on independent expenditures "relative to a clearly identified candidate" precludes most associations from effectively amplifying the voice of their adherents, the original basis for the recognition of First Amendment protection of the freedom of association...

In sum, although the Act's contribution and expenditure limitations both implicate fundamental First Amendment interests, its expenditure ceilings impose significantly more severe restrictions on protected freedoms of political expression and association than do its limitations on financial contributions.

Contribution Limitations

We find that, under the rigorous standard of review established by our prior decisions, the weighty interests served by restricting the size of financial contributions to political candidates are sufficient to justify the limited effect upon the First Amendment freedoms caused by the $1,000 contribution ceiling.

Expenditure Limitations

The Act's expenditure ceilings impose direct and substantial restraints on the quantity of political speech...It is clear that the primary effect of these expenditure limitations is to restrict the quantity of campaign speech by individuals, groups, and candidates. The restrictions, while neutral to the ideas expressed, limit political expression "at the core of our electoral process and of the First Amendment freedoms."...

1. The $1,000 Limitation on Expenditures "Relative to a Clearly Identified Candidate"...[T]he constitutionality of 608(e)(1) turns on whether the governmental interests advanced in its support satisfy the existing scrutiny applicable to limitations on core First Amendment rights of political expression.

We find that the governmental interest in preventing corruption and the appearance of corruption inadequate to justify 608(e)(1)'s ceiling on independent expenditures...

It is argued, however, that the ancillary governmental interest in equalizing the relative ability of individuals and groups to influence the outcome of elections serves to justify the limitation on express advocacy of the election or defeat of candidates imposed by 608(e)(1)'s expenditure ceiling. But the concept that government may restrict the speech of some elements of our society in order to enhance the relative voice of others is wholly foreign to the First Amendment...The First Amendment's protection against governmental abridgement of free expression cannot properly be made to depend on a person's financial ability to engage in public discussion...

323

For the reasons stated, we conclude that 608(e)(1)'s independent expenditure limitation is unconstitutional under the First Amendment.

2. Limitation on Expenditures by Candidates from Personal or Family Resources

The ceiling on personal expenditures by candidates on their own behalf, like the limitations on independent expenditures contained in 608(e)(1), imposes a substantial restraint on the ability of persons to engage in protected First Amendment expression…

The ancillary interest in equalizing the relative financial resources of candidates competing for elective office, therefore, provides the sole relevant rationale for 608(e)(1)'s expenditure ceiling. The interest is clearly not sufficient to justify the provision's infringement of fundamental First Amendment rights…

3. Limitations on Campaign Expenditures

Section 608(c) places limitations on overall campaign expenditures by candidates seeking nomination for election and election to federal office…

No governmental interest that has been suggested is sufficient to justify the restriction on the quantity of political expression imposed by 608(c)'s campaign expenditure limitations. The major evil associated with rapidly increasing campaign expenditures is the danger of candidate dependence on large contributions. The interest of alleviating the corrupting influence of large contributions is served by the Act's contribution limitations and disclosure provisions rather than by 608(c)'s campaign expenditure ceilings…

The interest in equalizing the financial resources of candidates competing for federal office is no more convincing a justification for restricting the scope of federal election campaigns…

The campaign expenditure limitations appear to be designed primarily to serve the governmental interests in reducing the allegedly skyrocketing costs of political campaigns…The First Amendment denies government the power to determine that spending to promote one's political views is wasteful, excessive, or unwise. In the free society ordained by our Constitution it is not the government but the people—individually as citizens and candidates collectively as associations and political committees—who must retain control over the quantity and range of debate on public issues in a political campaign.

For these reasons we hold that 608(c) is constitutionally invalid…

Reporting and Disclosure Requirements

Each political committee is required to register with the Commission, 433, and to keep detailed records of both contributions and expenditures, 432(c), (d)…

Each committee and each candidate also is required to file quarterly reports, 434(a). The reports are to contain detailed information…

Every individual or group, other than a political committee or candidate, who makes "contributions: or "expenditures" of over $100 in a calendar year "other than by contribution to a political committee or a candidate" is required to file a statement with the Commission…

A. General Principle

Unlike the overall limitations on contributions and expenditures, the disclosure requirements impose no ceiling on campaign-related activities. But we have repeatedly found that compelled disclosure, in itself, can seriously infringe on privacy of association and belief guaranteed by the First Amendment...

We long have recognized that significant encroachments on First Amendment rights of the sort that compelled disclosure imposes cannot be justified by a mere showing of some legitimate governmental interest. Since *NAACP v. Alabama* [1958] we have required that the subordinating interests of the State must survive exacting scrutiny...

The strict test established by *NAACP v. Alabama* is necessary because compelled disclosure has the potential for substantially infringing the exercise of First Amendment rights. But we have acknowledged that there are governmental interests sufficiently important to outweigh the possibility of infringement, particularly when the "free functioning of our national institutions" is involved...

The governmental interests sought to be vindicated by the disclosure requirements are of this magnitude. They fall into three categories. First, disclosure provides the electorate with information "as to where political campaign money comes from and how it is spent by the candidate" in order to aid the voters in evaluating those who seek federal office. It allows voters to place each candidate in the political spectrum more precisely than is often possible solely on the basis of party labels and campaign speeches. The sources of a candidate's financial support also alert the voter to the interests to which a candidate is most likely to be responsive and thus facilitate predictions of future performance in office.

Second, disclosure requirements deter corruption and avoid the appearance of corruption by exposing large contributions and expenditures to the light of publicity...

Third, and not least significant, record keeping, reporting, and disclosure requirements are essential means of gathering the data necessary to detect violations of the contribution limitations described above.

The disclosure requirements, as a general matter, directly serve substantial governmental interests. In determining whether these interests are sufficient to justify the requirements we must look to the extent of the burden that they place on individual rights...

HOW WELL DID YOU UNDERSTAND THIS SELECTION?

1. In *Buckley V. Valeo* the Supreme Court draws a distinction between contributions and expenditures. What is the difference between the two and should either or both be a protected form of expression under the First Amendment to the Constitution?

2. Courts have consistently held that the First Amendment freedoms do not prohibit all forms of national government interference. Under what conditions can the national government constitutionally infringe upon the freedoms of speech, press, religion, and assembly?

When familial abuse or the inability of the family to ensure the child's safety and well being endangers a child, government agencies are empowered to remove the child from the home. In 1978 Congress passed the Indian Child Welfare Act to rectify a history of government agencies removing Indian children to non-Indian foster and adoptive homes and institutions. The law requires that Indian children be placed in homes that reflect the Indian culture. The law also gives the child's Indian tribe the right and power to intervene in any child custody proceedings involving an Indian child.

To establish standards for the placement of Indian children in foster or adoptive homes, to prevent the breakup of Indian families, and for other purposes.

Be it enacted by the Senate and House of Representatives of the United States of America in Congress assembled, That this Act may be cited as the "Indian Child Welfare Act of 1978."

Sec. 2 Recognizing the special relationship between the United States and the Indian tribes and their members and the Federal responsibility to Indian people, the Congress finds—

(1) that clause 3, section 8, article I of the United States Constitution provides that "The Congress shall have Power *** To regulate Commerce *** with Indian tribes" and, through this and other constitutional authority, Congress has plenary power over Indian affairs;

(2) that Congress, through statutes, treaties, and the general course of dealing with Indian tribes, has assumed the responsibility for the protection and preservation of Indian tribes and their resources;

(3) that there is no resource that is more vital to the continued existence and integrity of Indian tribes than their children and that the United States has a direct interest, as trustee, in protecting Indian children who are members of or are eligible for membership in an Indian tribe;

(4) that an alarmingly high percentage of Indian families are broken up by the removal, often unwarranted, of their children from them by nontribal public and private agencies and that an alarmingly high percentage of such children are placed in non-Indian foster and adoptive homes and institutions; and

(5) that the States, exercising their recognized jurisdiction over Indian child custody proceedings through administrative and judicial bodies, have often failed to recognize the essential tribal relations of Indian people and the cultural and social standards prevailing in Indian communities and families.

Sec. 3. The Congress hereby declares that it is the policy of this Nation to protect the best interests of Indian children and to promote the stability and security of Indian tribes and families by the establishment of minimum Federal standards for the removal of Indian children from their families and the placement of such children in foster or adoptive homes which will reflect the unique values of Indian culture, and by providing for assistance to Indian tribes in the operation of child and family service programs....

Title I—Child Custody Proceedings

Sec. 101. (a) An Indian tribe shall have jurisdiction exclusive as to any State over any child custody proceeding involving an Indian child who resides or is domiciled within the reservation of such tribe, except where such jurisdiction is otherwise vested in the State by existing Federal law. Where an Indian child is a ward of a tribal court, the Indian tribe shall retain exclusive jurisdiction, notwithstanding the residence or domicile of the child.

(b) In any State court proceeding for the foster care placement of, or termination of parental rights to, an Indian child not domiciled or residing within the reservation of the Indian child's tribe, the court, in the absence of good cause to the contrary, shall transfer such proceeding to the jurisdiction of the tribe, absent objection by either parent, upon the petition of either parent or the Indian custodian or the Indian child's tribe: *Provided,* That such transfer shall be subject to declination by the tribal court of such tribe.

(c) In any State court proceeding for the foster care placement of, or termination of parental rights to, an Indian child, the Indian custodian of the child and the Indian child's tribe shall have a right to intervene at any point in the proceeding.

(d) The United States, every State, every territory or possession of the United States, and every Indian tribe shall give full faith and credit to the public acts, records, and judicial proceedings of any Indian tribe applicable to Indian child custody proceedings to the same extent that such entities give full faith and credit to the public acts, records, and judicial proceedings of any other entity.

Sec. 102. (a) In any involuntary proceeding in a State court, where the court knows or has reason to know that an Indian child is involved, the party seeking the foster care placement of, or termination of parental rights to, an Indian child shall notify the parent or Indian custodian and the Indian child's tribe, by registered mail with return receipt requested, of the pending proceedings and of their right of intervention. If the identity or location of the parent or Indian custodian and the tribe cannot be determined, such notice shall be given to the Secretary in like manner, who shall have fifteen days after receipt to provide the requisite notice to the parent or Indian custodian and the tribe. No foster care placement or termination of parental rights proceeding shall be held until at least ten days after receipt of notice by the parent or Indian custodian and the tribe or the Secretary: *Provided,* That the parent or Indian custodian or the tribe shall, upon request, be granted up to twenty additional days to prepare for such proceeding.

(b) In any case in which the court determines indigency, the parent or Indian custodian shall have the fight to court-appointed counsel in any removal, placement, or termination proceeding. The court may, in its discretion, appoint counsel for the child upon a finding that such appointment is in the best interest of the child. Where State law makes no provision for appointment of counsel in such proceedings, the court shall promptly notify the Secretary upon appointment of counsel, and the Secretary, upon certification of the presiding judge, shall pay reasonable fees and expenses out of funds which may be appropriated pursuant to the Act of November 2, 1921.

(c) Each party to a foster care placement or termination of parental rights proceeding under State law involving an Indian child shall have the right to examine all reports or other documents filed with the court upon which any decision with respect to such action may be based.

(d)   Any party seeking to effect a foster care placement of, or termination of parental rights to, an Indian child under State law shall satisfy the court that active efforts have been made to provide remedial services and rehabilitative programs designed to prevent the breakup of the Indian family and that these efforts have proved unsuccessful.

(e) No foster care placement may be ordered in such proceeding in the absence of a determination, supported by clear and convincing evidence, including testimony of qualified expert witnesses, that the continued custody of the child by the parent or Indian custodian is likely to result in serious emotional or physical damage to the child.

(f) No termination of parental rights may be ordered in such proceeding in the absence of a determination, supported by evidence beyond a reasonable doubt, including testimony of qualified expert witnesses, that the continued custody of the child by the parent or Indian custodian is likely to result in serious emotional or physical damage to the child.

Sec. 103. (a) Where any parent or Indian custodian voluntarily consents to a foster care placement or to termination of parental rights, such consent shall not be valid unless executed in writing and recorded before a judge of a court of competent jurisdiction and accompanied by the presiding judge's certificate that the terms and consequences of the consent were fully explained in detail and were fully understood by the parent or Indian custodian. The court shall also certify that either the parent or Indian custodian fully understood the explanation in English or that it was interpreted into a language that the parent or Indian custodian understood. Any consent given prior to, or within ten days after, birth of the Indian child shall not be valid....

Sec. 105. (a) In any adoptive placement of an Indian child under State law, a preference shall be given, in the absence of good cause to the contrary, to a placement with (1) a member of the child's extended family; (2) other members of the Indian child's tribe; or (3) other Indian families.

(b) Any child accepted for foster care or preadoptive placement shall be placed in the least restrictive setting which most approximates a family and in which his special needs, if any, may be met. The child shall also be placed within reasonable proximity to his or her home, taking into account any special needs of the child. In any foster care or preadoptive placement, a preference shall be given, in the absence of good cause to the contrary, to a placement with—

(i) a member of the Indian child's extended family;

(ii) a foster home licensed, approved, or specified by the Indian child's tribe;

(iii) an Indian foster home licensed or approved by an authorized nonIndian licensing authority; or

(iv) an institution for children approved by an Indian tribe or operated by an Indian organization which has a program suitable to meet the Indian child's needs....

HOW WELL DID YOU UNDERSTAND THIS SELECTION?

1. What are the purposes of the Indian Child Welfare Act?

2. What part of the Constitution gives Congress the power to legislate the welfare of Indian children?

3. In your opinion, should an orphaned Native American child be raised exclusively by Native American adoptive parents? Support your response.

FLAG DESECRATION AND THE PROPOSED CONSTITUTIONAL AMENDMENT BANNING FLAG-BURNING

*Almost a century ago the Supreme Court upheld the right of a state to punish individuals who desecrate the American flag (**Halter v. Nebraska,** 205 U.S. 34, 43 (1907)). The question arose in subsequent years as to whether individuals who desecrated the flag in order to "communicate a message" were protected by the free speech clause of the First Amendment to the Constitution.*

*In the case of **Texas v. Johnson** (491 U.S. 397 (1989)), a flag burning case, the Supreme Court ruled that the First Amendment is applicable: the flag is a symbol and burning it is considered to be "symbolic" or non-verbal expression. The defendant in the case, Gregory Lee Johnson, who ignited the flag during a political protest in Dallas, Texas during the 1984 Republican National Convention, had been found guilty of violating a Texas law that prohibited the desecration of venerated objects and was fined two thousand dollars and sentenced to one year in jail. The decision was affirmed by the Dallas Court of Appeals but reversed by the Texas Court of Criminal Appeals. The Supreme Court of the United States, in a 5-4 ruling, sustained the decision of the Court of Criminal Appeals. Justice Brennan, who delivered the majority opinion of the Court, stated that the judgment of the Court of Criminal Appeals was affirmed because Johnson's action "did not threaten to disturb the peace...," and because, according to the free speech clause of the First Amendment, "the Government may not prohibit expression simply because it disagrees with its message .... "[1]*

*The decision was unpopular and highly controversial and Congress, in an attempt to circumvent it, passed the Flag Protection Act (1989). The Supreme Court ruled (**United States v. Eichman,** 110 S.Ct. 2404, 1990)) that this law—which stated that "whoever knowingly mutilates, defaces, physically defiles, burns, maintains on the floor or ground, or tramples upon any flag of the United States shall be fined under this title or imprisoned for not more than one year, or both"—was an unconstitutional abridgment of the right to free speech. It became clear that the only way that flag-burning could be banned was through a Constitutional amendment.*

President George Bush was an ardent supporter of such an amendment and he "felt compelled to push" the Congress to take action.[2] It did so. Having failed by 15 votes to obtain the two-thirds majority it needed in the Senate in 1989, Congress again considered amendments banning flag-burning in 1990, 1995, 1998 and 1999. Although these too were defeated (or not acted upon) it is likely, given the passion of its supporters, that an amendment aimed at protecting the flag will be proposed again.

The wording of the amendment, favored by President Bush, is very brief.

PROPOSED FLAG DESECRATION CONSTITUTIONAL AMENDMENT

"The Congress and the States shall have power to prohibit the physical desecration of the flag of the United States."

[1]"*Texas v. Johnson*, 491 U.S. 397 (1989)." In May It Please the Court: The First Amendment: Transcripts of the Oral Arguments Made Before the Supreme Court in Sixteen Key First Amendment Cases, ed. Peter Irons, 217-231. New York: The New Press, 1997.

[2]Toner, Robin. "President to Seek Amendment to Bar Burning the Flag." *The New York Times.* 28 June 1989, l(A) and 7(B).

HOW WELL DID YOU UNDERSTAND THIS SELECTION?

1. Which clause of which amendment to the Constitution did the Supreme Court find protects an individual's right to burn the American flag?

In June 1989 the Supreme Court determined that flag burning is a constitutionally protected form of free speech. (See "Flag Desecration and the Proposed Constitutional Amendment Banning Flag Burning") The selection below, written by presidential observer and scholar Hugh Sidey, is a commentary on President Bush's reaction to the Court's decision.

GIVING HONOR TO OLD GLORY
"No matter whether th' constitution follows th' flag or not, th' supreme coort follows th' iliction returns."

—Mr. Dooley

Not this time. Neither the flag nor the returns. "That flag decision," allowed political analyst Horace Busby, "shows that old Mr. Dooley [Finley Peter Dunne's fictional Chicago bartender] sometimes didn't know what he was talking about. The Supreme Court must not even read the newspapers." Busby plans to monitor the July 4th festivities across the nation. If the flag burners come out in force, there could be quite a political ruckus and possibly a constitutional amendment in less time than it takes to sing **The Star Spangled Banner**.

On the morning after the court had, with great heaving and sighing, delivered the flag decision, George Bush hit the Oval Office about 7:15. He did not even want to hear about the state of the world from his CIA briefer until he had dealt with flag burning. In the three-minute walk from his apartment upstairs, he probably saw the flag in the Yellow Room or maybe the one in the Blue Room. Maybe he glanced down toward the Mall and spied the 50 flags at the base of the Washington Monument. If he missed all those flags, there was one right behind his desk in the Oval Office.

Bush called flag burning reprehensible. He vowed that he would say so publicly later in the day. Where he left off, his senior staff picked up. "Seems to me," said one aide, "any virtue if carried to an extreme becomes a vice. No right is absolute if it is outweighed by damage to that society."

There is nothing hokey about Bush's indignation. He has carried his reverence for the symbols of freedom on his sleeve as long as he has been in politics and used them a time or two for political advantage. Back in the presidential primary campaign of 1988, Bush's field surveys showed that the controversy over requiring the Pledge of Allegiance in schools was a warm issue, the pro-Pledge stand wildly favored in many audiences. His visit to a New Jersey flag factory during the campaign drew some boos from the political commentators, but Bush never blushed.

Handling the flag at that level of power is tricky. Lyndon Johnson quite literally ground his teeth when he looked out his White House window and saw the Viet Nam protesters desecrate flags. But he was a prisoner of jingoism gone sour. Richard Nixon used the Stars and Stripes as a weapon against the marchers, ordering extraordinary displays of flags, pointedly wearing a flag lapel pin. Air Force One pilot Colonel Ralph Albertazzie had a better idea. When traveling abroad with the President, he was moved by the sight of people weeping when the plane taxied up. But he often flew and landed at night, and the long, graceful fuselage was swallowed by the dark. Albertazzie had small spotlights installed in the plane's horizontal stabilizers to illuminate the flag painted on its towering rudder. Wherever and whenever the President flies, the flag glows; the darker the night, the more spectacular the effect. That, in a way, is the history of the flag. It is not going to change, whatever the court may say.

Source: Sidey, Hugh. "The Presidency: Giving Honor to Old Glory," *Time*, 3 July 1989, 16.

HOW WELL DID YOU UNDERSTAND THIS SELECTION?

Give one specific example from the article that illustrates that author Hugh Sidey sympathizes with President Bush's antiflag burning position.

Lobbyists try to influence the behavior of public officials. Because lobbyists tend to be experts in their field, members of Congress often turn to them for information. This sharing of information is often done in informal environments, for example, during a round of golf, at a dinner or other fundraiser. As early as 1946, the government sought to regulate lobbying. The 1946 Federal Regulation of Lobbying Act required foreign lobbyists to register and report their actions. The Ethics in Government Act of 1978 attempted to ban contributions that would create conflicts of interest by government officials. The latest attempt to regulate lobbying occurred in 1994, with the passage of an act to regulate lobbying and gift giving to Congress.

When Push Comes to Shove,
House Votes for Gift Ban

…The bill updates and strengthens the 1946 lobbying disclosure law, which for years has been derided as ineffective. The measure requires anyone paid to lobby members of Congress, their staffs or senior executive branch officials to register at a new Office of Lobbying Registration and public Disclosure…

The bill would ban registered lobbyists from giving members gifts, meals or entertainment. It would, however, allow clients of lobbyists to buy meals for members and permit members to accept free travel for charity functions. Both activities would have to be disclosed…

Lobbying and Gift Provisions

Following are the highlights, which are similar to the Senate bill:

• Registration would be required for any organization that spends or receives more than $2,500 from all clients it lobbies for.

• Lobbying contacts would be defined as any communications with congressional members, aides or high-level executive branch officials with regard to legislation or official actions, including money spent on grass-roots campaigns.

• Any organization that employs a lobbyist would have to file a report covering all of its lobbying activities.

• Reports would be required twice a year specifying clients, lobbyists, amount spent or received, issues involved, agencies and committees contacted and interests of foreign affiliates.

• The gift provisions of the bill are not included in the Senate bill, which required disclosure by lobbyists of any gift worth more than $20 to a member.

Following are the highlights of the House gift language:
- Registered lobbyists would be barred from providing meals, entertainment or gifts to members directly or indirectly.
- Companies, unions or other groups that employ a lobbyist could pay for members' travel to political events, conventions, retreats, symposiums and receptions, including meals and entertainment.
- A company or union that employs a lobbyist could provide meals and entertainment for a member as long as a company official who is not a lobbyist is present.

HOW WELL DID YOU UNDERSTAND THIS SELECTION?

1. Why do you think the Lobby Acts require lobbyists to register and report their activities?

2. What benefits can a member of Congress legally receive under the Lobby Acts?

To date, sexual preference has not been recognized by the Supreme Court as a fundamental right guaranteed to individuals by the U.S. Constitution. In light of this, state and local governments have moved to protect sexual preference by passing "fairness" laws that have made it illegal to discriminate on the basis of sexual preference in the areas of hiring and housing. Several states have also begun to evaluate their marital laws to consider granting same-gender unions the same legal standing as heterosexual marriages.

In 1996, in reaction to state and local measures and ostensibly to insure the "full faith and credit" clause of the Constitution, Congress has passed federal legislation to define marriage as the heterosexual union between one man and one woman. Since the legislation is federal, a state would still be free to recognize homosexual marriages; however, for purposes of national law, such as for social security benefits, those unions would not be recognized. Recognizing that marital contracts have traditionally fallen within the area of state policy-making, the Defense of Marriage Act also provides that no state would have to recognize married homosexuals who were married under the laws of another state that recognized homosexual marriages.

To define and protect the institution of marriage.

Be it enacted by the Senate and House of Representatives of the United States of America in Congress assembled,

SECTION 1. SHORT TITLE.

This Act may be cited as the "Defense of Marriage Act".

SEC. 2, POWERS RESERVED TO THE STATES.

(a) In General—Chapter 115 of title 28, United States Code, is amended by adding after section 1738B the following:

"**§1738C. Certain acts, records, and proceedings and the effect thereof**

"No State, territory, or possession. of the United States, or Indian tribe, shall be required to give effect to any public act, record, or judicial proceeding of any other State, territory, possession, or tribe respecting a relationship between persons of the same sex that is treated as a marriage under the laws of such other State, territory, possession, or tribe, or a right or claim arising from such relationship.".

SEC. 3. DEFINITION OF MARRIAGE.

(a) In General.—Chapter 1 of title 1, United States Code, is amended by adding at the end the following:

"**§ 7. Definition of 'marriage' and 'spouse'**

"In determining the meaning of any Act of Congress, or of any ruling, regulation, or interpretation of the various administration bureaus and agencies of the United States, the word 'marriage' means only a legal union between one man and one woman as husband and wife, and the word 'spouse' refers only to a person of the opposite sex who is a husband or a wife.

Source: Public Law 104-199-Sept. 21, 1996   110 Stat.2419

HOW WELL DID YOU UNDERSTAND THIS SELECTION?

1. How is the concept of federalism infused in this legislation?

2. Does this legislation alter the intent of Article IV of the Constitution?

BURLINGTON INDUSTRIES, INC. V. ELLERTH (1998)
United States Supreme Court

Sexual harassment has been a serious problem in the American workplace. Under Title VII of the Civil Rights Act of 1964, the problem was addressed, and women were given a legal remedy. In this case, the plaintiff, Kimberly Ellerth, was harassed for 15 months by a supervisor while she was working at Burlington Industries. She refused all the supervisor's advances and yet suffered no tangible retaliation and was even promoted once. She did not report the harassment because the supervisor who she felt was harassing her would have seen the report. She sued under Title VII.

Justice Kennedy delivered the opinion of the Court.

We decide whether, under Title VII of the Civil Rights Act of 1964, 78 Stat. 253, as amended, 42 U.S.C. 2000e *et seq.*, an employee who refuses the unwelcome and threatening sexual advances of a supervisor, yet suffers no adverse, tangible job consequences, can recover against the employer without showing the employer is negligent or otherwise at fault for the supervisor's actions.

I

Summary judgment was granted for the employee, so we must take the facts alleged by the employee to be true...The employer is Burlington Industries, the petitioner. The employee is Kimberly Ellerth, the respondent. From March 1993 until May 1994, Ellerth worked as a salesperson in one of Burlington's divisions in Chicago, Illinois. During her employment, she alleges, she was subjected to constant sexual harassment by her supervisor, one Ted Slowik.

In the hierarchy of Burlington's management structure, Slowik was a mid-level manager. Burlington has eight divisions, employing more than 22,000 people in some 50 plants around the United States. Slowik was a vice president in one of five business units within one of the divisions. He had authority to make hiring and promotion decisions subject to the approval of his supervisor, who signed the paperwork...According to Slowik's supervisor, his position was "not considered an upper-level management position," and he was "not amongst the decision-making or policy-making hierarchy." Slowik was not Ellerth's immediate supervisor. Ellerth worked in a two-person office in Chicago, and she answered to her office colleague, who in turn answered to Slowik in New York.

Against a background of repeated boorish and offensive remarks and gestures which Slowik allegedly made, Ellerth places particular emphasis on three alleged incidents where Slowik's comments could be construed as threats to deny her tangible job benefits. In the summer of 1993, while on a business trip, Slowik invited Ellerth to the hotel lounge, an invitation Ellerth felt compelled to accept because Slowik was her boss...When Ellerth gave no encouragement to remarks Slowik made about her breasts, he told her to "loosen up" and warned, "[y]ou know, Kim, I could make your life very hard or very easy at Burlington."

In March 1994, when Ellerth was being considered for a promotion, Slowik expressed reservations during the promotion interview because she was not "loose enough." The comment was followed by his reaching over and rubbing her knee. Ellerth did receive the promotion; but when Slowik called to announce it, he told Ellerth, "you're gonna be out there with men who work in factories, and they certainly like women with pretty butts/legs."

In May 1994, Ellerth called Slowik, asking permission to insert a customer's logo into a fabric sample. Slowik responded, "I don't have time for you right now, Kim—unless you want to tell me what you're wear-

339

ing." Ellerth told Slowik she had to go and ended the call. A day or two later, Ellerth called Slowik to ask permission again. This time he denied her request, but added something along the lines of, "are you wearing shorter skirts yet, Kim, because it would make your job a whole heck of a lot easier."

A short time later, Ellerth's immediate supervisor cautioned her about returning telephone calls to customers in a prompt fashion. In response, Ellerth quit. She faxed a letter giving reasons unrelated to the alleg3ed sexual harassment we have described. About three weeks later, however, she sent a letter explaining she quit because of Slowik's behavior.

During her tenure at Burlington, Ellerth did not inform anyone in authority about Slowik's conduct, despite knowing Burlington had a policy against sexual harassment. In fact, she chose not to inform her immediate supervisor (not Slowik) because "it would be his duty as my supervisor to report any incidents of sexual harassment." On one occasion, she told Slowik a comment he made was inappropriate...

III

We must decide, then, whether an employer has vicarious liability when a supervisor creates a hostile work environment by making explicit threats to alter a subordinate's terms or conditions of employment based on sex, but does not fulfill the threat.

A

Section 219(1) of the Restatement sets out a central principle of agency law:
"A master is subject to liability for the torts of his servants committed while acting in the scope of their employment."

An employer may be liable for both negligent and intentional torts committed by an employee within the scope of his or her employment. Sexual harassment under Title VII presupposes intentional conduct. While early decisions absolved employers of liability for the intentional torts of their employees, the law now imposes liability where the employee's "purpose, however misguided, is wholly or in part to further the master's business...For example, when a saleperson lies to a customer to make a sale, the tortuous conduct is within the scope of employment because it benefits the employer by increasing sales, even though it may violate the employer's policies.

As Courts of Appeal have recognized, a supervisor acting out of gender-based animus or a desire to fulfill sexual urges may not be actuated by a purpose to serve the employer...

The general rule is that sexual harassment by a supervisor is not conduct within the scope of employment.

B

Scope of employment does not define the only basis for employer liability under agency principles. In limited circumstances, agency principles impose liability on employers even where employees commit torts outside the scope of employment. The principles are set forth in the much-cited 219(2) of the Restatement:

"(2) A master is not subject to liability for the torts of his servants acting outside the scope of their employment, unless:

"(a) the master intended the conduct or the consequences, or

"(b) the master was negligent or reckless, or

"(c) the conduct violated a non-delegable duty of the master, or

"(d) the servant purported to act or to speak on behalf of the principal and there was reliance upon apparent authority, or he was aided in accomplishing the tort by the existence of the agency relation."...

D

We turn to the aided in the agency relation standard. Ina sense, most workplace tortfeasors are aided in accomplishing their tortuous objective by the existence of the agency relation: Proximity and regular contact may afford a captive pool of potential victims. Were this to satisfy the aided in the agency relation standard, an employer would be subject to vicarious liability not only for all supervisor harassment, but also for all co-worker harassment, a result enforced by neither the EEOC nor any court of appeals to have considered this issue…The Aided in the agency relation standard, therefore, requires the existence of something more than the employment relation itself.

At the outset, we can identify a class of cases where, beyond question, more than the mere existence of the employment relation aids in commission of the harassment: when a supervisor takes a tangible employment action against the subordinate. Every Federal Court of Appeals to have considered the question has found vicarious liability when the discriminatory act results in the tangible employment action…

In the context of this case, a tangible employment action would have taken the form of a denial of a raise or a promotion. The concept of a tangible employment action appears in numerous cases in the Courts of Appeals discussing claims involving race, age, and national origin discrimination, as well as sex discrimination. Without endorsing the specific results of those decisions, we think it prudent to import the concept of a tangible employment action for resolution of the vicarious liability issue we consider here. A tangible employment action constitutes a significant change in the employment status, such as hiring, firing, failing to promote, reassignment with significantly different responsibilities, or a decision causing a significant change in benefits…

When a supervisor makes a tangible employment decision, there is assurance the injury could not have been inflicted absent the agency relation. A tangible employment action in most cases inflicts direct economic harm. As a general proposition, only a supervisor, or other person acting with the authority of the company, can cause this sort of injury. A co-worker can break a co-worker's arm as easily as a supervisor, and anyone who has regular contact with an employee can inflict psychological injuries by his or her offensive conduct…But one co-worker (absent some elaborate scheme) cannot dock another's pay, nor can one co-worker demote another. Tangible employment actions fall within the special province of the supervisor. The supervisor has been empowered by the company as a distinct class of agent to make economic decisions affecting other employees under his or her control.

Tangible employment actions are the means by which the employer brings the official power of the enterprise to bear on subordinates. A tangible employment decision requires an official act of the enterprise, a company act. The decision in most cases is documented in official company records, and may be subject to review by higher level supervisors…

For these reasons, a tangible employment action taken by the supervisor becomes for Title VII purposes the act of the employer. Whatever the exact contours of the aided in the agency relation standard, its requirements will always be met when a supervisor takes a tangible employment action against a subordinate. In that instance, it would be implausible to interpret agency principles to allow an employer to escape liability…

Whether the agency relation aids in commission of supervisor harassment which does not culminate in a tangible employment action is less obvious. Application of the standard is made difficult by its malleable terminology, which can be read to either expand or limit liability in the context of supervisor harassment. On the one hand, a supervisor's power and authority invests his or her harassing conduct with a particular threatening character, and in this sense, a supervisor always is aided by the agency relation…

In order to accommodate the agency principles of vicarious liability for harm caused by misuse of supervisory authority, as well as Title VII's equally basic policies of encouraging forethought by employers and saving action by objecting employees, we adopt the following holding in this case and in *Faragher* v. *Boca*

341

Raton, post, also decided today. An employer is subject to vicarious liability to a victimized employee for an actionable hostile environment created by a supervisor with immediate (or successively higher) authority over the employee. When no tangible employment action is taken, a defending employer may raise an affirmative defense to liability or damages, subject to proof by a preponderance of the evidence, see Fed. Rule Civ. Proc. 8©. The defense comprises two necessary elements: (a) that the employer exercised reasonable care to prevent and correct promptly any sexually harassing behavior, and (b) that the plaintiff employee unreasonably failed to take advantage of any preventive or corrective opportunities provided by th employer or to avoid harm otherwise. While proof that an employer had promulgated an anti-harassment policy with complaint procedure is not necessary in every instance as a mater of law, the need for a stated policy suitable to the employment circumstances may appropriately be addressed in any case when litigating the first element of the defense. And while proof that an employee failed to fulfill the corresponding obligation of reasonable care to avoid harm is not limited to showing any unreasonable failure to use any complaint procedure provided by the employer, a demonstration of such failure will normally suffice to satisfy the employer's burden under the second element of the defense. No affirmative defense is available, however, when the supervisor's harassment culminates in a tangible employment action, such as discharge, demotion, or undesirable reassignment...

Although Ellerth has not alleged she suffered a tangible employment action at the hands of Slowik, which would deprive Burlington of the availability of the affirmative defense, this is not dispositive. In light of our decision, Burlington is still subject to vcarious liability for Slowik's activity, but Burlington should have an opportunity to assert and prove the affirmative defense to liability...

For these reasons, we will affirm the judgment of the Court of Appeals, revising the grant of summary judgment against Ellerth. On remand, the district Court will have the opportunity to decide whether it would be appropriate to allow Ellerth to amend her pleading or supplement her discovery.

The judgment of the Court of Appeals is affirmed.

HOW WELL DID YOU UNDERSTAND THIS SELECTION?

1. How does the Court define sexual harassment?

2. Under what conditions will a company be liable for one of its employee's harassment of another employee?

A president's state of the union address is his/her opportunity to set the legislative agenda for the coming year. This 1999 State of the Union Address was delivered by President Clinton in the shadow of the Senate impeachment trial that had begun only days before, and many Republicans demanded that he refrain from giving the address. When he did, many Republicans refused to attend and many others sat in stony silence.

Mr. Speaker, Mr. Vice President, Members of Congress, honored guests, my fellow Americans: Tonight I have the honor of reporting on the State of the Union.

The Aging of 21st Century America

Our fiscal discipline gives us an unsurpassed opportunity to address a remarkable new challenge: the aging of America.

With the number of elderly Americans set to double by 2030, the baby Boom will become a Senior Boom.

So first and above all, we must save Social security for the 21st Century.

Early in this century, being old meant being poor. When President Roosevelt created Social Security, thousands wrote to thank him for eliminating what one woman called the "stark terror of penniless, helpless old age." Even today, without Social Security, half our nation's elderly would be forced into poverty.

Today, Social Security is strong. But by 2013, payroll taxes will no longer be sufficient to cover monthly payments. And by 2032, the Trust Fund will be exhausted, and Social Security will be unable to pay out the full benefits older Americans have been promised.

The best way to keep Social Security a rock-solid guarantee is not to make drastic cuts in benefits; not to raise payroll tax rates; and not to drain resources from Social Security in the name of saving it.

Instead, I propose that we make the historic decision to invest the surplus to save Social Security...

Second, once we have saved Social Security, we must fulfill our obligation to save and improve Medicare. Already, we have extended the life of Medicare by 10 years—but we should extend it for at least another decade. Tonight I propose that we use one out of every six dollars in the surplus over the next 15 years to guarantee the soundness of Medicare until the year 2020.

But again, we should aim higher. We must be willing to work in a bipartisan way and look at new ideas, including the upcoming report of the bipartisan Medicare commission. If we work together, we can secure Medicare for the next two decades and cover seniors' greatest need—affordable prescription drugs.

Third, we must help all Americans, from their first day on the job, to save, invest, to create wealth. From its beginning, Americans have supplemented Social Security with private pensions and savings. Yet today, millions of people retire with little to live on other than Social Security. Americans living longer than ever must save more than ever.

Therefore, in addition to saving Social Security and Medicare, I propose a new pension initiative for retirement security in the 21st Century. I propose that we use 11 percent of the surplus to establish Universal Savings Accounts—USA Accounts—to give all Americans the means to save. With these new accounts, Americans can invest as they choose, and receive funds to match a portion of their savings, with extra help for those least able to save…

Fourth, we must invest in long-term care. I propose a tax credit of $1,000 for the aged, ailing or disabled and the families who care for them. Long-term care will become a bigger and bigger challenge with the aging of America—and we must help our families deal with it.

21st Century Schools

There are more children, from more diverse backgrounds, in our public schools than at any time in our history. Their education must provide the knowledge and nurture the creativity that will allow our nation to thrive in the new economy…

Later this year, I will send to Congress a plan that for the first time holds states and school districts accountable for progress and rewards them for results. My Education Accountability Act will require every school district receiving federal help to take the following steps.

First, all schools must end social promotion.

No child should graduate from high school with a diploma he or she can't read. We do our children no favors when we allow them to pass from grade to grade without mastering material…

Second, all states and school districts must turn around their worst performing schools—or shut them down. That is the policy established by Gov. Jim Hunt in North Carolina, where test scores made the biggest gains in the nation last year. My budget includes $200 million to help states turn around their failing schools.

Third, all states and school districts must be held responsible for the quality of their teachers. The great majority of teachers do a fine job. But in too many schools, teachers don't have college majors—or even minors—in the subjects they teach.

Fourth, we must empower parents, with more Information and more choices. In too many communities, it is easier to get information on the quality of the local restaurants than on the quality of the local schools. Every school district should issue report cards on every school.

And parents should have more choice in selecting their public schools. When I became president, there was one independent, public charter school ion all of America. With our support, there are 1100 today. My budget assures that early in the next century, there will be 3000.

Fifth, to ensure that our classrooms are truly places of learning, all states and school districts must adopt and implement discipline policies…

21st Century Support For American Families

We must do more to help the millions of parents who give their all every day at home and at work.

The most basic tool of all is a decent income. Let's raise the minimum wage by a dollar and hour over the next two years.

And let's make sure women and men get equal pay for equal work by strengthening enforcement of equal pay laws.

Working parents also need quality childcare. Again, I ask Congress to support our plan for tax credits and subsidies for working families, improved safety and quality, and expanded after-school programs. Our plan also included a new tax credit for stay-at-home parents. They need support too.

The Family Medical Leave Act—the first bill I signed into law—has helped millions of Americans care for a new baby or an ailing relative without risking their jobs. We should extend Family Leave to 10 million more Americans working in smaller companies.

Parents should never face discrimination in the workplace. I will ask Congress to prohibit companies from refusing to hire or promote workers simply because they have children.

America's families deserve the world's best medical care.

Thanks to bipartisan federal support for medical research, we are on the verge of new treatments to prevent or delay diseases from Parkinson's to Alzheimer's, from arthritis to cancer…

A 21st Century Economy

Today, America is the most dynamic, competitive, job creating economy in history.

But we can do better—in building a 21st Century economy for all Americans.

Today's income gap is largely a skills gap. Last year, Congress passed a law enabling workers to get a skills grant to choose the training they need. This year, I recommend a fi8ve year commitment in this new system so that we can provide that training for all Americans who lose their jobs, and rapid response teams to help towns where factories have closed. And I ask for a dramatic increase in federal support for adult literacy, so we can mount a national campaign aimed at millions of working people who read at less than a fifth grade level.

In the past six years, we have cut the welfare rolls nearly in half. Two years ago, from this podium, I asked five companies to lead a national effort to hire people off welfare.

Tonight, our Welfare to Work Partnership includes 10,000 companies who have hired hundreds of thousands of people. Our balanced budget will help another 20,000 people move to the dignity and pride of work.

We must bring the spark of private enterprise to every community in America—to inner cities and remote rural areas—with more support for community development banks, empowerment zones and 100,000 vouchers for affordable housing. And I ask Congress to support our bold plan to help businesses raise $15 billion of private sector capital to bring jobs and opportunity to our inner cities and rural areas—with tax credits and loan guarantees, including new American Private

Investment Companies modeled on our Overseas Private Investment Corporation. Our greatest untapped markets are not overseas—they are right here at home...

At the same time, we will continue to work on a global basis to build a financial system for the 21st Century that promotes prosperity and tames the cycles of boom and bust. This June I will meet with other world leaders to advance this historic purpose.

We must also create a freer and fairer trading system for the 21st Century. Trade has divided Americans for too long. We must find the common ground on which business, workers, environmentalists, framers and government can stand together...

A Strong America in a New World

No nation in history has had the opportunity and responsibility we now have to shape a world more peaceful, secure, and free...

As we work for peace, we must also meet threats to our nation's security—including increased dangers from outlaw nations and terrorism. We will defend our security wherever we are threatened—as we did this summer when we struck at Osama bin Laden's network of terror. The bombing of our embassies in Kenya and Tanzania reminds us of the risks faced every day by those who represent America to the world. Let's give them our support, the safest possible workplaces, and the resources they need so America can continue to lead...

The new century demands new partnerships for peace and security.

The United Nations plays a crucial role, with allies sharing burdens America might otherwise bear alone. America needs a strong and effective UN. I want to work with this new Congress to pay our dues and our debts.

We must support security in Europe and Asia—expanding NATO and defining new missions at the 50th Anniversary summit this year in Washington, maintaining our alliance with Japan and Korea, and our other Asian allies, and engaging China...

21st Century Communities

As the world has changed, so have our own communities. We must make them safer, more livable, more united. This year, we will reach our goal of 100,000 community police officers—ahead of schedule and under budget. The Brady Bill has stopped a quarter million felons, fugitives, and stalkers from buying handguns. Now, the murder rate is the lowest in 30 years, and the crime rate has dropped for six straight years.

Tonight, I propose a 21st Century Crime Bill to deploy the latest technologies and tactics to make the communities even safer.

My balanced budget will help put up to 50,000 more police on the beat in the areas hardest hit by crime, and to equip them with new tools, from crime-mapping computers to digital mug shots.

We must break the deadly cycle of drugs and crime. My budget expands support for drug testing and treatment. It says to prisoners: If you stay on drugs, you stay behind bars. And it says to those on parole: To keep your freedom, keep free of drugs.

Congress should restore the five-day waiting period for buying a handgun. And you should extend the Brady Bill to prevent juveniles who commit violent crimes from buying a gun.

We must keep our schools the safest places in our communities…

A century ago, President Theodore Roosevelt defined our "great, central task" as "leaving this land even a better land for our descendants than it is for us."

Today, we are restoring the Florida Everglades, saving Yellowstone, preserving the red rock canyons of Utah, protecting California's redwoods and our precious coasts.

But our most fateful new challenge is the threat of global warning. Nineteen ninety-eight was the warmest year ever recorded. Last year's heat waves, ice storms, and floods are but a hint of what future generations may endure if we don't act now.

So tonight, I propose a new clean air fund to help communities reduce pollution, and tax incentives and investments to spur clean energy technologies. And I will work with Congress to reward companies that take early, voluntary action to reduce greenhouse gases…

The Millennium

My fellow Americans, this is our moment. Let us lift our eyes as one nation, and from the mountaintop of this American century, look ahead to this next one—asking God's blessing on our endeavors and our beloved country.

HOW WELL DID YOU UNDERSTAND THIS SELECTION?

1. What are the president's priorities for 1999?

2. Approval ratings for the president soared to over 70 percent after he delivered this speech. What does this tell you about the power of the presidency?

Article II, Section 4 of the Constitution of the United States provides that "the President, Vice President and all civil Officers of the United States shall be removed from Office on Impeachment for, and on conviction of, Treason, Bribery, or other high Crimes and Misdemeanors." It also provides that the House of Representatives has "the sole power of impeachment" (Article I, Section 2) and that the Senate has "the sole power to try all impeachments." (Article I, Section 3)

Although no president has been convicted by the Senate, two (Andrew Johnson in 1868 and William Jefferson Clinton in 1998) have been impeached by the House. In addition, the House Committee on the Judiciary had voted in favor of three of five articles of impeachment against President Richard M. Nixon on July 27, 1974, but he resigned from office before they were considered by the entire membership of the House of Representatives. In Clinton's case, the full House did get to consider and vote upon four articles of impeachment, which had been approved by the Judiciary Committee on December 11-12, 1998. What follows is the full text of those articles as they appeared in House Resolution 611 and the results of the full House vote on December 19, 1998.

HOUSE RESOLUTION 611

Resolution impeaching William Jefferson Clinton, president of the United States, for high crimes and misdemeanors.

Resolved, That William Jefferson Clinton, president of the United States, is impeached for high crimes and misdemeanors, and that the following articles of impeachment be exhibited to the United States Senate:

Articles of impeachment exhibited by the House of Representatives of the United States of America in the name of itself and of the people of the United States of America, against William Jefferson Clinton, president of the United States of America, in maintenance and support of its impeachment against him for high crimes and misdemeanors.

Article I

In his conduct while president of the United States, William Jefferson Clinton, in violation of his constitutional oath faithfully to execute the office of president of the United States and, to the best of his ability, preserve, protect, and defend the Constitution of the United States, and in violation of his constitutional duty to take care that the laws be faithfully executed, has willfully corrupted and manipulated the judicial process of the United States for his personal gain and exoneration, impeding the administration of justice, in that:

On August 17, 1998, William Jefferson Clinton swore to tell the truth, the whole truth, and nothing but the truth before a Federal grand jury of the United States. Contrary to that oath, William Jefferson Clinton willfully provided perjurious, false and misleading testimony to the grand jury concerning one or more of the following: (1) the-nature and details of his relationship with a subordinate Government employee; (2) prior perjurious, false and misleading testimony he gave in a Federal civil rights action brought against him; (3) prior false and misleading statements he allowed his attorney to make to a Federal judge in that civil rights action; and (4) his corrupt efforts to influence the testimony of witnesses and to impede the discovery of evidence in that civil rights action.

In doing this, William Jefferson Clinton has undermined the integrity of his office, has brought disrepute on the presidency,' has betrayed his trust as president, and has acted in a manner subversive of the rule of law and justice, to the manifest injury of the people of the United States.

Wherefore, William Jefferson Clinton, by such conduct, warrants impeachment and trial, and removal from office and disqualification to hold and enjoy any office of honor, trust or profit under the United States.

Article II

In his conduct while president of the United States, William Jefferson Clinton, in violation of his constitutional oath faithfully to execute the office of president of the United States and, to the best of his ability, preserve, protect, and defend the Constitution of the United States, and in violation of his constitutional duty to take care that the laws be faithfully executed, has willfully corrupted and manipulated the judicial process of the United States for his personal gain and exoneration, impeding the administration of justice, in that:

(1) On December 23, 1997, William Jefferson Clinton, in sworn answers to written questions asked as part of a Federal civil rights action brought against him, willfully provided' perjurious, false and misleading testimony in response to questions deemed relevant by a Federal judge concerning conduct and proposed conduct with subordinate employees.

(2) On January 17, 1998, William Jefferson Clinton swore under oath to tell the truth, the whole truth, and nothing but the truth in a deposition given as part of a Federal civil rights action brought against him. Contrary to that oath, William Jefferson Clinton willfully provided perjurious, false and misleading testimony in response to questions deemed relevant by a Federal judge concerning the nature and details of his relationship with a subordinate Government employee, his knowledge of that employee's involvement and participation in the civil rights action brought against him, and his corrupt efforts to influence the testimony of that employee.

In all of this, William Jefferson Clinton has undermined the integrity of his office, has brought disrepute on the presidency, has betrayed his trust as president, and has acted in a manner subversive of the rule of law and justice, to the manifest injury of the people of the United States.

Wherefore, William Jefferson Clinton, by such conduct, warrants impeachment and trial, and removal from office and disqualification to hold and enjoy any office of honor, trust or profit under the United States.

Article III

In his conduct while president of the United States, William Jefferson Clinton, in violation of his constitutional oath faithfully to execute the office of president of the United States and, to the best of his ability, preserve, protect, and defend the Constitution of the United States, and in violation of his constitutional duty to take care that the laws be faithfully executed, has prevented, obstructed and impeded the administration of justice, and has to that end engaged personally, and through his subordinates and agents, in a course of conduct or scheme designed to delay, impede, cover up, and conceal the existence of evidence and testimony related to a Federal civil rights action brought against him in a duly instituted judicial proceeding.

The means used to implement this course of conduct or scheme included one or more of the following acts:

(1) On or about December 17, 1997, William Jefferson Clinton corruptly encouraged a witness in a Federal civil rights action brought against him to execute a sworn affidavit in that proceeding that he knew to be perjurious, false and misleading.

(2) On or about December 17, 1997, William Jefferson Clinton corruptly encouraged a witness in a Federal civil rights action brought against him to give perjurious, false and misleading testimony if and when called to testify personally in that proceeding.

(3) On or about December 28, 1997, William Jefferson Clinton corruptly engaged in, encouraged, or supported a scheme to conceal evidence that had been subpoenaed in a Federal civil rights action brought against him.

(4) Beginning on or about December 7, 1997, and continuing through and including January 14, 1998, William Jefferson Clinton intensified and succeeded in an effort to secure job assistance to a witness in a Federal civil rights action brought against him in order to corruptly prevent the truthful testimony of that witness in that proceeding at a time when the truthful testimony of that witness would have been harmful to him.

(5) On January 17, 1998, at his deposition in a Federal civil rights action brought against him, William Jefferson Clinton corruptly allowed his attorney to make false and misleading statements to a Federal judge characterizing an affidavit, in order to prevent questioning deemed relevant by the judge. Such false and misleading statements were subsequently acknowledged by his attorney in a communication to that judge.

(6) On or about January 18 and January 20-21, 1998, William Jefferson Clinton related a false and misleading account of events relevant to a Federal civil rights action brought against him to a potential witness in that proceeding, in order to corruptly influence the testimony of that witness.

(7) On or about January 21, 23, and 26, 1998, William Jefferson Clinton made false and misleading statements to potential witnesses in a Federal grand jury proceeding in order to corruptly influence the testimony of those witnesses. The false and misleading statements made by William Jefferson Clinton were repeated by the witnesses to the grand jury, causing the grand jury to receive false and misleading information.

In all of this, William Jefferson Clinton has undermined the integrity of his office, has brought disrepute on the presidency, has betrayed his trust as president, and has acted in a manner subversive of the rule of law and justice, to the manifest injury of the people of the United States.

Wherefore, William Jefferson Clinton, by such conduct, warrants impeachment and trial, and removal from office and disqualification to hold and enjoy any office of honor, trust or profit under the United States.

Article IV

Using the powers and influence of the office of president of the United States, William Jefferson Clinton, in violation of his constitutional oath faithfully to execute the office of president of the United States and, to the best of his ability, preserve, protect, and defend the Constitution of the United States, and in disregard of his constitutional duty to take care that the laws be faithfully executed, has engaged in conduct that resulted in misuse and abuse of his high office, impaired the due and proper administration of justice and the conduct of lawful inquiries, and contravened the authority of the legislative branch and the truth, seeking purpose of a coordinate investigative proceeding in that, as president, William Jefferson Clinton, refused and failed to respond to certain written requests for admission and willfully made perjurious, false and misleading sworn statements in response to certain written requests for admission propounded to him as part of the impeachment inquiry authorized by the House of Representatives of the Congress of the United States.

William Jefferson Clinton, in refusing and failing to respond, and in making perjurious, false and misleading statements, assumed to himself functions and judgments necessary to the exercise of the sole power of impeachment vested by the Constitution in the House of Representatives and exhibited contempt for the inquiry.

In doing this, William Jefferson Clinton has undermined the integrity of his office, has brought disrepute on the presidency, has betrayed his trust as president, and has acted in a manner subversive of the rule of law and justice, to the manifest injury of the people of the United States.

Wherefore, William Jefferson Clinton, by such conduct, warrants impeachment and trial, and removal from office and disqualification to hold and enjoy any office of honor, trust, or profit under the United States.

RESULTS OF THE VOTE ON THE ARTICLES IMPEACHMENT
House of Representatives - Saturday, December 19, 1998

Article I

Article I charged that the President willfully provided perjurious, false and misleading testimony to the grand jury in August 1998.

Votes for impeachment:	228	
Votes against impeachment:	206	
Not voting:		1

Article II

Article II charged that the President willfully provided perjurious, false and misleading testimony in both his written responses and in a deposition in the sexual harassment lawsuit brought against him by Paula Jones.

Votes for impeachment:	205	
Votes against impeachment:	229	
Not voting:		1

Article III

Article III charged that the President "obstructed and impeded the administration of justice" in the Paula Jones case.

Votes for impeachment:	205	
Votes against impeachment:	229	
Not voting:		1

Article IV

Article IV charged that during the impeachment inquiry conducted by the House of Representatives the President both failed to respond to requests for information and lied to the Congress.

Votes for impeachment:	148	
Votes against impeachment:	285	
Not voting:		2

Articles II and IV were defeated. Articles I and III were, however, approved and thus President Clinton became the only elected U.S. president to ever be impeached. The two Articles of Impeachment were then, as the Constitution specifies, sent up to the Senate for trial.

The House of Representatives passed two of the four articles of impeachment under its consideration. These two articles (Article I and Article III) went to the Senate as Article I and Article II.

The Senate trial, with Chief Justice William Rehnquist presiding, began on January 14, 1999. For the first three days the House managers, headed by the Chair of the Committee on the Judiciary, Henry J. Hyde (R-Illinois), presented the case against President Clinton. After a two day adjournment, the counsel to the president presented the defense case from January 19 - 21. What followed were two days in which Senators submitted questions to the Chief Justice who directed them to either the House managers or to the defense team for responses. The Senate then took several more days to debate various motions (including a motion to dismiss the case against the president), and allowed a few more days for taking and viewing videotaped depositions from witnesses (including Monica Lewinsky). Closing arguments were made on February 8, and the Senate voted to acquit the president on February 12.

The document below summarizes the last four days in which the Senate sat a Court of Impeachment.

THE SENATE TRIAL OF WILLIAM JEFFERSON CLINTON
THE DEBATE AND THE VOTE
FEBRUARY 9-12

On Tuesday, February 9, fourteen Republicans and all forty-five Democrats voted to open the debate—eight short of the two-thirds vote required to suspend the secrecy rules. Shortly before 2 P.M., reporters, spectators, prosecutors, and defense lawyers were ordered from the chamber, and the senators began their deliberations in private.

Over the course of three days, the debate continued. Participants described it as collegial, sometimes impassioned. And several senators announced publicly how they would vote. Three Republicans—John Chafee of Rhode Island, James Jeffords of Vermont, and Arlen Specter of Pennsylvania—declared that they would reject both articles of impeachment; two more, Slade Gorton of Washington and Ted Stevens of Alaska said they would oppose the perjury article, but support the obstruction-of-justice article.

On the morning of Friday, February 12, after a final closed session in which the last few debaters finished their remarks, the Senate again opened its doors. The chief justice recognized Majority Leader Lott.

Mr. Lott: Mr. Chief Justice, Members of the Senate, the Senate has met almost exclusively as a Court of Impeachment since January 7, 1999, to consider the articles of impeachment against the president of the United States. The Senate meets today to conclude this trial by voting on the articles of impeachment, thereby, fulfilling its obligation under the Constitution. I believe we are ready to proceed to the votes on the articles. And I yield the floor.

The Chief Justice: The clerk will now read the first article of impeachment.

Article I, charging President Clinton with perjury, was read aloud. Then the chief justice called for the vote.

The Chief Justice: The question is on the first article of impeachment. Senators, how say you? Is the respondent, William Jefferson Clinton, guilty or not guilty? A roll call vote is required.
    The clerk will call the roll.
The results: guilty 45, not guilty 55. Ten Republicans joined the Democrats in voting to acquit.

The Chief Justice: On this article of impeachment, 45 Senators having pronounced William Jefferson Clinton, president of the United States, guilty as charged, 55 Senators having pronounced him not guilty, two-thirds of the Senators present not having pronounced him guilty, the Senate adjudges that the respondent, William Jefferson Clinton, president of the United States, is not guilty as charged in the first article of impeachment.

Article II, charging President Clinton with obstruction of justice, was read aloud.

The Chief Justice: The question is on the second article of impeachment. Senators, how say you? Is the respondent, William Jefferson Clinton, guilty or not guilty?
    The clerk will call the roll.
The results: guilty 50, not guilty 50. This time, five Republicans joined the Democrats for acquittal.

The Chief Justice: ... On this article of impeachment, 50 Senators having pronounced William Jefferson Clinton, president of the United States, guilty as charged, 50 Senators having pronounced him not guilty, two-thirds of the Senators present not having pronounced him guilty, the Senate adjudges that the respondent, William Jefferson Clinton, president of the United States, is not guilty as charged in the second article of impeachment ....

It was almost over. A bipartisan majority did try to force through a resolution censuring the president, but only 56 senators—short of the required two-thirds—voted to suspend the rules.

At 12:43 P.M., the Senate, sitting as a Court of Impeachment, adjourned.

Source: McLoughlin, Merrill, ed. "The Debate and the Vote." In the Impeachment and Trial of President Clinton: The Official Transcripts, from the House Judiciary Committee Hearings to the Senate Trial, edited by Merrill McLoughlin, 433-435. New York: Random House, 1999.

SENATORS TALK ABOUT THEIR VOTES IN
THE IMPEACHMENT TRIAL

After the Senate voted to acquit President Clinton of the charges brought against him by the House of Representatives, many Senators explained why they voted (for or against impeachment) as they did and/or expressed their opinions about the impeachment process. Excerpts of the statements made by thirty-five of them were published in **The New York Times** *the following day. Segments of six of these excerpts, three from Democrats and three from Republicans, are presented below.*

Susan Collins, Republican of Maine

As this case has been argued in this chamber, I have become convinced that the perjury charges of Article I are not fully substantiated by the record ....

The evidence supporting Article II is more convincing. Indeed, the case presented by the House managers proves to my satisfaction that the President did, in fact, obstruct justice in Paula Jones's civil rights case ....

Nevertheless, I do not think that the President's actions constitute a high crime or misdemeanor ....

Ben Nighthorse Campbell, Republican of Colorado

I took a solemn oath—perhaps it is the only thing in common I share with John F. Kennedy, Harry Truman and Daniel Webster as well as the founders of this nation—and that is why honoring it is all the more important to me.

Simply speaking, the President did, too. And, so even though I like him personally, I find I can only vote one way. And that is guilty on both articles.

Phil Gramm, Republican of Texas

... I have tried to screen out my own strong partisan sentiments by asking a simple question: Would I vote to convict President Ronald Reagan or President George Bush if they had committed the acts that President Clinton has committed ? The answer is a sad but firm yes ....

I have asked myself how men from an era when honor was valued above all other traits, men like George Washington, Thomas Jefferson, John Adams and James Madison, might have viewed a President who committed perjury and obstruction of justice for personal and political gain.

Would they believe that denying another citizen equal protection of the law was a betrayal of a public trust? It seems to me the men who pledged their lives, their fortunes and their sacred honor in order to establish our nation of laws would find President Clinton's behavior to be a high crime and misdemeanor.

Edward M. Kennedy, Democrat of Massachusetts

Clearly, the framers [of the Constitution] intended the House and the Senate to use the impeachment power cautiously, and not wield it promiscuously for partisan political purposes. Sadly, in this case, Republicans in the House of Representatives, in their partisan vendetta against the President, have wielded the impeachment power in precisely the way the framers rejected recklessly and without regard for the Constitution or the will of the American people ....

Barbara A. Mikulski, Democrat of Maryland

The House managers' case on both counts was thin and circumstantial ....

Overall, the House managers' assertions about perjury rested on President Clinton's vague and unhelpful responses to the independent counsel's [Ken Starr] questions. While those responses many have been frustrating to the independent counsel, the Republican House managers, and perhaps the American public, they were not perjurious as defined by law.

Similarly, the case presented by the Republican House managers did not present sufficient direct evidence to prove beyond a reasonable doubt that the President obstructed justice.

Daniel Patrick Moynihan, Democrat of New York

Impeachment is a power singularly lacking any of the checks and balances on which the framers depended .... Do not doubt that it could bring radical instability to the American Government ....

Senators, do not take the imprudent risk that removing William Jefferson Clinton for low crimes will not in the end jeopardize the Constitution itself. Censure him by all means. He will be gone in less than two years. But do not let his misdeeds put in jeopardy the Constitution we are sworn to uphold and defend.

Source: "Excerpts: Senators Talk About Their Votes in the Impeachment Trial." *The New York Times*, 13 February 1999, 13-14 (A).

HOW WELL DID YOU UNDERSTAND THIS SELECTION?

1. Two of the four Articles of Impeachment were approved by the House of Representatives. Which two passed?

2. What "high crimes and misdemeanors" was the president charged with?

3. What data in the readings can be used to support the argument that both the impeachment proceedings by the House of Representatives and the trial in the Senate were highly partisan in nature?

*One of the enduring questions asked of political scientists is "who **really** has power in the United States: the people? elected officials? the bureaucracy? large interest groups?" It is interesting to note that for many political scholars who have investigated the matter, the response to the question is "no one of the above." They would contend that the powerful are those relatively few individuals who set the country's political agenda and who benefit the most from the policies and decisions made by the government. These few individuals, or as C. Wright Mills called them, "the higher circles," constitute the power elite. Excerpts from Mills' classic mid-twentieth century work **The Power Elite** and Thomas R. Dye's more recent **Who's Running America? The Clinton Years** provide two views of the nature of those with power in the United States and two estimates of the size of America's elite.*

WHO'S RUNNING AMERICA?

Great power in America is concentrated in a handful of people. A few thousand individuals out of 250 million Americans decide about war and peace, wages and prices, consumption and investment, employment and production, law and justice, taxes and benefits, education and learning, health and welfare, advertising and communication, life and leisure.... These are the individuals who possess the formal authority to formulate, direct and manage programs, policies and activities of the major corporate, governmental, legal, educational, civic and cultural institutions in the nation....

Our definition of an institutional elite resulted in the identification of 7,314 elite positions. These top positions, taken collectively, control almost three quarters of the nation's industrial assets; one half of all assets in communication and utilities; over one half of all U.S. banking assets; over three quarters of all insurance assets; and they direct Wall Street's largest investment firms. They control the television networks, the influential news agencies, and the major newspaper chains. They control nearly 40 percent of all the assets of private foundations and two thirds of all private university endowments. They direct the nation's largest and best-known New York and Washington law firms as well as the nation's major civic and cultural organizations. They occupy key federal governmental positions in the executive, legislative, and judicial branches. And they occupy all the top command positions in the Army, Navy, Air Force, and Marines. These aggregate figures—roughly 7,300 positions—are themselves important indicators of the concentration of authority and control in American society....

On the whole, those at the top are well-educated, older, affluent, urban, WASP, and male.

Source: Dye, Thomas R. *Who's Running America? The Clinton Years.* Englewood Cliffs, New Jersey: Prentice-Hall, 1995.

THE HIGHER CIRCLES

Some men come to occupy positions in American society from which they can look down upon, so to speak, and by their decisions mightily affect, the every day worlds of ordinary men and women. They are not made by their jobs; they set up and break down jobs for thousands of others; they are not confined by simple family responsibilities; they can escape.

They rule the big corporations. They run the machinery of the state and claim its prerogatives. They direct the military establishment.... They have a greater share than other people of the things and experiences that are most highly valued. From this point of view, the elite are simply those who have the most of what there is to have, which is generally held to include money, power, and prestige....

The people of the higher circles may also be conceived as...a set of groups whose members know one another, see one another socially and at business, and so, in making decisions, take one another into account..... [T]hey have become self-conscious members of a social class. People are either accepted into this class or they are not...and they behave toward one another differently from the way they do toward members of other classes. They accept one another, understand one another, marry one another, tend to work and to think if not together at least alike...they mingle with one another on the golf course, in the gentleman's clubs, at resorts, on transcontinental airplanes, and on ocean liners. They meet at the estates of mutual friends, face each other in front of the TV camera, or serve on the same philanthropic committee....

[There are] forty-one members of the very rich, ninety-three political leaders, and seventy-nine chief executives of corporations.

Source: Mills, C. Wright. *The Power Elite*. New York: Oxford University Press, 1959.

HOW WELL DID YOU UNDERSTAND THESE SELECTION?

1. According to Thomas Dye what personal characteristics are shared by the elite in America?

2. The top of what three "domains" or "higher circles," according C. Wright Mills, constitutes the elite?

3. Compare and contrast Mills description of the power elite with that of Thomas Dye.

U.S. policy had always forbidden homosexuals from serving in the military. This did not mean that there were no gays and lesbians enlisted in the armed forces but rather that they had to pretend to be heterosexual or suffer the legal consequences. Early in his presidency, Clinton attempted to honor his promise to the gay and lesbian community and end this long-standing policy. President Clinton had originally intended to end the ban on military service based on sexual orientation. This would grant gay and lesbians the opportunity to serve in the military without concealing their sexual preference.

Clinton's position turned out to be extremely controversial, and he was highly criticized for pursuing this policy. Many political pundits believed that he expended important political capital during his "honeymoon" period with Congress that could have been used on other more "popular" issues, such as health-care reform. After months of highly sensitive debates, a compromise was reached between Clinton and Congress that appeared to satisfy no one. The following is the text of the "Don't Ask, Don't Tell" policy of the Department of Defense that allows homosexuals to serve in the military as long as they do not express their sexual preference.

*From its inception, this policy has been challenged in the courts in such cases as **Able v USA** claiming that the "Don't Ask, Don't Tell" policy violates the First and Fifth Amendments to the Constitution. Although the issue has been addressed in several lower federal courts, the Supreme Court to date has declined to hear any cases that would allow it to consider the constitutionality of the policy.*

U.S. Code - Title 10, Section 654

Sec. 654. Policy concerning homosexuality in the armed forces

(a) Findings. - Congress makes the following findings:

(1) Section 8 of article I of the Constitution of the United States commits exclusively to the Congress the powers to raise and support armies, provide and maintain a Navy, and make rules for the government and regulation of the land and naval forces.

(2) There is no constitutional right to serve in the armed forces.

(3) Pursuant to the powers conferred by section 8 of article I of the Constitution of the United States, it lies within the discretion of the Congress to establish qualifications for and conditions of service in the armed forces.

(4) The primary purpose of the armed forces is to prepare for and to prevail in combat should the need arise.

(5) The conduct of military operations requires members of the armed forces to make extraordinary sacrifices, including the ultimate sacrifice, in order to provide for the common defense.

(6) Success in combat requires military units that are characterized by high morale, good order and discipline, and unit cohesion.

(7) One of the most critical elements in combat capability is unit cohesion, that is, the bonds of trust among individual service members that make the combat effectiveness of a military unit greater than the sum of the combat effectiveness of the individual unit members.

(8) Military life is fundamentally different from civilian life in that –

(A) the extraordinary responsibilities of the armed forces, the unique conditions of military service, and the critical role of unit cohesion, require that the military community, while subject to civilian control, exist as a specialized society; and

(B) the military society is characterized by its own laws, rules, customs, and traditions, including numerous restrictions on personal behavior, that would not be acceptable in civilian society.

(9) The standards of conduct for members of the armed forces regulate a member's life for 24 hours each day beginning at the moment the member enters military status and not ending until that person is discharged or otherwise separated from the armed forces.

(10) Those standards of conduct, including the Uniform Code of Military Justice, apply to a member of the armed forces at all times that the member has a military status, whether the member is on base or off base, and whether the member is on duty or off duty.

(11) The pervasive application of the standards of conduct is necessary because members of the armed forces must be ready at all times for worldwide deployment to a combat environment.

(12) The worldwide deployment of United States military forces, the international responsibilities of the United States, and the potential for involvement of the armed forces in actual combat routinely make it necessary for members of the armed forces involuntarily to accept living conditions and working conditions that are often spartan, primitive, and characterized by forced intimacy with little or no privacy.

(13) The prohibition against homosexual conduct is a longstanding element of military law that continues to be necessary in the unique circumstances of military service.

(14) The armed forces must maintain personnel policies that exclude persons whose presence in the armed forces would create an unacceptable risk to the armed forces' high standards of morale, good order and discipline, and unit cohesion that are the essence of military capability.

(15) The presence in the armed forces of persons who demonstrate a propensity or

intent to engage in homosexual acts would create an unacceptable risk to the high standards of morale, good order and discipline, and unit cohesion that are the essence of military capability.

(b) Policy. - A member of the armed forces shall be separated from the armed forces under regulations prescribed by the Secretary of Defense if one or more of the following findings is made and approved in accordance with procedures set forth in such regulations:

(1) That the member has engaged in, attempted to engage in, or solicited another to engage in a homosexual act or acts unless there are further findings, made and approved in accordance with procedures set forth in such regulations, that the member has demonstrated that

(A) such conduct is a departure from the member's usual and customary behavior;

(B) such conduct, under all the circumstances, is unlikely to recur;

(C) such conduct was not accomplished by use of force, coercion, or intimidation;

(D) under the particular circumstances of the case, the member's continued presence in the armed forces is consistent with the interests of the armed forces in proper discipline good order, and morale; and

(E) the member does not have a propensity or intent to engage in homosexual acts.

(2) That the member has stated that he or she is a homosexual or bisexual, or words to that effect, unless there is a further finding, made and approved in accordance with procedures set forth in the regulations, that the member has demonstrated that he or she is not a person who engages in, attempts to engage in, has a propensity to engage in, or intends to en age in homosexual acts.

(3)That the member has married or attempted to marry a person known to be of the same biological sex.

(c) Entry Standards and Documents. - (1) The Secretary of Defense shall ensure that the standards for enlistment and appointment of members of the armed forces reflect the policies set forth in subsection (b).

(2) The documents used to effectuate the enlistment or appointment of a person as a member of the armed forces shall set forth the provisions of subsection (b).

(d) Required Briefings. - The briefings that members of the armed forces receive upon entry into the armed forces and periodically thereafter under section of this title (article 1 3   7 of the Uniform Code of Military Justice) shall include a detailed explanation of the applicable laws and regulations governing sexual conduct by members of the armed   forces, including the policies prescribed under subsection (b).

(e) Rule of Construction. - Nothing in subsection (b) shall be construed to require that a member of the armed forces be processed for separation from the armed forces when a determination is made in accordance with regulations prescribed by the Secretary of defense that –

(1) the member engaged in conduct or made statements for the purpose of avoiding or terminating military service; and

(2) separation of the member would not be in the best interest of the armed forces.

(f) Definitions. - In this section:

(1) The term "homosexual" means a person, regardless of sex, who engages in, attempts to engage in, has a propensity to engage in, or intends to engage in homosexual acts, and includes the terms "gay" and "lesbian."

(2) The term "bisexual" means a person who engages in, attempts to engage in, has a propensity to engage in, or intends to engage in homosexual and heterosexual acts.

(3) The term "homosexual act" means—

(A) any bodily contact, actively undertaken or passively permitted, between members of the same sex for the purpose of satisfying sexual desires; and

(B) any bodily contact which a reasonable person would understand to demonstrate a propensity or intent to engage in an act described in subparagraph (A).

PENTAGON ISSUES NEW GUIDELINES FOR GAYS IN MILITARY

The "Don't Ask, Don't Tell" policy continues to be ineffective. The following article discusses the recent changes the Pentagon has made in an attempt to clarify it. However, until the Supreme Court is willing to consider sexual preference as a fundamental right, policies such as these will always be open to interpretation.

August 13, 1999, Web Posted at: 4:12 p.m. EDT (2012 GMT)
From staff and wire reports

WASHINGTON — The U.S. military Friday issued new directives intended to end abuses of the "don't ask, don't tell" policy toward gays and lesbians in the armed forces.

The revised specifications require that troops receive anti-gay harassment training throughout their military careers, starting with boot camp.

"I've made it clear there is no room for harassment or threats in the military," Defense Secretary William Cohen said in issuing the new directives.

The guidelines also mandate that any investigation into the sexual orientation of a soldier be handled at a more senior level of the military justice system than before.

The revisions follow the beating death last month of a soldier at Fort Campbell, Kentucky, who was rumored to be gay. Barry Winchell was bludgeoned to death in his barracks.

The Army conducted a hearing this week to determine whether the murder case against Pvt. Calvin Glover, 18, of Sulphur, Oklahoma, will go to a general court-martial. The decision is expected in about two weeks.

Some activists have charged that gay harassment and investigation of gays have surged to record levels in the military, despite the "don't ask, don't tell" policy.

Last year, 1,145 people were discharged from the armed forces for homosexuality, according to a Pentagon report. In 1997, the total was 997, the highest number since 1987. The number of discharges hit a low of 617 in 1994, the year the "don't ask, don't tell" policy took effect.

Pentagon officials have defended the policy, contending that roughly 80 percent of the discharges occur because the individual has come forward.

The new guidelines do not make any major changes in the procedures that have been followed since 1994, but try to spell them out more clearly, the officials said.

Michelle Benecke, a former Army officer now with the Service members Legal Defense Network, said she "seriously doubts'" the new guidelines will be an adequate response to the problem.

Still, officials said it is hoped that the intended clarifications — and mandatory anti-gay harassment, training — will end what they claim are a relatively small number of abuses.

Under the policy, those who are openly homosexual are still barred from serving in the in the military.

Gays can remain in the services so long as they do not discuss their sexual orientation openly. Commanders and investigators are not permitted to ask troops about their sexual orientation.

The policy was a compromise developed after Congress rejected an earlier proposal by President Clinton for an outright ban on discrimination based on sexual orientation.

Source: CNN, August 13, 1999. Correspondent David Ensor and the Associated Press contributed to this report.

HOW WELL DID YOU UNDERSTAND THIS SELECTION?

1. Explain how the discussion over gays in the military in part stems from the constitutional tension between Congress's power to organize the military and the president's role as Commander-in-chief.

2. Is sexual preference a constitutionally protected right?

3. Do you believe that it is important that the military reflect the value of the society that it is defending?

The election of 2000 was one of the closest and most controversial presidential elections in U.S. history. Many would say that it was decided by one vote, not on election day but on December 12, 2000, in an extraordinary 5-4 Supreme Court decision. The election was a lesson in advanced citizenship and centered America's attention on the constitutional concepts of federalism, separation of power, and checks and balances. It challenged the legal systems at both the state and national levels.

The question was who had won Florida's twenty-five electoral votes. It was clear that Al Gore had won the overall popular vote; however, he had not secured the majority of electoral votes he needed to become president. Without Florida's electoral votes, Gore would be unable to win the presidency. If Gore lost Florida's electors, it would be the first time in over 100 years, that the candidate who had won the popular vote would not become the president.

In the early morning of November 8, George Bush held a razor-thin lead in Florida that would have entitled him to the state's electoral votes. However, the lead was so small that it triggered the state's automatic recount law. This was the beginning of legal maneuverings that would wind its way though the Florida state court system ultimately ending up in the hands of the U.S. Supreme Court. Both the Bush and Gore campaigns sought legal solutions to their electoral dilemmas.

In the end, the Supreme Court of the United States ruled that the Florida Supreme Court had erred in its order for a manual recount of thousands of ballots in the state's hotly contested election. A court not known for rendering decisions based on the XIV Amendment's "equal rights" clause rendered a surprise late-night decision. It said that the Florida Supreme Court had violated "equal rights" by ordering selective recounts in Florida counties. The justices found constitutional problems with the manual recounting process order by the Florida Supreme Court and concluded that there was not enough time to fix the problem and complete the counting by the compressed electoral college timetable. Without a recount, George Bush was declared the winner of Florida's twenty-five electoral votes, and the Supreme Court decision transformed George Bush, the candidate, into George Bush, president-elect.

SUPREME COURT OF THE UNITED STATES
GEORGE W. BUSH, ET AL., PETITIONERS v. ALBERT GORE, JR., ET AL.
No. 00-949
[December 12, 2000]
PER CURIAM.
ON WRIT OF CERTIORARI TO THE FLORIDA SUPREME COURT

I

On December 8, 2000, the Supreme Court of Florida ordered that the Circuit Court of Leon County tabulate by hand 9,000 ballots in Miami-Dade County. It also ordered the inclusion in the certified vote totals of 215 votes identified in Palm Beach County and 168 votes identified in Miami-Dade County for Vice President Albert Gore, Jr., and Senator Joseph Lieberman, Democratic Candidates for President and Vice President. The Supreme Court noted that petitioner, Governor George W. Bush asserted that the net gain for Vice President Gore in Palm Beach County was 176 votes, and directed the Circuit Court to resolve that dispute on remand. The court further held that relief would require manual recounts in all Florida counties where so-called "undervotes" had not been subject to manual tabulation. The court ordered all manual recounts to begin at once. Governor Bush and Richard Cheney, Republican Candidates for the Presidency and Vice Presidency, filed an emergency application for a stay of this mandate. On December 9, we granted the application, treated the application as a petition for a writ of certiorari, and granted certiorari.

The proceedings leading to the present controversy are discussed in some detail in our opinion in Bush v. Palm Beach County Canvassing Bd. On November 8, 2000, the day following the Presidential election, the Florida Division of Elections reported that petitioner, Governor Bush, had received 2,909,135 votes, and respondent, Vice President Gore, had received 2,907,351 votes, a margin of 1,784 for Governor Bush. Because Governor Bush's margin of victory was less than "one-half of a percent . . . of the votes cast," an automatic machine recount was conducted under §102.141(4) of the election code, the results of which showed Governor Bush still winning the race but by a diminished margin. Vice President Gore then sought manual recounts in Volusia, Palm Beach, Broward, and Miami-Dade Counties, pursuant to Florida's election protest provisions. Fla. Stat. §102.166 (2000). A dispute arose concerning the deadline for local county canvassing boards to submit their returns to the Secretary of State (Secretary). The Secretary declined to waive the November 14 deadline imposed by statute. §§102.111, 102.112. The Florida Supreme Court, however, set the deadline at November 26. We granted certiorari and vacated the Florida Supreme Court's decision, finding considerable uncertainty as to the grounds on which it was based. On December 11, the Florida Supreme Court issued a decision on remand reinstating that date.

On November 26, the Florida Elections Canvassing Commission certified the results of the election and declared Governor Bush the winner of Florida's 25 electoral votes. On November 27, Vice President Gore, pursuant to Florida's contest provisions, filed a complaint in Leon County Circuit Court contesting the certification. Fla. Stat. §102.168 (2000). He sought relief pursuant to §102.168(3)(c), which provides that "[r]eceipt of a number of illegal votes or rejection of a number of legal votes sufficient to change or place in doubt the result of the election" shall be grounds for a contest. The Circuit Court denied relief, stating that Vice President Gore failed to meet his burden of proof. He appealed to the First District Court of Appeal, which certified the matter to the Florida Supreme Court.

Accepting jurisdiction, the Florida Supreme Court affirmed in part and reversed in part. The court held that the Circuit Court had been correct to reject Vice President Gore's challenge to the results certified in Nassau County and his challenge to the Palm Beach County Canvassing Board's determination that 3,300 ballots cast in that county were not, in the statutory phrase, "legal votes."

The Supreme Court held that Vice President Gore had satisfied his burden of proof under §102.168(3)(c) with respect to his challenge to Miami-Dade County's failure to tabulate, by manual count, 9,000 ballots on which the machines had failed to detect a vote for President ("undervotes"). Noting the closeness of the election, the Court explained that "[o]n this record, there can be no question that there are legal votes within the 9,000 uncounted votes sufficient to place the results of this election in doubt." A "legal vote," as determined by the Supreme Court, is "one in which there is a 'clear indication of the intent of the voter. '" The court therefore ordered a hand recount of the 9,000 ballots in Miami-Dade County. Observing that the contest provisions vest broad discretion in the circuit judge to "provide any relief appropriate under such circumstances," Fla. Stat. §102.168(8) (2000), the Supreme Court further held that the Circuit Court could order "the Supervisor of Elections and the Canvassing Boards, as well as the necessary public officials, in all counties that have not conducted a manual recount or tabulation of the undervotes . . . to do so forthwith, said tabulation to take place in the individual counties where the ballots are located."

The Supreme Court also determined that both Palm Beach County and Miami-Dade County, in their earlier manual recounts, had identified a net gain of 215 and 168 legal votes for Vice President Gore. Rejecting the Circuit Court's conclusion that Palm Beach County lacked the authority to include the 215 net votes submitted past the November 26 deadline, the Supreme Court explained that the deadline was not intended to exclude votes identified after that date through ongoing manual recounts. As to Miami-Dade County, the Court concluded that although the 168 votes identified were the result of a partial recount, they were "legal votes [that] could change the outcome of the election." The Supreme Court therefore directed the Circuit Court to include those totals in the certified results, subject to resolution of the actual vote total from the Miami-Dade partial recount.

The petition presents the following questions: whether the Florida Supreme Court established new standards for resolving Presidential election contests, thereby violating Art. II, §1, cl. 2, of the United States Constitution and failing to comply with 3 U. S. C. §5, and whether the use of standardless manual recounts violates the Equal Protection and Due Process Clauses. With respect to the equal protection question, we find a violation of the Equal Protection Clause.

II

A

The closeness of this election, and the multitude of legal challenges which have followed in its wake, have brought into sharp focus a common, if heretofore unnoticed, phenomenon. Nationwide statistics reveal that an estimated 2% of ballots cast do not register a vote for President for whatever reason, including deliberately choosing no candidate at all or some voter error, such as voting for two candidates or insufficiently marking a ballot… In certifying election results, the votes eligible for inclusion in the certification are the votes meeting the properly established legal requirements.

This case has shown that punch card balloting machines can produce an unfortunate number of ballots which are not punched in a clean, complete way by the voter. After the current counting, it is likely legislative bodies nationwide will examine ways to improve the mechanisms and machinery for voting.

B

The individual citizen has no federal constitutional right to vote for electors for the President of the United States unless and until the state legislature chooses a statewide election as the means to implement its power to appoint members of the Electoral College. U. S. Const., Art. II, §1. This is the source for the statement in McPherson v. Blacker, 146 U. S. 1, 35 (1892), that the State legislature's power to select the manner for appointing electors is plenary; it may, if it so chooses,

369

select the electors itself, which indeed was the manner used by State legislatures in several States for many years after the Framing of our Constitution. History has now favored the voter, and in each of the several States the citizens themselves vote for Presidential electors. When the state legislature vests the right to vote for President in its people, the right to vote as the legislature has prescribed is fundamental; and one source of its fundamental nature lies in the equal weight accorded to each vote and the equal dignity owed to each voter. The State, of course, after granting the franchise in the special context of Article II, can take back the power to appoint electors…

The right to vote is protected in more than the initial allocation of the franchise. Equal protection applies as well to the manner of its exercise. Having once granted the right to vote on equal terms, the State may not, by later arbitrary and disparate treatment, value one person's vote over that of another…It must be remembered that "the right of suffrage can be denied by a debasement or dilution of the weight of a citizen's vote just as effectively as by wholly prohibiting the free exercise of the franchise." <u>Reynolds v. Sims</u>, 377 U. S. 533, 555 (1964).

There is no difference between the two sides of the present controversy on these basic propositions. Respondents say that the very purpose of vindicating the right to vote justifies the recount procedures now at issue. The question before us, however, is whether the recount procedures the Florida Supreme Court has adopted are consistent with its obligation to avoid arbitrary and disparate treatment of the members of its electorate.

Much of the controversy seems to revolve around ballot cards designed to be perforated by a stylus but which, either through error or deliberate omission, have not been perforated with sufficient precision for a machine to count them. In some cases a piece of the card — a chad — is hanging, say by two corners. In other cases there is no separation at all, just an indentation.

The Florida Supreme Court has ordered that the intent of the voter be discerned from such ballots. For purposes of resolving the equal protection challenge, it is not necessary to decide whether the Florida Supreme Court had the authority under the legislative scheme for resolving election disputes to define what a legal vote is and to mandate a manual recount implementing that definition. The recount mechanisms implemented in response to the decisions of the Florida Supreme Court do not satisfy the minimum requirement for non-arbitrary treatment of voters necessary to secure the fundamental right. Florida's basic command for the count of legally cast votes is to consider the "intent of the voter." This is unobjectionable as an abstract proposition and a starting principle. The problem inheres in the absence of specific standards to ensure its equal application. The formulation of uniform rules to determine intent based on these recurring circumstances is practicable and, we conclude, necessary.

The law does not refrain from searching for the intent of the actor in a multitude of circumstances; and in some cases the general command to ascertain intent is not susceptible to much further refinement. In this instance, however, the question is not whether to believe a witness but how to interpret the marks or holes or scratches on an inanimate object, a piece of cardboard or paper which, it is said, might not have registered as a vote during the machine count. The factfinder confronts a thing, not a person. The search for intent can be confined by specific rules designed to ensure uniform treatment.

The want of those rules here has led to unequal evaluation of ballots in various respects…As seems to have been acknowledged at oral argument, the standards for accepting or rejecting contested ballots might vary not only from county to county but indeed within a single county from one recount team to another.

The record provides some examples. A monitor in Miami-Dade County testified at trial that he observed that three members of the county canvassing board applied different standards in defining a legal vote. 3 Tr. 497, 499 (Dec. 3, 2000). And testimony at trial also revealed that at least one county changed its evaluative standards during the counting process. Palm Beach County, for example, began the process with a 1990 guideline which precluded counting completely attached chads, switched to a rule that considered a vote to be legal if any light could be seen through a chad, changed back to the 1990 rule, and then abandoned any pretense of a per se rule, only to have a court order that the county consider dimpled chads legal. This is not a process with sufficient guarantees of equal treatment.

An early case in our one person, one vote jurisprudence arose when a State accorded arbitrary and disparate treatment to voters in its different counties. <u>Gray v. Sanders</u>, 372 U. S. 368 (1963). The Court found a constitutional violation. We relied on these principles in the context of the Presidential selection process in <u>Moore v. Ogilvie</u>, 394 U. S. 814 (1969), where we invalidated a county-based procedure that diluted the influence of citizens in larger counties in the nominating process. There we observed that "[t]he idea that one group can be granted greater voting strength than another is hostile to the one man, one vote basis of our representative government."

The State Supreme Court ratified this uneven treatment. It mandated that the recount totals from two counties, Miami-Dade and Palm Beach, be included in the certified total. The court also appeared to hold sub silentio that the recount totals from Broward County, which were not completed until after the original November 14 certification by the Secretary of State, were to be considered part of the new certified vote totals even though the county certification was not contested by Vice President Gore. Yet each of the counties used varying standards to determine what was a legal vote. Broward County used a more forgiving standard than Palm Beach County, and uncovered almost three times as many new votes, a result markedly disproportionate to the difference in population between the counties.

In addition, the recounts in these three counties were not limited to so-called undervotes but extended to all of the ballots. The distinction has real consequences. A manual recount of all ballots identifies not only those ballots which show no vote but also those which contain more than one, the so-called overvotes. Neither category will be counted by the machine. This is not a trivial concern. At oral argument, respondents estimated there are as many as 110,000 overvotes statewide. As a result, the citizen whose ballot was not read by a machine because he failed to vote for a candidate in a way readable by a machine may still have his vote counted in a manual recount; on the other hand, the citizen who marks two candidates in a way discernable by the machine will not have the same opportunity to have his vote count, even if a manual examination of the ballot would reveal the requisite indicia of intent. Furthermore, the citizen who marks two candidates, only one of which is discernable by the machine, will have his vote counted even though it should have been read as an invalid ballot. The State Supreme Court's inclusion of vote counts based on these variant standards exemplifies concerns with the remedial processes that were under way.

That brings the analysis to yet a further equal protection problem. The votes certified by the court included a partial total from one county, Miami-Dade. The Florida Supreme Court's decision thus gives no assurance that the recounts included in a final certification must be complete. Indeed, it is respondent's submission that it would be consistent with the rules of the recount procedures to include whatever partial counts are done by the time of final certification, and we interpret the Florida Supreme Court's decision to permit this…This accommodation no doubt results from the truncated contest period established by the Florida Supreme Court in Bush I, at respondents' own urging. The press of time does not diminish the constitutional concern. A desire for speed is not a general excuse for ignoring equal protection guarantees.

In addition to these difficulties the actual process by which the votes were to be counted under the Florida Supreme Court's decision raises further concerns. That order did not specify who would recount the ballots. The county canvassing boards were forced to pull together ad hoc teams comprised of judges from various Circuits who had no previous training in handling and interpreting ballots. Furthermore, while others were permitted to observe, they were prohibited from objecting during the recount.

The recount process, in its features here described, is inconsistent with the minimum procedures necessary to protect the fundamental right of each voter in the special instance of a statewide recount under the authority of a single state judicial officer. Our consideration is limited to the present circumstances, for the problem of equal protection in election processes generally presents many complexities.

The question before the Court is not whether local entities, in the exercise of their expertise, may develop different systems for implementing elections. Instead, we are presented with a situation where a state court with the power to assure uniformity has ordered a statewide recount with minimal procedural safeguards. When a court orders a statewide remedy, there must be at least some assurance that the rudimentary requirements of equal treatment and fundamental fairness are satisfied.

Given the Court's assessment that the recount process underway was probably being conducted in an unconstitutional manner, the Court stayed the order directing the recount so it could hear this case and render an expedited decision. The contest provision, as it was mandated by the State Supreme Court, is not well calculated to sustain the confidence that all citizens must have in the outcome of elections. The State has not shown that its procedures include the necessary safeguards. The problem, for instance, of the estimated 110,000 overvotes has not been addressed, although Chief Justice Wells called attention to the concern in his dissenting opinion.

Upon due consideration of the difficulties identified to this point, it is obvious that the recount cannot be conducted in compliance with the requirements of equal protection and due process without substantial additional work. It would require not only the adoption (after opportunity for argument) of adequate statewide standards for determining what is a legal vote, and practicable procedures to implement them, but also orderly judicial review of any disputed matters that might arise. In addition, the Secretary of State has advised that the recount of only a portion of the ballots requires that the vote tabulation equipment be used to screen out undervotes, a function for which the machines were not designed. If a recount of overvotes were also required, perhaps even a second screening would be necessary. Use of the equipment for this purpose, and any new software developed for it, would have to be evaluated for accuracy by the Secretary of State, as required by Fla. Stat. §101.015 (2000).

The Supreme Court of Florida has said that the legislature intended the State's electors to "participat[e] fully in the federal electoral process," as provided in 3 U. S. C. §5…That statute, in turn, requires that any controversy or contest that is designed to lead to a conclusive selection of electors be completed by December 12. That date is upon us, and there is no recount procedure in place under the State Supreme Court's order that comports with minimal constitutional standards. Because it is evident that any recount seeking to meet the December 12 date will be unconstitutional for the reasons we have discussed, we reverse the judgment of the Supreme Court of Florida ordering a recount to proceed.

Seven Justices of the Court agree that there are constitutional problems with the recount ordered by the Florida Supreme Court that demand a remedy…The only disagreement is as to the remedy. Because the Florida Supreme Court has said that the Florida Legislature intended to obtain the safe-harbor benefits of 3 U. S. C. §5, JUSTICE BREYER's proposed remedy — remanding to the Florida Supreme Court for its ordering of a constitutionally proper contest until December 18-contemplates action in violation of the Florida election code, and hence could not be part of an "appropriate" order authorized by Fla. Stat. §102.168(8) (2000).

* * *

None are more conscious of the vital limits on judicial authority than are the members of this Court, and none stand more in admiration of the Constitution's design to leave the selection of the President to the people, through their legislatures, and to the political sphere. When contending parties invoke the process of the courts, however, it becomes our unsought responsibility to resolve the federal and constitutional issues the judicial system has been forced to confront.

The judgment of the Supreme Court of Florida is reversed, and the case is remanded for further proceedings not inconsistent with this opinion.

Pursuant to this Court's Rule 45.2, the Clerk is directed to issue the mandate in this case forthwith.

It is so ordered.

HOW WELL DID YOU UNDERSTAND THIS SELECTION?

1. What is the "equal protection" clause of the Constitution and how did the Supreme Court apply it to this particular case?

2. How does a case come before the Supreme Court?

3. What elements of federalism and separation of power do you see at work in the election of 2000?

4. In your opinion, did the Supreme Court decide the election of 2000? If so, how so?

There are four possible categories for any Supreme Court decision: unanimous opinion, majority opinion, concurring opinion, and dissenting opinion. If a decision is not unanimous, it can be any combination of the others. All opinions of the Court are important because they set precedents for future cases throughout the judicial system.

The majority opinion is extremely important because it reflects the sentiments of the "majority" of the Court. By tradition, the assignment of who is to write the majority opinion is left up to the Chief Justice, if he is in the majority, or to the most senior justice if the Chief Justice is on the dissenting side. Once the majority opinion is drafted, it is circulated to the other justices. Some members of the majority may find fault with the specific language of the opinion and choose to pen a "concurring" opinion. This type of opinion supports the majority decision but presents a somewhat different rationale or emphasis.

*In **Bush v Gore**, Chief Justice Rehnquist was in the majority and chose to write the opinion himself. Since the decision was 5-4, those justices not voting with the majority had the option of writing a dissenting opinion. There may be one or more dissenting opinions each explaining a justice's constitutional rational for voting against the majority. These dissenting views are very important because they are often used as a basis for argument to appeal and establish new precedents at a later date. Judge Ginsberg wrote a dissenting opinion in **Bush v Gore**.*

Ginsberg did not see constitutional flaws in the recounts prescribed by the Florida Supreme Court. To show her disdain for the majority's decision, she concluded her opinion with "I dissent," pointedly omitting the customary modifier "respectfully." This is extremely strong language for a Supreme Court justice. Those writing dissenting opinions usually find no reason to please the majority and consequently can be less guarded than the majority in their writing. Some of the most eloquent and memorable opinions of the Court were "dissenting" ones, and Justice Ginsberg's outspoken response to the majority may prove to be more memorable than the decision itself.

SUPREME COURT OF THE UNITED STATES

No. 00-949
GEORGE W. BUSH, ET AL., PETITIONERS v.ALBERT GORE, JR., ET AL.
ON WRIT OF CERTIORARI TO THE FLORIDA SUPREME COURT
[December 12, 2000]

JUSTICE GINSBURG, with whom **JUSTICE STEVENS** joins, and with whom **JUSTICE SOUTER** and **JUSTICE BREYER** join as to Part I, dissenting.

I

The CHIEF JUSTICE acknowledges that provisions of Florida's Election Code "may well admit of more than one interpretation." Ante, at 3. But instead of respecting the state high court's province to say what the State's Election Code means, THE CHIEF JUSTICE maintains that Florida's Supreme Court has veered so far from the ordinary practice of judicial review that what it did cannot properly be called judging. My colleagues have offered a reasonable construction of Florida's law. Their construction coincides with the view of one of Florida's seven Supreme Court justices. I might join THE CHIEF JUSTICE were it my commission to interpret Florida law. But disagreement with the Florida court's interpretation of its own State's law does not warrant the conclusion that the justices of that court have legislated. There is no cause here to believe that the members of Florida's high court have done less than "their mortal best to discharge their oath of office," Sumner v. Mata, 449 U. S. 539, 549 (1981), and no cause to upset their reasoned interpretation of Florida law.

This Court more than occasionally affirms statutory, and even constitutional, interpretations with which it disagrees. For example, when reviewing challenges to administrative agencies' interpretations of laws they implement, we defer to the agencies unless their interpretation violates "the unambiguously expressed intent of Congress." Chevron U. S. A. Inc. v. Natural Resources Defense Council, Inc., 467 U. S. 837, 843 (1984). We do so in the face of the declaration in Article I of the United States Constitution that "All legislative Powers herein granted shall be vested in a Congress of the United States." Surely the Constitution does not call upon us to pay more respect to a federal administrative agency's construction of federal law than to a state high court's interpretation of its own state's law. And not uncommonly, we let stand state-court interpretations of federal law with which we might disagree. Notably, in the habeas context, the Court adheres to the view that "there is 'no intrinsic reason why the fact that a man is a federal judge should make him more competent, or conscientious, or learned with respect to [federal law] than his neighbor in the state courthouse.'" Stone v. Powell, 428 U. S. 465, 494, n. 35 (1976)...

No doubt there are cases in which the proper application of federal law may hinge on interpretations of state law. Unavoidably, this Court must sometimes examine state law in order to protect federal rights. But we have dealt with such cases ever mindful of the full measure of respect we owe to interpretations of state law by a State's highest court. In the Contract Clause case, General Motors Corp. v. Romein, 503 U. S. 181 (1992), for example, we said that although "ultimately we are bound to decide for ourselves whether a contract was made," the Court "accord[s] respectful consideration and great weight to the views of the State's highest court." And in Central Union Telephone Co. v. Edwardsville, 269 U. S. 190 (1925), we upheld the Illinois Supreme Court's interpretation of a state waiver rule, even though that interpretation resulted in the forfeiture of federal constitutional rights. Refusing to supplant Illinois law with a federal definition of waiver, we explained that the state court's declaration "should bind us unless so unfair or unreasonable in its application to those asserting a federal right as to obstruct it."

In deferring to state courts on matters of state law, we appropriately recognize that this Court acts as an " 'outside[r]' lacking the common exposure to local law which comes from sitting in the jurisdiction." Lehman Brothers v. Schein, 416 U. S. 386, 391 (1974). That recognition has sometimes prompted us to resolve doubts about the meaning of state law by certifying issues to a State's highest court, even when federal rights are at stake. Cf. Arizonans for Official English v. Arizona, 520 U. S. 43, 79 (1997) ("Warnings against premature adjudication of constitutional questions bear heightened attention when a federal court is asked to invalidate a State's law, for the federal tribunal risks friction-generating error when it endeavors to construe a novel state Act not yet reviewed by the State's highest court."). Notwithstanding our authority to decide issues of state law underlying federal claims, we have used the certification devise to afford state high courts an opportunity to inform us on matters of their own State's law because such restraint "helps build a cooperative judicial federalism."

Just last Term, in <u>Fiore v. White</u>, 528 U. S. 23 (1999), we took advantage of Pennsylvania's certification procedure. In that case, a state prisoner brought a federal habeas action claiming that the State had failed to prove an essential element of his charged offense in violation of the Due Process Clause. Instead of resolving the state-law question on which the federal claim depended, we certified the question to the Pennsylvania Supreme Court for that court to "help determine the proper state-law predicate for our determination of the federal constitutional questions raised."... THE CHIEF JUSTICE's willingness to reverse the Florida Supreme Court's interpretation of Florida law in this case is at least in tension with our reluctance in Fiore even to interpret Pennsylvania law before seeking instruction from the Pennsylvania Supreme Court. I would have thought the "cautious approach" we counsel when federal courts address matters of state law, Arizonans, 520 U. S., at 77, and our commitment to "build[ing] cooperative judicial federalism," Lehman Brothers, 416 U. S., at 391, demanded greater restraint.

Rarely has this Court rejected outright an interpretation of state law by a state high court. <u>Fairfax's Devisee v. Hunter's Lessee</u>, 7 Cranch 603 (1813), <u>NAACP v. Alabama ex rel. Patterson</u>, 357 U. S. 449 (1958), and <u>Bouie v. City of Columbia</u>, 378 U. S. 347 (1964), cited by THE CHIEF JUSTICE, are three such rare instances. See ante, at 4, 5, and n. 2. But those cases are embedded in historical contexts hardly comparable to the situation here. Fairfax's Devisee, which held that the Virginia Court of Appeals had misconstrued its own forfeiture laws to deprive a British subject of lands secured to him by federal treaties, occurred amidst vociferous States' rights attacks on the Marshall Court. G. Gunther & K. Sullivan, Constitutional Law 61-62 (13th ed. 1997). The Virginia court refused to obey this Court's Fairfax's Devisee mandate to enter judgment for the British subject's successor in interest. That refusal led to the Court's pathmarking decision in Martin v. Hunter's Lessee, 1 Wheat. 304 (1816). Patterson, a case decided three months after <u>Cooper v. Aaron</u>, 358 U. S. 1 (1958), in the face of Southern resistance to the civil rights movement, held that the Alabama Supreme Court had irregularly applied its own procedural rules to deny review of a contempt order against the NAACP arising from its refusal to disclose membership lists. We said that "our jurisdiction is not defeated if the nonfederal ground relied on by the state court is without any fair or substantial support."... Bouie, stemming from a lunch counter "sit-in" at the height of the civil rights movement, held that the South Carolina Supreme Court's construction of its trespass laws — criminalizing conduct not covered by the text of an otherwise clear statute — was "unforeseeable" and thus violated due process when applied retroactively to the petitioners.

THE CHIEF JUSTICE's casual citation of these cases might lead one to believe they are part of a larger collection of cases in which we said that the Constitution impelled us to train a skeptical eye on a state court's portrayal of state law. But one would be hard pressed, I think, to find additional cases that fit the mold. As JUSTICE BREYER convincingly explains, see post, at 5-9 (dissenting opinion), this case involves nothing close to the kind of recalcitrance by a state high court that warrants extraordinary action by this Court. The Florida Supreme Court concluded that counting every legal vote was the overriding concern of the Florida Legislature when it enacted the State's Election Code. The court surely should not be bracketed with state high courts of the Jim Crow South.

THE CHIEF JUSTICE says that Article II, by providing that state legislatures shall direct the manner of appointing electors, authorizes federal superintendence over the relationship between state courts and state legislatures, and licenses a departure from the usual deference we give to state court interpretations of state law. Ante, at 5 ("To attach definitive weight to the pronouncement of a state court, when the very question at issue is whether the court has actually departed from the statutory meaning, would be to abdicate our responsibility to enforce the explicit requirements of Article II."). The Framers of our Constitution, however, understood that in a republican government, the judiciary would construe the legislature's enactments. See U. S. Const., Art. III; The Federalist No. 78 (A. Hamilton). In light of the constitutional guarantee to States of a "Republican Form of Government," U. S. Const., Art. IV, §4, Article II can hardly be read to invite this Court to disrupt a State's republican regime. Yet THE CHIEF JUSTICE today would reach out to do just that. By holding that Article II requires our revision of a state court's construction of state laws in order to protect one organ of the State from another, THE CHIEF JUSTICE contradicts the basic principle that a State may organize itself as it sees fit....

The extraordinary setting of this case has obscured the ordinary principle that dictates its proper resolution: Federal courts defer to state high courts' interpretations of their state's own law. This principle reflects the core of federalism, on which all agree. "The Framers split the atom of sovereignty. It was the genius of their idea that our citizens would have two political capacities, one state and one federal, each protected from incursion by the other." Saenz v. Roe, 526 U. S. 489, 504, n. 17 (1999) THE CHIEF JUSTICE's solicitude for the Florida Legislature comes at the expense of the more fundamental solicitude we owe to the legislature's sovereign. U. S. Const., Art. II, §1, cl. 2 Were the other members of this Court as mindful as they generally are of our system of dual sovereignty, they would affirm the judgment of the Florida Supreme Court.

II

I agree with JUSTICE STEVENS that petitioners have not presented a substantial equal protection claim. Ideally, perfection would be the appropriate standard for judging the recount. But we live in an imperfect world, one in which thousands of votes have not been counted. I cannot agree that the recount adopted by the Florida court, flawed as it may be, would yield a result any less fair or precise than the certification that preceded that recount....

Even if there were an equal protection violation, I would agree with JUSTICE STEVENS, JUSTICE SOUTER, and JUSTICE BREYER that the Court's concern about "the December 12 deadline," ante, at 12, is misplaced. Time is short in part because of the Court's entry of a stay on December 9, several hours after an able circuit judge in Leon County had begun to superintend the recount process. More fundamentally, the Court's reluctance to let the recount go forward — despite its suggestion that "[t]he search for intent can be confined by specific rules designed to ensure uniform treatment," ante, at 8 — ultimately turns on its own judgment about the practical realities of implementing a recount, not the judgment of those much closer to the process.

Equally important, as JUSTICE BREYER explains, post, at 12 (dissenting opinion), the December 12 "deadline" for bringing Florida's electoral votes into 3 U. S. C. §5's safe harbor lacks the significance the Court assigns it. Were that date to pass, Florida would still be entitled to deliver electoral votes Congress must count unless both Houses find that the votes "ha[d] not been . . . regularly given." 3 U. S. C. §15. The statute identifies other significant dates. See, e.g., §7 (specifying December 18 as the date electors "shall meet and give their votes"); §12 (specifying "the fourth Wednesday in December" — this year, December 27 — as the date on which Congress, if it has not received a State's electoral votes, shall request the state secretary of state to send a certified return immediately). But none of these dates has ultimate significance in light of Congress' detailed provisions for determining, on "the sixth day of January," the validity of electoral votes. §15.

The Court assumes that time will not permit "orderly judicial review of any disputed matters that might arise." Ante, at 12. But no one has doubted the good faith and diligence with which Florida election officials, attorneys for all sides of this controversy, and the courts of law have performed their duties. Notably, the Florida Supreme Court has produced two substantial opinions within 29 hours of oral argument. In sum, the Court's conclusion that a constitutionally adequate recount is impractical is a prophecy the Court's own judgment will not allow to be tested. Such an untested prophecy should not decide the Presidency of the United States.
I dissent.

HOW WELL DID YOU UNDERSTAND THIS SELECTION?

1. How does Ginsberg define separation of power in her dissent?

2.Ginsberg's dissent is based in part on her opinion that the Supreme Court overstepped its bounds by reversing a Florida Supreme Court interpretation of a state law. How does this fit into the evolving relationship between federal and state government?

PREDICTING PRESIDENTIAL PERFORMANCE:
MEASURING BUSH'S MOTIVES

*Evaluating the first hundred days in office of a new president has become a ritual in American politics. Newspaper editorials, magazine and journal articles and television, radio and Internet commentaries on the novice prsident's job performance abound. Implied (and sometimes implicit) in all the media specu- lation is the notion that this "honeymoon" period provides clues about both the future behavior of the chief executive and the welfare of the country. As the April 29, 2001 editorial in The **New York Times** put it, "the glimpses we get often can be valuable and even prophetic." It should be noted, however, that many, if not most, of the early prophesies are somewhat limited in that they are based solely on subjective interpretations of presidential behavior. What sets political psychologist David G. Winter's analysis of President George W. Bush's first few months in office apart, and what makes it particularly valuable, is that it is based on empirical methodology (content analysis). The full text of Professor Winter's article, "Measuring Bush's Motives," is reprinted below.*

MEASURING BUSH'S MOTIVES

By the time you receive this issue [Spring 2001] of the newsletter [ISPP (International Society of Political Psychology) News,] President George W. Bush will have been in office for a few months. Can we predict what kind of president he will be over four years? Political leaders, journalists, and ordinary citizens—we all try to predict presidents' performance. When new presidents assume of- fice, we speculate about their strengths and vulnerabilities. Will they accomplish a lot? Where will they stumble? Sometimes we extrapolate from a new president's past record, although being a U.S. president is really not comparable to any earlier office or experience. Thus presidents' futures do not always resemble their pasts, as the administrations of Harry Truman and Chester Authur have taught us. Sometimes we look to presidents' platforms or campaign promises, though these are often quickly thrown overboard as the captain of the Ship of State navigates through unfamiliar and dangerous political waters.

   Political psychologists usually don't have access to important leaders; if they do, they can't talk about their clients. (Remember what happened to psychiatrist James Coburn in the amusing 1967 movie, "The President's Analyst"?) Thus to study presidents, they have to rely on indirect methods, such as systematic content analysis of presidential words and verbal imagery. Of course speechwriters script virtually everything presidents say in public, but presidents do choose their writers and usually edit their work. For several years now, I have used content analysis to score political speeches for motive imagery, or reference to three kinds of goals: **achievement** (references to excellence, unique accomplishments, overcoming failure), **affiliation** (concern for warmth and close relations), and **power** (having impact). These motive images do not measure particular policy goals, but rather the way leaders talk about their goals.

So what about George W. Bush? Measured in this way and compared to previous presidents, Bush's inaugural address was a little below average in achievement motive imagery ("America, at its **best**, is also courageous"). It was very high in affiliation ("principles that **unite** us") and power ("and we **will not allow** it") [.] In standard score units, Bush's speech scored -.5 for achievement, +2.6 for affiliation, and +2.2 for power.

What does this profile mean for the Bush presidency? Based on past research about presidential motives and performance, we can predict that Bush will enjoy being president (rather than becoming frustrated in the manner of a Jimmy Carter). He may also demonstrate greater political effectiveness than some might expect (high power and below-average achievement). In making decisions, however, he may rely on small, secluded groups of close friends and advisers who are similar to himself (high affiliation), which may alienate people with different views and experience. Further, he might be vulnerable to scandals arising from the excessive influence of advisors and friends (also high affiliation). In foreign affairs, he may endorse more aggressive policies (high power), for example on Iraq, depending particularly on whether the "hawk" or "dove" faction of his foreign policy advisors comes to have the most influence over him. Overall, George W's motive profile suggests a more aggressive and less entrepreneurial version of his father. Interestingly enough, it closely resembles John F. Kennedy's inaugural motive profile.

One of the most striking and unusual features of Bush's speech is the very frequent use of "not," which psychologists take as a measure of **activity inhibition**. Bush used that three-letter word almost 17 times per 1000 words, which is greater than any other American president (standard-score of +2.6). Interestingly enough, activity inhibition is often high among people who, like Bush, have given up liquor or don't drink. What else does frequent use of "not" mean? Some pychologists, following Freud, believe that the word attempts to negate or deny repressed wishes even while expressing them (recall Nixon's "I am not a crook"). For example, several of Bush's negations involved denial of aggression ("to protect but **not** to possess, to defend but **not** to conquer") or cynicism ("civility is **not** a tactic"). However, many others were directed against what may be latent core beliefs of his right-wing religious supporters: for example, "children at risk are **not** at fault," "abandonment and abuse are **not** acts of God," "Americans in need are **not** strangers," and "encouraging responsibility is **not** a search for scapegoats." Perhaps these negations are really directed against Bush's allies on the right. Or perhaps they suggest his own ambivalence about divine will, blame, and those in need. Only time can tell whether Bush's mantra of compassionate conservatism is meant to fool some of his staunchest supporters, or himself.

Source: David G. Winter, "Measuring Bush's Motives," in ISPPNews, spring 2001 vol. 12(1), p. 9.

HOW WELL DID YOU UNDERSTAND THIS SELECTION?

1. Why does the author, Dr. David Winter, reject extrapolating a president's future behavior from his past record and his platform or campaign promises?

2. The author uses content analysis to score political speeches for motive imagery, or reference to what three kinds of goals?

3. How does the author compare George W. Bush's motive profile to that of his father?

PART III

Social and Environmental Issues

Tocqueville was a keen observer of American political culture. He did not fail to notice, in his travels throughout the United States during the nineteenth century, that race (white, black and red) was an issue that could possibly undermine democracy in America. Tocqueville's thoughts on the race problem in **Democracy in America** *are analyzed in an article. Presented below are sections of that article entitled "Race and Democracy."*

THE DILEMMA OF RACE IN AMERICA

What appeared to Tocqueville to constitute the greatest threat to the new republic was the presence of a large black (slave) population and the failure of the three races—white, black, and red—that then inhabited the United States to assimilate.

The systematic removal of Indians from their tribal lands constitutes one of the darker chapters in American history. But it contains a number of harsh, yet universal and timeless, lessons- - for example, the struggle for racial dominance, the resettlement of contested land by the dominant race, the territorial basis of racial survival, the ubiquitous risks of minority racial status, and vulnerability of civil liberties and rights in a multiracial society—.

To his credit, Tocqueville deplored the "great evils" of this [Indian] expulsion, but saw them as "irremediable." The Indian nations of North America were "doomed to perish," he predicted, because they were afforded "only the alternative of war or civilization"; they could "either destroy the Europeans or become their equals." But he felt the Indians were incapable of civilizing themselves in time.

The expulsion of the Indians was clearly a shameful repudiation of the new republic's humanitarian ideals. But it was the peculiar institution of slavery, peculiar in the sense that it went against everything America stood for, that Tocqueville thought constituted the greatest physical threat to whites and the ultimate survival of the republic itself. In his view, slavery posed a race dilemma that came in three interrelated parts: the presence of a large black population on American soil, the segregated condition of the white and black races, and the racial prejudices of white Americans.

Given Tocqueville's analysis of the race problem... his pessimism about a multiracial future becomes at least understandable. He could only conceive of two paths: total separatism or total integration. "The negroes and the whites must either wholly part or wholly mingle," he warned. There was no middle ground .... Tocqueville then stated his ... belief that the white and black races would never live in any country on an equal footing, and that achieving equality would be more difficult in the United States than elsewhere. A despot might be able to "succeed in commingling" the races, he predicted, but, as long as the country remains democratic, "no one will undertake so difficult a task; and it may be foreseen that the freer the white population of the United States becomes, the more isolated will it remain."

Although Tocqueville could envision a race war and the breakup of the Union, he could not foresee the bloody and costly Civil War, fought mostly by whites over the slavery issue. Neither could he foresee, although it would not have surprised him, a new system of racial subjugation in the South that would negate the civil rights amendments passed after the war and last until the middle of the twentieth century.

However, many other changes in race relations, mostly positive, fall within the purview of Tocqueville's analysis and his predictions that American democracy would move, steadily and inexorably, toward greater political and social equality.

Source: Lieske, Joel. "Race and Democracy." *PS: Political Science and Politics* 32 (June 1999): 217-224.

HOW WELL DID YOU UNDERSTAND THIS SELECTION?

Many of Tocqueville's predictions about race relations in America turned out to be accurate. Give an example of a an accurate prediction. Give an example of an inaccurate prediction.

THEODORE ROOSEVELT PUBLICIZES CONSERVATION, 1908

The quest for protecting this nation's environment actually began during Theodore Roosevelt's presidential administration. He initiated legislation mandating the creation of national parks as a means of preserving animal life, primarily game. An avid hunter himself, Roosevelt was concerned that advancement of urban growth would eventually render large herds of deer, buffaloes, birds, and so on extinct. His speech, therefore, emphasizes that the preservation of the environment and our natural resources is vital to the existence of this country.

Governors of the several States; and Gentlemen:

I welcome you to this Conference at the White House. You have come hither at my request, so that we may join together to consider the question of the conservation and use of the great fundamental sources of wealth of this Nation. . . .

This Conference on the conservation of natural resources is in effect a meeting of the representatives of all the people of the United States called to consider the weightiest problem now before the Nation; and the occasion for the meeting lies in the fact that the natural resources of our country are in danger of exhaustion if we permit the old wasteful methods of exploiting them longer to continue.

With the rise of peoples from savagery to civilization, and with the consequent growth in the extent and variety of the needs of the average man, there comes a steadily increasing growth of the amount demanded by this average man from the actual resources of the country. And yet, rather curiously, at the same time that there comes that increase in what the average man demands from the resources, he is apt to grow to lose the sense of his dependence upon nature. He lives in big cities. He deals in industries that do not bring him in close touch with nature. He does not realize the demands he is making upon nature. . . .

In [George] Washington's time anthracite coal was known only as a useless black stone; and the great fields of bituminous coal were undiscovered. As steam was unknown, the use of coal for power production was undreamed of. Water was practically the only source of power, save the labor of men and animals; and this power was used only in the most primitive fashion. But a few small iron deposits had been found in this country, and the use of iron by our countrymen was very small. Wood was practically the only fuel, and what lumber was sawed was consumed locally, while the forests were regarded chiefly as obstructions to settlement and cultivation. The man who cut down a tree was held to have conferred a service upon his fellows.

Such was the degree of progress to which civilized mankind had attained when this nation began its career. It is almost impossible for us in this day to realize how little our Revolutionary ancestors knew of the great store of natural resources whose discovery and use have been such vital factors in the growth and greatness of this Nation, and how little they required to take from this store in order to satisfy their needs.

Since then our knowledge and use of the resources of the present territory of the United States have increased a hundred-fold. Indeed, the growth of this Nation by leaps and bounds makes one of the most striking and important chapters in the history of the world. Its growth has been due to the rapid development, and alas that it should be said! to the rapid destruction, of our natural resources. Nature has supplied to us in the United States, and still supplies to us, more kinds of resources in a more lavish degree than has ever been the case at any other time or with any other people. Our position in the world has been attained by the extent and thoroughness of the control we have achieved over nature; but we are more, and not less, dependent upon what she furnishes than at any previous time of history since the days of primitive man....

The wise use of all of our natural resources, which are our national resources as well, is the great material question of today. I have asked you to come together now because the enormous consumption of these resources, and the threat of imminent exhaustion of some of them, due to reckless and wasteful use, ... calls for common effort, common action.

We want to take action that will prevent the advent of a woodless age, and defer as long as possible the advent of an ironless age. . . .

Natural resources . . . can be divided into two sharply distinguished classes accordingly as they are or are not capable of renewal. Mines if used must necessarily be exhausted. The minerals do not and can not renew themselves. Therefore in dealing with the coal, the oil, the gas, the iron, the metals generally, all that we can do is to try to see that they are wisely used. The exhaustion is certain to come in time. We can trust that it will be deferred long enough to enable the extraordinarily inventive genius of our people to devise means and methods for more or less adequately replacing what is lost; but the exhaustion is sure to come.

The second class of resources consists of those which can not only be used in such manner as to leave them undiminished for our children, but can actually be improved by wise use. The soil, the forests, the waterways come in this category. Every one knows that a really good farmer leaves his farm more valuable at the end of his life than it was when he first took hold of it. So with the waterways. So with the forests. In dealing with mineral resources, man is able to improve on nature only by putting the resources to a beneficial use which in the end exhausts them; but in dealing with the soil and its products man can improve on nature by compelling the resources to renew and even reconstruct themselves in such manner as to serve increasingly beneficial uses—while the living waters can be so controlled as to multiply their benefits....

In the past we have admitted the right of the individual to injure the future of the Republic for his own present profit. In fact there has been a good deal of a demand for unrestricted individualism, for the right of the individual to injure the future of all of us for his own temporary and immediate profit. The time has come for a change. As a people we have the right and the duty, second to none other but the right and duty of obeying the moral law, of requiring and doing justice, to protect ourselves and our children against the wasteful development of our natural resources, whether that waste is caused by the actual destruction of such resources or by making them impossible of development hereafter.

Finally, let us remember that the conservation of our natural resources, though the gravest problem of today, is yet but part of another and greater problem to which this Nation is not yet awake but to which it will awake in time, and with which it must hereafter grapple if it is to live — the problem of national efficiency, the patriotic duty of insuring the safety and continuance of the Nation. [Applause.] When the People of the United States consciously undertake to raise themselves as citizens, and the Nation and the States in their several spheres, to the highest pitch of excellence in private, State, and national life, and to do this because it is the first of all the duties of true patriotism, then and not till then the future of this Nation, in quality and in time, will be assured.

[Great applause]

HOW WELL DID YOU UNDERSTAND THIS SELECTION?

1. What did Roosevelt feel was the "weightiest" problem confronting the United States?

2. According to Roosevelt, what are the two distinct classes of natural resources? Provide examples for each category.

3. What solution(s) did Roosevelt propose to address the deterioration of the nation's natural resources?

Particularly in the South, African Americans were the targets of racial slurs, abuses, and public lynchings. The horrific party-like atmosphere of these lynchings caught the attention of southern women who formed the Association of Southern Women for the Prevention of Lynching. They were able to gain the support of the major newspapers in drawing public attention to these all too frequent displays of hatred towards African Americans. The first article emphasizes the concern the predominately Anglo women's suffrage movement had for the plight of minority women, particularly African Americans. The second article was issued by a predominately African-American woman association. It is interesting to note that both organizations expressed similar issue concerns.

Women's Council of the Methodist Episcopal Church, South, 1920

We, a company of Southern white women, in conference assembled on the invitation of the Commission on Inter-Racial Cooperation, find ourselves with a deep sense of responsibility to the womanhood and childhood of the Negro race, and also with a great desire for a Christian settlement of the problems that overshadow the homes of both races....

We recognize and deplore the fact that there is friction between the races, but we believe that this can be largely removed by the exercise of justice, consideration, and sympathetic cooperation.

In order that the results of this conference may be perpetuated and enlarged, we recommend:

That a Continuation Committee be appointed to devise ways and means for carrying out the work considered by this conference; that this committee be composed of one woman from each denomination and Christian agency here represented, and that it be empowered to add to its membership as may seem necessary; that each local community form a Woman's Inter-Racial Committee, which may include representatives from all religious, civil and social service bodies working in the community, and that this Continuation Committee recommend plans by which this may be accomplished.

Desiring that everything that hinders the establishment of confidence peace justice and righteousness in our land shall be removed in order that there shall be better understanding and good will in our midst, we call attention to the following points as possible causes of friction, which if corrected, may go far toward creating a better day.

Domestic Service. We acknowledge our responsibility for the protection of the Negro women and girls in our homes and on the streets. We therefore recommend: That the domestic service be classed as an occupation and coordinated with other world service in order that better relations may be established by both employer and employee.

Child Welfare. We are persuaded that the conservation of the life and health of Negro children is of the utmost importance to the community. We therefore urge: That day nurseries and kindergartens be established in local communities for the Protection, care and training of children of Negro mothers who go out to work; that free baby clinics be established and that government leaflets on child welfare be distributed to expectant mothers, thus teaching the proper care of themselves and their children; that adequate playgrounds and recreational facilities be established for Negro children and young people.

Sanitation and Housing. Since good housing and proper sanitation are necessary for both physical and moral life, we recommend: That a survey of housing and sanitary conditions be made in the Negro section in each local community, followed by an appeal to the proper authorities for improvements when needed.

Education. Since sacredness of personality is the basis for all civilization, we urge: That every agency touching the child life of the nation shall strive to create mutual respect in the hearts of the children of different races. We are convinced that the establishment of a single standard of morals for men and women, both black and white, is necessary for the life and safety of a nation. We therefore pledge ourselves to strive to secure respect and protection for womanhood everywhere, regardless of race or color. Since provision for the education of Negro children is still inadequate, we recommend: More equitable division of the school fund, suitable school buildings and equipment, longer school terms, higher standards and increased pay for teachers.

Travel. Since colored people frequently do not receive fair treatment on street cars, on railroads and in railway stations and recognizing this as one of the chief causes of friction between the races, we urge: That immediate steps be taken to provide for them adequate accommodations and courteous treatment at the hands of street car and railway officials.

Lynching. As women, we urge those who are charged with the administration of the law to prevent lynching at any cost. We are persuaded that the proper determination on the part of the constituted officials, upheld by public sentiment, would result in the detection and prosecution of those guilty of this crime. Therefore we pledge ourselves to endeavor to create a public sentiment which will uphold these officials in the execution of justice.

Justice in the Courts. We recommend: That our women everywhere raise their voices against all acts of violence to property and person, wherever and for whatever cause occurring. We further recommend: That competent legal assistance be made available for colored people in the local communities in order to insure to them the protection of their rights in the courts.

Public Press. Since the public press often gives undue prominence to the criminal element among Negroes, and neglects the worthy and constructive efforts of law-abiding citizens, we pledge ourselves to cooperate with the men's committees in endeavoring to correct this injustice, and to create a fair attitude to Negroes and Negro news....

Southeastern Federation of Colored Women's Clubs, 1921

We desire to state our position on some matters relating to the welfare of colored people, and to enlist the sympathy and cooperation of Southern white women in the interest of better understandings and better conditions, as these affect the relations between white and colored people.

We take this opportunity to call to your attention certain conditions which affect colored women in their relations with white people and which if corrected will go far toward decreasing friction, removing distrust and suspicion and creating a better atmosphere in which to adjust the difficulties which always accompany human contacts.

Conditions in Domestic Service. The most frequent and intimate contact of white and colored women is in domestic service. Every improvement made in the physical, moral and spiritual life of those so employed must react to increase the efficiency of their service to their employers.

We, therefore, direct your attention to: Long and Irregular Working Hours; (1) lack of provision for wholesome recreation; (2) undesirable housing conditions. We recommend, therefore, (1) definite regulation for hours and conditions of work; (2) sanitary, attractive and wholesome rooming facilities; (3) closer attention to personal appearance and deportment; (4) provision for and investigation of character of recreation.

Child Welfare. The large burden of economic responsibility which falls upon many colored women results in their prolonged absence from home and the consequent neglect of the children of the homes. We direct your attention to: Child Welfare — (1) neglected homes (irregularity in food, clothing, conduct, training); (2) truancy; (3) juvenile delinquency. We therefore recommend — Welfare Activities — (1) day nurseries, play grounds, recreation centers; (2) home and school visitation; (3) probation officers and reform schools.

Conditions of Travel. Race friction is perhaps more frequent in street cars and railroad trains than in any other public places. To reduce this friction and remove causes for just complaint from colored passengers we call your attention to: (1) seating accommodations on street cars; (2) unsanitary surroundings, at stations and on trains; (3) toilet facilities, at stations and on trains; (4) difficulty in securing tickets, Pullman accommodations and meals; (5) abuse of rights of colored passengers by train crew and white passengers occupying seats while colored passengers stand, smoking, profane language, overcrowding; (6) as corrective measures we suggest provision of equal accommodations in all public carriers and courteous treatment at the hands of street car and railway officials, for all passengers.

Education. Without education for all the children of all the people we cannot sustain a democracy. Ignorance and crime are the twin children of neglect and poverty. We urge your increasing effort for better educational facilities so that there may be provided: adequate accommodations for all Negro children of school age, vocational training in all secondary schools, improved rural schools — longer terms, suitable buildings, training schools for teachers, adequate salaries for teachers.

Lynching. We deplore and condemn any act on the part of any men which would tend to excite the mob spirit. We believe that any man who makes an assault upon any woman should have prompt punishment meted out to the limit of the law, but not without thorough investigation of the facts and trial by the courts. The continuance of lynching is the greatest menace to good will between the races, and a constant factor in undermining respect for all law and order. It is our opinion that mob violence incites to crime rather than deters it; and certainly it is less effective in discouraging crime than the watchful, thorough and deliberate processes of a fair and just trial.

Toward the suppression of this evil, we appeal to white women to: (1) raise their voices in immediate protest when lynchings or mob violence is threatened; (2) encourage every effort to detect and punish the leaders and participants in mobs and riots; (3) encourage the white pulpit and press in creating a sentiment among law-abiding citizens and urge outspoken condemnation of these forms of lawlessness.

The Public Press. In the great majority of cases the white press of the South gives undue prominence to crime and the criminal element among Negroes to the neglect of the worthy and constructive efforts of law-abiding Negro citizens. We feel that a large part of friction and misunderstanding between the races is due to unjust, inflammatory and misleading headlines, and articles appearing in the daily papers. We suggest that white women include in their local community program a united effort to correct this evil and to secure greater attention to worthy efforts of Negro citizens.

Suffrage. We regard the ballot as the democratic and orderly method of correcting abuses and protecting the rights of citizens; as the substitute of civilization for violence. As peace loving, law-abiding citizens we believe the ultimate and only guarantee of fair dealing and justice for the Negro, as well as the wholesome development of the whole community, lies in the peaceful, orderly exercise of the franchise by every qualified Negro citizen. We ask therefore, that white women, for the protection of their homes as well as ours indicate their sanction of the ballot for all citizens as representing government by the sober, reasoned and deliberate judgment of all the people.

In these articles offered at your request we are stating frankly and soberly what in our judgement, you as white women may do to correct the ills from which our race has so long suffered, and of which we as a race are perhaps more conscious now than ever. We recall how in the recent days of our nation's peril so many of us worked side by side for the safety of this land and defense of this flag which is ours as it is yours. In that same spirit of unselfishness and sacrifice we offer ourselves to serve again with you in any and every way that a courageous facing of duty may require as you undertake heroically this self-appointed yet God-given task. We deeply appreciate the difficulties that lie before you, but as you undertake these things which are destined to bless us all, we pledge you our faith and loyalty in consecration to God, home and country.

HOW WELL DID YOU UNDERSTAND THIS SELECTION?

1. Why did the membership of the Southeastern Federation of Colored Women's Clubs believe that the only way to address their concerns was through influential white women's organizations?

2. In turn, why did the predominately white membership of the Women's Council of the Methodist Episcopal Church (WCMEC) "find ourselves with a deep sense of responsibility to the womanhood and childhood of the Negro race"?

3. What was the connection between white and African-American women regarding domestic services?

4. In what ways are ignorance and crime the twin children of neglect and poverty?

The Great Depression caused physical and mental hardships to millions of Americans. It seemed to be endless. In 1929, more than four million Americans, approximately 9 percent of the workforce, were out of work. By 1932, more than 12 million people, approximately 25 percent of the workforce, were out of work. Particularly hard hit were individuals living in the overcrowded cities where many had congregated to find work. Conditions in Philadelphia were not unique but rather representative of circumstances that existed in cities all across the country.

Relief stopped in Philadelphia on June 25 [1932]. For months previously 52,000 destitute families had been receiving modest grocery orders and a little milk.

The average allowance to a family at that time was about $4.35 per week, no provision being made for fuel, clothing, rent or any of the minimum accessories that go to make up the family budget.

Their rent was unpaid, their credit and their borrowing power exhausted. Most of them were absolutely dependent for existence on the food orders supplied through State funds administered by the Committee for Unemployment Relief. Then there were no more funds, and relief—except for a little milk for half-sick children, and a little Red Cross flour—was suddenly discontinued. And Philadelphia asked itself what was happening to these 52,000 families. There were no reports of people starving in the streets, and yet from what possible source were 52,000 families getting enough food to live on?

It was a fair question and the Community Council under the direction of Mr. Ewan Clague, a competent economist and in charge of its Research Bureau, set out to find the answer by a special study of 400 families who had been without relief for a period varying from 10 to 25 days. The families were not picked out as the worst cases, but as stated before were fairly typical of the 52,000.

According to Mr. Clague, and I am quoting him quite liberally, the count of the 400 families showed a total of 2,464 persons. The great majority ranged from five to eight persons per family.

In their effort to discover how these 2,464 human beings were keeping themselves alive the investigators inquired into the customary sources of family maintenance, earnings, savings, regular help from relatives, credit and, last but not least, the neighbors.

Some current income in the form of wages was reported by 128 families, though the amounts were generally small and irregular, two or three dollars a week perhaps, earned on odd jobs, by selling knickknacks on the street or by youngsters delivering papers or working nights. For the whole 128 the average wage income was $4.16 a week and 272 families of the 400 had no earnings whatsoever.

Savings were an even more slender resource. Only 54 families reported savings and most of these were nothing more than small industrial insurance policies with little or no cash surrender value, technically an asset, actually an item of expense. This does not mean that these families had not had savings—take for instance, the Baker family—father, mother, and four children. They had had $1,000 in a building and loan association which failed. They had had more than $2,000 in a savings bank, but the last cent had been withdrawn in January, 1931. They had had three insurance policies, which had been surrendered one by one. Both the father and the oldest son were tubercular, the former at the moment being an applicant for sanitarium care. This family—intelligent, clean, thrifty, and likable—one of thousands at the end of their rope—had had savings as a resource even a year ago, but not now.

The same situation, it was found, prevailed in regard to regular help from relatives. In the early stages of the depression a large proportion of relief families could count on this help in some form. But of our 400 families only 33 reported assistance from kinsfolk that could be counted on, and this assistance was slender indeed: A brother paid the rent to save eviction, a brother-in-law guaranteed the gas and electric bills, a grandmother, working as a scrubwoman, put in a small sum each week. Most of the relatives it was found were so hard pressed that it was all they could do to save themselves. As a matter of fact many relatives had moved in with the families and were recorded as members of the household.

In the absence of assets or income the next line of defense is credit. But most of the 400 families were bogged down in debt and retained only a vestige of credit. Take the item of rent or building and loan payments: Three hundred and forty-nine of the families were behind—some only a month or two, some for a year, a few for two or three years, with six months as the average for the group....

Thus, then, the picture of the 400 families shaped itself. Generally no income, such as there was slight, irregular and undependable; shelter still available so long as landlords remained lenient; savings gone, credit exhausted.

But what of food, the never ending, ever pressing necessity for food? In this emergency the outstanding contribution has been made by neighbors. The poor are looking after the poor. In considerably more than a third of the 400 families the chief source of actual subsistence when grocery orders stopped was the neighbors. The supply was by no means regular or adequate but in the last analysis, when all other resources failed the neighbors rallied to tide the family over a few days. Usually it was leftovers, stale bread, meat bones for soup, a bowl of gravy. Sometimes the children are asked in for a meal. One neighbor sent two eggs a day regularly to a sick man threatened with tuberculosis. This help was the more striking since the neighbors themselves were often close to the line of destitution and could illy spare the food they shared. The primitive communism existing among these people was a constant surprise to the visitors. More than once a family lucky enough to get a good supply of food called in the entire block to share the feast. There is absolutely no doubt that entire neighborhoods were just living from day to day sharing what slight resources any one family chanced to have. Without this mutual help the situation of many of the families would have been desperate.

As a result of all these efforts, what did these families have? What meals did they get and of what did these meals consist? About 8 per cent of the total number were subsisting on one meal a day. Many more were getting only two meals a day, and still others were irregular, sometimes one meal, sometimes two, occasionally by great good fortune, three. Thirty-seven per cent of all families were not getting the normal three meals a day.

When the content of these meals is taken into consideration the facts are still more alarming. Four families had absolutely no solid food whatever— nothing but a drink, usually tea or coffee. Seventy-three others had only one food and one drink for all meals, the food in many cases being bread made from Red Cross flour. Even in the remaining cases, where there were two or three articles of food, the diets day after day and week after week consisted usually of bread, macaroni, spaghetti, potatoes, with milk for the children. Many families were getting no meat and very few vegetables. Fresh fruits were never mentioned, although it is possible that the family might pick these up in the streets occasionally.

These diets were exceedingly harmful in their immediate effects on some of the families where health problems are present. In a number of cases the children are definitely reported on a hospital diagnosis as anemic. Occasionally the adults are likewise affected. The MacIntyre family for instance: These two older people have an adopted child 8 years of age. The husband is a bricklayer by trade and the wife can do outside housework. They have had occasional odd jobs over the past year but have been very hard pressed. For the three meals immediately preceding the visit they reported the menus as follows: Dinner, previously day, bread and coffee; breakfast, bread and coffee; lunch, corn, fish, bread, and coffee; one quart of milk for the little girl for the entire three meals.

Also their health problems were serious. The wife has had several operations, the husband is a possible tuberculosis case, and the child is under-weight. All three have also been receiving medical attention from a hospital for the past three years. The little girl has been nervous, has fainted at times, and is slightly deformed from rickets. Being undernourished, she needs cod-liver oil, milk, oranges, and the food which was possible only when the family was on relief. She went to camp for two weeks, and returned up to weight and in good spirits. But relief was cut off while she was away, and she came back to meals of milk, coffee, and bread. In short time at home she had become fretful and listless, refusing to take anything but milk. This whole family promised to be in serious health difficulties if their situation were long continued.

Source: Jacob Billikopf, *Federal Aid for Unemployment Relief*, 72nd Cong, 2d session, 1933, 8-11.

HOW WELL DID YOU UNDERSTAND THIS SELECTION?

1. Does the government have the responsibility to take proactive measures in times of emergency? Explain your answer in terms of the Constitution?

2. What would constitute an emergency?

President Johnson believed that his presidential legacy would be in the area of domestic affairs. Prior to becoming president, Johnson had been an extremely powerful Senator. He believed that he could use the relationships he had built in Congress to push through major domestic legislation that Kennedy had been unable to accomplish. Johnson developed a package of legislation that he called the Great Society. The agenda of the legislation covered a myriad of progressive issues from Medicare and Medicaid to what has become known as the War on Poverty. In this speech at the University of Michigan graduation ceremonies in May 1964, he clearly outlined what he envisioned the Great Society in America would be like.

I have come today from the turmoil of your capital to the tranquility of your campus to speak about the future of your country.

The purpose of protecting the life of our nation and preserving the liberty of our citizens is to pursue the happiness of our people. Our success in that pursuit is the test of our success as a nation.

For a century we labored to settle and to subdue a continent. For half a century we called upon unbounded invention and untiring industry to create an order of plenty for all of our people.

The challenge of the next half century is whether we have the wisdom to use that wealth to enrich and elevate our national life, and to advance the quality of our American civilization.

Your imagination, your initiative, and your indignation will determine whether we build a society where progress is the servant of our needs, or a society where old values and new visions are buried under unbridled growth. For in your time we have the opportunity to move not only toward the rich society and the powerful society, but upward to the Great Society.

The Great Society rests on abundance and liberty for all. It demands an end to poverty and racial injustice, to which we are totally committed in our time. But that is just the beginning.

The Great Society is a place where every child can find knowledge to enrich his mind and to enlarge his talents. It is a place where leisure is a welcome chance to build and reflect, not a feared cause of boredom and restlessness. It is a place where the city of man serves not only the needs of the body and the demands of commerce but the desire for beauty and the hunger for community.

It is a place where man can renew contact with nature. It is a place which honors creation for its own sake and for what it adds to the understanding of the race. It is a place where men are more concerned with the quality of their goals than the quantity of their goods.

But most of all, the Great Society is not a safe harbor, a resting place, a final objective, a finished work. It is a challenge constantly renewed, beckoning us toward a destiny where the meaning of our lives matches the marvelous products of our labor.

So I want to talk to you today about three places where we begin to build the Great Society - in our cities, in our countryside, and in our classrooms. Many of you will live to see the day, perhaps fifty years from now, when there will be 400 million Americans - four-fifths of them in urban areas. In the remainder of this century urban population will double, city land will double, and we will have to build homes, highways, and facilities equal to all those built since this country was first settled. So in the next forty years we must rebuild the entire urban United States.

Aristotle said: "Men come together in cities in order to live, but they remain together in order to live the good life." It is harder and harder to live the good life in American cities today.

The catalogue of ills is long: there is the decay of the centers and the despoiling of the suburbs. There is not enough housing for our people of transportation for our traffic. Open land is vanishing and old landmarks are violated.

Worst of all expansion is eroding the precious and time- honored values of community with neighbors and communion with nature. The loss of values breeds loneliness and boredom and indifference.

Our society will never be great until our cities are great. Today the frontier of imagination and innovation is inside those cities and not beyond their borders....

A second place where we begin to build the Great Society is in our countryside. We have always prided ourselves on being not only America the strong and America the free, but America the beautiful. Today that beauty is in danger. The water we drink, the food we eat, the every air that we breathe, are threatened with pollution. Our parks are overcrowded, our seashores overburdened. Green fields and dense forests are disappearing.

A few years ago we were greatly concerned about the "Ugly American." Today we must act to prevent an ugly America.

For once the battle is lost, once our natural splendor is destroyed, it can never be recaptured. And once man can no longer walk with beauty or wonder at nature his spirit will wither and his sustenance be wasted.

A third place to build the Great Society is in the classrooms of America. There your children's lives will be shaped. Our society will not be great until every young mind is set free to scan the farthest reaches of thought and imagination. We are still far from that goal....

Each year more than 100,000 high school graduates, with proved ability, do not enter college because they cannot afford it. And if we cannot educate today's youth, what will we do in 1970 when elementary school enrollment will be 5 million greater than 1960? And high school enrollment will rise by 5 million. College enrollment will increase by more than 3 million.

In many places, classrooms are overcrowded and curricula are outdated. Most of our qualified teachers are underpaid, and many of our paid teachers are unqualified. So we must give every child a place to sit and a teacher to learn from. Poverty must not be a bar to learning, and learning must offer an escape from poverty.

But more classrooms and more teachers are not enough. We must seek an educational system which grows in excellence as it grows in size. This means better training for our teachers. It means preparing youth to enjoy their hours of leisure as well as their hours of labor. It means exploring new techniques of teaching, to find new ways to stimulate the love of learning and the capacity for creation.

These are three of the central issues of the Great Society. While our government has many programs directed at those issues, I do not pretend that we have the full answer to those problems....

But I do promise this: We are going to assemble the best thought and the broadest knowledge from all over the world to find those answers for America. I intend to establish working groups to prepare a series of White House conferences and meetings - on the cities, on natural beauty, on the quality of education, and on other emerging challenges. And from these meetings and from this inspiration and from these studies we will begin to set our course toward the Great Society.

The solution to these problems does not reset on a massive program in Washington, nor can it rely sorely on the strained resources of local authority. They require us to create new concepts of cooperation, a creative federalism, between the national capital and the leaders of local communities.

Within your lifetime powerful forces, already loosed, will take us toward a way of life beyond the realm of our experience, almost beyond the bounds of our imagination.

For better or for worse, your generation has been appointed by history to deal with those problems and to lead America toward a new age. You have the chance never before afforded to any people in any age. You can help build a society where the demands of morality, and the needs of the spirit, can be realized in the life of the nation.

So, will you join in the battle to give every citizen the full equality which God enjoins and the law requires, whatever his belief, or race, or the color of his skin?

Will you join in the battle to give every citizen an escape from the crushing weight of poverty?

Will you join in the battle to make it possible for all nations to live in enduring peace - as neighbors and not as mortal enemies?

Will you join in the battle to build the Great Society, to prove that our material progress is only the foundation on which we will build a richer life of mind and spirit?

There are those timid souls who say this battle cannot be won; that we are condemned to a soulless wealth. I do not agree. We have the power to shape the civilization that we want. But we need your will, your labor, your hearts, if we are to build that kind of society.

Those who came to this land sought to build more than just a new country. They sought a new world. So I have come here today to your campus to say that you can make their vision our reality. So let us from this moment begin our work so that in the future men will look back and say: It was then, after a long and weary way, that man turned the exploits of his genius to the full enrichment of his life.

Source: Public Papers of the Presidents of the United States: Lyndon B. Johnson~ 1963-1964. Vol. I (Washington, D.C.: U.S. Government Printing Office, 1965), pp. 704-707.

HOW WELL DID YOU UNDERSTAND THIS SELECTION?

1. Under the Constitution does the federal government have the power to enact all the elements of the Great Society discussed in this article? Explain your answer and quote sources from the Constitution.

2. How did the Great Society impact the separation of power between the national and state governments?

A PROCLAMATION FROM THE INDIANS OF ALL TRIBES, ALCATRAZ ISLAND, 1969

Alcatraz Prison, housed on a small island off the coast of San Francisco, was closed in 1964. Within a year of the closing, a handful of Sioux Indians landed on the island and staked out claims under a 100-year-old treaty, the Sioux Treaty of 1868, permitting non-reservation Indians to claim land the government had once taken for forts and other uses and had later abandoned. The Sioux landing on Alcatraz Island lasted only four hours, but it succeeded in drawing media attention to the plight of the American Indian. The Indians had lost nineteen of every twenty acres they once owned and in exchange had been given some of the poorest quality of land yet remaining in the United States. The landing also dramatized the fact that over 600 treaties with the Indians had been broken by the United States government. The Indians also wanted to draw attention to the ridiculous offer of 47 cents per acre that the government was then proposing to California Indians in compensation for the tribal lands stolen from them since the Gold Rush.

On November 20, 1969, the Indians once again occupied Alcatraz, this time for nineteen months. Many factors conspired against the success of the occupation. The sanitary conditions on the island, its physical isolation, and a disastrous fire on the island in June of 1970 undermined the Indians' resolve to hold the island. Finally, on June 11, 1971, the Coast Guard recaptured Alcatraz Island, rounded up and removed the Indians, and secured the island with chain link fencing.

To the Great White Father and All His People—

We, the native Americans, re-claim the land known as Alcatraz Island in the name of all American Indians by right of discovery.

We wish to be fair and honorable in our dealings with the Caucasian inhabitants of this land, and hereby offer the following treaty:

We will purchase said Alcatraz Island for twenty-four dollars (24) in glass beads and red cloth, a precedent set by the white man's purchase of a similar island about 300 years ago. We know that $24 in trade goods for these 16 acres is more than was paid when Manhattan Island was sold, but we know that land values have risen over the years. Our offer of $1.24 per acre is greater than the 47 cents per acre the white men are now paying the California Indians for their land.

We will give to the inhabitants of this island a portion of the land for their own to be held in trust by the American Indian Affairs and by the bureau of Caucasian Affairs to hold in perpetuity—for as long as the sun shall rise and the rivers go down to the sea. We will further guide the inhabitants in the proper way of living. We will offer them our religion, our education, our life-ways, in order to help them achieve our level of civilization and thus raise them and all their white brothers up from their savage and unhappy state. We offer this treaty in good faith and wish to be fair and honorable in our dealings with all white men.

We feel that this so-called Alcatraz Island is more than suitable for an Indian reservation, as determined by the white man's own standards. By this we mean that this place resembles most Indian reservations in that:

1. It is isolated from modem facilities, and without adequate means of transportation.
2. It has no fresh running water.
3. It has inadequate sanitation facilities.

4. There are no oil or mineral rights.

5. There is no industry and so unemployment is very great.

6. There are no health care facilities.

7. The soil is rocky and non-productive, and the land does not support game.

8. There are no educational facilities.

9. The population has always exceeded the land base.

10. The population has always been held as prisoners and kept dependent upon others.

Further, it would be fitting and symbolic that ships from all over the world, entering the Golden Gate, would first see Indian land, and thus be reminded of the true history of this nation. This tiny island would be a symbol of the great lands once ruled by free and noble Indians.

What use will we make of this land?

Since the San Francisco Indian Center burned down, there is no place for Indians to assemble and carry on tribal life here in the white man's city. Therefore, we plan to develop on this island several Indian institutions:

1. A Center for Native American Studies which will educate them to the skills and knowledge relevant to improve the lives and spirits of all Indian peoples.

2. An American Indian Spiritual Center which will practice our ancient tribal religious and sacred healing ceremonies....

3. An Indian Center of Ecology which will train and support our young people scientific research and practice to restore our lands and waters to their pure and natural state....

4. A Great Indian Training School will be developed to teach our people how to make a living in the world, improve our standard of living, and to end hunger and unemployment among all our people....

Some of the present buildings will be taken over to develop an American Indian Museum which will depict our native food & other cultural contributions we have given to the world. Another part of the museum will present some of the things the white man has given to the Indians in return for the land and life he took: disease, alcohol, poverty and cultural decimation (As symbolized by old tin cans, barbed wire, rubber tires, plastic containers, etc.)....

In the name of all Indians, therefore, we re-claim this island for our Indian nations....

HOW WELL DID YOU UNDERSTAND THIS SELECTION?

1. Why did the Indians holding Alcatraz Island offer to purchase the island from the federal government for only $24 in glass beads and red cloth?

2. What was the underlying rationalization for the seizure of Alcatraz Island by Native American leaders?

Different generations of students have often manifested their discontent in seemingly unique ways. However, the underlying problems of discontent seem to remain relatively constant. Student discontent in the nineties appears to have resulted in students perpetuating violence against each other. Recent violent outbursts in high schools across the country have resulted in numerous student deaths. These deaths have resulted in society evaluating its attitudes towards violence and Congress evaluating its policy towards gun control and the right to bear arms.

Student discontent, however, has not always resulted in rage against its own generation. During the sixties, students did not focus their discontent against each other but rather at the establishment. A sizeable number of students focused their anger against the Vietnam war and the political establishment. In a larger sense, student discontent of this generation forced society to re-examine its attitudes towards war and in a more limited and political context, Congress to re-examine its foreign policy towards Vietnam.

It is my conviction that Vietnam and the bomb serve youth as a screen for what really ails them: their feeling that youth has no future because modem technology has made them obsolete - socially irrelevant, and, as persons, insignificant. Youth feels its future is bleak not with the prospect of nuclear war... but because of their feeling that nobody needs them, that society can do nicely without them. This is the even bleaker anxiety behind their feeling that youth has no future. Because, if a young man does not feel it is he who will be building the future, is sorely needed to bring it about, then the feeling is that he has none. That is why, in hopes of denying such an anxious conviction, students insist that their mission is to build a wholly new and different future. Their anxiety is not - as they claim -about a future atomic war. It is not that society has no future. Their existential anxiety is that they have no future in a society that does not need them to go on existing....

It is education that prepares us for our place in the work of society, and if education today prepares us only to be replaceable items in the production machine, to program its computers, then it seems to prepare us not for a chance to emerge in importance as persons, but only to serve the machine better.

Behind all this lie more fundamental reasons why adolescent malaise grows so widespread. These begin to emerge when we look in quite another direction - when we recognize that adolescent revolt is not a stage of development that follows automatically from our natural makeup, because what makes for adolescent revolt is the fact that society keeps the next generation too long dependent in terms of mature responsibility and a striving for independence. This I believe, is the common denominator wherever student rebellion occurs. And the fact that it occurs where affluence exists, only the modem, industrial state, is merely the same common denominator as seen from the outside.

Years ago, when schooling ended for the vast majority at 14 or 15, and therefore one became self-supporting, got married and had children, there was no need for adolescent revolt. Because while puberty is a biological fact, adolescence as we know it with its identity crises is not. All children grow up and become pubertal. By no means do they all become adolescents. To be adolescent means that one has reached and even passed the age of puberty, is at the very height of one's physical development—healthier, stronger, even handsomer than one has been, or will be, for the rest of one's life—but must nevertheless postpone full adulthood till long beyond what any other period in history has considered reasonable.

With no more open frontiers left, our society has no special place for adolescents today, with the single exception of our colleges and universities. Moreover, we push our young people toward maturity nowadays even while over-extending the years of their dependence. We start them sooner and sooner in school and make a farce of graduations - even from kindergarten now - until school becomes a rat race with never a home stretch in sight. And, so, by the time they get to college, they have had it. I doubt whether life was ever less of a rat race than today.
But it only became a senseless rat race when more and more people got to feeling they were racing after goals that were not really worthwhile or urgent, because survival seems assured by the affluent state.

At the same time, the educational experience today, whether in the home or the school, prepares only a small minority of youth well for such a pro-longed waiting, for controlling their angry impatience. Here we should not overlook the symbolic meaning of the student's invading the office of the president or dean, violently, or through sit- ins. Big in size and age, those who sit-in feel like little boys with a need to play big by sitting in papa's big chair. They want to sit in the driver's seat, want to have a say in how things are run, not because they feel competent to do so, but because they cannot bear to feel incompetent a moment longer.

I think it is unnatural to keep a young person in dependence for some twenty years attending school. This may be a way of life for that small elite which would always have chosen it in the past. There were always those who could go to school for twenty years, but they were never more than a small percentage of the population - even of the university population which included those attending a matter of caste. Now the tremendous push on everyone to go to college has brought incredibly large numbers to the university who do not find their self-realization through study or the intellectual adventure - or not at that point in their lives. What they still want urgently, however, is to find their manhood.

To make matters worse, our institutions of higher learning have expanded too fast. Under public pressure for more education for all, they have steadily increased enrollment without the means to parallel adjustments in the learning situation. One result is far too large classes. Another is the anonymity, the impersonal nature of student-faculty contacts that students rightly complain of.

But essentially it is the waiting for things - for the real life to come - that creates a climate in which a sizable segment of the students are chronically seduced into following the lead of a small group of militants. In the words of Jerry Rubin, yippie organizer, "Who the hell wants to 'make it' in America any more? The American economy no longer needs young whites and blacks. We are waste material. We fulfill our destiny in life by rejecting a system which rejects us."
Campus rebellion seems to offer youth a chance to shortcut the empty waiting and prove themselves real adults. This can be seen from the fact that most rebellious students, here and abroad, are either undergraduates or those studying the social sciences and humanities. There are precious few militants among students of medicine, chemistry, engineering, the natural sciences. Student power has no meaning in the laboratory; there no one doubts the need for leadership by the most experienced of the less experienced. Moreover, while the social science student can easily convince

himself that he knows precisely what is wrong with society, particularly if his friends all agree, it is impossible for the medical student to fool himself that he knows what went wrong in the cancerous cell. Nor can such a student believe that what he is doing, or the discipline it demands, is irrelevant.

Those who cannot find themselves in their studies or their work are hence the most vocal in finding the university irrelevant. Typically, the militant finds his largest following among the newcomers, those with least time or chance as yet to find a place for themselves at the university. This place some try to find quickly by plunging into active, even violent, battle against the existing order. Except that if they should win they would be changing the university into an institution that no longer serves inquiry and study, but a belligerent reshaping of society.

I maintain that, despite the high-sounding moral charges against the sins of our society, leaders to find a mass following without which their efforts at disruption would soon collapse or could readily be contained.

Source: Hearings on Riots, Civil and Criminal Disorders (Washington, D.C., 1969), pp. 3069-79.

HOW WELL DID YOU UNDERSTAND THIS SELECTION?

1. Do the elite retain civil rights until the masses demand them?

2. What constitutes civil disobedience and when is it most effectively used? Explain your answer.

The Women's Suffrage Amendment was ratified on August 18, 1920. State laws, however, continued to discriminate against women. Women were denied control equal to that of men over their children and their earnings. The National Woman's Party organized to put an end to such discriminatory state laws.

The removal of all forms of the subjection of women is the purpose to which the National Woman's Party is dedicated. Its present campaign to remove the discriminations against women in the laws of the United States is but the beginning of its determined effort to secure the freedom of women, an integral part of the struggle for human liberty for which women are first of all responsible. Its interest lies in the final release of woman from the class of a dependent, subservient being to which early civilization committed her.

The laws of various States at present hold her in that class. They deny her a control of her children equal to the father's; they deny her, if married, the right to her own earnings; they punish her for offences for which men go unpunished; they exclude her from public office and from public institutions to the support of which her taxes contribute. These laws are not the creation of this age, but the fact that they are still tolerated on our statute books and that in some States their removal is vigorously resisted shows the hold of old traditions upon us. Since the passage of the Suffrage Amendment the incongruity of these laws, dating back many centuries, has become more than ever marked....

The National Woman's Party believes that it is a vital social need to do away with these discriminations against women and is devoting its energies to that end. The removal of the discriminations and not the method by which they are removed is the thing upon which the Woman's Party insists. It has under consideration an amendment to the Federal Constitution which, if adopted, would remove them at one stroke, but it is at present endeavoring to secure their removal in the individual States by a blanket bill, which is the most direct State method. For eighty-two years the piecemeal method has been tried, beginning with the married women's property act of 1839 in Mississippi, and no State, excepting Wisconsin, where the Woman's Party blanket bill was passed in June, 1921, has yet finished....

The present program of the National Woman's Party is to introduce its Woman's Equal Rights Bill, or bills attaining the same purpose, in all State legislatures as they convene. It is building up in Washington a great headquarters from which this campaign can be conducted, and it is acting in the faith that the removal of these discriminations from our laws will benefit every group of women in the country, and through them all society.

413

HOW WELL DID YOU UNDERSTAND THIS SELECTION?

1. Why did the members of the National Woman's Party believe the equal rights for women could only be achieved through federal and not state legislation?

2. What were some of the legal restrictions confronting women in the 1920s?

It took almost half a century for an Equal Rights Amendment to the Constitution to be approved by both houses of Congress and sent to the States for ratification. First introduced in Congress in 1923, and reintroduced in every subsequent Congress for the next fifty years, the amendment was authored by the head of the National Women's Party (NWP)—suffrage leader Alice Paul. The 1923 ERA proposed that:

> *Men and women shall have equal rights throughout the United States and in every place subject to its jurisdiction. Congress shall have power to enforce this article by appropriate legislation.*

In order to make the wording of the ERA more compatible with that of the Nineteenth Amendment, which gave women the right to vote, new language was subsequently drafted with the assistance of Alice Paul. The revised wording, provided below, was never altered again.

The amendment, which consists of three Sections, was passed without change (in a vote of 354-24) by the United States House of Representatives in 1971 and approved (in a vote of 84-8) by the U.S. Senate the following year. The 92nd Congress, which passed the amendment on March 22, 1972, imposed a ratification deadline of seven years (March 22, 1979). The 95th Congress extended that deadline to June 30, 1982.

As specified in Article V of the U.S. Constitution, which deals with the amending process, a change in the document requires the approval of three fourths of the state legislatures. Thirty-five states (representing 72 percent of the U.S. population) of the required thirty-eight had ratified the Equal Rights Amendment when time ran out. The fifteen states legislatures which did not approve were: Alabama, Arizona, Arkansas, Florida, Georgia, Illinois, Louisiana, Mississippi, Missouri, Nevada, North Carolina, Oklahoma, South Carolina, Utah and Virginia. The complete text (with the added congressional preamble) of the narrowly defeated amendment follows.

The Proposed Equal Rights Amendment (1972)

Resolved by the Senate and House of Representatives of the United States of America in Congress assembled (two-thirds of each House concurring therein) that the following Article is proposed as an amendment to the Constitution of the United States, which shall be valid to all intents and purposes as part of the Constitution when ratified by the legislatures of three-fourths of the several States within seven years of the date of its submission by the Congress.

Section 1.
Equality of rights under the law shall not be denied or abridged by the United States or by any State on account of sex.

Section 2.

The Congress shall have the power to enforce, by appropriate legislation, the provisions of this Article.

Section 3.

The Amendment shall take effect two years after the date of ratification.

HOW WELL DID YOU UNDERSTAND THIS SELECTION?

1.   In order to amend the Constitution two thirds of each House of Congress and three quarters (38) of the fifty states have to approve the proposed change. The ERA failed to secure the approval of which?

Some of the arguments in defense of the proposed Equal Rights Amendment were reflected in Gloria Steinem's testimony before Congress.

My name is Gloria Steinem. I am a writer and editor. I have worked in several political campaigns, and am currently a member of the Policy Council of the Democratic National Committee.

During twelve years of working for a living, I've experienced much of the legal and social discrimination reserved for women in this country. I have been refused service in public restaurants, ordered out of public gathering places, and turned away from apartment rentals; all for the clearly-stated sole reason that I am a woman. And all without the legal remedies available to blacks and other minorities. I have been excluded from professional groups, writing assignments on so-called "unfeminine" subjects such as politics, full participation in the Democratic Party, jury duty, and even from such small male privileges as discounts on airline fares. Most important to me, I have been denied a society in which women are encouraged, or even allowed, to think of themselves as first-class citizens and responsible human beings.

However, after two years of researching the status of American women, I have discovered that I am very, very lucky. Most women, both wage-earners and housewives, routinely suffer more humiliation and injustice than I do.

As a freelance writer, I don't work in the male-dominated hierarchy of an office. (Women, like blacks and other visibly-different minorities, do better in individual professions such as the arts, sports, or domestic work; anything in which they don't have authority over white males.) I am not one of the millions of women who must support a family. Therefore, I haven't had to go on welfare because there are no day care centers for my children while I work, and I haven't had to submit to the humiliating welfare inquiries about my private and sexual life, inquiries from which men are exempt. I haven't had to brave the sex bias of labor unions and employers, only to see my family subsist on a median salary 40% less than the male median salary.

I hope this committee will hear the personal, daily injustices suffered by many women-professionals and day laborers, women housebound by welfare as well as suburbia. We have all been silent for too long. We won't be silent anymore.

The truth is that all our problems stem from the same sex-based myths. We may appear before you as white radicals or the middle-aged middleclass or black soul sister, but we are ALL sisters in fighting against these outdated myths. Like racial myths, they have been reflected in our laws. Let me list a few:

That Women Are Biologically Inferior To Men

In fact, an equally good case can be made for the reverse. Women live longer than men, even when the men are not subject to business pressures. Women survived Nazi concentration camps better, keep cooler heads in emergencies currently studied by disaster-researchers, are protected against heart attacks by their female sex hormones, and are so much more durable at every state of life that nature must conceive 20 to 50 percent more males in order to keep some balance going.

Man's hunting activities are forever being pointed to as tribal proof of superiority. But while he was hunting, women built houses, tilled the fields, developed animal husbandry, and perfected language. Men, being all alone in the bush, often developed into a creature [sic] as strong as women, fleeter of foot, but not very bright.

However, I don't want to prove the superiority of one sex to another. That would only be repeating a male mistake. English scientists once definitively proved, after all, that the English were descended from the angels, while the Irish were descended from the apes: it was the rationale for England's domination of Ireland for more than a century. The point is that science is used to support current myth and economics almost as much as the church was.

What we do know is that the difference BETWEEN two races or two sexes is much smaller than the differences to be found WITHIN each group. Therefore, in spite of the slide show on female inferiorities that I understand was shown to you yesterday, the law makes much more sense when it treats individuals, not groups bundled together by some condition of birth.

A word should be said about Dr. Freud, the great 19th Century perpetuator of female inferiority. Many of the differences he assumed to be biological, and therefore changeless, have turned out to be societal, and have already changed....

That Women Are Already Treated Equally In This Society

I'm sure there has been ample testimony to prove that equal pay for equal work, equal chance for advancement, and equal training or encouragement is obscenely scarce in every field, even those-like food and fashion industries-that are supposedly "feminine."

A deeper result of social and legal injustice, however, is what sociologists refer to as "Internalized Aggression." Victims of aggression absorb the myth of their own inferiority, and come to believe that their group is in fact second class.

Women suffer this second class treatment from the moment they are born. They are expected to BE rather than achieve, to function biologically rather than learn. A brother, whatever his intellect, is more likely to get the family's encouragement and education money, while girls are often pressured to conceal ambition and intelligence to "Uncle Tom."

I interviewed a New York public school teacher who told me about a black teenager's desire to be a doctor. With all the barriers in mind, she suggested he be a veterinarian instead.

The same day, a high school teacher mentioned a girl who wanted to be a doctor. The teacher said, "How about a nurse?"

Teachers, parents, and the Supreme Court may exude a protective, well-meaning rationale, but limiting the individual's ambition is doing no one a favor. Certainly not this country. It needs all the talent it can get.

That American Women Hold Great Economic Power

51% of all shareholders in this country are women. That's a favorite male-chauvinist statistic. However, the number of shares they hold is so small that the total is only 18% of all shares. Even those holdings are often controlled by men.

Similarly, only 5% of all the people in the country who receive $10,000 a year or more, earned or otherwise, are women. And that includes all the famous rich widows.

The constantly-repeated myth of our economic power seems less testimony to our real power than to the resentment of what little power we do have.

That Children Must Have Full-Time Mothers

American mothers spend more time with their home and children than those of any other society we know about. In the past, joint families, servants, a prevalent system in which grandparents raised the children, or family field work in the agrarian systems-all these factors contributed more to child care than the labor-saving devices of which we are so proud.

The truth is that most American children seem to be suffering from too much Mother, and too little Father. Part of the program of Women's Liberation is a return of fathers to their children. If laws permit women equal work and pay opportunities, men will then be relieved of their role as sole breadwinner. Fewer ulcers, fewer hours of meaningless work, equal responsibility for his own children: these are a few of the reasons that Women's Liberation is Men's Liberation, too.

As for the psychic health of the children, studies show that the quality of time spent by parents is more important than the quantity. The most damaged children were not those whose mothers worked, but those whose mothers preferred to work but stayed home out of role-playing desire to be a "good mother."

That The Women's Movement Is Not Political, Won't Last, Or Is Somehow Not "Serious"

When black people leave their 19th Century roles, they are feared., When women dare to leave theirs, they are ridiculed. We understand this, and accept the burden of ridicule. It won't keep us quiet anymore.

Similarly, it shouldn't deceive male observers into thinking this is somehow a joke. We are 51% of the population, we are essentially united on these issues across boundaries of class or race or age, and we may well end by changing this society more than the civil rights movement. That is an apt parallel. We, too, have our right wing and left wing, our separatists, gradualists, and Uncle Toms. But we are changing our own consciousness, and that of the country. [Friedrich] Engels noted the relationship of the authoritarian, nuclear family to capitalism: the father as capitalist, the mother as means of production, and the children as labor. He said the family would change as the economic system did, and that seems to have happened, whether we want to admit it or not. Women's bodies will no longer be owned by the state for the production of workers and soldiers: birth control and abortion are facts of everyday life. The new family is an egalitarian family.

Gunnar Myrdal noted thirty years ago the parallel between women and Negroes in this country. Both suffered from such restricting social myths as: smaller brains, passive natures, inability to govern themselves (and certainly not white men), sex objects only, childlike natures, special skills and the like. When evaluating a general statement about women, it might be valuable to substitute "black people" for "women"-just to test the prejudice at work. And it might be valuable to do this Constitutionally as well. Neither group is going to be content as a cheap labor pool anymore. And neither is going to be content without full Constitutional rights.

Finally, I would like to say one thing about this time in which I am testifying.

I had deep misgivings about discussing this topic when National Guardsmen are occupying our campuses, the country is being turned against itself in a terrible polarization, and America is enlarging an already inhuman and unjustifiable war. But it seems to me that much of the trouble this country is in has to do with the Masculine Mystique; with the myth that masculinity somehow depends on the subjugation of other people. It is a bi-partisan problem: both our past and current Presidents seem to be victims of this myth, and behave accordingly.

Women are not more moral than men. We are only uncorrupted by power. But we do not want to imitate men to join this country as it is, and I think our very participation will change it. Perhaps women elected leaders-and there will be many more of them-will not be so likely to dominate black people or yellow people or men; anybody who looks different from us.

After all, we won't have our masculinity to prove.

Source: Testimony of Gloria Steinem, U.S. Congress, Senate Committee on the Judiciary, Subcommittee on Constitutional Amendments, Hearings, 91st Congress, 32nd Session, 1970, pp. 335-337.

HOW WELL DID YOU UNDERSTAND THIS SELECTION?

1. How does Steinem describe discrimination against women?

2. What are the myths concerning women that she deals with?

3. What are her arguments in defense of an equal rights amendment?

In the seventy-two years between the Declaration of Sentiments introduced at Seneca Falls in 1848 and the passage of the Nineteenth Amendment in 1920, the demand for women's suffrage was articulated in many ways. The right to vote was couched in reasonable, legal, angry and, as the statement below demonstrates, even in humorous and somewhat cynical terms. The tongue-in-cheek list that follows was written by the novelist and poet Alice Duer Miller in 1915.

WHY WE DON'T WANT MEN TO VOTE

1. Because man's place is in the army.

2. Because no really manly man wants to settle any question otherwise than by fighting about it.

3. Because if men should adopt peaceable methods women will no longer look up to them.

4. Because men will lose their charm if they step out of their natural sphere and interest themselves in other matters than feats of arms, uniforms and drums.

5. Because men are too emotional to vote. Their conduct at baseball games and political conventions shows this, while their innate tendency to appeal to force renders them unfit for government.

Source: "Why We Don't Want Men to Vote." **The New York Times.** 30 September 1990, 6(4A).

HOW WELL DID YOU UNDERSTAND THIS SELECTION?

Explain why poet Miller's list is referred to as both "cynical" and "tongue-in-cheek."

A truly marginalized group in society are the homeless. By the very virtue of their homelessness, they are disenfranchised from the electoral process and the political system. As such, their plight is often overlooked by politicians concerned with re-election and constituent concerns. The homeless must continue to rely on others to speak for them or their voice would go unheard in the political system.

It is difficult to assess how many Americans are homeless on any given day. Official estimates vary. The U.S. Census Bureau, in its last census, reported that 228,621 Americans were homeless. Many other institutions believe that this statistic greatly underestimates the number of homeless. The Urban Institute estimates that there are about 600,000 homeless. The Department of Health and Human Services reports two million and various interest groups that serve as advocates for the homeless state that the number is well over three million. One disturbing recent trend has been in the increase of homelessness among families. Whereas the traditional profile of a homeless individual was a single male, today, woman as heads of households and families make up the largest number of homeless.

You see them now in every American city — the homeless people, who sleep by night in doorways, under highway bridges, in tents, on steaming grates, in bus stations. By day they wander warily from park bench to soup kitchen to abandoned building to public library or museum, watching the long hours slip away into nothingness. On frigid winter nights, they jam into emergency shelters that more closely resemble concentration camps than warm havens. These hundreds of thousands, if not millions, of homeless represent a national epidemic — the most severe housing crisis since the Depression. It is a problem that most agree will only get dramatically worse, growing far faster than the remedies.

Wide disagreement exists over the number of homeless, with the most frequently cited national figures ranging from a low of 250,000 (estimated by the Department of Housing and Urban Development in 1984) to four million (a 1982 estimate by the Community for Creative Non-Violence, an advocacy group located in Washington, D.C.). In a report to the National Governors' Association, New York Gov. Mario Cuomo gave the following estimates for 1983: 20,000 to 25,000, Chicago; 12,000 to 15,000, Baltimore; 2,500, Denver; 8,000 to 10,000, San Francisco; 2,000, Boston; 7,700, St. Louis:; 22,000, Houston.

One difficulty in accurately counting the homeless population is that the number changes constantly in response to such factors as national economic policy, unemployment rates, availability of social services, availability of low-rent housing, season of the year, weather, day of the month. In addition, definitions of homelessness vary, as do counting methodologies. However, as Congressman Bruce Vento (D. Minn.) says, "We shouldn't be diverted by an argument about numbers. The obvious fact is that we have a growing number of homeless."

The real issue is not the precise number of homeless, but the gravity of their situation. The Department of Health and Human Services reports: 'They [the homeless live brutal, debilitating, stressful lives of great hardship." In New York City alone, some 25 to 50 homeless people are thought to die on the streets during each of the winter months. The causes are violence; weather related illnesses (pneumonia, frostbite, gangrene, stroke, heart failure); alcohol-induced illnesses, among others.

Public awareness of the plight of the homeless has heightened. Yet grave misconceptions still abound as to who the homeless are, why they are on the streets, and what is needed to remedy their situation. Some communities acknowledge the problem by shipping the homeless out of town.

Elsewhere, homelessness has become the latest fashion fad: In the spring of 1983, Bloomingdale's department store in New York City opened in its second floor boutique a new display called "Street Couture." The clothing was designed to mimic the dress of the homeless poor: disheveled, wrinkled, patched, and mismatched. A jacket with torn sleeves listed for $190. An employee insisted that the "street look" sells. "Bag ladies are in," she explained.

The insensitivity continues on a daily basis in every city by those who more easily tell a joke about the homeless on the streets than acknowledge the homeless as human beings. D.C. homeless advocates Mary Ellen Hombs and Mitch Snyder offer the following as an example:

"In all of the years that Red and Willie [two homeless men] have spent on the down town [Washington, D.C.] heat grates, millions of people have walked or driven by them, but only a handful have stopped to talk, to see if they could be of any help. Some furtively scan the scene; others stare in amazement. For most, expressions do not change. Red and Willie, their pain and their loneliness, are invisible. If not invisible, then surely untouchable."

Dr. Michael Vergare, a psychiatrist with the Albert Einstein Medical Center in Philadelphia, suggests, "We struggle to comprehend how, in this day and age when so many people are so well off, we have people who cannot find shelter."

John Philips, AIA, 1985 chairman of AIA's housing committee says, "The epidemic of homelessness to some Americans, maybe to many, is so unthinkable that they refuse to recognize the visible homeless although the homeless are all around.... We must acknowledge that homelessness is a major social crisis today."

Often the homeless are identified by their tattered appearance; bizarre behavior; belongings carried in plastic bags or cardboard boxes tied with string or stuffed into shopping carts; swollen, ulcerated legs; apparent aimlessness. But, as Hombs and Snyder describe, "There are also those who have been able to maintain a reasonably good personal appearance and whose behavior betrays no apparent sign of disorder," which allows them to more easily find food, daytime shelter in libraries or museums, and public washroom facilities and to escape threats, violence, and harassment.

Generally, a homeless person is someone who has no stable residence, which is defined as a place to sleep and receive mail. This person is usually destitute and has either minimal or no resources or income. In addition, a homeless person is not likely receiving any government assistance.

Perhaps the first step in understanding the homeless is to dispel the myth that the homeless are on the streets by choice, having voluntarily rejected any available assistance. "It is an overstatement to say even a small minority of these people live on the streets by choice. There is no evidence that people live on the streets by choice," says Robert Hayes, founder and legal counsel of the National Coalition for the Homeless, headquartered in New York City. "It is essential to see the homeless as suffering individuals," Hayes adds, and to illustrate his point offers the following examples:

Alice is an elderly woman who has lived her entire life in quite a normal way. She raised children, then moved out of her home town to the Midwest. Her husband died. Then her rent went up dramatically. She first moved to a cheap hotel, an SRO (single-room-occupancy hotel). She lost that suddenly, at the age of 73, for the first time in her life, Alice could not find a place to live. She wound up in a train terminal. She became confused, and suddenly people were describing her as a "bag lady."

Joey is a six-year-old boy in New York City. He's been homeless for three years—half of his life. He's been shunted from welfare hotels to what we euphemistically call "barrack shelters" in New York —refugee camps where cots and cribs are lined up on large, open rooms with common sleeping areas. When I first met Joey, he was a little fellow. He was playful and had that glint in his eyes. And that glint was, to me, something that I thought would get him through. But he's six now. The glint's gone. Joey has struggled. Joey has suffered. But most of all, he's lost his playfulness, his right to that commodity that every child should have — his childhood.

Hayes maintains that "if people are offered safe, decent, humane shelters, they will go in off the streets."

A barometer of the problem's seriousness in the incidence of hunger, since hunger is considered the handmaiden of homelessness. In a survey of 181 food pantries and soup kitchens in 12 states, the National Governors' Association found a "dramatic increase" in the numbers seeking emergency food aid between February 1982 and February 1983. In that single year, demand in over half of the programs surveyed rose by 50 percent or more.

In a survey of 25 major cities, the U.S. Conference of Mayors found that hunger and homelessness rose sharply during 1985. Demand rose an average of 28 percent for emergency food and an average of 25 percent for shelter. In fact, the survey of cities ranging in size from New York to Charleston, S. C., found that "in none of the cities surveyed has the economic recovery lessened the problems of homelessness." There are also indications of a growing disparity between the have and have nots. For example, in Chicago "there has been no significant shift in the economic status of the city's poor and near poor." In Salt Lake City, "the national economic recovery has not alleviated the problems of low-income people. In fact, it appears that there are more people in need and that they are worse off, than previously."

Hayes reports, "What we saw in most parts of the country was a 20 to 30 percent increase during 1985 in the number of people seeking help   I don't know any place that had spare beds."

Hayes noted last year, "In understanding homelessness, we have to start out by realizing that here we are in 1985 in a period without precedence in the history of the United States. By that I mean, sure there have been a lot of homeless folks in this country over the past few hundred years, but always mass homelessness in this country has been accompanied by system-wide economic dislocations — serious depressions or recessions. But something peculiar is happening because maybe [homelessness was understandable] in the 1930s, maybe even in 1982 or 1983 when there were serious economic problems. But in 1985, it does not seem so simple to understand. It seems that something fairly severe has to be undertaken because the old systems of dealing with mass homelessness in this country aren't working in the 1980s."

What makes the '80s feel like the '30s is the make-up of the homeless population. Now, as in the Depression, the homeless represent a broad cross section of American society — the young and old, single people and families, the mentally and physically disabled, and the able-bodied. The most dramatic change in the last 10 years has been a sharp increase in the number of women, children, young men, and families.

The New York State Department of Social Services reports: "Increasingly, the problem of homelessness is affecting people and families who are in most respects like other poor people, except that they cannot find or afford housing. The homeless transient, the wandering loner who may be alcoholic or mentally disabled, is no longer typical of the great majority of people without shelter. More and more, those sleeping in emergency shelters include parents and children whose primary reason for homelessness is poverty or family disruption. They have arrived in shelters not from the streets but from some dwelling (typically not their own) where they are no longer welcome or where they can no longer afford to stay."

The homeless population is now vastly different from the homogeneous skid row population of the post-World War II era, the majority of whom were older white men suffering from alcoholism and/or drug addiction. Since many cities and states had anti-vagrancy laws (until the 1970s), most skid rowers were actually not homeless, but sheltered — in jails, if not seedy hotels, flophouses, or missions,. But, regardless, many were considered the derelicts of society, as often the homeless are today. Now, though, according to the U.S. General Accounting Office (GAO), the average age of homeless persons is 34. Single women make up 13 percent of the homeless population, minorities 44 percent, and families 21 percent, the GAO reported in 1985. The U.S. Conference of Mayors reported in 1985 that the most significant recent change in the homeless population was the growing number of families with children; the number of young single adults also increased. It is especially poignant to see young children as miniature bag people dragging their toys in plastic bags.

A microcosm of the homeless population is found in Los Angeles County, where the number of homeless in not only large—HUD estimated 33,800 as of July '84— but is thought to be increasing rapidly. The compositional changes in that population parallel shifts in the national homeless population. For example- single males who had became homeless 12 months prior to a survey of homeless shelters (conducted over a six month period ending in May '84) were younger and better educated, and more likely to be non-white, recently unemployed, and veterans than those homeless for more than 12 months. Increased numbers of families with children, single women, and youths were visible throughout the county.

"A whole new wave of homeless people in the U.S. is made up of the young and able-bodied who have little chance of winning a place in a tight [employment] market and consequently no ability **to** win the competition for housing in a tighter and tighter housing market;" Hayes suggests, Marita Dean, of the Washington D.C., office of Catholic Charities, reported in 1984: We're seeing people now that no agency ever saw before, people who never had **to** beg before. They're frightened, so you help them this month, but they're not going to be any better off next month."

In addition to its demographic diversity, the homeless population varies significantly in duration of homelessness. Vergare and his associate, Dr. Anthony Arce, have suggested three groupings: the chronic, who are homeless for more than 30 continuous days — although many, if not most, have been homeless for months or years; the episodic, who tend to alternate for varying periods of time between being domiciled and homeless, with homelessness usually lasting less then 30 days; and the situational, for whom homelessness is the temporary result of an acute life crisis.

What looms ahead? One clue may be the number of people doubling up (living with one or two other persons or families). The National Coalition for the Homeless estimated at the end of 1985 that there were as many as 10 to 20 million doubling up, with as many as 500,000 in New York City alone. Seattle's Mayor Charles Royer noted in May 1985, "For every homeless person in Seattle, there are 10 others who are at risk and who need some kind of housing assistance."

A recent needs assessment in New York State found "disturbing information — the numbers of homeless people were far larger than imagined. But even more distressing was the consensus among service providers of the tremendous number of persons and families doubling up," says Nancy Travers, assistant commissioner, New York State Department of Social Services. She suggests that if New York State continued providing shelter to the homeless at the level it did in 1984, "it would take 20 years to meet the needs of the homeless. Clearly this is a housing problem of a scale that is hard to imagine."

Meanwhile, the numbers keep growing. In its Dec. 16, 1985, issue, *Newsweek* reported: "Across the frost belt last week, cities set records in sheltering the homeless: New York, Boston, Philadelphia have emergency policies requiring police and city employees to round up the homeless and take them to shelters after the temperature turns frigid. But the hundreds of shelter beds — in the case of New York City, 23,000 — come nowhere close to meeting the need."

Source: *Subcommittee on Housing and Community Development.* January 26, 1988. *pp.* 303-306.

HOW WELL DID YOU UNDERSTAND THIS SELECTION?

1. Much of the discussion in this article centers on discovering the exact number of homeless or hungry, or at the very least, proving that the number of homeless and hungry is rising. In the United States, is there a numerical threshold above which an issue becomes defined as a political problem?

2. Who has the power to define a social problem and when and why would they?

3. Is it implicitly required in our process that the majority take into account the needs of the minority whoever and whatever they might be?

PART IV

Social and Cultural Perspectives

Beginning with the conquest of Mexico by Cortez, the Spanish government extended its colonial empire into the New World. The royal edict clearly indicates that the Spanish government would take these lands by whatever means necessary including war and invasion. The reader should note the benevolent tone of the edict promising the good life for those who would willingly surrender themselves to their conquerors. Those who wished to fight the inevitable invasion risked war and punishment.

On the part of the King, don Fernando [Ferdinand], and of donia Juana, his daughter, Queen of Castile and Leon, subduers of the barbarous nations, we their servants notify and make known to you, as best we can, that the Lord our God,

Living and Eternal, created the Heaven and the Earth, and one man and one woman, of whom you and 1, and all the men of the world, were and are descendants, and all those who come after us. But, on account of the multitude which has sprung from this man and woman in the five thousand years since the world was created, it was necessary that some men should go one way and some another, and that they should be divided into many kingdoms and provinces, for in one alone they could not be sustained.

Of all these nations God our Lord gave charge to one man, called St. Peter, that he should be Lord and Superior of all the men in the world, that all should obey him, and that he should be head of the whole human race, wherever men should live, and under whatever law, sect, or belief they should be; and he gave him the world for his kingdom and jurisdiction.

And he commanded him to place his seat in Rome, as the spot most fitting to rule the world from; but also he permitted him to have his seat in any other part of the world, and to judge and govern all Christians, Moors, Jews, Gentiles, and all other sects. This man was called Pope, as if to say, Admirable Great Father and Governor of men. The men who lived in that time obeyed that St. Peter, and took him for Lord, King, and Superior of the universe; so also have they regarded the others who after him have been elected to the Pontificate, and so it has been continued even until now, and will continue until the end of the world.

One of these Pontiffs, who succeeded that St. Peter as Lord of the world, in the dignity and seat which I have before mentioned, made donation of these isles and *terra firme* [mainland] to the aforesaid King and Queen and to their successors, our lords, with A that there are in these territories, as is contained in certain writings which passed upon the subject as aforesaid, which you can see if you wish.

So their Highnesses are kings and lords of these islands and land of *terra firme* by virtue of this donation; and some islands, and indeed almost all those to whom this has been notified, have received and served their Highnesses, as lords and kings, in the way that subjects ought to do, with good will, without any resistance, immediately, without delay, when they were informed of the aforesaid facts. And also they received and obeyed the priests whom their Highnesses sent to preach to them and to teach them our Holy Faith; and all these, of their own free will, without any reward or condition, have become Christians, and are so, and their Highnesses have joyfully and benignantly received them, and also have commanded them to be treated as their subjects and vassals; and you too are held and obliged to do the same. Wherefore as best we can, we ask and require you that you consider what we have said to you, and that you take the time that shall be necessary to understand and deliberate upon it, and that you acknowledge the Church as the Ruler and Superior of the whole world and the high priest called Pope, and in his name the King and Queen dona Juana our lords, in his place, as superiors and lords and kings of these islands and this *terra firme* by virtue of the said donation, and that you consent and give place that these religious fathers should declare and preach to you the aforesaid.

If you do so, you will do well… and we… shall receive you in all love and charity, and shall leave you your wives, and your children, and your lands, free without servitude, that you may do with them and with yourselves freely that which you like and think best, and they shall not compel you to turn Christians, unless you yourselves, when informed of the truth, should wish to be converted to our Holy Catholic Faith, as almost all the inhabitants of the rest of the islands have done. And besides this, their Highnesses award you many privileges and exceptions and will grant you many benefits.

But if you do not do this, and wickedly and intentionally delay to do so, I certify to you that, with the help of God, we shall forcibly enter into your country and shall make war against you in all ways and manners that we can, and shall subject you to the yoke and obedience of the Church and of their Highnesses; we shall take you and your wives and your children, and shall make slaves of them, and as such shall sell and dispose of them as their Highnesses may command; and we shall take away your goods, and shall do all the harm and damage that we can, as to vassals who do not obey, and refuse to receive their lord, and resist and contradict him; and we protest that the deaths and losses which shall accrue from this are your fault, and not that of their Highnesses, or ours, nor of these gentlemen who come with us. And that we have said this to you and made this Requirement, we request the notary here present to give us his testimony in writing, and we ask the rest who are present that they should be witnesses of this Requirement.

HOW WELL DID YOU UNDERSTAND THIS SELECTION?

1. What was the relationship between the Catholic Church and the Spanish monarchy?

2. What benefits did the Spanish government extend to those Native Americans who became Christians?

3. What punitive sanctions would be confronted by those who chose not to convert to Christianity?

Throughout history, white men have exhibited an unwillingness and inability to understand Indian customs and practices. The religious beliefs and ceremonies of the Indians were commonly seen as foreign and strange. In 1721, a Frenchman in Canada wrote of his observations of Indian religious practices. Note how he finds them "ill contrived," "ill digested," and "wild."

Fort at the River Saint Joseph, September 8, 1721

Madam,

This letter will in all likelihood be a very long one, unless some unforeseen hindrance should oblige me to put off to some other opportunity what I have been able to collect, relating to the belief, traditions and religion of our Indians.

Nothing is more certain than that the Indians of this continent, have an idea of a supreme Being, though nothing at the same time can be more obscure. They all in general agree in looking upon him as the first spirit, and the governor and creator of the world, but when you press them a little close on this article, in order to know what they understand by the sovereign spirit, you find no more than a tissue of absurd imaginations, of fables so ill contrived, of systems so ill digested and so wild, that it is impossible to give any regular or just account of them. It is pretended that the Sioux approach much nearer than the other Indians towards a just conception of this first principle, but the little commerce we have hitherto had with them, does not permit me to be sufficiently informed of their traditions, to enable me to speak of them with any degree of certainty.

Almost all of the nations of the Algonquin language, give this foreign Being the appellation of the great Hare; some again call him Michabou, and others Atahocan. Most of them hold the opinion that he was born upon the waters, together with his whole court, entirely composed of four footed animals like himself; that he formed the earth of a grain of sand, which he took from the bottom of the ocean, and that he created man of the bodies of the dead animals. There are likewise some who mention a god of the waters, who opposed the designs of the great Hare, or at least refused to be assisting to him. This god is according to some, the great Tyger, but it must be observed, that the true tyger is not to be found in Canada; thus this tradition is probably of foreign extraction. Lastly, they have a third god called Matcomek, whom they invoke in the winter season, and concerning whom, I have learned nothing particular....

The gods of the Indians have bodies, and live much in the same manner with us, but without any of the inconveniences to which we are subject. The word *spirit* amongst them, signifies only a being of a more excellent nature than others. They have no words to express what passes the bounds of their own understanding, their conceptions being extremely limited, with respect to whatever is not the object of their senses, or to any thing besides the common occurrences of life. They however ascribe to those imaginary beings, a kind of immensity and omnipresence, for in whatever place they are, they invoke them, and act in consequence. To all the questions you put to these barbarians, in order to obtain a farther account of their belief, they answer that this is all they have been taught or know of the matter; nay, there are only a few old men who have been initiated in their mysteries who know so much....

Besides the first being, or the great spirit, and the other gods who are often confounded with them, there is likewise an infinite number of genii or inferior spirits, both good and evil, who have each a peculiar form of worship.

The Iroquois place Atahentsic at the head of these latter, and make Jouskeka the chief of the former; they even sometimes confound him with the god, who drove his grandmother out of heaven, for suffering herself to be seduced by a mortal. They never address themselves to the evil genii, except to beg of them to do them no hurt, but they suppose that the others are placed as so many guardians of mankind, and that every person has his own tutelary. In the Huron language these are called Okkis, and in the Algonquin Manitous: it is to them that they recourse in all perils and undertakings, as also when they would obtain some extraordinary favour; there is nothing but what they may think they may beg of them, let it be ever so unreasonable or contrary to good morals....

There is nothing in all nature, if we believe the Indians, which has not its genius, of which there are some of all ranks, but with different powers. When they are at a loss to conceive any thing, they attribute it to superior genius, and their manner of expressing themselves then is, "This is a Spirit." This is said of greater justice of them, who have any singular talent, or who have performed an extraordinary action, "These are Spirits," that is they have a tutelary genius of an order superior to the common....

HOW WELL DID YOU UNDERSTAND THIS SELECTION?

1. What did the author mean by the statement: "Nothing is more certain than that the Indians of this continent, have an idea of a supreme Being, though nothing at the same time can be more obscure?"

2. Give specific examples of the struggles between good and evil spirits experienced by the tribes observed by the author.

In 1773, Phillis Wheatley wrote about the bountiful and beautiful countryside of the New World.

An Hymn to the Morning

Attend my lays, ye ever honour'd nine,
Assist my labours, and my strains refine;
In smoothest numbers pour the notes along,
For bright Aurora now demands my song.
Aurora, hail, and all the thousand dyes,
Which deck thy progress through the vaulted skies;
The morn awakes, and wide extends her rays,
On ev'ry leaf the gentle zephyr plays;
Harmonious lays the feather'd race resume,
Dart the bright eye, and shake the painted plume.
Ye shady groves, your verdant gloom display
To shield your poet from the burning day:
Calliope, awake the sacred lyre,
While thy fair sisters fan the pleasing fire:
The bow'rs, the gales, the variegated skies
In all their pleasures in my bosom rise.
See in the east th' illustrious king of day!
His rising radiance drives the shades away-
But oh! I feel his fervid leaves too strong,
And scarce begun, concludes th' abortive song.

An Hymn to the Evening

Soon as the sun forsook the eastern main
The pealing thunder shook the heav'nly plain;
Majestic grandeur! From the zephyr's wing,
Exhales the incense of the blooming spring,
Soft purl the streams, the birds renew their notes,
And through the air their mingled music floats.
Through all the heav'ns what beauteous dyes are spread!
But the west glories in the deepest red:
So may our breasts with every virtue glow,

The living temples of our God below!
Fill'd with the praise of him who gives the light,
And draws the sable curtains of the night,
Let placid slumbers soothe each weary mind,
At morn to wake more heav'nly, more refin'd;
So shall the labors of the day begin
More pure, more guarded from the snares of sin.
Night's leaden sceptre seals my drowsy eyes,
Then cease, my song, till fair Aurora rise.

HOW WELL DID YOU UNDERSTAND THIS SELECTION?

1. Briefly summarize how the author views her environment. Include her descriptive adjectives in your response.

The buffalo was extremely important to the Indian tribes. The meat and skins filled many tribal needs, including food and clothing. Images of buffalo appeared in religious symbols and ceremonial dress. The buffalo were abundant, vast herds literally darkening the western horizon. As gunpowder and the railroad came to the range, the number of buffalo fell rapidly. Non-Indian traders sought buffalo for fur coats, hide for leather, and heads for trophies. Army commanders encouraged the killing of buffalo, accurately predicting that starvation would prove the most effective means of breaking tribal resistance to the white man's presence. In the following selection, Old Lady Horse tries to paint a kinder picture of the fate of the American buffalo.

Everything the Kiowas had came from the buffalo. Their tipis were made of buffalo hides, so were their clothes and moccasins. They ate buffalo meat. Their containers were made of hide, or of bladders or stomachs. The buffalo were the life of the Kiowas.

Most of all, the buffalo was part of the Kiowa religion. A white buffalo calf must be sacrificed in the Sun Dance. The priests used parts of the buffalo to make their prayers when they healed people or when they sang to the powers above.

So, when the white men wanted to build railroads, or when they wanted to farm or raise cattle, the buffalo still protected the Kiowas. They tore up the railroad tracks and the gardens. They chased the cattle off the ranges. The buffalo loved their people as much as the Kiowas loved them.

There was war between the buffalo and the white men. The white men built forts in the Kiowa country, and the woolly-headed buffalo soldiers [the Tenth Cavalry, made up of black troops] shot the buffalo as fast as they could, but the buffalo kept coming on, coming on, even into the post cemetery at Fort Sill. Soldiers were not enough to hold them back.

Then the white men hired hunters to do nothing but kill the buffalo. Up and down the plains those men ranged, shooting sometimes as many as a hundred buffalo a day. Behind them came the skinners with their wagons. They piled the hides and bones into the wagons until they were full, and then took their loads to the new railroad stations that were being built, to be shipped east to the market. Sometimes there would be a pile of bones as high as a man, stretching a mile along the railroad track.

The buffalo saw that their day was over. They could protect their people no longer. Sadly, the last remnant of the great herd gathered in council, and decided what they would do.

The Kiowas were camped on the north side of Mount Scott, those of them who were still free to camp. One young woman got up very early in the morning. The dawn mist was still rising from Medicine Creek, and as she looked across the water, peering through the haze, she saw the last buffalo herd appear like a spirit dream.

Straight to Mount Scott the leader of the herd walked. Behind him came the cows and their calves, and the few young males who had survived. As the woman watched, the face of the mountain opened.

Inside Mount Scott the world was green and fresh, as it had been when she was a small girl. The rivers ran clear, not red. The wild plums were in blossom, chasing the red buds up the inside slopes. Into this world of beauty the buffalo walked, never to be seen again.

HOW WELL DID YOU UNDERSTAND THIS SELECTION?

1. Why was the buffalo so valuable to Native American tribes?

2. What was the significance of the birth of a white buffalo to the Kiowas?

3. According to Old Lady Horse, what was the ultimate fate of the buffalo?

A WHITE MAN'S RATIONALE FOR KILLING INDIANS
ON THE OVERLAND TRAIL, 1849

In the 1840s, the United States government sought to deal with the Indians in two ways. First, it initiated a reservation policy under which individual tribes would live within clearly defined zones. Secondly, it sought to annihilate the nomadic tribes with whom the white settlers were coming into conflict as they competed for land and buffalo. The enormous violence entailed in this annihilation demanded some justification. In the following selection, such justification is offered. The Indian is characterized as a violent enemy of the emigrant moving westward.

... One evening, after camping, a scout of the Oregon party rode in and reported a party of Indians camped about five miles ahead, about twenty in number; that having seen signs of the band, he had followed on unobserved until he found them camped; that they had evidently been there some time, as they had built huts. All were up in arms in a few minutes, and ready to start for them. The women were as much excited as the men. But the captain put a stop to their haste; told them the better plan would be to wait till night and crawl carefully out and bag the whole party. His plan was adopted, and guns were cleaned and ammunition looked after. It was arranged that some should remain with the women and children, and the rest to start about eleven o'clock, surround their camp, and at a signal rush in and surprise the ferocious native. Three of our party volunteered—there was no lack of volunteers, the trouble was, all wanted to go, which would leave the home-guard too small. But the women were not afraid to remain alone; they wanted the "red devils rubbed out," as they expressed it. While the preparation was being made for the raid upon the Indian camp, an amusing little incident occurred. The captain had a little dumpy stub of a boy, some six or seven years old, about as thick as he was long, who came stubbing up to his father, saying: "Fader, fader, I want you to buy me a wyfle." "What do you want a rifle for, my son?" said the father. "I want to shoot the Ingins," replied the precocious son and heir, emphasizing his answer with one of his father's most profane curses. "That's right, my son," said his father, "I'll buy you a rifle," and his eye beamed with fatherly pride. He was proud of his son's speech, and, doubtless, regarded him as a rising young [hero]. I think if that boy had cut down all the cherry trees in Oregon, and then lied about it, the old man would have cheerfully gone his bail and carried up the case. If the biography of that father has ever been written and placed in the libraries of Oregon, it will probably be found that he was not a descendant of a Puritan family.

It was midnight when we started, and half-past two when we arrived in sight of the Indian camp. Their fires were burning dimly. The captain ordered a halt, and then he crawled up a little nearer and reconnoitered. There were eighteen of our party. The captain returned, placed the men about equal distance apart around the camp, and ordered each to crawl silently to within about one hundred yards of the camp, and there lie perfectly quiet till a signal from him, when we should come down upon them. It was understood that the raid was to be made just at break of day, or when light enough to see that none escaped. Judging from the systematic manner in which he went about the work, I think it was not the first Indian camp he had surprised. I had lain full three-quarters of an hour when the signal was given by one most unearthly yell from the captain. The prime object thereof was to bring the redskins out of their tents. In an instant every man was on his feet, running and yelling at the top of his voice, and in less time than it takes to tell the story, twenty-seven wild and ferocious Indians were changed into harmless spirits of the air, never more to take the war-path or surprise and slaughter a party of emigrants.

Some may think it was a cruel and unmanly proceeding, but had those who think so been situated as we were — whose companions had been massacred before our eyes; whose dead of a few days before still lay naked and unburied in the canon, and those we hastily buried exhumed and stripped of their grave clothes; driven to the extreme verge of starvation; saved from death only by the mere chance of having fallen in with another party; standing guard by night, and sending out scouts by day to look out for a ferocious enemy, as the man-eating tiger lurking near villages and isolated homes in Hindustan is watched for and hunted by the natives — I think, if happily they survived to return, it would be with modified views of the emigrants' dealings with the plundering and murderous tribes of the interior of the continent in the year of grace '49.

Still, if anyone thinks otherwise, and believes that a free and roving tribe, uncontrolled by military force, can be humanized and civilized by any process known to civilized or Christianized man, I nevertheless would warn him not to risk his person among them. Powder, not prayer, is their only civilizer. You cannot manage him by reasoning with him and persuading him, as the wag said he controlled his vicious and cantankerous mule. Nothing will convert an Indian like convincing him that you are his superior, and there is but one process by which even that can be done, and that is to shut off his wind. I never knew but one "truly good" Indian, and he was dead. I have heard considerable romance, from persons inexperienced, about the brave and noble red man, but I never yet have met one. All I have ever known have been cowardly and treacherous, never attack like men, but crawl upon you, three or four to one, and shoot you down, as they did sixteen of our party in the canon. Then why not attack them, not wait to be attacked by them, and then only in self-defense take, perhaps, one of their worthless lives? In all modern civilized warfare, to surprise the enemy and kill, if they do not surrender, is the climax of military renown. The world applauds, congress promotes, parliament does likewise, graciously voting the hero of the hour, at the same time, a little hundred thousand pounds and a dukedom, and even bishops, priests and clergy offer prayers and incense to divine Providence for the delivery of their equally civilized and equally honorable and patriotic enemy into their hands! But if a party of emigrants surprise and annihilate a band of Indians, who, perhaps, only the day before had murdered every man, woman and child of a large train, and spattered the wagon wheels with the brains of babes, why, the Christian world holds up its hands in breathless horror. But what is the difference? The Indian is the emigrant's enemy. If the emigrant gets the advantage, why should he not take it, for most surely the Indian will? I do not believe in wanton cruelty to the Indian, but when you are in a country where you know he is your enemy, and is not only waiting his chance but looking out for his opportunity, why not cut him down, as otherwise he most surely will you?

HOW WELL DID YOU UNDERSTAND THIS SELECTION?

1. Explain the underlying rationale for the author's belief that powder not prayer is the only civilizer of American Indians.

2. In your opinion, did the actions taken by the emigrants against Native Americans an act of civilized warfare? Support your response.

MARY CHURCH TERRELL,
"LYNCHING FROM A NEGRO'S POINT OF VIEW," 1904

In the following selection, Mary Church Terrell, the first President of the National Association of Colored Women, dispels the myths surrounding the lynching of African Americans. She argues that lynching was never retribution for rapes perpetrated by African-American males on white women. Rather, she argues, a lynching is an act of race hatred and a symptom of a lawless society.

Before 1904 was three months old, thirty-one negroes had been lynched. Of this number, fifteen were murdered within one week in Arkansas, and one was shot to death in Springfield, Ohio, by a mob composed of men who did not take the trouble to wear masks. Hanging, shooting and burning black men, women and children in the United States have become so common that such occurrences create but little sensation and evoke but slight comment now.... In the discussion of this subject, four mistakes are commonly made.

In the first place, it is a great mistake to suppose that rape is the real cause of lynching in the South. Beginning with the Ku Klux Klan the negro has been constantly subjected to some form of organized violence ever since he became free. It is easy to prove that rape is simply the pretext and not the cause of lynching. Statistics show that, out of every 100 negroes who are lynched, from 75-85 are not even accused of this crime, and many who are accused of it are innocent....

In the second place, it is a mistake to suppose that the negro's desire for social equality sustains any relation whatsoever to the crime of rape.... It is safe to assert that, among the negroes who have been guilty of ravishing white women, not one had been taught that he was the equal of white people or had ever heard of social equality....

The third error on the subject of lynching consists of the widely circulated statement that the moral sensibilities of the best negroes in the United States are so stunted and dull, and the standard of morality among even the leaders of the race is so low, that they do not appreciate the enormity and heinousness of rape.... Only those who are densely ignorant of the standards and sentiments of the best negroes, or who wish wilfully *[sic]* to misrepresent and maliciously slander a race already resting under burdens greater than it can bear, would accuse its thousands of reputable men and women of sympathizing with rapists, either black or white, or of condoning their crime....

What, then, is the cause of lynching? At the last analysis, it will be discovered that there are just two causes of lynching. In the first place, it is due to race hatred, the hatred of a stronger people toward a weaker who were once held as slaves. In the second place, it is due to the lawlessness so prevalent in the section where nine-tenths of the lynchings occur....

Lynching is the aftermath of slavery. The white men who shoot negroes to death and flay them alive, and the white women who apply flaming torches to their oil-soaked bodies today, are the sons and daughters of women who had but little, if any, compassion on the race when it was enslaved. The men who lynch negroes today are, as a rule, the children of women who sat by their firesides happy and proud in the possession and affection of their own children, while they looked with un-pitying eye and adamantine heart upon the anguish of slave mothers whose children had been sold away, when not overtaken by a sadder fate.... It is too much to expect, perhaps, that the children of women who for generations looked upon the hardships and the degradation of their sisters of a darker hue with few if any protests, should have mercy and compassion upon the children of that oppressed race now. But what a tremendous influence for law and order, and what a mighty foe to mob violence Southern white women might be, if they would arise in the purity and power of their womanhood to implore their fathers, husbands and sons no longer to stain their hands with the black man's blood! ...

HOW WELL DID YOU UNDERSTAND THIS SELECTION?

1. According to the author, what were the prevailing rationalizations used by the white community to lynch African Americans?

2. Why does the author believe that lynching was the aftermath of slavery?

THE BUREAU OF INDIAN AFFAIRS LAUDS INDIAN PARTICIPATION IN WORLD WAR II, 1942

For much of its history, the Bureau of Indian Affairs was criticized for imposing its image of what was desirable behavior upon the Indians. Little encouragement was given to what was uniquely part of Indian culture and civilization. The Bureau attempted to assimilate the Indian populations through education and had at times interfered with Indian religious affairs and tribal customs. In the 1930s, under the leadership of John Collier, the Bureau did become more sensitive to Indian cultural and religious freedom but the tendency to measure Indians according to Anglo-American criteria continued. In the following selection, the Bureau praises the "special aptitudes" of Indians and celebrates the Indians' contribution to the American efforts in the Second World War. The Indians are lauded for enlisting in the armed services, buying Treasury bonds, and supplying goods and services to the military.

Indians, the truest Americans, everywhere in the United States are deeply concerned and intensely occupied with the prosecution of the war for freedom. From Alaska to Mississippi and from Arizona to Maine, the Indians are giving their lands, their savings, their skills and their lives in the service of their country. In numbers, it is believed, exceeding the per capita contributions of any racial group, including the white, Indians are enlisting in the Navy, the Marine Corps, the Coast Guard and the Army. Their peculiar, inherited talents make them uniquely valuable.

In civilian war work they are equally zealous, and equally effective. Technical training of recent years has converted many Indian men from laborers to specialists. Natural gifts of precision, endurance, poise and high intelligence add great value to their services. War industries are seeking Indian workmen in greater numbers than they can be supplied.

Indians in Every Branch of Service

Prior to the Japanese assault at Pearl Harbor, Indians in the Army alone numbered 4,481, of whom approximately 60 per cent had enlisted in either the Regular Army or the National Guard. In addition to Indians who are Naval Officers, there are 40 Indians in the Navy in branches exclusive of the Marine Corps and the Coast Guard. Perhaps the outstanding Indian Naval Officer is Commander Francis J. Mee, a Chippewa born in Detroit Lakes, Minnesota. Commander Mee has just been promoted from the rank of Lieutenant Commander and has been shifted from the United States destroyer Ellet to a post on the heavy cruiser Portland, where he commands several hundred men. His colleagues and superiors express a deep respect and regard for Commander Mee, who is familiarly identified as "Chief" Mee.

One reason why the service of Indians in the armed forces is important is because of the special skills which are part of the Indian heritage. As scouts, runners, in signal work and in other fields, the modern Indian has demonstrated special aptitudes which are being rapidly recognized and utilized by their commanders.

Items rewritten from the Nation's newspapers reveal typical instances of Indian military performances:

The fortitude of Private Charley Ball, a 24-year-old Indian boy from the Fort Belknap Reservation in northern Montana, while fighting with General MacArthur's forces on Bataan Peninsula in the Philippines, has won him the Distinguished Service Cross. In a dispatch from the Bataan fighting front, it is related that Private Ball was wounded in a battle against Japanese forces, but despite his wounds he helped cover the withdrawal of his comrades in the 21st Infantry. Ball has two brothers in the armed forces.

During the opening weeks of the war, it was reported that about 15 young braves from the Sac and Fox Reservation near Tama, Iowa, enlisted in the Army.

The great, great grandson of old Chief Winnemucca, young Stanley Winnemucca, of Nixon, Nevada, has been accepted by the Marine Corps. Almost a century ago Chief Winnemucca led his warriors to one of the greatest victories ever won by Indian fighters over whites in the battle of Pyramid Lake. He later was a leader in preserving peace in Nevada.

Kitus Tecumseh, descendant of famous Chief Tecumseh and a member of the United States Navy in World War I, visited the Cedar Rapids, Iowa, Naval Recruiting Station to ask for enlistment in the present war. He served on a submarine chaser in 1918 and is classed as 33 per cent disabled as a result of wounds received then.

Indian soldiers at Fort Benning, Georgia, have shown adeptness in the white man's war games. One of the top Sergeants has reported that they're making good soldiers. At the time of this report, which was made before war was declared, there were 16 Indians from Oklahoma in the Fourth Signal Battalion at Fort Benning. "Those Indians are the best morale tonic on the shelf," maintains the First Sergeant. "They take a hard job and make a game of it. We could use more like 'em." . . .

Buy Defense Bonds

... Purchase of Treasury Stamps and Bonds by Indian groups and individuals has been considerable. A great many of these transactions do not come officially to the attention of the Indian Service because the purchases are made locally with funds not under Government jurisdiction. On record in Washington are purchases of $1,270,000 in Treasury Bonds from April, 1941 to the present.

These are not Defense Bonds but the money is, nevertheless, available to the Government. Applications now pending for the purchase of Treasury and Defense Bonds total $19,000. The money for these purchases came from both tribal and individual funds from the sale of land, timber, oil and gas leases, etc.

Applications have been received from various tribes for the purchase of approximately $750,000 in Defense Bonds, but as the funds involved are already in the United States Treasury, nothing would be gained by the purchases and, therefore, the Interior Department disapproved the requests. The spirit of the Indians in making these requests provides further evidence of their patriotic spirit.

Chee Dodge, last of the Navajo war chiefs, has purchased $20,000 of United States Defense Bonds, and has urged Navajos in New Mexico, Arizona and Utah to buy Bonds "as generously as possible." In response to the establishment of sales committees over the Navajo Reservation, Indians are buying Bonds in mounting numbers, Superintendent Fryer of the Navajo Agency has reported.

The Crow Tribe of Montana offered to the Government all of its resources and all of its man power for the prosecution of the war. The Superintendent, himself a Crow Indian, has reported that approximately 70 men and boys of the Tribe have gone into the Service. This is a very large proportion of the eligible man power on the reservation. His son is among those who have already gone into the Army. Even the girls and women of the Crow Tribe are reportedly desirous of entering active military service. The Superintendent stated that several women have already applied for enlistment and he seeks information as to how such service can be arranged.

In Alaska, the Indians and Eskimos are making many contributions which for military reasons cannot be discussed. However, it is no secret that in a considerable area centering at Nome more than 300 women and children (and one man) are working day and night to fashion mukluks (skin boots), parkas (fur outer garments), fur caps, mittens and fur pants for the soldiers. The Army has just ordered 5,000 additional mukluks. All of the work is being done through the Nome Skin Sewers Association, a cooperative organized by the Indian Service under the provisions of the Alaska Act of 1936, a counterpart of the Indian Reorganization Act of 1934.

Many natives are turning over their boats to the armed forces. In one case the incorporated members of a tribe offered land for an air base, without compensation. The land has been accepted but, in the interests of fairness, some payment was provided....

HOW WELL DID YOU UNDERSTAND THIS SELECTION?

1. According to the author, what peculiar, inherited talents made Native American participation in World War II uniquely valuable? Provide specific examples.

The role of women in the workforce was an absolute necessity as the nation's commitment to WW II began to drain the workforce of its able-bodied men. The tanks had to be built, the bullets prepared, and the guns assembled so our soldiers would be able to fight a successful campaign against the Germans and the Japanese. The workforce was changing from the traditional career-minded single woman to the married woman with dependent children. How would these women be able to keep a job while at the same time fulfill their roles as mothers and, in some cases, as fathers to their children? Would their children be adversely impacted by their absence? Would these children be left without the constant supervision children so often need? Would these children become juvenile delinquents? These questions are addressed in Dr. Hohman's article.

The task of working women who are mothers, too, involves unquestionable difficulties which we must face squarely. Yet it gives women and their husbands a chance to prove dramatically and quickly where their deepest interests are.

If I had had any doubts on the question, my trip to the Hartford home of Fred and Mary Berckman would have converted me. Their whole household teems with evidence that their children are to them the most important consideration in the world. Their unflagging interest is the solid foundation for the first of the specific rules to be drawn from their highly successful experience.

The first rule is that mothers who are working must deliberately and determinedly plan to spend ample time with their children. To Mary this is not in the least burdensome. She delights in helping with the lessons of all her merry brood – second-grader son Junie, and the daughters Eileen, Fredrica and the eldest, Catherine, in the fifth grade. Mary sings with them, laughs with them, tells them stories in her fine Irish brogue of County Mayo, where she was born and lived until she came to America nineteen years ago.

"We make things interesting in this house," Mary said — an excellent boost for girls and boys along the road to happiness and security.

With all her fondness for her children, Mary could not accomplish so much time with them if both she and Fred had not organized their days carefully with that very purpose in mind. Her early shift at the Colt arms plant brings her home in the afternoons about the time the children arrive from school. She mixes them a malted milk, does preliminary work on dinner, then lies down for an hour until the children call out that their father is home from work. Fred is there at noon, too, from the Royal Typewriter plant just across the street, to help the youngsters prepare the lunch that has been arranged by Mary before she left for work.

Not much is to be gained by a detailed study of the exact schedule Fred and Mary use. Each working mother will have to arrange a schedule according to her individual working hours and her individual problems. We can be sure in advance that those who haven't the will to succeed will seek excuses for not doing so well as Fred and Mary - such as, "Neither my husband nor I can **come** home at noon." We can be equally sure that those who sincerely try will find some way to make certain that their children are well cared for while they are at work.

One mother I know who has an important executive position and commutes every working day to her desk rises much earlier every morning than she otherwise would have to, so that she can have breakfast and a long chat with her daughter. In the evenings, also, she always manages to spend some time with the child. They talk gaily of topics which interest the little girl. Their companionship is far closer than that of most daughters with mothers who haven't any outside work to do.

A writing assistant on a daily radio program who has few unfilled hours at home during the week still arranges to find brief and happy intervals for her young son every day. The main feature of her admirable plan comes every Sunday. The entire day is her son's. Any reasonable suggestion he makes on how they shall spend his day, she follows merrily. They have grand fun. The scheme often means that she and her husband decline weekend invitations, but they hold to their plan and enjoy themselves more than they would on the missed parties. The result is that the son is held to his parents by the strongest possible bonds of wholesome affection.

The general attitude of mothers— and fathers too — is a more powerful influence than the actual number of hours they spend with their children. Couples who want to act childless and who find association with their children irksome and dull, do not fool their children by staying home and snapping at them. Fewer hours and more companionship would be much better.

A child's sense of security is fostered psychologically by stability in his environment. Despite all protestations of love at odd moments, young children in a harum-scarum household are likely to develop unstable emotional habits and a feeling of insecurity.

I am convinced that jobs for mothers outside the home generally help to create the stability of environment that is so essential. The gain usually more than offsets the loss of the hours in which the mother has to be away. Besides the scheduling of household routine imposed by regular employment, there is the added advantage for children that the inefficient mothers whose home management is hit-or-miss and disturbingly unreliable will learn to be more efficient by working where efficiency is required.

The skill and willingness in housework which Fred acquired when he took it over completely while his heart would not permit more strenuous exertion, makes him an ideal partner for a working wife. This suggests still another flat rule:

If children are to be reared successfully in families with employed mothers who haven't enough money for nursemaids and servants, it is absolutely necessary for husbands to help their wives with home duties and with the children's training.

Many unemployed wives would say offhand that their husbands could never learn. They probably would be pleasantly surprised. An outside job for a wife usually seems to cause a striking improvement in the husband's domesticity. Every husband of a working wife to whom I have mentioned the problem assured me that he felt obligated to help. "I never did before my wife got a job," several said. "After all, why should I when I had done my part and she had nothing else to do?" Not taking the husbands' statements of their own virtues as final, I made extensive inquiries